THE SETTLER SEA

MANY WESTS

SERIES EDITORS:
Thomas G. Andrews, University of Colorado
Ari Kelman, University of California, Davis
Amy Lonetree, University of California, Santa Cruz
Mary E. Mendoza, Pennsylvania State University
Christina Snyder, Pennsylvania State University

THE SETTLER SEA

CALIFORNIA'S SALTON SEA and the
CONSEQUENCES of COLONIALISM

Traci Brynne Voyles

UNIVERSITY OF NEBRASKA PRESS   LINCOLN

Acknowledgments for the use of previously
published material appear on pages xi–xii, which
constitute an extension of the copyright page.

Publication of this volume was assisted by the McCabe
Greer Book Manuscript Workshop, the George
and Ann Richards Civil War Era Center, and the
Pennsylvania State University Department of History.

Library of Congress Cataloging-in-Publication Data
Names: Voyles, Traci Brynne, author.
Title: The settler sea: California's Salton Sea and the
consequences of colonialism / Traci Brynne Voyles.
Description: Lincoln: University of Nebraska
Press, [2021] | Series: Many wests | Includes
bibliographical references and index.
Identifiers: LCCN 2021006475
ISBN 9781496216731 (hardback)
ISBN 9781496229618 (epub)
ISBN 9781496229625 (pdf)
Subjects: LCSH: Salton Sea (Calif.)—Environmental
conditions. | Salton Sea (Calif.)—Political aspects. | Salton
Sea (Calif.)—History. | BISAC: HISTORY / United States /
State & Local / West (AK, CA, CO, HI, ID, MT, NV, UT,
WY) | NATURE / Ecosystems & Habitats / Oceans & Seas
Classification: LCC GE155.C2 V69 2021 |
DDC 304.209794/99—dc23
LC record available at https://lccn.loc.gov/2021006475

Set in Charis by Mikala R. Kolander.
Designed by N. Putens.

CONTENTS

PART 3

ILLUSTRATIONS

ACKNOWLEDGMENTS

I began writing this book with a newborn in my arms and finished it during a pandemic. Every page owes something to the people around me who took care of me, my work, and my family in the years in between.

I thank the colleagues who lifted me up during my time at Loyola Marymount University (LMU): Stella Oh, Mairead Sullivan, Sina Kramer, Nicolas Rosenthal, Eliza Rodriguez y Gibson, Jennifer Williams, Elizabeth Drummond, Andrew Dilts, Tahereh Aghdasifar, Brian Treanor, Jennifer Moorman, Marne Campbell, Amy Woodson Boulton, and Carla Bittel. Upon moving to the University of Oklahoma (OU), I found new depths of collegial sustenance; thank you to David Wrobel, Jill Irvine, Elyssa Faison, Megan Sibbett, Lisa Funnell, Carrie Schroeder, Jennifer Davis, Kathleen Brosnan, Kalenda Eaton, Sandy Holguín, Raymond Orr, Laura Harjo, Zev Trachtenberg, Karlos Hill, Jennifer Holland, and Sarah Hines. I could not have done anything at OU without the expertise of Susy Jorgenson. Special thanks to Mark Boxell, who lent a hand to the project at a crucial juncture, and to Sara Raines and Maureen Bemko, both of whom went above and beyond to bring the book to fruition.

My community of scholars outside of LMU and OU made this effort—and all my work—joyful. I thank Dina Gilio-Whitaker, Natale Zappia, Chris Finley, Maile Arvin, Finis Dunaway, Ross Frank, Lisa Sun-Hee Park, Matt Basso, and Susan Burch. Karen Leong offered indispensable comments at a critical stage, as did Elyssa Faison. Will Madrigal Jr. shared important guidance, spot-on book recommendations, and great conversations about Cahuilla history. This book owes much of its inspiration (and more than a few of its words) to Elaine Nelson, Cathleen Cahill, Virginia Scharff, Ellen Stroud, Kathy Morse, Christina Snyder, and Mary E. Mendoza. Major frameworks of this project emerged through the rich conversations that took place at the 2016 meeting of the Environmental Justice/Climate Justice Hub at the University of Santa Barbara, particularly with David Naguib Pellow, John Foran, Julie Sze, Joni Adamson, Kari Norgaard, and ann-elise lewallen.

Special thanks to LMU's Academy for Catholic Thought and Imagination for awarding me a fellowship that allowed me to complete crucial portions of the research. I am also grateful to the selection committee for the Graves Award in the Humanities for finding this project worthy of their generous support.

The bulk of this book was written when I was living on the homelands of Tongva peoples and researching on the homelands of the Cahuilla, Kumeyaay, Quechan, and Payómkawichum Nations. I thank the peoples of those nations for their continued practices of sovereignty and self-determination in the context of ongoing settler colonialism. I am grateful to the Executive Board of the Malki Museum, particularly Amanda Castro and Andie Geyer, for their generous and patient help with this project. I appreciate conversations with Sandonne Goad, tribal council chairwoman of the Gabrielino/Tongva Nation, and Edgar Perez of the Gabrielino/Tongva Nation. I am grateful to everyone who fielded my calls and emails at Torres Martinez and at the Sonny Bono National Wildlife Refuge. Special gratitude goes to Selina Santillanes and Hans Bauman for sharing their time and expertise. Thank you to the members of the California Indian Basketweavers Association, who gave permission for me to quote from their archives.

A number of texts have been indispensable guides for how to hone better and more ethical methodologies and writing practices when one is a white settler writing about Native peoples, although there is still much left to learn and do. I am especially grateful for important works about methodologies in Native American and Indigenous studies, particularly the contributions of Linda Tuhiwai Smith, James Riding In, Alyssa Mt. Pleasant, Jennifer Nez Denetdale, Gregory Younging, Norman K. Denzin, and Yvonna S. Lincoln. As I sought to understand this desert world and the Salton Sea's place in it, books and articles by Benny Andrés, William DeBuys, Karen Isaksen Leonard, Clifford Trafzer, Tanis Thorne, Michael Connolly Miskwish, and Florence Connolly Shipek were never far out of reach.

The editors of the Many Wests series guided this project and made it possible: Christina Snyder, Ari Kelman, Thomas Andrews, Mary E. Mendoza, and Amy Lonetree. I am deeply grateful to the other readers who participated in a workshop on the book manuscript at Pennsylvania State University in the spring of 2018. In addition to the series editors, important contributions came from Ellen Stroud, Julie Reed, and Jacob Lee. Joshua Reid and Christina Snyder both offered comments and suggestions at multiple stages of this project that proved to be nothing short of transformative—this would have been a poor work indeed without their guidance. It might not have existed at all without Bridget Barry's stewardship, encouragement, and editorial genius, or the tireless efforts of Emily Wendell. Mary E. Mendoza, as always, has been my first and best interlocutor for every harebrained idea and barely completed draft. Thank you for always pulling me back to earth where I belong.

Joy Browne and Wyatt Voyles gave me the space and support to finish final edits and, more importantly, fed me while I worked. Jamie Voyles kept a keen eye on the science and steered me clear of the kind of magical thinking a historian might want to apply to biology.

Finally, to Juan, Coco, and Beni: what can I say? I had just enough words to write this book. I would need millions more—more words than there are stars in the sky—to tell you what you mean to me.

This book is for Benicio, the newborn who was there at the beginning. I love you, my little big one.

Portions of the introduction and chapters 1 and 2 previously appeared in "Environmentalism in the Interstices: California's Salton Sea and the Borderlands of Nature and Culture," *Resilience: A Journal of the Environmental Humanities* 3 (2016): 211–14.

Portions of chapter 5 previously appeared in "The Invalid Sea: Disability Studies and Environmental Justice History," in *Disability Studies and the Environmental Humanities: Toward an Eco-Crip Theory*, ed. Sarah Jaquette Ray and Jay Sibara (Lincoln: University of Nebraska Press, 2017), 448–73.

Portions of chapter 6 previously appeared in "Toxic Masculinity: California's Salton Sea and the Environmental Consequences of Manliness," *Environmental History* 26, no. 1 (2021): 127–41.

A NOTE ON NAMING

The Salton Sea, the subject of this book, has gone by many names. Native peoples who live in its vicinity sometimes call it "Lake Cahuilla" to emphasize that it belongs to a long, unbroken story of lacustrine ebbs and flows in the desert. The water has other names too.[1] The decision to differentiate between the past's Lake Cahuilla and the current stand of water in the desert was made by a railroad engineer named William Phipps Blake in 1909. Blake was not the first to call water in the desert the "Salton Sea," a moniker borrowed from the nearby settlement of Salton, but he made it stick. More important, he drew a firm line between it and the stands of water that had regularly shaped the desert's past. Blake made this pronouncement: "As the original discoverer and describer of the ancient lake, I claim the right to give it a name." The new Salton Sea, he mused, was distinct enough from its watery ancestors to warrant a different appellation altogether.[2] Like other colonizers who declared themselves discoverers, Blake was wrong in almost every way.

Unlike Blake, I claim no such right to rename this complex body of water or to differentiate it from its marine antecedents. Throughout this book I use "Salton Sea" to describe the twentieth-century stand of water in the desert, in keeping with its most recognizable toponym. But I also note that what we call the Salton Sea is contiguous with a long and complex history of lakes in the desert that belies Blake's insistence on drawing a line between old and new bodies of water. Lake Cahuilla is the Salton Sea's past, it shapes its present, and it offers possibilities for its future. The Salton Sea—the *settler* sea—is but one part of Lake Cahuilla's long and enduring story.

Like nearly everything about the Salton Sea, right down to what it is called, the name of the place it occupies is complicated too. Here again we find Blake's influence: while handing out names, he also dubbed the desert in which the sea now sits the "Colorado Desert," choosing to label it after the great Colorado River rather than after the state of California. The Colorado Desert is the triangular, northwesternmost tip of the greater Sonoran ecoregion that extends east into present-day Arizona and south into the Mexican states of Baja California and Sonora. It is bounded by mountain ranges—the Chocolate Mountains to the east, San Jacintos to the north, and Cuyamacas to the west—and bounded on one side by the Algodones Dunes, where vast mounds of sand ripple and shift in the wind. In between mountains and sand, the Colorado Desert dips almost three hundred feet below sea level in a giant bowl in the earth's floor perfect for hosting a great body of water—which, of course, is how it came to be there in the first place.[3]

In what follows, I trace the comings-and-goings of people, water, fish, and birds in this complex, sometimes confounding place. Along the way, this history also requires attending to the changes wrought by dams, guns, bombs, bacteria, weeds, pesticides, and prisons. The Salton Sea, as you might surmise from this wide-ranging list of main characters, is as hard to understand as it has been to name; it is one sea and many seas. To find out why, read on.

THE SETTLER SEA

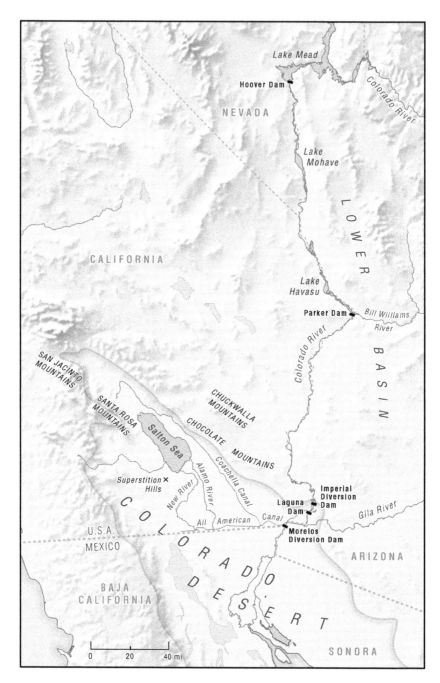

1. River systems, mountains, and ecological zones connecting the Salton Sea to the Lower Colorado River basin. Created for the author by Erin Greb Cartography.

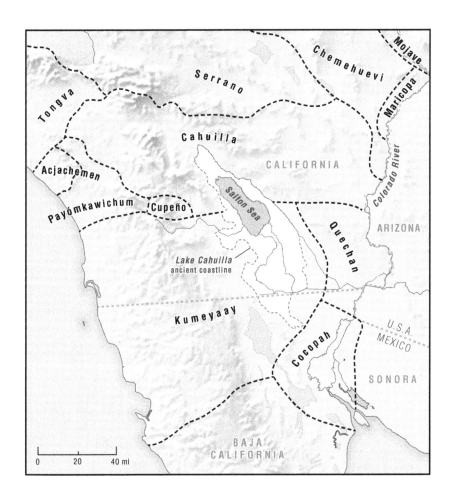

2. Indigenous homelands and the bed of ancient Lake Cahuilla, with a current-day outline of the Salton Sea within the area once covered by Lake Cahuilla. Created for the author by Erin Greb Cartography.

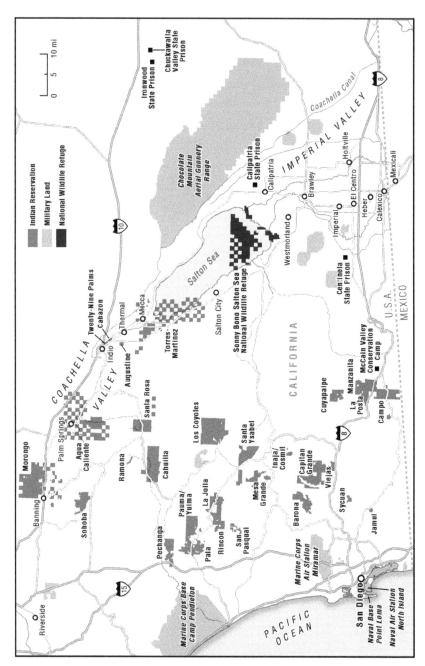

3. Contemporary political map showing reservations, towns and cities, federal and state land, and the international border. Created for the author by Erin Greb Cartography.

INTRODUCTION

A WORLD ON THE BRINK

Are not the laws of nature the same in a tea-kettle as they are in a universe?
—K. D. Shugart, "The Local Climatic Effect of Salton Lake," 1891

PARADOX AND PRECARITY

In the lowlands of Southern California the state's largest inland body of water teeters between worlds. Runoff trickles from agricultural valleys to the north and the south thick with fertilizer, salt, and pesticides. Once there, the water has nowhere to go but up, called skyward by the blazing heat of a desert sun. It rarely condenses into overhead clouds, though, and almost never lets loose drops of fresh water to replenish the lake's offerings. Birds dip in and out, resting in the shallows and rooting around in the mud for food. That mud delivers nutrients into the birds' bodies—and toxins as well. Gatherers arrive to pick arrowweed, saltcedar, and desert saltgrass, to harvest beans from mesquite trees, and to seek out feathers shed from sacred desert birds that pass overhead.

Every year less water flows in to replenish that which the sun dries up. The shoreline recedes; the bleached band encircling the water grows wider. Mudflats dry and crack. Windstorms blow in from the mountains as they have always done, kicking up dust from the sandy desert floor, newly exposed, as well as particles made of the pulverized shells of mollusks and the desiccated carcasses of millions of fish. Every year the temperatures get hotter, the weather less predictable, and the water shallower. People hold on to their homes around the ever-expanding shoreline, breathing in the dusty air—including those whose ancestors have lived in this place since time immemorial.

It would be a mistake, however, to see *only* the dead fish, dusty shoreline, and a flat slate of water stretched toward a hazy horizon. Turn around. Creosote bush and saltbushes thrive in thin, alkaline soil. Scrub cactus plants grow on the rocky slopes of the horizon's aptly named Chocolate Mountains, glowing the color of burnt sienna in the glare of a desert sunset. Long, whip-like tendrils of the distinctive ocotillo wave in the dry air, erupting every spring in flutes of bright red flowers. An impressive range of legume trees furnish valuable protein for human and nonhuman desert dwellers: blue palo verde, ironwood, honey and screwbean mesquite, and catclaw, among others. Ghostly smoke trees, distinctive features in this part of the larger Sonoran ecosystem, emanate weightlessly from the ground. To the southwest the smooth-faced Algodones Dunes host vibrant ecological communities, including what one scholar has called "the largest number of dune-endemic plants in North America."[1]

Notice the birds. They are everywhere. Eared grebes, white and brown pelicans, terns, cormorants, herons, and egrets all congregate here, splashing in the shallows and hunting for food. They soar over the water's still surface, the tips of their wings drawing long smooth lines to mark their passage. Those you can see are just a handful of the more than 3.5 million birds, representing four hundred bird species, that rely on the Salton Sea as a wetland resource. From their airborne point of view, the sea glints in the sunshine with the promise of water and sustenance—a sight that has become all too uncommon as wetlands across the west coast of North America disappear, yielding to cities and suburbs, farms and parks.[2]

This is the Salton Sea, an ecological conundrum and a study in paradoxes: a wetland in a desert; one of California's last remaining water resources for migrating birds, as well as a polluted hazardscape; both natural and human-made; a rich ecosystem and an environmental catastrophe; a sacred part of the local Indigenous past, present, and future; and an artifact of the dispossessive settler world that surrounds the area's Native peoples.

In the deep reaches of geologic time, water came to this part of the desert over and over again. The great river to the east, which colonizers would name the Colorado River, spilled over its banks in breaches big and small, sending water in thin trickles and great floods. This world was made in cycles of inundation over the course of epochs; Native peoples had plenty of time to learn the water's lessons. In dry years the lowest reaches of the desert—the bottomlands of an ephemeral and transitory sea—knitted together a map of nations. Quechans, Cahuillas, Kumeyaays, Chemehuevis, Cocopahs, and other Native peoples traversed the desert for trade, using well-worn paths and forming a zone of international migration. They shared commodities, stories, and songs and maintained sacred sites along trails marked with deep wells and stands of mesquite trees. There was intranational migration as well: desert Cahuilla clans, whose homeland encompasses the northern half of the deepest part of the sink, migrated regularly in lateral territorial holdings, from the bottom of the desert, up to the foothills, into the mountains, and back again.[3]

In the breathless period of time since non-Native settlers arrived here, flooding and drying have continued to be an enduring part of its story. For more than a century, outsiders of many kinds arrived and left again, either passing through or turning back after seeing the apparent bareness of the desert stretched out before them. Outsiders did not come to stay until the turn of the twentieth century, when schemes to irrigate the desert finally rooted themselves, albeit shallowly, in the alkaline desert soil.

The arrival of these outsiders did not dissuade the river from its centuries of work. Nor did the new colonizers listen to Native peoples who told them that the farms they busily etched in the earth with little more than promises and paper would end in watery ruin.

In 1905 the river, as it always had in the past, rushed in. It washed away the settlers' meager homesteads, chased the railroad out of the desert basin, and cut enormous new courses—some more than one hundred feet deep—through the dry soil.[4] It would take nearly two years, thousands of laborers, and hundreds of thousands of pounds of dirt and rock to persuade the river to return to its southbound course and thence toward its delta.

At first the colonizers looked out at this new sea in a desert with a kind of startled wonder. It was not that they were unused to the nature-borne demise of outlandish irrigation schemes. In those decades, stories of nature's agency turning colonizers' dreams to nightmares were as common as desert jackrabbits. The Colorado River, however—never a river to do things by halves—had brought its penchant for drama to this particular scene. Its ruddy water washed away would-be farms, newly picked out on the desert floor in the negative space of cleared sagebrush. It chased out the Southern Pacific Railroad, forcing railroad employees to frantically pry up and move the tracks five times before the train could pass safely above the high-water mark. It carved chasms a hundred feet deep in the thin desert soil, rendering the previously flat plain of land unrecognizable and impossible to navigate. The life the colonizers imagined they would live in their "Imperial Valley," the river insisted, would be a precarious one, forever bound up in the drama and the paradox of a river and a desert.

In the wake of the floods that created it, colonizers put the Salton Sea to a new purpose, seeing it as a "natural dumping basin" for the water that flowed across their fields and seeped into the soil below.[5] Colorado River water wetted the roots of cantaloupe and alfalfa, asparagus and lettuce. As it gave these crops what they needed to grow, it also leached salt from the soil, preventing the saliferous desert soil from poisoning the colonizers' plants. But a layer of clay below the surface meant that the salty water needed to go somewhere, lest it turn the fields to briny mire. Over the subsequent decades Imperial Valley settlers crafted an underground drainage infrastructure, building under their shimmering green fields pathways that corralled the salty wastewater and ushered it downhill to the Salton Sea.[6]

Of course, making the desert bloom required more than power over the nonhuman world. It required power over a wide variety of humans too. Since the first capitalist ventures in the desert, agricultural workers have been overwhelmingly nonwhite, grossly underpaid, and among the most vulnerable in a system of large-scale farming that grows workers' vulnerability as abundantly as it grows melons and carrots.[7] Accordingly, the region has produced astonishing amounts of wealth for very few people. The whole thing, in the words of cultural studies scholar Mike Davis, amounts to an "agricultural caste system"—one that, in the tradition of U.S. agricultural labor writ large, was deeply defined by race.[8]

In the deep bowl in the desert where the Salton Sea sits, this history takes on new meaning. Here the sea serves as a relic and reminder of these feats of engineering prowess and a paradox of settler success, settler failure, Native dispossession, environmental degradation, and labor exploitation. Here is the Imperial Valley, a mantle of green in the midst of the Sonoran Desert, watered by the Colorado River and the supplier of vast quantities of food to U.S. markets. The immense wealth of landowners and water managers emerges from the staggering poverty of farm laborers and their families.[9] The Salton Sea itself hosts some of the richest wildlife diversity in the West, the wildlife refuge on its southern shores providing resources for a stunning array of endangered and protected bird species. Here is a place described in the same breath as a toxic wasteland and an indispensable environmental resource: a place of paradox and precarity but also one of promise.

THE SETTLER SEA

Is the Salton Sea natural or human-made? Is it a product of nature or technology? For the sea—and for the birds, fish, and people that rely on it—these are questions of real consequence. In the waning years of the twentieth century, environmentalists struggled to mobilize support for conservation work at the Salton Sea.[10] Elsewhere I have argued that the reticence of mainstream environmental actors to "protect" the Salton Sea as they mobilize to protect places like Lake Tahoe emerged in part from the sea's ambivalent origins. The tendency to view the sea as a human creation, the lamentable result of an engineering accident and a body of water that never should have been there in the first place, made it difficult to muster much action. The stench of rotten eggs emanating from its surface and the crunch of fish bones and mollusk shells under visitors' boots as they walked along the shore didn't help either. Nor did endless images of bird carcasses washing up on the beach.[11]

No matter where one falls on the sides of this debate about the formation of the sea (or if one slips and slides into the murky, liminal, middle space of its having been made by both nature and humans), one thing is clear: its current state of decline is unambiguously the result of the actions, decisions, and interferences of particular kinds of humans pursuing particular kinds of economic activities. If the sea is not clearly human- or nature-made, it is certainly—undeniably—settler-maintained.

The Settler Sea examines the ways that settlers maintain, shape, manage, and mismanage the nonhuman world, arguing that colonizers have restructured physical landscapes in ways that exert and reinforce processes that are part and parcel of colonial power relations in the United States: Indigenous dispossession, nationalist enclosure, and racial capitalism, as well as environmental degradation.[12] In a sense the history of the Salton Sea can most clearly be understood as a physical manifestation of settler colonial power; settler colonialism, in turn, can be tracked in terms of its physical consequences for landscapes as well as people.[13] "Settler colonialism" refers to a set of power relations that seeks to colonize Indigenous peoples and claim their homelands as settlers' own through intersecting forces of racism, sexism, heteronormativity, environmental degradation, dispossession, ableism, and capitalism.[14] Settler colonialism is not, in other words, a binary power relation with unilateral impacts from white settler to Native but a web of relationships that reinforces white supremacy, control over land, exploitation of racialized workers, and unsustainable resource use for capitalist accumulation.

To look for the ways that colonizers have reshaped landscapes to their own ends means to track the material consequences of oppression on the nonhuman as well as the human world. This is not the first study to undertake such an analysis. Cultural geographers have explored many ways in which humans have shaped physical space to produce or reinforce dominant notions of social organization: gender-segregated bathrooms organize and reinforce the gender binary; cities and parks organize and reinforce the dichotomy between culture and nature; racial segregation organizes and reinforces white supremacy and the idea of racial difference; borders reify nation-states and may often do the same with racist and classist systems of exclusion; and so on. Environmental historians, too, have unpacked all manner of other built and curated environments: from riparian zones to wildernesses, from national parks to vast metropolises. Researchers in environmental justice studies have created an entire scholarly field out of the study of the co-constitution of harm to the environment and oppression of people by racism, classism, and colonization.[15]

These forms of intersectional analysis suggest that the Salton Sea's story is not simply a staid narrative of environmental decline, in which humans endlessly, and universally, destroy nature.[16] *The Settler Sea* tracks a more nuanced argument: that the functions of social power built into settler colonial processes—racism, sexism, classism, heteropatriarchy, ableism—are *themselves* environmentally ruinous. In this formulation, oppression of humans is a primary threat to the nonhuman world. Here the central line of thinking in environmental justice studies and some major works of environmental history (notably Connie Chiang's *Nature behind Barbed Wire*)—that environmental problems compound social inequities—is inverted to argue that social inequities also cause vast environmental problems.[17] The morass of devastating environmental conditions at the Salton Sea illustrates how the dispossessive and exploitative conditions inherent to settler colonialism in this part of California have restructured the natural world in deeply troubling ways.

Nor does *The Settler Sea* posit that these forces of settler colonial power have been homogenous, consistent, or even always successful. Settler colonialism is an aspirational process, but it is far from perfect.[18] In fact it often fails. At the Salton Sea this failure is reflected in the daily lives of Native peoples whose homelands are in the vicinity of its receding shoreline. The Salton Sea has been sitting atop at least 40 percent of the Torrez Martinez Cahuillas' reservation land since 1907. At present its rapid evaporation releases polluted particulate matter into the air, causing high rates of respiratory illness for Native and non-Native people alike, including and especially children.[19] These are manifestations of the sea's settler history and the consequences of the uses to which it has been put. And yet the water has other stories and other purposes. Desert Cahuillas and desert Kumeyaays hold it as a crucial part of the ecosystem of their homelands, a rich and complex body of water that has always been part, in one way or another, of their ancestors' lives. They have engaged in ongoing work to conserve the sea, seeking to mitigate the environmental harms inflicted on it by a century of colonial uses.[20]

In 1986 historian Alfred Crosby mused that "perhaps the success of European imperialism has a biological, an ecological, component." Ultimately, this book tracks that idea, noting that the century-long mismanagement of the Salton Sea has constituted a manifestation of "ecological imperialism."[21] Although Crosby did not engage deeply with analysis of race, gender, and other forms of oppression, ecological imperialism has never taken place outside of these structures of power relations. The Salton Sea, faltering in the desert under a hot sun after a century of settlers mismanaging both it and the river that created it, reminds us that Crosby might have been too quick to describe imperialism as a "success." If colonization has had a "biological, an ecological, component," perhaps its failure does too. There are lessons in these tensions between settler failure and Indigenous futures. *The Settler Sea* seeks to trace their contours, following paths, ancient and new, etched along a rocky shoreline.

WHERE WATER AND DESERT MEET

Environmental histories of the U.S. West have been preoccupied with water. For a region defined by aridity, this is something of a paradox. Rivers and lakes, aqueducts and ditches, wetlands and creeks, dams and bridges—these watery topics have loomed large in the West precisely *because* of the region's aridity. Control over water and access to it have been an essential feature of western life; as environmental historian Nancy Langston points out, riparian areas, where land and water meet, have been where humans concentrated their activity in the West for thousands of years (to say nothing of nonhumans).[22] It is safe to say that historians' preoccupation with water emerges from the irrefutable fact that the history of settler experiences in the West can in many ways be boiled down to a collection of stories of "making wet lands drier and dry lands wetter."[23]

Historians assert that such preoccupation with water, in historiography and in actual human life alike, emerged from water's role as a metaphor and a vehicle for power. Throughout western history wealth flowed along rivulets of water. So did stability, settlement, and community. The manipulation of nature and the transformation of great rivers into organic machines that created hydraulic empires in the West have organized the power of the settler colonial nation state and a great many of its citizens.[24] Water, and control of it, became a central vehicle for struggles over regional influence and access to federal resources; water policy shaped power relations on scales ranging from the family farm to the halls of the U.S. Congress and back again.[25] As climate change transforms water politics the world over, access to and control over water takes on new meanings and new urgency, amplifying the struggles over water scarcity that defined much of western history.[26]

If water has been both a metaphor and a vehicle for power in the West, deserts are something else altogether. Where water means promise, deserts have represented antagonism and barriers.[27] Environmental histories of western deserts, taking up scanty space on library shelves as compared to the groaning weight of their watery counterparts, focus on the ways in which non-Indigenous people in the West have encountered deserts: settlers avoid them, cross them, die in them, fear them, irrigate them, urbanize them, and sometimes inadvertently create them.[28] In mainstream perspectives on deserts water symbolizes abundance while arid lands symbolize waste—wasted lands, wasted space, wasted lives.[29] Rivers shape and animate maps of the West; deserts are marked with forebodingly blank spaces.

Deserts, in short, represent water's inverse, the shadow self of power and control that has etched the contours of western history. Deserts have not by and large been written about as ecosystems with their own value, worth, and human and nonhuman communities but as landscapes of scarcity with, in historian Donald Worster's words, "potential to desiccate and shrivel," provoking in humans "the deepest anxiety, the sorriest desperation, forcing them to make radical changes to their

4. Cahuillas dug deep wells in the desert floor to access fresh water from underground aquifers. Charles C. Pierce, *Indian Well at Martinez, Showing the Heavy Vegetation around It,* circa 1903. California Historical Society Collection, 1860–1960; Title Insurance and Trust, and C. C. Pierce Photography Collection, 1860–1960. University of Southern California Libraries. California Historical Society.

behavior and institutions."[30] In these accounts, humans universally reacted to deserts by undertaking massive transformations to their physical environs, constructing leviathan works of engineering to shift water from wet to dry places.[31]

But this tendency in scholarly works to see deserts and rivers only coming together as the result of landscape-altering transformations of rivers' courses does not align with the realities of the Colorado Desert. First appearances notwithstanding, this desert world has never been in any way waterless. In reality its residents—human, plant, and animal alike—historically have relied on the vast freshwater aquifers just below the hardscrabble surface. Cahuillas accessed this water by building deep walk-in wells lined with mesquite branches and descending diagonally as far as 120 feet beneath the hot crust of the earth. Cahuillas etched steps into these massive wells, reinforced the walls, and stored the water drawn from underground in watertight baskets woven of rushes or deer grass and decorated in patterns of red and black. Across the sink to the south, Kumeyaays found water closer to the surface, excavating shallower bowls in the earth using mesquite-handled shovels with carved stone heads.[32] Add to that a rich and complex relationship among the desert, its peoples, and the Colorado River, and it becomes clear that environmental history of this desert world will grapple with water as much as with aridity.

Any study of the Salton Sea, this quagmire of paradoxes, must contend with these extremes. Using environmental histories of water and deserts in the West as a jumping-off point, I explore how the juxtaposition of these subfields of environmental history and the material imbrication of desert and wetland in Southern California offer new ways to look at the environmental conditions that have shaped human history in this unlikely place. In so doing, *The Settler Sea* makes two historiographical interventions: first, an argument for centering settler colonialism in environmental history; and second, a reimagining of the historical contexts and scales of environmental justice. Below, I briefly outline each of these interventions.

Settler Colonialism

This book brings together environmental history, settler colonial studies, and Indigenous history to explore how Indigenous perspectives can help us better understand the power structures that organize our relationships to each other and to the nonhuman world.[33] Placing Indigenous peoples at the center of analysis means reframing normative (settler) perspectives on the world and calls into question nearly all of our standard narratives about human relationships to nature. It certainly places a question mark at the end of every sentence non-native environmental historians have written about "our" impacts on the natural world.

The Settler Sea makes an argument for the importance of settler colonialism as a crucial framework for understanding environmental and western history in the United States.[34] Settler colonialism has been and continues to be a primary organizing framework of power relations in the United States, extending to all areas where power relations affect human and nonhuman life: bodies and health, labor, politics, economics, cultural representation, and so on. Settler colonialism has been understood by scholars as being, in its essence, about *land*—the very soil we till and the ground we stand on. In a useful definition of the term provided by social theorist Glen Coulthard, settler colonialism is "a structure of domination predicated on dispossession."[35] As such, it has special resonance with environmental history as a field of intellectual engagement.[36] Important contributions to this conversation have expanded what we mean by *land*; sometimes, as historian Joshua Reid demonstrates, this framework applies to marine worlds in ways similar to how it applies to terrestrial ones.[37]

Indigenous studies scholars have recently added complexity to this conversation, however, in ways that create new potential for environmental history and its engagement with settler colonialism. As Dian Million, Winona LaDuke, Leanne Betasamosake Simpson, and Kyle Powys Whyte have argued, seeing land and territory as the zero-sum game of Indigenous struggles against settler colonialism is not enough; it runs the risk of centering the property orientation of settlers as the principal politics of decolonization.[38] In fact, settler colonialism has sought a dual strategy of colonizing land and superimposing settler *relations* on that land (including racist relations to non-Native people of color). The duality is both *epistemological* (how things are known) and *ontological* (how things are lived). Indigenous epistemological and ontological relations to the land, and between human and nonhuman people, matter just as much as the physical landscapes themselves.[39]

Centering *relations* in turn suggests that Indigenous perspectives on settler history call into question relations of all kinds. To be sure, this requires a focus on the relations between white settlers and Indigenous nations. But settler colonialism is a racial as well as a political-economic structure in which multiple populations are "marked for erasure and early death."[40] As historian Kelly Lytle Hernández points out, settler colonialism is marked by Native elimination, but settler societies also strive to block, erase, or remove non-Native outsiders of color from their claimed territory.[41] Even as many settler societies depend on racialized workforces, settler cultures, institutions, and politics simultaneously trend toward excluding racialized workers from full inclusion in the body politic, corralling their participation in community life and, largely due to rising and falling labor demands, deporting, hiding, or criminalizing them or otherwise revoking the right of racialized outsiders to be within the invaded territory.[42]

Racism, as cultural theorist Iyko Day argues, is "internal" to settler colonialism and functions to differentiate and define whiteness as a category that stipulates the settler claim to land; in Day's words, "settler colonialism abides by a dual logic that is originally driven to eliminate Native peoples from land and mix the land with enslaved black labor. If land is the basis of settler colonialists' relationship to Indigenous peoples, it is labor that frames that relationship with enslaved peoples."[43] Rather than erasing white settlers' relationships to (and oppression of) other non-Native people of color, those relationships of enslavement, racialized labor, and criminalization function on an "inherited background field" of Native dispossession.[44] In this book I take that "background field" as a material object: a landscape, curated through settler-imposed relations between land and people, that facilitates ongoing Native dispossession, the exploitation of racial labor, and the exclusion of nonwhite Others from the privileges of full settler citizenship.

Environmental Justice

In its most fundamental formulation, environmental injustice occurs when people who are marginalized by racism, classism, settler colonialism, or heteropatriarchy are disproportionately targeted to bear the burdens of environmental harm.[45] Scholars have frequently treated environmental injustices as the result of industrial pollution in the late twentieth century; environmental historians and others, however, have pointed out how patterns of unjust distribution of environmental burdens have appeared throughout U.S. history.[46] Some studies have examined, in fact, how environmental degradation has influenced the ways racial difference is understood and acted upon. For instance, in *Clean and White*, Carl Zimring shows how whiteness and cleanliness have been co-constituted in part by environmentally unjust practices of urban housing segregation and racialized patterns in sanitation work. Relatedly, in *Wastelanding* I argued that perceptions of particular landscapes as wastelands—easily polluted, ecologically worthless, and uninhabited or unimportantly inhabited—relied on perceptions of the people who occupy those landscapes as unworthy of protection from environmental harm.

If landforms like the Salton Sea function in ways that maintain and advance the dispossessive and exploitative nature of settler colonialism, it extends what we can think of as cases of environmental injustice. When environmental conditions exacerbate existing social inequities—as, for example, happens around the Salton Sea when evaporation exposes nearby poor and nonwhite communities to noxious dust storms—they become part of the structure of those community members' experiences of oppression. When social inequities contribute to harm done against the nonhumans and the environment, they become part of the ways in which human oppression of other humans degrades environmental quality. Each of these functionalities expands and transforms the scope of what we understand to be environmental injustices. Environmental injustice thus can include more commonly studied examples, such as racist patterns in toxic waste siting, but also can be used as a framework to analyze a wide range of sites and scales, from the network of dams that alternately flood and desiccate Native lands (chapter 4), to the impacts on wild fish and birds from racial capitalism in agricultural labor (chapter 5). Feminist ecologists note this reality, arguing, as Sherilyn MacGregor does, that "one cannot have environmental sustainability without social and economic sustainability."[47]

Approaching environmental *injustice* in this way has the potential to transform how we imagine environmental *justice*. David Pellow, a leading scholar in environmental justice studies, calls for a "critical" approach to this field, one that can "comprehend the complex spatial and temporal causes, consequences, and possible resolutions of [environmental justice] struggles."[48] Indigenous studies scholars, in turn, have sought to reframe environmental justice in ways that position it, as Indigenous studies scholar Jaskiron Dhillon puts it, "within historical, social, political, and economic contexts and larger structures of power that foreground the relationships among settler colonialism, nature, and planetary devastation." Environmental justice, in this framework, encompasses not just demands for redistribution but demands for decolonizing settler relations to nature as well as to Indigenous people and territory.[49] In arguing that settler colonialism has restructured nature in the form of "organic machines" that then themselves produce the outcomes of settler colonial power over people and nature, I suggest that decolonization necessarily entails these larger concerns about "planetary devastation." Planetary devastation is not an incidental outcome, or accident, of settler history; it is built into the very machinations that move it forward.

THE PATHS AT OUR FEET

Each of the chapters in *The Settler Sea* tells the history of the Salton Sea through a thematic lens. Although each chapter offers its own internal chronology, the chapters move the book forward chronologically, from deep geological time in part 1, to the 1880s through the early 1940s in part 2, and the mid- to late twentieth century in part 3. For each of these broad swaths of time, I have identified the primary agents of change at the Salton Sea: desert and flood in part 1; birds, concrete, and bodies in part 2; and bombs, chains, and toxins in part 3.

Chapter 1 presents a long view of the sea's history through Indigenous oral history and ecological knowledge, mapped closely onto geological understandings of the region's formation. Chapter 2 eyes the Salton Sea from the perspective of rivers and limnological systems, looking at the history of human relationships to riverborne resources in the desert from the 1880s to the flooding that created the Salton Sea in 1905–7.

Chapter 3 looks at the Salton Sea from a bird's-eye view, seeking out the relationships between humans and their avifaunal relations, as well as their consequences. Chapter 4 pays heed to the role of dams and other settler-built infrastructure of the West's hydraulic empire, noting that the Salton Sea's existence has hinged as much on the Hoover Dam as it has the Colorado River. Chapter 5 presents a history of the sea through bodies of various sizes and scales—from human bodies and their impacts on the Salton Sea (and vice versa), to the roles of insect bodies and other "pests," to vector bodies such as bacteria that, though small, have had giant physical and ideological consequences.

The mid- to late twentieth-century history of the Salton Sea, as well as its status in the early twenty-first century, revolves around the roles of bombs, chains, and toxins. Chapter 6 examines the uses of the Salton Sea by the U.S. military—as a base, a target, and a test site—during and after World War II, and it also maps the sea into the history of the broader militarization of the West since the 1940s. Chapter 7 pays heed to the deeply carceral nature of settler relationships to the desert surrounding the Salton Sea from the 1880s on, with those relationships intensifying in the later decades of the twentieth century. Chapter 8 concludes the main body of the book by telling the Salton Sea's history through the lens of toxic pollution, including pesticides, bacteria and viruses, and dump sites near its shores.

The result of this approach is less a step-by-step chronological account of change over time at the Salton Sea than it is a kaleidoscope. Turn the Salton Sea one way, you see a diverse wetland for water birds; tilt it a bit more, and witness an intensely polluted hazardscape; a clockwise twist reveals a disregarded place of poverty and destitution occupied by families pulled there by low-wage labor; turn it the other way and see the quirky counterculture that sprouted here in celebration of the sea's paradoxical strangeness.[50] A full rotation lays bare a sacred Indigenous world, maintained since time immemorial with balance between human communities and their nonhuman relations in mind.[51]

The Settler Sea does not provide an exhaustive account of the major settlements that surround the Salton Sea, from Palm Springs, Banning, and Indio, to Imperial, Brawley, and Holtville, to Mexicali and Calexico. Each of these places has its own micro-history, its own nuanced tales of culture, politics, environment, and change over time. Other works will have to trace those contours of life in this desert world. Nor is *The Settler Sea* a political economic history of the forces of capital and governance that shaped, and were shaped by, events at and near the Salton Sea.

This could have been a very different book. As anyone who has been there knows, the Salton Sea resists representation. No camera can capture its vastness, no single perspective can quite reconcile its vibrant communities of birds with the rotting detritus of settler life—moldy armchairs and abandoned trailers, empty pools and shuttered motels—that litters its shoreline. A book about its history could have focused on any number of different ways of framing its past. *The Settler Sea* offers one angle of vision with which to regard this rich and complex place, with the promise and the caveat of a final set of paradoxes: that the Salton Sea, this place of environmental crisis and decline, is also a place of astounding abundance. A *settler* sea that has facilitated the dispossession of Indigenous peoples remains home to those same peoples, who assert their sovereignties, speak their languages, tell their histories, weave their baskets, and hold their ceremonies in contiguous connections with their ancestors. This is a place of limitless stories and limitless ways to tell them.

This book traces these paths toward and away from the Salton Sea, a body of water teetering somewhere between nature and culture, settler and Native, past and future. The routes might not always be clear, the story often as murky as the sea's bacteria-choked water. But, etched along ancient water lines, overblown by gusty winds, lined with straggly creosote, they unfailingly guide us toward a better understanding of our world, each other, and where we might go from here.

PART 1

1

DESERT

The land itself is an archive.

—Lisa Brooks, *Our Beloved Kin*, 2018

THE RIVER

Viewed through the macro lens of geologic time, the Colorado River might look like a skinny serpent undulating languidly across the high desert landscapes of the U.S. Southwest—a rattlesnake lazily taking in the late afternoon sun. Its headwaters emerged nearly eight and a half thousand feet above sea level at Grand Lake, Colorado, from which it flowed south and west, over time nestling itself thousands of feet deep in the warm red earth of the Colorado Plateau. It created vast canyons and chasms as it flowed rapidly downhill.

At the very tip of its tail, where a diamondback's rattle would be, the river flicked back and forth across the lowlands of present-day Imperial County. When it turned to the north, water poured into the desert, weighed down by the salt and silt of its 1,400-mile-long journey from the Rocky Mountains. Eventually the river carved out a giant bowl in the earth's floor, shifting aside the thin desert soil until the earth sank two hundred feet below sea level. In Cahuilla oral history describing the formation of this bowl in their desert homeland, the Cahuilla creators,

Múkat and Témayawet, "turned up the edges of the earth" so that the water could not spill over when the basin was flooded by the Colorado.[1]

In this way, per the creators' design, the water steadied the earth and the earth cupped the water. Years passed, the basin filling with water so choked by the sediment of dissolved mountains, plains, and canyons that it shone red in the sunlight; as outsiders would later quip, the Colorado was "too thick to drink, too thin to plow."[2] Eventually this displaced soil and silt pressed against the earth, pushing the river back toward its former bed with a levee of its own creation. Then the river turned south again, seeking a free and unimpeded course to the ocean. Above the crook of the continent's western elbow, where the lower California peninsula met the mainland, the Colorado spread out in its delta with the relief of water set loose over broad, flat, and arid ground. Back in the Cahuilla homeland, the great body of water the river had created slowly retreated skyward.

From its headwaters in the Rocky Mountains all the way to the sea, people cared for the Colorado River. At Grand Lake, where the river began, members of the Ute, Cheyenne, and Arapaho Nations regarded the water as a relative, and they offered prayers in exchange for the bounties of fish and game it provided. Where it buried itself hundreds of feet deep in the land, carving through sedimentary rock across the Colorado Plateau, the Diné, Hopi, Havasupai, and Hualapi Nations cared for it and for the fish it sustained. Along its lower lengths, the Mojave (Pipa Aha Macav), Chemehuevi, and Quechan (Kwatsan) peoples used the river to irrigate their crops, their gods having given them this gift by fixing the river's course across their lands so that the river would not flood but run sometimes fast and sometimes slow. For the Mojaves, Mastamho, the grandchild of Earth and Sky, guided the river with his boat so that it would spread itself flat and wide across the earth. Quechans taught that Kumastamxo, son of the god Kwikumat, etched the Colorado's course in the ground with his spear, ensuring that it would run to the ocean and not flood Quechans' homeland.

Cahuillas and Kumeyaays had no such divine reassurance against the threat of flooding. Whenever the Colorado River changed course to send water flowing north into their homelands, it created a vast sea in this desert world. The water brought new relatives to the desert tribes: fish and fowl, as well as mammals, reptiles, and plants. It dispersed seeds across the land, which sprouted and bloomed and grew into squat trees with wide overstories, casting shade across the hot ground and sprouting plentiful beans rich in protein and fiber. By most estimates, full inundations of the desert—when the whole contents of the Colorado poured north into the Salton Sink—occurred three times in the last millennium.[3] Today geologists estimate that large floods have periodically filled the entire basin nearly as far south as the Colorado River delta, creating vast lakes every few hundred years that stretched more than a hundred miles, dramatically altering the desert ecosystem.

One long human lifetime might be enough to measure the epic ebbs and flows produced by the twitchy tail of the Colorado River. A child born when the first trickles of river water collected at the bottom of the sink would be an adult by the time the river turned south again and sought free passage to the sea. Near the end of her life, with great-grandchildren playing at her feet, she would have lived to see the desert laid bare and waterless again by the furious heat of the sun. Historians have called the great body of water in the desert Lake Cahuilla; before Americans arrived in the desert, it probably last filled the basin and evaporated in the mid- to late sixteenth century.

Contending with a river that sometimes, with a flick of its tail, flooded their lands, these desert peoples needed to adapt to vastly different environmental conditions depending on the presence or absence of water. When the desert flooded, Cahuillas moved whole villages to the mountains, out of reach of the wayward river. When the new lake reached its apex, they returned to its northern and western shorelines to build stone fish traps that looked like giant U- and V-shaped colanders in the desert floor and that trapped and held fish when the tide receded. Here they caught the various fish species supplied by the river—bonytail, striped mullet, and razorback sucker—and used bows and obsidian-tipped arrows to bring down the birds that, like their human neighbors, also feasted on the newly plentiful fish.[4]

After each flood the water slowly receded. Memories of it did not. Flooding figured prominently in the oral histories of desert Cahuilla,

Kumeyaay, and Quechan peoples. In the 1940s Francisco Patencio, a historian of the Agua Caliente band of the Cahuilla Nation, recounted this history in a way that speaks to the ever-changing nature of the Cahuillas' experiences of water in the desert: "The water did not come in one moment, no. It came rolling along slowly, so that the people who heard and saw, ran up the mountain sides and saved their lives. But nothing down in the valley lived, either animals or men."[5] These floods displaced entire clans to other parts of the desert and to the mountains.[6] A Cahuilla community in the present-day Santa Rosa Mountains originally formed due to a flood that filled the Salton Sink. When that incarnation of the great lake evaporated, some people stayed in that mountain community and others returned to the now-dry valley below. Many of the most sacred sites for the Cahuilla Nation are related to the presence, absence, or evaporation of water in the Salton Sink. Cahuillas consider petroglyphs at the fish traps their "'national treasures,' [and] a symbol of their sacred past."[7] The lake served as a landmark for places where obsidian could be gathered to make tools and weapons, or for trade with other desert nations.[8] When the water evaporated, the desert valley was home to village sites where a number of families and clans made their homes, including Túva', the village of the Wanticiñakik-tamianawitcem clan, and Ulicpatciat, home to the Mumkwitcem clan.[9]

The landscape itself remembered these inland seas, its visitations from the intemperate Colorado. Strata like bathtub rings marked high-water lines. Shells and the fossils of lacustrine animals lie scattered across the shallow surface of rocks and soil. The ephemeral New and Alamo Rivers provided channels for the water heading north into the sink, etched into the earth during dry times and floods alike. Few visitors to the area failed to notice the evidence left behind by the inland sea, so clear that "it was not difficult to imagine [hearing] the measured swell of the waves" and worry that the "waters might suddenly return and claim their former sway" over the desert.[10]

Farther to the south, where desert Kumeyaay people dwelled, Colorado River water was life. In between the great floods that occurred at intervals of several hundred years, the Colorado regularly lapped over its banks into floodplains that stretched through the land where the U.S.-Mexico border now scores the map. These smaller bodies of water ran ten to fifteen miles long and only a few feet deep. In heat that caused standing water to evaporate at a rate of six feet per year, smaller lakelets appeared and disappeared regularly. Along the two sloughs referred to on present-day maps as the New River and the Alamo River, desert Kumeyaays could expect water to flow north toward the Salton Sink in the summer, although in many years the riverbeds remained dry.[11] Kumeyaays in the desert chose their planting sites carefully, surveying their wide swath of territory from the mountains in the west to the Colorado River in the east. Floods flushed the desert with fresh water, bringing fish and fowl, and replenishing vegetation. When Americans began poking their way through the region in the 1840s, they noticed these trickling overflows and the caches of fresh water left behind—by one count, at least fifteen of these floods slaked the desert's thirst between 1840 and 1900.

When Lake Cahuilla filled the basin sometime around 1600, desert Kumeyaays, like their Cahuilla neighbors to the north, adapted to their new lake environment. On the southern shores of the great body of water, Kumeyaays fished from seasonal village sites. They hunted the diverse species of birds that were called to the desert by the water; a favorite by far was the American coot, which the Kumeyaay could hunt by laying vast nets in the muddy shallows and driving the birds into them. When a community member died, Kumeyaays conducted their mourning ceremonies—the *keruk* ceremony to cremate the deceased and the *watlma* to burn their clothing—along the lake's beloved shoreline.[12]

As these nations developed flexible relations with water, plants, and desert, so too did they develop interactions with each other. In 1540, prior to Spanish arrival in what would become the U.S. Southwest, intricate trading networks linked nations, from the northern coastal Chumash to the Tohono O'odham east of the Colorado River and beyond. Quechans traded gourds, eagle feathers, tobacco, and baskets for Kumeyaay shellfish, yucca fiber, and carrying nets. Shell beads—what the Cahuilla called *múkyat*—traded from the Chumash islands not far from the coast functioned as currency for trade with the Cahuilla, Xawiłł kwñchawaay, and many peoples beyond.[13] The Cahuillas bartered with Parry

y psychological stress which does not appear to be directly relate
) the cause of the stress, as Rappaport and Vayda have demor
rated with regard to the function of pig feasts in Melanesi
Rappaport, 1964:17–40; Vayda, 1961:69–77).

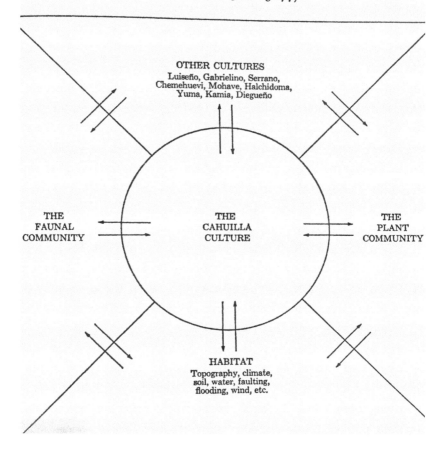

5. Anthropologist Lowell John Bean mapped the entangling influences of the Cahuilla
world as a system of mutually constitutive forces interacting between the habitat,
the faunal community, the plant community, and other cultures. Lowell John Bean,
Mukat's People: The Cahuilla Indians of Southern California (Berkeley: University of
California Press, 1974), fig. 1.

pinyon nuts, which could be used to make nutritious baby food, porridge, beverages, and, when dried, caches of food for lean times. They traded arrowheads made from obsidian gathered on the northwestern shore of Lake Cahuilla, and those arrow points could be tipped with poison from desert elephant trees.[14] Marriage relations connected the Chemehuevi people in familial bonds to members of the Cahuilla, Hopi, Payómkawichum, Mojave, Diné, and Yavapai Nations. Trading networks traversed the land from west to east and from south to north, as did well-trod pathways, songs, histories, and shared vocabulary.[15] Desert Kumeyaays maintained such close relationships with the Quechans to the east that white observers could never decide if they belonged to the Kumeyaay Nation, the Quechans, or were their own people entirely (the Kamias).[16] The region saw conflict at times: raids and territorial skirmishes, interpersonal conflict and strife.[17] But these nations existed largely as peaceful and cooperative neighbors, each closely connected to their homelands.[18]

During dry times the Colorado Desert served as a crossing-over place: a zone of migration and interaction, a terrestrial version of connective tissue for peoples engaged in travel and trade. Well-worn paths formed a zone of international migration, with intricate networks of trails lining the Colorado Desert like arteries delivering the lifeblood of human communities: commerce, stories, conflict, debates, gossip, technology, art, songs, resources, and relationships.[19] The trails carried people in every direction, the enmeshing of their worlds along the desert paths marked with "pot drops," shrines, wells, rock cairns, and engravings.[20] Cahuilla historian Katherine Siva Saubel described the relationships between these nations as a grid of intersecting trails: "Everywhere their trails crisscrossed the terrain they traveled on, where the Indians would meet each other."[21] In Saubel's telling, the territorial borders of the Cahuillas served as rendezvous places where different nations overlapped. People gathered food in the borderlands, coming together to share languages, stories, and songs. "They would never get into skirmishes," she attested; "[the borders] were entirely open."[22]

As people migrated between nations, so did their songs. Across the desert, people sang their shared histories and relationships with local ecosystems in the form of the Bird Songs. Sung over a period of four days with a driving, syncopating rhythm that invited listeners to dance along with the singers' voices and the beat they kept with rattles, Bird Songs traveled across the Colorado Plateau and down from the Great Basin. They came up from the south and traveled west to east along the Gila River. Each nation crafted them to its own language and independent history, but together the syncretic cultural form of the Bird Songs came to share similar features and purposes: to inform and to entertain, to educate and build community.[23]

At the heart of this world made of multiple dynamic and evolving nations sat either the dry bowl carved by Colorado River water into the floor of the northern Sonoran desert or a vast lake, depending on the moods of the region's most important river. Together the river, desert, and people constructed a place built around cyclical changes, responding to shifts in the human and nonhuman world in ways that emerged from their history, close care for the environmental conditions of their homelands, and deep epistemological knowledge that their physical world frequently changed, sometimes without warning. According to one anthropologist, Cahuillas adopted a "basic assumption of unpredictability," which reflected the role of water and its irregular comings and goings.[24]

In 2017 a book examining the natural history of California asserted, like so many other sources have, that "before 1905, the Salton Sea did not exist."[25] This common declaration erases a long history of this region and the crucial role of multiple bodies of water in shaping its human and nonhuman past, but it also, however inadvertently, suggests compelling counterhistories for this body of water. From a Cahuilla point of view, the notion that the Salton Sea never existed before 1905 might make a certain kind of sense; the body of water now occupying the sink has never been artificially maintained or seen as a permanent feature of the landscape. In this sense the Salton Sea is starkly different from past bodies of water.

From a settler point of view, it suggests the power of historical amnesia, a reckless overlooking of environmental history and conditions that give context for contemporary ecological conditions; the settler notion that the Salton Sea did not exist before 1905 reveals how, as critical race theorists Eve Tuck and K. Wayne Yang have put it, "the horizons of the settler colonial nation-state are total."[26] In other words, possibilities external to the settler colonial nation-state, its drives and desires, its hegemonies and histories, are consistently in danger of being forgotten or even erased. In the end, how we remember the Salton Sea and tell its story, whether and how we recognize its existence before 1905, depends to a large extent on how we remember these other bodies of desert water, and their connections—spanning nearly half a continent—to the Colorado River and the river's many peoples.[27]

A DESERT AND ITS PEOPLES

To understand a mesquite tree, you must first look underground. Under the surface of the earth a strong taproot travels as far as two hundred feet in search of water, reaching toward deep aquifers. No other tree is known to reach as far into the ground for its water. As thick around as a human leg, long and conical like a giant carrot, the taproot provides a profound anchorage for what above the earth might look comparatively insubstantial. The lateral roots, meanwhile, spread out parallel to the surface, their long, thin branches reaching fifty feet in every direction to pull in moisture from shallower soil. This network of roots can draw wetness from desperately dry earth, and for this reason its below-ground body is nearly always larger than the parts that glimmer in the hot sun above the surface. In lean times the roots can even shift from a flagging water source to a more promising one.[28]

Above ground the tree moves the water upward through at least one main trunk before branching into a canopy wider than it is tall. It casts a broad swath of precious shade across the sun-baked ground, offering more shade from a short and squat tree dappled with small leaves than any tall and narrow counterpart could hope to provide.[29] In spring and summer the branches burst into fuzzy yellow blossoms the length and width of your finger, calling out to bees for pollination. The upper branches offer nesting places for birds. The tree, however, does not give itself over entirely to hospitality: inch-long thorns await roaming herbivores who stray too near the branches.

In early summer comes the first harvest: successive bounties of bean pods, still green in the sun and growing anywhere from three to eight inches long, encasing smooth bundles of protein and fiber, carbohydrates and vitamins, sugar and fat—all the component parts of good food.[30] The second harvest arrives before autumn, the bean pods toasted to a crisp brown by long months of summer sunshine. For thousands of years the tree's people, spreading far and wide over the continent, from the California mountain ranges through the southern tips of the Yucatán Peninsula, have found a thousand ways to eat mesquite beans. Nonhuman animals—particularly herbivores such as deer, mountain sheep, and antelope—thrived on the bean pods plucked from the branches.[31] Coyotes and other scavengers waited until the late summer and fall, when the brown pods fell to the ground and scattered under the trees' shade.

Humans put their opposable thumbs to good use. Drying the pods and grinding the beans to a fine meal in stone metates, they transformed the mesquite harvest into porridge, pancakes, crackers, soup, bread, fermented and unfermented beverages, tea, candy, and flour. Across the continent mesquites offered food, shelter, firewood, and medicine to a staggering variety of Indigenous nations: Kiowa, Mescalero and Chiricahua Apache, Comanche, Isleta, Keres, Acoma, Laguna, Pima, Yavapai, Havasupai, Kumeyaay, Payómkawichum, Mahuna, Maricopa, Mojave, Paiute, Papago, Seri, Kwatsan, Diné, Cahuilla, Cocopah, Kawaiisu, Tewa, and Hualapai.[32] The Spanish borrowed a name for the mesquite tree from Nahuatl; they called it "meszquite," after the Nahua people's reverential term for their arboreal relation, *mizquitl*.

Cahuillas honored the trees by naming their seasons after its lifecycle stages: eight seasons made up the Cahuilla year, moving from the season when mesquites budded (Taspa), to the season in which they blossomed (Sevwa), through the season when seed pods formed (Hevawiva), the season when they ripened (Menukis-kwasva), the season when they fell (Merukis-chaveva), and then to midsummer (Talpa), the season of cool days (Uche-wiva), and the season of cold days before the mesquites budded again (Tamiva).[33] In addition to this mesquite-based calendar, Cahuillas named their clans for the mesquite's various types and virtues.[34] They used its fibers and wood for clothes and clothing fasteners, diapers, paper, tools, cooking implements, rope, building materials, dermatological salve, hunting bows, and eye medicine. Its sap made excellent glue.[35] From the late nineteenth century on, non-Native settlers relied on the trees as indications of the presence of water not far under the surface of the ground, and they assumed that large trees equated to a full and shallow water table, while short trees marked places where water would be less abundant.[36]

The tree cared for its plant relations in addition to its human neighbors. Cacti and bushes clustered nearby to share in its shade. Its deep taproot brought water near the surface of the ground to dampen the shallower roots of these plants, making them doubly welcome to grow next door.[37] Humans too wanted to be nearby and often cultivated stands of the trees near their village sites. In these villages Cahuillas considered trees communal resources, not the property of individuals or families.[38] One should not, however, harvest the beans without first asking the person who grew and cared for them. Not asking before picking could spark arguments. Some stands were known for growing particularly sweet beans, others for high yields; Cahuilla women, who took on most of the work of cultivating mesquite stands and harvesting from them, often knew how to nurture the beans and when to pick them to make the creamiest teas or the richest flours.[39]

The tree's people reciprocated its many blessings by taking on responsibility for its health and prosperity. In fact, the impressive range of the mesquite's natural habitat has its animal relations to thank: reaching back to the Miocene and Pleistocene epochs, mastodons and giant sloths feasted on mesquite pods and spread the seeds far and wide across the continent via the vector of their scat.[40] In more recent history its human relations, including Cahuillas, cared for it by pruning its crowded branches, digging ditches and deep wells for irrigation, and using controlled burns to protect it from parasites, such as desert mistletoe.[41]

The people treated mesquites as they treated their other plant relations: by asking before taking, harvesting only what they needed, and always leaving something behind so there would be more in the future.[42] As Saubel put it, "They did not abuse it"; "they treated the mesquite

6. Cahuillas constructed granaries for storing huge quantities of mesquite beans. Charles C. Pierce, *Coahuilla Indian Mesquite Granary at Torres, East of Palm Springs*, circa 1903. California Historical Society Collection, 1860–1960; Title Insurance and Trust, and C. C. Pierce Photography Collection, 1860–1960. University of Southern California Libraries. California Historical Society.

trees with respect."[43] The women prepared themselves and the trees for harvest by talking to the trees. "*Ne pishkal*," they might say, or "'I have come' *henyekawish* 'to gather' *etu'i* 'your fruit.'" I will store it for later, they told the trees, before offering a final word of deep gratitude: "*alawa* 'thank you.'"[44] Harvesting, in other words, was also a time to practice being a good relative.

Cahuillas called the beans they harvested from mesquites *méñikiš*. The Cahuillas' homeland, with their help, provided an excellent ecological setting for people with a *méñikiš*-based diet to thrive—at least, when it was a desert and not a lake. Large inundations of the water from the Colorado River wiped out stands of mesquites even as they displaced the Cahuillas who cultivated and relied on them. These times

7. Alena Levi (*left*) photographed on the Torres Martinez Reservation, October 30, 1917. Levi leans over a granary basket while another woman observes her work. Edward H. Davis, Alena Levi (also known as Helena Levi and Mrs. Louis Levy), desert Cahuilla (Torres Martinez Reservation/Torres Martinez band), circa 1853–1922, Torres Martinez Reservation, National Museum of the American Indian.

of great flooding came to be known as the Starving Time, when new resources would need to be found to sustain whole communities, and people who only knew how to fish based on their grandparents' stories had to draw on those intergenerational memories to put recollections into practice.[45] Small overflows, on the other hand, dispersed new seeds and water to the desert floor for new growth of these trees.

During long stretches of time when no great lakes occupied the desert—spanning the concurrent lifetimes of "four or five very old men," as reported by Cahuillas in 1909—mesquites provided a key resource that allowed the Cahuilla to re-adapt to desert, as opposed to lacustrine, lifeways.[46] Fish-based diets turned back to *méñikiš*-based diets. Mesquite porridge replaced aquatic birds as a source of protein.

The mesquite roots' ability to shift underground from one water source to another served as an ecological metaphor for Cahuillas' ability to thrive in radically different ecological conditions: from mountains to desert, from a lacustrine world of birds and fish to a spare and arid one of plant fibers and beans. They navigated complex cultural conditions as well, developing relationships of trade, negotiation, and shared space with communities throughout the region. These ecological and cultural influences, in combination with the exigencies of the faunal and plant worlds, produced a flexible and adaptive worldview among the Cahuillas.[47]

Over time the Cahuilla Nation divided itself into three roughly geographical subgroups: mountain Cahuillas, desert Cahuillas, and pass Cahuillas. Each geographical subgroup relied on hunting, gathering, and cultivating food, as well as trading with neighboring nations. Villages formed around water sources, and each village comprised from 150 to several hundred people, organized into clans. Most clans got their names from sacred plants or the animals present at their creator, Múkat's, funeral: Ativalem, the dog clan; Wietem, grasshopper clan; Iswatem, mountain lion clan; Tokut, bobcat clan; Univetem, bear clan; Unal, the badger clan; and so on.[48] Each clan had a *net* (leader) chosen by a council of clan members and *puls* (medicine people, including men and women) who had been chosen by Múkat. Clans gathered in their own *kish umna*, or ceremonial house, for funerals and dances, feasts and *kewéts* (or festive social gatherings).[49] The *net* lived in the *kish umna* and cared for the sacred eagles they raised there. Today these groups are dispersed in a diaspora among a number of Southern California reservations, as well as on nonreservation land.[50]

Desert Cahuillas, occupying what is currently called the Coachella Valley—named for the preponderance of shells embedded in the valley's soil and rock, each one a memento of the region's watery past—established village sites all along the northern stretches of the Sonoran Desert, from the edges of the deepest parts of the Salton Sink to the foothills of the mountains. These villagers developed sophisticated uses and cultivation of desert resources. They dug canals to divert water from streams and freshwater springs to their fields of melons, beans, and squash.[51] They maximized ecological conditions for herbaceous plants by use of controlled burns, including burning palm trees that had become infested with parasitic insects.[52] As Saubel described this process, "When something would infest them, when they would get wormy, then they would burn the (infected) palm tree." Saubel went on, saying that this "was the way the Indians took care of the earth."[53] They transplanted nutritious root plants nearer their villages so they could better tend to them.[54] They planted palm trees in well-watered areas, growing whole stands and harvesting the trees' rich fruit.[55] They cultivated kitchen gardens of chia and deer grass.[56] In addition to wild plants, they harvested beans, corn, and tobacco, which were gifts from their creator, Múkat, upon his death.[57] When he died, Múkat told the people he had created "tobacco . . . for the old people to smoke. The melons grow from my skull; pumpkins from my stomach; corn from my teeth," and Múkat instructed the people that these things would nurture them.[58] They diverted natural springs into reservoirs for irrigation of these gifts and kept keen eyes out for pests that might ruin the harvest, singing to the bugs that ate wild oats and corn kernels. "'I am watching over [this plant],'" a singer would caution the insects. To save the plant, the singer warned, "En meknan kuai kavi'"—"I will kill you."[59]

Mesquites provided a primary way in which Cahuillas navigated this ever-changing world. But in addition to the bounty harvested from mesquites, Cahuillas tended other wild and domesticated members of their plant community: arrow weed, juniper, agave, oak, palm, and a cornucopia of fruits. Roasted agave oozed a rich molasses-like sap. Cahuilla women cooked stalks of yucca and boiled their flowers. They harvested wild plums and the sweet fruits of native palm trees, collecting these and other food plants in coiled baskets crafted from wiregrass, deer grass, and sumac.[60] When floods from the Colorado River brought water to the desert and sprouted stands of reeds, they culled the plants' fibers to weave hammocks for carrying their babies. Meanwhile, men and boys hunted rabbits with bows and arrows and ribbonwood hunting sticks, returning with heavy clutches of cottontails and jackrabbits. Young men and boys did not eat their own kills but rather distributed them to other families, a practice that built into Cahuilla life a reliance on others and a practice of community interdependency.[61]

Mesquite trees, in combination with the exercise of these agricultural practices, provided some stability for Cahuilla people in a world where instability was literally part of the firmament. Located on top of a vast seam in the earth, where two tectonic plates knit together along a line that geologists later named the San Andreas Fault, the ground under Cahuilla feet shifted, rocked, and trembled with alarming frequency. The deep wells Cahuilla people dug to access underground aquifers were regularly disturbed by these quakes, meaning that the Colorado River was not the only fickle water source in their lives: well water would be plentiful one week and gone the next, shifting along with the temperamental ground beneath them.[62] Rather than causing alarm, the regularity of earthquakes made this a normal part of Cahuilla life; as Pedro Chino, a Cahuilla *pa'vu'ul* (the most powerful of *puls*, or shamans), put it, "The earth is just breathing."[63] Cahuillas honored the earthquakes with songs that mimicked the rhythm of the "'pulsating'" earth.[64]

Thus, in addition to the Colorado River flicking its watery tail periodically across their homeland, giving water and then taking it away again, Cahuillas contended with often-unpredictable moods of land and climate. Flash floods resulted from rare inundations of heavy rainfall. Water rose and fell. The earth shook when it breathed. All of these conditions of the natural world that surrounded them figured into Cahuilla stories, ceremonies, and ecological practices, together forming a worldview that understood, according to Cahuilla historian Anthony Madrigal, that "the circumstances of life are often unstable and unpredictable." In a world that breathed and flooded, Cahuillas' ecological knowledge emphasized "the value of working diligently and carefully, a necessary virtue in an uncertain world and changing environment."[65]

Their worldview entailed more than a deep understanding of ecology, however. In her autobiography, Cahuilla *pul* and anthropologist Ruby Modesto spoke wryly of settler researchers from universities who traveled to the desert to learn about her peoples' uses of plants. "They believe everything we tell them," she reported, having witnessed too many of these outsiders busily scribbling down the various uses of mesquite, palo verde, and desert chia. "But," she noted, "when we say the most important part they smile and turn away." The part they missed made up a universe of Modesto's knowledge as a *pul*: the reality that "plants

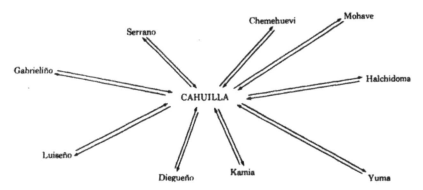

FIGURE 2. Schematic Diagram Showing Intertribal Relationships with the Cahuilla.

8. A chart of Cahuilla relationships to nearby Native nations, as interpreted by Lowell John Bean. Lowell John Bean, *Mukat's People: The Cahuilla Indians of Southern California* (Berkeley: University of California Press, 1974), fig. 2.

have a spirit too." Learning their spirits, Modesto knew, provided the key to the Cahuillas' long tenure in an often shifting world.[66]

To the south, along sacred desert trails that traversed the Salton Sink, Kumeyaays likewise cultivated strong connections to their arid homeland, despite—and possibly because of—its natural fluctuations and startling ecological diversity.[67] At the eastern base of the mountains, where the slopes eased into alluvial plains at the seams of mountain and desert, Kumeyaays used agricultural terracing to maximize runoff; they lined up parallel rows of rocks to catch water and spread it over their fields, wetted seasonally with overflow water from the Colorado River.[68] They also used brush, anchored with rocks, to more evenly distribute runoff and moisten dry ground.[69] Like the Cahuillas, they transplanted wild tuber roots, wild onions, and tobacco near their villages and in areas well suited for these plants' growth. Recognizing the multitude of blessings brought by mesquites, they transplanted these trees across their homeland.[70] Across the Kumeyaays' broad swath of land, the people cultivated gardens, transplanted vegetation for food and medicinal purposes, and used stands of cacti as fences around communities.[71]

The desert reaches of the Kumeyaays' homeland constituted just one part of a vast expanse containing a range of ecological conditions. The Kumeyaay Nation stretched from the desert area around the Salton Sink all the way west to the salty spray of the Pacific Ocean. Kumeyaays cultivated resources from shellfish on the coast, to pinyon and oak in the In-Ko-Pah and Jacumba Mountains and foothills, to low-lying medicinal gardens along the Tijuana River.[72] In the desert to the south of the Salton Sink, Kumeyaays planted according to the overflows of the Colorado River, waiting for the summer season. When the constellations Hachaa and Anyehai (the Pleiades and Hyades to European-descended astronomers) appeared in the night sky, these stars marked the beginning of the month Hellyaa Hachaa and the planting season.[73]

Changes in population density roughly 1,300 years ago corresponded to more intensive resource use among Kumeyaays; development of new material culture, including ceramics and hard projectile points; and more complex relations with their neighboring nations. Nevertheless, seasonal migration, deep knowledge of their homeland and its ecological and botanical conditions, and organization of the larger nation into small groups or bands meant that Kumeyaays left a relatively light ecological and archeological footprint. Because of their long tenure on a vast and diverse homeland, Kumeyaays benefited from Colorado River overflows but did not entirely rely on these irregular inundations.[74] Like the Cahuillas to their north, they dug wells for fresh water. Unlike the Cahuillas and their deep walk-in wells, however, the Kumeyaays needed to dig just below the surface, scooping water into clay pots and tightly woven baskets.[75]

The autobiography of Delfina Cuero, a Kumeyaay woman born around 1900, vividly illustrated Kumeyaay relationships to their diverse ecosystems. Those relationships required mobility across a broad swath of land, from foothills and mountains to tide pools and sea, *as well as* regular access to planted areas of cultivated crops. In Cuero's account, this work of tending the wild was both laborious and rewarding; she reflected on memories of how her family would travel to the coast and spend their days gathering shellfish and then preserving it with salt harvested from San Diego Bay. They would "pound the meat of abalone soft with a rock" and use its shells as spoons. They dug holes big enough to hold ollas that could be used to harvest clams and trapped and cleaned fish, sometimes with nets woven from agave fiber and sometimes with the aid of boats woven so tightly of reeds that water would not seep through.[76]

To the east Quechans and Cocopahs benefited from greater proximity to the Colorado River and its less capricious nature there in its main riverbed (thanks, according to Quechan history, to the engineering prowess of Kumastamxo). Here, agriculture thrived despite the near total absence of rainfall. Instead of relying on water from the sky, Quechans organized their growing seasons around annual overflow of the Colorado River: in early summer, the snowmelt from faraway mountains swelled the river, and it seeped over its banks into Quechan fields. In late spring they cleared the fields adjacent to the river. When the water arrived, Quechans used sharpened sticks to make seed holes in the fields, planting the seeds in mud as quickly as possible before the parching summer heat dried the ground again. Corn and beans, adapted to a lightning-quick growing season, thrived here, as did squash: together, these crops were the Three Sisters that sustained many Native Nations across North America.[77]

In and around the Salton Sink these peoples created an international borderland where multiple nations came together. Together the forces of water and desert shaped the lifeways of these nations, influencing their ecological practices, the ways their societies changed (seasonally and over the course of decades), and how they related to one another. In its regular ebbs and flows, Lake Cahuilla mattered a great deal for the region and its human and nonhuman inhabitants.

FROM BORDERLAND TO SHATTER ZONE

In the mid- to late sixteenth century the last stand of the great Lake Cahuilla slowly evaporated under the glare of the desert sun. On its northern and southern shores, Cahuilla and Kumeyaay families fished in the lake's shallows and hunted the birds that cruised over its surface. By the 1540s troubling rumors had arrived from the east and southeast along trading networks. From their neighbors—the Tohono O'odham, the Hohokam, the Quechan, and the Nde peoples—came stories of violence, sickness, strange animals, and even stranger people. News of these portentous arrivals traveled west from these nations to reach the Kumeyaay clans on the Pacific coast; in 1543, when a Spanish ship appeared in what is currently San Diego Bay, the Kumeyaays responded by firing arrows at the Spanish, driving them away to their great relief.[78] A generation later, knowledge of these strangers and the consequences that trailed along behind them prompted the Chumash to respond likewise to the appearance of a boat in their harbor: they attacked it and the men onboard, driving it back to the open sea.

For the next hundred years the Spanish presence in the lives of Cahuilla, Kumeyaay, Quechan, and Payómkawichum peoples took the form of irregular expeditions that never seemed to yield concrete outcomes, as well as, and much more dangerously, new diseases that appeared in their communities seemingly from nowhere and wiped out whole swaths of population. Spanish people, however, were seen only rarely.

By 1684 these Native peoples' southern neighbors could not say the same. In that year the first Spanish missions in the Californias began their slow march north, beginning in present-day Baja. To the Indigenous peoples of this peninsula, they brought a new god, new germs, new creatures, new seeds and plants, new architecture, and—perhaps most disastrously—new soldiers. The missions formed the ballast for Spanish military occupation of the Baja California Peninsula, a religious cover for military conquest. The Jesuit padres exerted little control over the violent impulses of the soldiers. Along with dying from overwork, starvation, disease, and other miscellaneous perils of their conversion to Christianity, the Native peoples of Baja suffered violence, rape, humiliation, and death at the hands of the Spanish military. Within a century of the establishment of the first mission on the peninsula, the Indigenous population of Baja—comprising Paipai, Pericú, Guaycura, Monqui, Cochimí, Kiliwa, Akwa'ala, Xawiłł kwñchawaay, and Kumeyaay peoples—decreased by 82.5 percent, from forty thousand persons to seven thousand.[79]

Given this devastation of their southern neighbors, the establishment of Franciscan missions along the California coastline met almost immediate resistance by Native peoples. The first mission in what the Spanish called Alta California, Mission San Diego de Alcalá, was founded in 1769 in the heart of the Kumeyaay homeland. Just six years and several hundred conversions later, six hundred Kumeyaays attacked the mission in the dead of night, setting fire to the buildings and killing the man in charge, Father Luis Jayme, by arrow and bludgeon. Ten years later, eight years after its founding, Mission San Gabriel saw an uprising of its own, with Tongva warriors led by the medicine woman Toypurina plotting to assault the priests in the dark of a moonless night. In 1780 Quechan people attacked the Purísima Concepción mission near present-day Yuma; the following year they did the same at the only other mission on their land, the Mission San Pedro y San Pablo de Bicuñer, just six months after it was founded. On top of these assaults on the missions, the Spanish discovered and thwarted untold other attempted rebellions.[80] As the mission system sprawled northward along the coast, eventually expanding to twenty-one missions in just over sixty-four years, the Spanish contended with daily acts of quotidian resistance: work stoppages and slowdowns, runaways, secrecy, guerrilla assaults, revivals of Native religious practices, and poisoned food.[81]

Seeking to quash rebellions big and small, soldiers defended the missions with violence and bloody spectacle, in one instance murdering an insurgent Tongva *tomyaar* (chief) and mounting his severed head on a pike for the edification of other would-be rebels. Spanish soldiers committed unspeakable acts of sexual violence against Native women and girls and routinely snatched children from their families to bring to the missions or sold them as enslaved laborers to Spanish families. Soldiers trampled the cultivated wealth of crops grown by the Kumeyaay, Payómkawichum, Tongva, and Chumash peoples; missionaries fenced off the land that hosted these crops and pulled them up by their roots to make way for rows of corn, beans, and squash—meaning that, in addition to infectious diseases and violence, the Native people also faced hunger and starvation. These conditions drove them by the thousands, ironically, *to* the missions, where workforces of Native *neofitos* (Christian initiates) had already been put to work growing food for missionaries and their new dependents.[82]

Preoccupied by their missions in the rich coastal zones, the Spanish only cast ambivalent eyes east toward the deserts. They desperately sought a foothold in the area where Yuma now sits, on Quechan land near the convergence of the Colorado and Gila Rivers, as the base of an overland connection between Sonora and California. In 1775 the Anza expedition represented the first sustained Spanish interest in inland explorations. Spanish military officer Juan Bautista de Anza's reports of dry, barren wastes did not encourage the Spanish to prioritize this part of their colonial project. Five years later the Quechans put an end to Spanish interest in the desert with their repeated attacks on the nascent missions. Thanks to this sustained and successful resistance, and to the European interlopers' discomfort with the exceptionally forbidding terrain, the Spanish never could establish a strong presence in the desert reaches of Alta California. The Kuupangaxwichem (Cupeño) people, in their homeland just northwest of the Colorado Desert, did not encounter Spaniards until 1795.

Even without establishing missions in the desert, Spanish colonization nevertheless had an impact on the lives and homelands of desert peoples. Spanish presence brought disease and invasive species, destroyed long-cultivated crops, redrew territorial boundaries, pushed people into the mountains and deserts from the more densely populated coastal areas, and ended or transformed centuries-long Indigenous trading relationships. Captives fled the missions and traveled hundreds of miles to escape, moving into other peoples' homelands and bringing stories of horror and dread—as well as deadly diseases. The fracturing of coastal Kumeyaay, Tongva, and Chumash lifeways sent fissures spreading eastward, where they creaked under the feet of the Cahuilla, Kuupangaxwichem, desert Kumeyaay, and Cocopah communities.[83]

The cracks first took the form of new, nonhuman relations: germs, seeds, and livestock. Germs made themselves known through deadly epidemics. On the other side of the continent, as English settlers observed cataclysmic population collapse among their Indigenous neighbors and wondered if outbreaks portended divine endorsement of English colonies (they did not), diseases in the Spanish sphere of contact spread along historical trading routes between Native communities. By the end of the sixteenth century smallpox, in combination with the other cataclysms of missionization, had devastated Native peoples as far north in New Spain as Sonora. Smallpox and measles outbreaks spread west to east and south to north for the next three centuries, cresting every few years, bringing death and disability and hindering Native peoples' capacity to maintain traditional ecological, cultural, familial, and economic practices, particularly when combined with the violent conditions created by Spanish colonization. As Rosalie Robertson, a Kumeyaay descendant of survivors of the mission system, reported, "My people got very sick in [the Spanish] missions. When you put the people all crowded together and pen them up in one dirty place, and those places were dirty, of course they get sick, and that's how the diseases got them." In and out of the missions, Spanish colonialism created unhealthy conditions that allowed diseases to flourish.[84]

Other transformations clopped through California on the hooves of horses, sheep, cows, and goats. Spanish livestock trod over and through the plants that Native peoples had carefully cultivated and harvested up and down the coast. By Robertson's account, some plants disappeared completely from Kumeyaay land, pulled up by the roots by the hoofed interlopers. On the other hand, as elsewhere on the continent, Native Nations of the desert adopted and indigenized European livestock, integrating horses in particular into Indigenous cultural and economic systems. The success of Quechan attacks on Spanish missions in 1780 and 1781 derived, in part, from their stellar equestrian skills. This indigenization of livestock also transformed spatial relations of Native Nations. Land that had been sufficient for people with no livestock was suddenly insufficient for people looking to graze flocks of horses, cows, and sheep.[85] An area that would be traversed in weeks by human strides could be crossed in days on horseback. Across the continent space suddenly became tighter, boundaries closer, and territorial conflicts hotter.[86]

Exacerbating these growing conflicts, Spanish influence also brought a new kind of exchange and traffic to a world that had long thrived on trade in shellfish and gourds, baskets and pots: that of human bodies. Spanish reliance on captive labor radiated east from the coastal missions and west from the New Mexican settlements. A booming slave trade expanded the reach of Spanish colonization to places where Spanish colonists never set foot, the effects spreading to even the unlikeliest of locales: the desert borderlands, hundreds of feet below sea level, where the territories of the Kumeyaay, Cahuilla, Payómkawichum, and Cocopah peoples came together, this place where the Colorado River deigned to flood from time to time and Natives had for centuries been learning to navigate the whims of a river and the strictures of a desert.[87]

By the time Mexico declared its independence from Spain in 1821, significant changes had reshaped the desert world between these nations. Successive epidemics prevented the population from maintaining crops, migration routes, and trade relationships. Refugees from the mission corridor moved continuously east toward the mountains and deserts. Territories shrank and, with them, life-sustaining resources.[88]

The Mexican period, lasting from 1821 to 1845, would again reconfigure life in the desert. Just as the establishment of missions produced ripple effects in the surrounding Native population, so did the decommissioning of these cruel institutions.[89] Mexico's secularization of the missions ostensibly liberated mission-dependent *neofitos* and invited Natives into the Mexican nation—nominally, at least—as full citizens. After nearly six decades of Spanish colonization and now under Mexican control, coastal Natives saw their homelands carved up into land grants and ranchos. Seeking to recover from the brutality of the pitiless mission period and having been kicked off their mission-adjacent lands by newly expanded ranchos, many former mission-dependent Indigenous people moved east toward the desert, "pushed into the rocks," as one historian put it, by the forces of coastal Mexican settlement.[90]

The shatter zone of the coastal mission corridor and the Mexican aftermath pushed Indigenous people east, toward the mountains and desert.[91] The traditional borderlands between the Colorado River tribes (Quechans, Cocopahs, Chemehuevis, Mojaves) and the desert and mountain nations (Cahuillas, Kumeyaays, Kuupangaxwichems) bore new burdens of instability and change: new disease ecologies; new patterns of resource consumption for food, water, and commodities; and new kinds of human relations. By the mid-nineteenth century these nations had responded with transformations of their political systems and adaptations of ecological relations.[92] They also developed rigorous anticolonial alliances. In 1833 an alliance of Kumeyaay and Quechan leaders asserted Native sovereignty over mission lands. The following year Kumeyaays worked together with Paipais and Cocopahs to attack Santa Catalina Mission in Baja California, while Cahuillas and Kumeyaays attacked the mission at San Bernardino repeatedly throughout 1835.[93] In general the Mexican period of California history gives the impression of persistent indigenization; seeing the padres routed from the missions by Mexican independence, Indigenous peoples sought to reclaim their homelands, even as Mexicans rushed to carve them into vast ranchos.[94] The trend toward indigenization was helped along by a weak Mexican government, with often only nominal control over the extreme northern reaches of its territory.

The mid-nineteenth century, however, brought new devastations to the land tenure, nationhood, and health of Native Nations in what became the state of California in 1850.

THE CROSSING-OVER PLACE

On a blazing hot afternoon in June 1853 a geologist named William Phipps Blake stood on a rocky outcrop above a vast depression in the earth's floor. He saw mesquite stands dotting what his contemporaries called a saline plain, with Cahuilla villages clustered around the valuable trees. As his companions ranged over the sink below him, collecting samples of univalve fossils then unknown to science and observing "bathtub rings" that revealed the high-water mark of the vast and ancient sea, Blake exulted.

Here he found a crossing-over place—though not the place of migration for people, seeds, river, and birds, as it had been for thousands of years. Instead, Blake saw promise in this place for a new kind of crossing-over: that of a railroad that could move people, goods, food, and supplies through the desert from east to west and back again. Cartographers had long sought an easy route through California's difficult central and eastern topography, noting that the unending mountains and deserts made travel to its storied coasts a deadly and trying prospect for emigrants to the gold fields and for other new settlers traveling from the East.[95]

Blake was not the first intruder to the Indigenous world of the Colorado Desert to recognize its potential. In 1776 the Spanish had sent Juan Bautista de Anza to find a route that would connect Spanish settlements in Sonora to the coastal corridor of missions. To show him the route, Anza hired Sebastián Tarabal, a Cochimí who had escaped from San Gabriel Mission with his wife and returned to the Cochimí homeland in Sonora via the desert. Tarabal's escape route was not unique; these desert passages were known to other Indigenous refugees as a haven from the bleakness and violence of the Spanish mission system. Nearly a century later John Butterfield established a portion of the Overland Mail route through the northern portion of the desert—through Cahuilla and Kuupangaxwichem homelands—along what Butterfield called the Anza Trail but would have been more accurately dubbed the Tarabal Trail.

If the desert was a place of refuge for Native people fleeing Spanish violence, settlers took the opposite view: the forbidding desert was something to flee *from*, not to, and a place to be crossed over as quickly and efficiently as possible. When settlers first began arriving in and near the Salton Sink, general non-Native attitudes about land—particularly that land was only good if you could till it or mine it—meant that this particularly desolate-seeming section of the Sonoran Desert held little promise. Settlers had little interest in the desert and dark memories of the hapless gold seekers who had succumbed to the dunes and blistering heat in the summer of 1849. A few imaginative speculators, witnessing clear evidence that the sink used to hold a vast sea, fantasized about diverting the Colorado River here to make an "irrigated Eden," a version of the numerous irrigation schemes that were happening all across the West in the mid- to late nineteenth century. Among these, a government-appointed Indian agent named Oliver M. Wozencraft dreamed the most fervently of an irrigated wonderland in the desert, going so far as to petition Congress for funding to construct an irrigation canal to draw Colorado River water to the Salton Sink.[96]

Again and again these schemes failed, dying with their proponents or faltering in the face of more promising projects. Still, settlers' hope sprang eternal: if tilling was out, at least for the time being, mining might still be a possibility for profit from the land. Some hopefuls sought gold in the Chocolate Mountains, ranging around the north edge of the sink and in the Pacific Mining District to the east, rich in deposits of gold, silver, and lead.[97] The exigencies of boom-and-bust cycles of mining economies brought settlers in and ushered them out again. As they came and went, they altered the nonhuman and human landscape alike, in ways that had strikingly different outcomes than Indigenous changes wrought on the same environments.

Settlers arrived from all directions. Within a year of the discovery of gold at Sutter's Mill in January 1848, tens of thousands of people—white Americans to be sure, but also Chinese, Mexicans, French, Chileans, Germans, and Russians—worked in California's goldfields. Cherokees came from Indian Territory. Free and enslaved Black people traveled from the east. Germans and Russians arrived from the north.[98] A "Sonoran migration" of Mexican prospectors, many of them Yaquis, traveled north from the Mexican states of Sonora, Chihuahua, and Durango through the blistering heat of the Colorado Desert en route to the gold diggings, carrying with them the "Indian baskets" that preceded iron gold pans for swirling pay dirt in water.[99] Newcomers from China labored in mining camps, opened hotels, started farms, and took jobs as wage laborers.[100] White Californians responded to the growth in Asian immigration to California with a crescendo of racist rhetoric, policy, and violence, matched only by the virulent racism against Native peoples and Mexicans that had characterized white California life since 1847.[101] "Their touch," wrote the poet Bayard Taylor of Chinese immigrants in 1855, "is pollution."[102] The California legislature concurred, passing laws that barred Chinese people from testifying in court against white people, placed heavy taxes on Chinese businesses to prevent them from competing with white businesses, and barred the entry of Chinese women without special permits.[103]

Some of the transformations to Native life that attended the shift to U.S. colonization after 1848 exaggerated the tragedies and injustices of Spanish and Mexican colonization. In 1850 the new California legislature, as one of its first orders of business, passed the mendaciously titled Act for the Governance and Protection of Indians, which gave legal cover for what became a voracious branch of a region-wide and centuries-old system of Native enslavement.[104] Passing as a benevolent codification of indenture and adoption of Native orphans, the law resulted in a statewide assault on Native families through the systematic kidnapping of thousands of their children. Settlers murdered resistant parents who sought to save their kin from this forced removal. The act, in short, amounted to a codification of tyranny and served as a state-backed helpmate to the raging fire of genocidal violence occurring just outside the boundaries of legality.[105]

At the same time, the act assaulted Native sovereignty and land tenure in other, more nuanced, ways. It banned, for example, Native peoples' use of fire to maintain ecological relations. Brushfires and other kinds of controlled burns had long been a key technique by which California Natives cared for their environments, from the Maidus' arboreal homeland to the Cahuillas' desert world and everywhere in between. If the act's assaults on Native families codified tyranny, its strictures on Native fire management codified settler forms of ecological relations over Indigenous ones. The result further debased Native peoples' ability to maintain their relations to their homelands.

Not that California settlers needed the incentive of codification. With or without the backing of state law, settlers turned their rifles on any Native people in their way. The period between 1846 and 1870 in California saw perhaps the most blatant, bloody, and sustained genocide in the history of U.S. settler colonialism.[106] As best as can be estimated, California settlers, vigilantes, and militia members murdered at least 9,400 California Natives between 1846 and 1873.[107] Tens of thousands more died from exposure, starvation, epidemics, and overwork. In total, from 1846 (the beginning of the American period of colonization in California) to 1870, the population of Native Californians went from about 150,000 people to 30,000—an 80 percent decline in barely twenty-four years.[108] The first decades of California's statehood, in other words, bent toward genocide, the new state's policy and settler population intent on elimination of its Native peoples. In Southern California, settlers so desperately desired the coastal homelands of Kumeyaays, Luiseños, and

Tongvas that even the meager legal protections for these peoples failed to prevent them from being shunted away from their homelands.[109] "We were just held down to . . . different areas," Cahuilla historian Katherine Saubel related, "sometimes to areas where we didn't even belong."[110]

In an ambivalent attempt to stymie the genocide, in 1853 the federal government began creating reservations for Native refugees of this undeclared war. These reservations, however, lacked firm boundaries. Mapmakers "floated" lines on maps, cartographically slicing good land out of reservations for the benefit of settlers. Settlers often came to their landholdings via the expedient of squatting on Native land and claiming it as their own.[111]

Three decades later, when Helen Hunt Jackson and Abbot Kinney arrived in California to study the condition and needs of the state's Indigenous peoples, they learned that most Native communities did not know the exact boundaries of their federally guaranteed lands. Compounding this confusion, leaders of many California Native Nations had already negotiated for significant land bases with federal agents in 1852, signing treaties that would have secured for them eight and a half million acres in a series of reservations running down the spine of the state. No one informed them that the U.S. Senate never ratified these treaties; rather, fearing the ire of California landowners, the Senate placed the treaties under seal for fifty years, lest anyone discover them and argue, per the U.S. Constitution, that "all Treaties made, or which shall be made, under the Authority of the United States, shall be the supreme Law of the Land."[112] In the words of Saubel, "They just hid them away somewhere," later finding them in "what the white people call a 'basement.'"[113]

As in the Spanish and Mexican periods, Southern California Indigenous leaders developed alliances to defend and protect themselves against this genocidal encroachment, part of an unbroken and continuous pattern of Native assertions of their self-determination and status as nations in the face of ongoing colonialism in California.[114] To the southeast, Quechans stood stalwart against American aggression, as they had against Spanish aggression a century before, at least in one instance with bloody results.[115] Meanwhile, Antonio Garrá, a Kuupangaxwichem leader, organized with Cahuillas, Kumeyaays, Payómkawichums, and Chemehuevis to seize control of the desert and Lower Colorado River. Under Garrá's leadership, they antagonized settlers from Yuma to San Bernardino and west all the way to coastal settlements. San Luis Rey in particular suffered repeated raids by Garrá and his forces, its American military personnel complaining that Garrá "openly committed depredations" against them. Adding literal insult to injury, the Americans also grumbled that Garrá "was on one occasion rude to Col. Cooke," in what they deemed an audacious transgression.[116] Entreating members of these various nations to work together against U.S. encroachment, Garrá implored them to understand that "if we lose this war, all will be lost. . . . This war," he stressed, "is for a whole life."[117]

The consequences of the early years of U.S. colonization of Southern California reshaped Cahuilla life in a way even the shatter zone of Spanish and Mexican colonization of coastal California had not. In a single decade, the 1860s, the Cahuillas experienced firsthand the twinned manifestations of settler colonialism that had devastated nations to their west, north, and east: smallpox and land dispossession. In 1863 smallpox tore through Cahuilla communities, killing entire clans already stressed by the pressures of colonization. The virus flourished because of a lack of immunity among Cahuillas, to be sure—part of the "virgin soil" epidemics that tore through Native communities on the continent for more than three centuries after European contact. But, as elsewhere, smallpox also gained a foothold among Southern California Native communities because of larger social and environmental conditions created by colonization; without these external factors, this viral wildfire would surely not have so thoroughly devastated Cahuillas in the 1860s.[118] This disease reached its deadly crescendo exactly ten years after the arrival of the first permanent white settler in the part of the Cahuilla homeland where the town of Banning now sits. Land dispossession compounded the pestilence. As in so many other Native homelands, the federal government ceded alternating sections of land to the railroad, carving up property in a checkerboard pattern that few bothered to explain to the people actually living on the land in question.[119]

By 1876, when President Ulysses S. Grant established mission Indian reservations by executive order, Cahuillas had experienced a series of devastating and deadly epidemics and had lost legal property rights to huge swaths of their land. Although settlers were still few and far between in the desert, settler colonial land policy, settler-borne epidemics, and new infrastructure had restructured Cahuilla life. In parts of inland Southern California, settlers often denied Natives access to public lands to graze their livestock, in addition to squatting on tribal land and hiring private surveyors to float lines and change boundaries on official maps.[120]

In the Cahuillas' desert world, the proximity of a heavily armed settler population had tragic and unjust consequences. In one of the most infamous of these episodes, a settler named Sam Temple shot and killed a Cahuilla man named Juan Diego, claiming that Juan Diego had stolen his horse. Temple followed Juan Diego, confronted him, and fired on him three times from a distance of four or five feet. Juan Diego's wife and two other Native women witnessed the murder but never had the chance to testify about what they saw; Temple promptly and unabashedly offered a full handwritten confession to a judge in San Jacinto. After reading his account, the judge dismissed all charges against the murderer "on grounds of justifiable homicide," opining that "no offense under the law [had] been committed."[121] The story took on national significance when Helen Hunt Jackson, incensed at the treatment of Native people throughout California, fictionalized the woes of Juan Diego and his widow, Ramona Lubo, in her novel *Ramona*.[122] At the time, Jackson wrote bitterly that "the killing of Indians is not a very dangerous thing in California."[123] Cahuillas and other Native peoples would likely have concurred, as would have other people of color, particularly Chinese immigrants, throughout the state—a view borne out in the violent life of Sam Temple himself, who spent his time in California tottering along a trail marked with bullets and blood. The decade after he killed Juan Diego, Temple shot and killed two Chinese men as they worked on the Santa Fe railway line to San Diego.[124]

As suggested by Temple's bloody biography, Native peoples' experiences of settler colonialism intersected with the effects of orientalist racism against Chinese immigrants. Anti-Chinese racism in coastal cities pushed Asian settlers eastward into Cahuilla and desert Kumeyaay land. Chinese farms and businesses that had sprouted along the coast and displaced Kumeyaay communities wilted in the face of codified discrimination and racist violence.[125] In the most notorious of these, a white mob attacked Chinese residents of Los Angeles in 1871, lynching seventeen Chinese men and spreading terror throughout the community.[126] In 1885 the Anti-Chinese Club formed in San Diego to protest the city's hiring of Chinese laborers for public works projects. During these years the Southern Pacific Railroad relied heavily on Chinese labor to build its Sunset Limited line connecting Yuma and Los Angeles. Workers increasingly found that staying in the desert reaches of Southern California posed fewer limitations from racist whites and more economic opportunity.[127]

In 1877, in the already transformed human and environmental landscape of the Colorado Desert, the first cars of the Southern Pacific Railroad cruised past the homesites of desert Cahuillas, chugging through the lowlands of the northern edge of the Salton Sink and away to the western edge of the continent. As the passengers gazed out their windows at the dry landscape running past, they measured their progress in the regular rise and fall of telegraph wires, which had begun spiriting messages from San Diego to Yuma and back again years before any railroad ties were hammered into the ground.

The railroad shrank the desert world by dint of new people and speedy and safe passage across what had before been a treacherous landscape. Settlers could now see and experience the desert in new ways. Changes to the material conditions of the landscape followed in due course. By 1900 oil companies had taken advantage of the railroad and new legal authority to stake claims on public domain land, sinking oil wells in the desert from Palm Springs to the U.S.-Mexico border.[128] During these years, oil drilling rigs rose from the desert like quills. The San Diego County clerk's office received claims from an energetic array of new concerns.[129] Their employees scoured Cahuilla and Kumeyaay land for petroleum reserves, used water from Cahuilla wells and natural springs, and burned stands of mesquite trees for the fuel they needed in their pursuit of fossil fuel energy to fire their works.

Using gas- and steam-powered drills, these companies sank wells nearly seven hundred feet into the desert floor, discovering what Cahuillas and Kumeyaays already knew: that underneath surface layers of clay and sandstone flowed vast aquifers of fresh water. Where Indigenous people had spent weeks digging wells laterally into the surface of the desert, these drillers punctured aquifers in hours. They capped wells Cahuillas had dug, effectively privatizing precious water sources that had previously been available to humans and nonhuman animals alike.[130] With this relatively quick access to plentiful aquifers, the *promise* of water in dreams of would-be agriculturalists like the federal Indian agent Oliver Wozencraft crashed into the *presence* of water in this unlikely place. If Cahuilla wells hewn into the desert floor signified Indigenous efforts to glean some stability from an inherently unstable world, settlers would put in place plans built on the faulty notion that this landscape was stable, static, and unchanging—a perfect stage for the dramas of teleological progress necessary for white settler worldviews in the West.

2

FLOOD

Then came the deluge.

—Alfred W. Crosby, *Ecological Imperialism*, 1986

LEAKS AND FISSURES

At the lowest part of the Salton Sink, two suns met face to face: one above, one below. The first sun blazed downward from the sky, baking the earth with the heat of an oven. From below, the second sun pulsed from a vast sheet of whiteness, reciprocating every degree of heat it received from above.

Here the tricks of centuries' worth of geological action on the desert—flooding and evaporating, flooding and evaporating, over and over again—left behind an underground wellspring of a particular kind of harvest: salt. As the sun vaporized water from the Colorado River into clouds, traveling upward in its purest molecular form—hydrogen, wed to oxygen—it shed the minerals that would keep it earthbound. Thousands of years of salt gathered here at this lowest point of the sink, a mother lode of purest sodium chloride in a vast salt marsh that continually regenerated itself.

Beneath a crust of pure white more than half a foot deep was a thick black brine the consistency of wet cement. Workers' boots crunched through the salt and sank into the muck below. Iron rods dropped into the white crust sank below the surface and disappeared, never to be recovered. Hands dug deep into this second sun, pulling back the white crust that made up its face. The heat, combined with the sweat of their labor, left those hands dried and cracked, looking like desiccated ground waiting for raindrops. These hands formed the whiteness into conical mounds standing as high as a man's waist, laid out in rows—an orchard of heat. As the workers scraped up the salt, more pushed up from below. At a time when salting was the most widespread means of preserving food in the United States (reliable refrigeration technology still being in the future), the salt fields of Salton represented a constant harvest of seemingly limitless profit for those who cared about such things.

One man, arriving in the desert from San Francisco via the Southern Pacific in the 1880s, cared very deeply about the profits this hot harvest promised. Early in that decade George Durbrow disembarked at the depot in Indio to take advantage of the young town's reputation as a vast open-air sanatorium. Afflicted with tuberculosis, Durbrow sought a climate that would ease his aching lungs. In the meantime, he cast about for a way to make money from this sparsely populated desert world. In 1883 he ordered a shipment of Guatemalan coffee trees to see if they would flourish in the foothills outside of Indio.[1] By the following year the coffee trees had failed, but the "climate cure" had worked. Durbrow filed a business license to mine salt from the low marshlands of the Salton Sink—somewhat delinquently, as he had initiated operations there the year before. He hired Henry Williamson McKay to oversee the saltworks.[2] Together, Durbrow and McKay gathered a workforce of local desert Cahuilla people, who had been harvesting the salt for trade since the evaporation of Lake Cahuilla in the mid-sixteenth century. Just a decade and a half out from a smallpox epidemic that had devastated desert Cahuilla clans and families, carrying away their powerful leader, Juan Antonio, these Cahuilla workers likely saw this as an opportunity for some stability and wage work at a time when agriculture was simply untenable on their too-small reservation.[3]

Their proximity to the abundance of salt on the surface of the desert (given that it was part of their homeland) and their experience with harvesting the salt probably made the Cahuillas seem like a natural

Plowing Salt at Salton.
Indio.

9. Workers harvesting salt from the Salton Sink for George Durbrow's New Liverpool Salt Works in the salt-encrusted prehistoric sea basin. Howard C. Tibbitts, *Plowing Salt at Salton. Indio*. 1894. Photographs of the Southern Pacific Route. The Bancroft Library, University of California, Berkeley.

workforce to Durbrow and McKay. But little was natural about the grueling labor they proceeded to do for the profit of Durbrow's company, christened the New Liverpool Salt Company. By 1891 nearly four hundred Cahuillas were spending long, hot days gathering the harvest from the salt fields. As they worked, they perspired so heavily in the heat that, as one observer noted, "you would imagine there was a garden hose playing on them all the time."[4] At night they slept in makeshift shelters, pieced together from surplus railroad ties scavenged from the Southern Pacific line. Where wide ribbons of sky could be seen in the gaps between the ties, workers covered the holes with tin from cans of fruit, split apart in a fire and hammered flat for makeshift shingles. They covered the roofs of these homes with earth to keep out any rain that might fall on this parched world. The work of domestic life occurred

THE SALTON SEA AND SALT WORKS.

10. Workers heaping salt from centuries' worth of deposits from the Colorado River into conical mounds to be packaged and shipped to settler consumers. *California South of Tehachapi: From Notes by the Agents Southern Pacific Company* (San Francisco: Southern Pacific, 1904), 89.

mostly outside, under arrow-weed ramadas, where women labored over zinc tubs and washboards.[5]

Few children, however, lived in the spare camps or played in the slatted shade from ramadas where their mothers and grandmothers cooked. During a decade that saw the rise of boarding schools for Native children across the United States, many Cahuilla children were already being removed from their families to Southern California's nascent system of missionary-run and industrial schools. As the 1880s came to a close, many of the children of Durbrow's Cahuilla workers faced removal to the St. Boniface Indian School at Banning. The schoolhouse had been built by the students themselves out of bricks made by Chinese laborers.[6] At St. Boniface, speaking Cahuilla within earshot of Catholic priests and nuns earned a child a whipping; the students subverted this attempt at exterminating their Native language by sneaking out behind the barn to speak together in their own tongue.[7]

While these Cahuilla students had their hair shorn short and their

Native languages banned, their adult relations pulled profit from the Salton Sink for Durbrow.[8] In late June 1891 Durbrow's Cahuilla employees, laboring between the sink's two suns, paused to note a strange new occurrence: small streams of water trickling in from the south and spreading out over the desert floor, in some places quite rapidly accumulating to more than a foot in depth. The workers were accustomed to strangeness. They were used to looking out over a "weird, bald desert," cupped around them, the bright shining white field uninterrupted by trees and rocks—and not a cache of shade in sight.[9] However, on that day in June the water made for something new, not least because it seemed to come from nowhere.[10] Over the course of two days the streams of water proved insistent—and worrisomely expansive. Water rapidly pooled at the lowest part of the sink, its volume increasing by the minute.

The Cahuilla workers did not wait to find out what the curious new flow of water portended; without delay, they packed their belongings, abandoned the salt field, and headed into the mountains—a move McKay and Durbrow furiously derided as an overreaction based on fear and superstition.[11] Of the roughly four hundred Cahuillas near the saltworks at that time, nearly all of them retreated to the mountains immediately after the first signs of flooding.[12] At Salton station they sent messages to the St. Boniface Indian School for their children to join them. Within days of the initial appearance of water, "there was not an Indian left at [Salton]. They had absolutely refused to remain, and had decamped to the high grounds in a panic."[13] Durbrow exasperatedly telegraphed Salton "asking that a gang of Chinamen be sent" to make up for the lost Cahuilla laborers. The Native residents of nearby Banning soon followed suit and began to pack up and leave as well. Rumors flew through desert communities that a "medicine man" had warned local Natives of a flood in which "all whites would be swept away and only the Indians saved"—perhaps a localized interpretation of the teachings of the Ghost Dance, which predicted similar results.[14] Laughing at this portent of (or wish for) their demise, white settlers in Banning gathered to form a yacht club, electing a few lucky men as their first officers, to celebrate the formation of a new lake in their vicinity.[15]

Within a few days, the water had increased from a collection of pooling streams to a rush of water so vigorous that its gushing could be heard by passengers on a Southern Pacific train en route to San Diego.[16] By June 30 the body of water in the sink was five miles wide and thirty miles long. By July 1, just a week after the first streams of water had appeared at the saltworks, the water's coverage had expanded astoundingly, to an estimated twelve miles long and forty miles wide.[17] At its fullest, the new body of water in the sink barely missed submerging the tracks of the Southern Pacific Railroad, which ran along the new lake's eastern edge. Soon, the saltworks had to be abandoned entirely— and the Cahuillas' early departure to the hills began to look less like superstition and more like prescience.[18]

The effects of the floods radiated out from the sink to the rest of the region. As if desert mirages had suddenly become real, water seemed to be disappearing from some places and reappearing elsewhere: at the Salton station on the Southern Pacific line and at Indio, recently sunk wells suddenly dried up; near Jacumba, horses unexpectedly mired down in spots in the road so soft and wet that the animals had to be lifted out.[19] Water was not the only barometer of the strange new effects associated with the flooding. Desert dwellers exclaimed that the air had suddenly turned as dry and hot as from a "vast furnace"—so hot it hurt to breathe.[20] This supremely dry and hot air blew across the desert in powerful new windstorms, the likes of which settlers had never experienced and which seemed irrefutably, albeit inexplicably, connected to the new lake in the Salton Sink.[21] San Diegans, on the other hand, experienced a strangely cool summer that brought too much rain, and they fretted that the new lake had somehow changed the very climate of the region.[22]

The settlers regarded the new lake of 1891 with utter perplexity.[23] Was the water's arrival biblical? Climactic? Natural? Was it a blessing or a menace? The result of a subterranean incursion of the Gulf of California in an attempt to "reconquer its old territory"? A "most peculiar freak of nature"?[24] Or perhaps the displacement of the ephemeral Whitewater River, another of nature's freaks that had caused no end of consternation among settlers when it disappeared for months before

The Beginnings of Salton [Sea]
L.A.C. Chamber of Commerce [?]

11. Settlers perplexed by the flooding of the Salton Sink, an anomaly in 1891; they puzzled over its provenance even as Cahuillas rightly predicted future—and bigger—inundations. *Beginnings of Salton Sea, Early View,* circa 1890. Security National Bank Photo Collection, Los Angeles Public Library.

reappearing in its previous channel?[25] Was it a mishap resulting from the sinking of new wells by Southern Pacific engineers?[26] Flooding from a particularly violent cloudburst?[27] Throughout the month of June no one knew nor could they agree on the most plausible theory.

By early July a consensus emerged that the water filling the sink resulted from flooding from the Colorado and Gila Rivers. Settlers dispatched local Cocopah and Quechan runners to find the source of the flooding. They launched boats into the new lake, only to have them run aground at its shallow and muddy southern shore. A group gathered together to report for the *San Francisco Examiner* climbed aboard a boat on the Colorado at its juncture with the Alamo River in the first week of July and found themselves running aground two hundred miles to the northwest at Salton five days later.[28] The river, swollen with summer floods, pushed them along. Just a few months before, Godfrey Sykes, who had been exploring the Colorado River delta to the south, attempted to "solve the riddle" of the water's provenance the same way; without being buoyed by high summer tides, however, Sykes ended up having to abandon his poor boat in the mud and walk some thirty-five miles to reach the nearest rail station.[29]

Different kinds of people viewed the flooding through starkly different lenses. White settlers seemed bemusedly incredulous, then alarmed, and finally resigned to what was frequently called a vast "waste of water"—an aquatic version of a wasteland—now holding court in the desert. One writer called the flooding "the most mysterious thing ever known since the white man has been here."[30] Another commented that passengers on the Southern Pacific seemed unable to comprehend the new sea "but gazed out on the watery waste and pronounced it a wondrous and magnificent mirage."[31]

At Durbrow's saltworks, the makeshift houses of the departed Cahuilla laborers and their families stood in utter ruin. In the flood's aftermath one journalist observed that "all day long the [Native women] can be seen traveling to the places from where the water has receded for the floated timbers and drag them to the nucleus of the settlement for the building of their homes." Moreover, the floods seemed to have made an impact on the village that went beyond what must have been a devastating annihilation of their homes: "the desert Indians," the same writer observed, "have been much unsettled during the past year. . . . Intelligent as these Indians are, this sudden lake has suddenly brought to the fore their superstitions and inspired them with vague, distrustful fears." The overseers of the saltworks took the flood as an opportunity to push an assimilationist agenda, encouraging the Native workers to construct "small cottages . . . regularly laid off into streets and squares" and lined with palm trees.[32]

The nonhuman world likewise responded in different ways to these 1891 floods, and at times settlers recognized what a crucial role a changeable nature played in the human story of life in the desert. The influx of fresh water from the flooding dispersed mesquite seeds to otherwise denuded parts of the sink's floor. The stands of mesquite sprouting from these seeds drew "many varieties of birds of bright hued plumage [and] sweet voices," and their root systems helped to anchor the dry and dusty desert floor against erosion. Their return in the aftermath of the floods, in addition to the grasses that "flourish only for a brief period on the overflowed lands," underscored the importance of regular flooding to this landscape and its human and nonhuman denizens. One observer also mused that the mesquite stands would aid attempts to divert the Colorado to its eastern bed and prevent future floods. "These trees," he noted, "will be the means of forming sand dunes" that would eventually "shut off all water communications of the Colorado River with the Salton," thus serving as a "natural" border to any further floods and protecting settlers and their homesites.[33]

The 1891 floods did not create the body of water now called the Salton Sea. *That* epic flooding would not take place for more than a decade. But when that larger flood occurred, it did lend weight and credence to Cahuilla history and ecological knowledge—as well as to the Cahuilla salt workers' choice to flee to the mountains on first sight of the rising water. John Wesley Powell, the famed director of the U.S. Geological Survey from 1881 to 1894, conceded that the flooding seemed to confirm "that the supposed traditions of the Indians are facts" and that the Colorado River had "been playing pranks of this sort" within the lifetimes of some of the older Cahuillas.[34] Indeed, almost every sojourn by non-Natives into the desert in the nineteenth century had yielded observations of small ephemeral bodies of water in the Salton Sink; there were reports of small lakes in the sink in 1828, 1840, 1849, 1852, 1862, and 1867.[35]

The flooding in 1891 would be the last of these relatively small inundations of the desert. The Colorado River, beginning to swell against three hundred years of silt buildup along its southern delta, was preparing to switch courses again, to flow north into the desert. Unaware of this, Durbrow reopened his saltworks as the 1891 flood slowly evaporated, exposing the salt beds once again. Durbrow insisted that he had tricked the Cahuilla workers into coming back by challenging their manhood, saying that if the laborers refused to come back he would hire their women instead because they possessed more bravery than the men.

The workers returned, perhaps having been cowed by Durbrow's taunts but more likely because for the moment the danger had clearly passed. When they did, their boss took to standing over them as they worked, fearful that they would abandon him again if he left them unsupervised.

In the brightness of the salt field Durbrow kept his paranoid watch over the workers, looking for signs of desertion. As he watched them, the workers kept their eyes on the southern horizon—"every one working with his face toward the gulf"—waiting for that next fateful change in course of the great river beyond the white horizon.[36]

Durbrow's salt scheme thrived for more than two decades before the saltworks dissolved in the flood that created the Salton Sea. From 1905 to 1907 the Colorado River reprised its regular history of turning to the north, away from its delta to the sea, to flow downhill into the Salton Sink. That fateful flooding reshaped the ecology and geography of the Colorado River delta and the Colorado Desert. It reshaped the built environment as well, washing out the Cahuillas' deep walk-in wells; destroying most of the buildings, brothels, and young boulevards of Mexicali; and uprooting the chicken wire fences Imperial Valley farmers had recently used to mark off their property. The floods coursed downhill to the sink and then cut back south again, carrying away the thin, dry soil as it went. Entire chunks of would-be farmland gave way to the water, collapsing into the rushing tide.

The floods also permanently ended Durbrow's salt mining enterprise, much to his frustration. Colorado River water unceremoniously swamped the buildings, equipment, and the salt itself, which all still sit under the murky water of the Salton Sea. After this early twentieth-century flooding, the water would not evaporate and let him return to his pursuits. Durbrow vented his frustration by suing the only entity he could blame for his losses: the California Development Company (CDC), which had ushered the Colorado River into the desert with a fateful mix of hastiness, greed, and incompetence.[37] Durbrow's lawsuit placed the blame for the flooding squarely in human hands, contributing to the larger narrative—still firmly entrenched in collective understandings of the Salton Sea's formation—that this was an accidental body of water, a mistake of engineering, rather than a natural fluctuation born of the long marriage between river and earth.[38]

If Durbrow, having experienced the 1891 flooding and its confirmation of Cahuillas' long experience in the region, knew that his ire at the CDC was misplaced, he did not let it stop his lawsuit. After all, blaming a river for flowing downhill held few profits for someone so well practiced at culling money from the dry ground of this salty desert world.

THE FUTURE WISH

The Imperial Valley began as a pretty mirage. In April 1901, as spring peeked through the desert and mesquite bean pods shone bright green in the early morning sun, settlers arrived on newly purchased plots of Kumeyaay land. They had no water but plenty of parched ground, yards of wire with which to etch their dreams in the dust, and buckets overflowing with extravagant promises from the CDC.

The men of the CDC, with help from the newborn *Imperial Valley Press*, went out of their way to promote a particularly grand vision of the as-yet-unwatered world. They hosted parties for boosters from San Francisco and Los Angeles and fetes for bankers and investors, journalists, and politicians. Imperial Valley's team of boosters urged them to report back to would-be settlers about the area's great promise. A journalist from Los Angeles named I. H. Rice gave form to the CDC's fantasy, enticing settlers to ignore the dusty reality below their feet and look off into the near distance. It helped to squint a little. "This is a great country," he reported. "Here the morning bath is taken in imaginary water; then a brisk walk is enjoyed down the imaginary boulevard; with the aid of a pipe the morning's news can be imagined, even to the cablegrams; in fact, all the comforts of civilization can be imagined by the nervy men who propose to make them realities."[39]

These boosters *had* to imagine their baths, boulevards, and cablegrams. In April 1901 none of those existed in the Imperial Valley. Rather, the valley consisted of a ragged scattering of settlers bartering their futures with promises from one of the many dryland farming companies that had formed—and, one by one, failed—throughout the West in the 1880s and 1890s. On the dusty path of what passed for the community's only street sat a tent hotel, run by a Chinese immigrant, and a church, the only wooden structure in the area. Settlers, most of whom arrived in the area by train and then stage, lived in glorified lean-tos propped up by mesquite posts and covered by thatches of arrow-weed. Large jars stored their only water.[40]

The *Imperial Valley Press* lent credibility to the dusty scene, publishing its first edition in April 1901. This first run of newspapers consisted of little more than endorsements like Rice's persuading settlers to ignore the evidence of their own eyes in favor of the CDC's comely mirage. Their land, punctuated with spiky ocotillos and crisscrossed by trails of jackrabbit footprints, represented "the most fertile body of arid land on the continent."[41] Or so they were told. Even water, the most essential ingredient to the development scheme, had yet to arrive in the CDC's main canal, which, in that hopeful spring of 1901, sat as dry as the settlers' newly fenced fields. The settlers "submitted cheerfully to some privations," one observer opined, "knowing that presently the lands would grow green under the magic touch of water, and be covered with homes." Until then, they waited, carting water in from a pond called Cameron Lake that, before long, also sat dry and empty.[42]

The imaginary Imperial Valley probably more strongly influenced its development than any of the political and economic machinations that brought the CDC and its grandiose promises to this part of California. Even renaming the Colorado Desert the "Imperial Valley" hinged on widespread notions that water could transform what was largely considered a desert waste into a colonial triumph of settler agriculture. Water would, according to one booster, coax "use and fruitfulness" out of "a desert waste."[43] More than perhaps any other example of western settlement in this period rife with audacious, even ludicrous, irrigation schemes, the Imperial Valley represented what postcolonial theorist Edward Said described as a colonial "future wish": the desire to "cancel and transcend an actual reality" by making the "land be empty for development by a more deserving power."[44] The less deserving power, in this equation, meant the Kumeyaay people on whose land the settlers strung their chicken wire fences.[45]

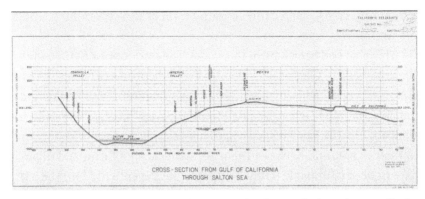

12. This cross section of the Colorado River and Salton Sink shows how easily the sink would flood and how precarious Imperial Valley settlements were in between river and sink. Lawrence Pratt, "Cross-Section from Gulf of California through Salton Sea" (195AD), Folder 2, Box 1, Lawrence Pratt Collection concerning Arizona v. California and the Colorado River, Beinecke Library, Yale University.

Miles away to the southeast, George Chaffey, the CDC's chief engineer, applied muscle to the future wish. In the cool spring months of 1901, Chaffey oversaw the construction of diversionary headgates that would siphon off a portion of the Colorado River's rushing, silt-clogged bulk into CDC canals. The water still had a long way to travel before wetting the dry farms of Imperial Valley settlers. Once diverted from the Colorado, it would turn south from Chaffey's main outpost—Hanlon Heading, just a few miles above the U.S.-Mexico border, in Quechan land—and flow across the border before careening west for another two or three miles. From there, it connected with the dry bed of the Alamo River, turning the water again toward the border, this time from south to north.[46] The Alamo River led through the Imperial Valley en route to the Salton Sink.

Before it rushed downhill toward the sink, its natural repository, the river water would be intercepted, in the CDC's plans, by settlers siphoning it off from the main canal to their thirsty fields. As long as the CDC could maintain control over the river—a river one historian has described as a "forty-pound wolverine that can drive a bear off its dinner" and one that crashed through one-twelfth of the U.S. continental land area, bringing with it a remarkable amount of the West's mountains, valleys, and canyons in the form of silt—everything would be just fine.[47]

This plan had been long in the works. The CDC formed in 1896 under the leadership of Charles Rockwood, a man described as a "wheedler and a plotter, a self-justifying advocate of the grandiose," and Rockwood's partner, Anthony Heber (a "small [and] viperish" man, a "comrade-in-flimflam").[48] The pair excelled at striking deals that quickly disintegrated in their hands, and between them the two had significant and diverse experiences with bankruptcy. Chaffey would eventually join the CDC as its chief engineer in the spring of 1900. But in the company's early years of chasing investors around New York City restaurants, technicalities like how to engineer canals, dams, and headgates for diverting irrigation water from an ornery and tempestuous western river seemed unimportant. When they recruited Chaffey to the company, the engineer saved the CDC thrice over: with his technical expertise, with his ability to raise funds, and with his idea for the scheme's name, a name that suggested that Rockwood was not the only "advocate of the grandiose" among them; it was Chaffey who dubbed it the *Imperial* Valley.[49]

The CDC did not sell land to settlers. Instead, it inverted many of the dryland farming schemes that had preceded it (and mostly failed) by dealing in rights to water alone. They set about creating subsidiary distribution companies on either side of the U.S.-Mexico border. The fact that the water had to cross the international line actually enabled the scheme, rather than causing additional headaches, in these early years. The water, which could not be privatized under U.S. law, left the United States and in doing so became property of the CDC's Mexican subsidiary. It then reentered the United States again as privately owned Mexican property—meaning that the CDC need not abide by U.S. regulations on the use and distribution of water from one of its major tributaries.[50] In effect, the CDC's main genius lay not in designing complex canal systems (those had mostly been engineered by the Colorado River and its centuries of overflow) or farming (its officials knew little about coaxing plants from dry land, and few had any foresight about what to do with the highly alkaline soil they proposed to water) but in designing a scheme for laundering water the way mobsters laundered money. What is more, when settlers defaulted on their expensive water rights, their land reverted to CDC ownership. It had the potential to be a beautiful, profitable, and not particularly legal grift.[51]

On May 14, 1901, just before lunchtime, Chaffey oversaw the first diversion of water into the CDC's border-crossing, part natural and part human-made canal system. Weeks later the water from Chaffey's diversion arrived in the Imperial Valley, greeted by a ragged scattering of settlers.[52] Their joy at the site of water in such a dry place must have been intense; after all, many of them likely felt as thirsty as their crops (fresh water notwithstanding, if they wanted a stronger beverage to take their minds off having bargained their futures on a spare and unwelcoming desert and mortgaged their futures to a man like Charles Rockwood, they would have to travel two hard days by stage to Calexico and then cross the line to Mexicali).[53] Within six months the Colorado had done the job demanded of it, and water coursed through the canals. It would be the last of Chaffey's services for the company he had saved with his money and expertise. By spring of 1902, just shy of a year after Chaffey delivered on his promise to send water to the CDC's customers, Rockwood drove him out. Maintenance of the four hundred miles of canals and laterals whose construction Chaffey had overseen now fell to someone whose only expertise in water lay in figuring out the most expedient way to exchange gallons for dollars.

When autumn arrived in 1901, the *Imperial Valley Press* estimated that settlers were staking up to fifty claims per day in the area around the nascent town. Needing a school that operated with regular hours in order to get funding for public education from the state, Imperial town founders constructed a mesquite and arrow-weed ramada—"*a la* Cocopah Indian[s]"—to shelter two dozen young children during school hours. As the settlers spread out across the desert, they stumbled over Kumeyaay and Cocopah pottery, as well as coffee mills, copper wash basins, bridle bits, silverware, and other odds and ends cast aside by gold seekers who had crossed the desert (or tried to) half a century before. The area around the New River, the heart of the desert Kumeyaays' agricultural lands, had "practically all been filed on" within months of the first arrival of settlers. Kumeyaays and Cocopahs earned wages where and when they could, working on the canal construction, as farm hands, and selling sacks of roasted mesquite beans to hungry settlers.[54]

By 1903 silt had clogged Chaffey's canals for four miles and the water ran low and muddy from there to Imperial. Proper construction and maintenance might have prevented the clogged canals and water shortages; the CDC, however, had no time, money, or patience to spare. Chaffey's work had been far from perfect, but Rockwood drove things from bad to worse. Despite his insistence on building waste gates and diversions, or even setting a dredge on the river to try to clear it of detritus from upstream, he could not clear the river of its interminable and infuriating silt. He spent a year engaged in this frustrated tinkering, but the water, thick with runoff, defeated him again and again.

Faced with another winter of water shortages in the fall of 1904, Rockwood did what he did best: he bet on a shortcut. Desperate to deliver the water he had promised to the roughly seven thousand Imperial Valley settlers, some of whom had started suing him for it, Rockwood ordered a ditch to be dug: fifty feet wide, more than three thousand feet long, and deep enough to drown a horse. It had no headgate to shut off the flow of the river in case of flooding. Water again flowed easily, its course unobstructed, veering inexorably downslope toward the Imperial Valley and the Salton Sink beyond.[55]

In that fall of 1904 the space in between the chicken wire fences of the audaciously named Imperial Valley and the shining white sheet of salt at Durbrow's New Liverpool saltworks existed more or less as it had since its creation by the gods Múkat and Témayawet: a hard, cracked desert bowl turned up at the edges and mirroring the curve of the sky above. The silty water flowing into Imperial Valley ditches and the cartloads of pure salt being loaded onto Southern Pacific railcars on the southern and northern rims of the bowl might as well have existed in different worlds; they shared a Sonoran ecosystem, but in the mental maps of most settlers their only connection was by the railroad that skirted the sink to the east.

In just a few short months these mental maps would be washed away by the muddy red water of the Colorado River. The Salton Sea would fill the space between them, creating a new kind of settler world, united by a perplexing body of water that no one would be sure had come to stay. In the past the floods that filled the Salton Sink had done the opposite for Cahuillas and Kumeyaays, interrupting their regular commerce and the connections they forged along the sink's desert trails; to continue their international trade and relationships, they would need to go around a lake rather than through a desert.

BOUND FOR THE SKY

In the fall of 1905 Mr. and Mrs. Lea, missionaries at Yuma, not far from Chaffey's Hanlon Heading diversion of the Colorado River, had to put their cottage on stilts to keep it from washing away. In the months between the Fourth of July and Thanksgiving, the Colorado River leaked over its banks and swamped the area at least four times. With each overflow, the river inundated missionary and Native gardens alike, washing away settlers' fenceposts and Quechans' latticework garden enclosures. When the water receded in rushing cutbacks to its former bed, the desert's most numerous reptilian denizens—lizards—sought shelter inside.

Driven mad by the repeated floods and by the plague of reptiles now underfoot in their home, the Leas commissioned their would-be human flock of Quechans, O'odhams, and Maricopas to assist them in lifting their house off the soggy ground. The couple moved back in the day before Thanksgiving, enjoying their new altitude and the absence of lizards. They were just in time: by Thanksgiving morning, the biggest flood yet covered the ground underneath them in three feet of river water. The Native people who had helped in the work of lifting the missionaries' home onto stilts fled to the mountains, despite lacking blankets or proper clothing for a winter in the foothills. They had to abandon their crops to the rising river.[56]

The missionaries' home sat in just the right place to foreshadow the flooding that would soon drown the Imperial Valley and create the Salton Sea. Yuma—on the Quechans' homeland, not far from where the Quechans had driven the Spanish away by attacking their missions in 1780—sat in the crook of the region's two most important rivers: the

Colorado and the Gila. Heavy discharge into both of these rivers caused the water to rise in the wide flat pan of land on which the Leas' home perched, the same pan of land the Quechans had been using since time immemorial for floodplain farming.

Here the Colorado's historic ambivalence—flow south to the gulf, or north, and downhill, into the Salton Sink?—played out over and over again in the course of hundreds of thousands of years. That ambivalence etched itself into the earth in the form of a network of ephemeral riverbeds, all of which led to a pair of dry channels dubbed by settlers the New and the Alamo Rivers, running from the Colorado to the Salton Sink.

The water rising below the Leas' newly lifted home rushed past them and directly toward Rockwood's ill-considered and unprotected cut from the Colorado River to the CDC's main canal. It was not the first flood that had headed that way in 1905. In fact, by Thanksgiving the same repeated risings that had persuaded the Leas to put their home on stilts had prompted a state of near panic among the CDC men, Rockwood in particular. A series of floods the previous winter had seemed big to Rockwood and his colleagues, but not unusually so. They noticed the overflow but did nothing, convinced that the floods were anomalies and not necessarily indicative of a larger pattern. The summer, they felt certain, would bring some respite in which they could install working headgates where Rockwood had put none.[57]

The Colorado and the Gila, however, had no interest in delivering the settlers their much-anticipated respite from floods. That summer the two rivers came together like two herds of stampeding horses just above Yuma. Their combined forces slammed into Rockwood's feebly constructed and unfinished dam, tearing it away. Rockwood scrambled to install another; the rivers made short work of it too. By the late summer months of 1905 engineers from the CDC, the Southern Pacific, and the federal Reclamation Service had visited the site of the breach, observing Rockwood's frantic attempts at damming the new path of the West's most vivacious waterway. Like the CDC men the previous winter, they registered muted alarm but did nothing. Their inaction reflected impotence more than lack of care; simply put, no one could come up with a workable plan for controlling the river. They signaled some alarm to higher-ups but, lacking a more workable plan, remained content to watch Rockwood try and fail, and try and fail again.

Their muted alarm, it turned out, would not cut it. Neither, probably, would any plan they could have concocted that summer of 1905, as evidenced by Rockwood's river-induced torture. Days after Thanksgiving, when the Leas escaped the rising water at their home in Yuma, the river, swollen with runoff from deep blankets of Rocky Mountain snow, hit the Lower Colorado's delta with the force of an avalanche. For an entire day the water rose a foot every hour.

At the island where Rockwood had made his fateful cut, 240 workers who had been laboring to anchor a jetty had mere hours to flee or risk drowning. By sheer luck they escaped onto a barge with wagons and horses just as the island sank under the voracious river. It might have seemed to them from their latter-day ark that it dissolved rather than sank; over the island where they had just been working rushed more than one hundred thousand cubic feet of water per second—roughly the same amount of water per second that crashes over Niagara Falls. Here, though, it did not run over hard limestone and shale rocks like the waters of Lake Erie cascading into the Niagara River a continent away; here the same volume of water coursed instead over (and through) thin desert topsoil, in which mesquite trees and ocotillos stood tentatively moored against a wall of river. The stampeding Colorado, heavy with silt, glowed cider-red in the sun. It carried the detritus of the desert world along with it: railroad ties and driftwood, rocks from CDC dams, whole mesquites uprooted from the desert floor, all pushed along in this vast rush of water.

By the first day of December almost all the Colorado had turned to flow west to the New and Alamo Rivers, where it veered north and charged downhill to the Salton Sink. It rushed past and through homesteads, most of which had to be abandoned in a hurry. Boats of explorers launched into the swirling red water to explore the extent of the damage, the waterborne investigators gazing out at the ruins of the settlers' future wishes for enclosed plots of productive desert land as they floated past on the Colorado's silt-clogged current. From their boats, they saw fences ripped from wooden posts. They gazed with melancholy at flower beds planted by farmers' wives near the doorways of newly built, and even more newly deserted, homes. Often the rushing water carried their boats through, rather than past, settlers' dismal homesites.

By the winter of 1905 the whole contents of the Colorado were flowing into the Salton Sink. In response, the CDC marshaled a workforce of local laborers, mostly Natives, who attempted to dam the breach. Their first attempt "had hardly been completed when a [second] flood came down the Colorado and swept it away."[58] A second dam met the same fate. This process of labor and flood repeated itself five times over the following year, with workers attempting to harness the river and pull it back into its eastern bed with dams of "piling, brush, sandbags, and earth," which were packed into enormous mattresses and heaved into the gushing river.[59] One of these floods raised the height of the Colorado more than fourteen feet in under twenty-four hours. As the water inundated the rail bed of the Southern Pacific line, workers frantically pulled up tracks and reset them on higher ground. The river chased them. They moved the tracks again and again, until the road had been pulled up and reset five times in one summer.

At the dam construction sites, laborers and their families formed small communities of up to two thousand people. The work sites were scenes of bustling activity, "there being giant drills, pile drivers, rock crushers, dredgers, and steam diggers all at work," employing hundreds of men in the attempt to amass enough earth and rock to stem the flood. As dam after dam failed to divert the Colorado, one observer noted that the river "in its wild flood has triumphed, and bidden the work to cease."[60] For one dam, built in August 1906, a massive workforce was garnered from what one writer described as "all the Indian tribes in that part of the southwest"—"Pimas, Papagoes, Maricopas and [Quechans]," as well as Cocopahs, Cahuillas, and Kumeyaays.[61] Meanwhile, as the Colorado rushed into the Salton Sink, its floodwaters swept away settlements and forced unlucky farmers to flee or drown.[62] "The Salton Sea," wrote naturalist John Muir in a letter to his daughters in January 1906, more than a year after the flooding began, "seems bound for the sky."[63]

The Southern Pacific engineers could not bring the river fully under control until February 1907, almost two years after the initial breach.

At that point crews of hundreds of workers had moved almost a million cubic yards of soil and rock to plug any and all potential leaks in the new dam system. Most of them were Natives who had been ordered to work by the Indian Agency and received less than three-quarters what their white counterparts earned. Together with the mostly white workers who labored in quarries to provide the ballast heaved into the river, these Native workers provided the collective strength it took to stymie the even more massive potential of the Colorado. In the rhetoric of writers who documented this work as it unfolded, the battle against the Colorado bordered on warfare: the cars used by the Southern Pacific were "battleships," the workers were an "army," and the noise of dynamite blasting boulders into manageable pieces "sounded like artillery in action."[64]

Though it had taken longer than anyone had anticipated, as one writer for the *Los Angeles Times* had predicted in 1905, "American engineering will not for long be baffled even by a mighty and treacherous Colorado River."[65]

Five years after the drama had subsided along with the rising floodwaters, a small party gathered around a campfire on the southeastern edge of the Salton Sink and told the region's stories. Three young boys listened intently as two elders explained the roles of the plants, animals, water, and rocks that surrounded them. Most of their stories revolved around various desert denizens' strategies for self-preservation. The plants, they posited, jealously guarded themselves against thirsty lizards and rodents by growing sharp thorns and emitting noxious smells. The jackrabbits possessed keen powers of speed and observation that kept them safe from predators. The horned toads wielded magic that allowed them to cloak themselves in different colors. Spiders and lizards secreted poisonous venom.

Plants and animals did not only need to protect themselves from each other, however. The elders described the floods that had risen in the sink, drowning settlements, denuding the landscape of its hardscrabble vegetation, and forcing animals—bipedal, quadrupedal, and so on—to flee. Grappling with the power of water, they explained to the young boys, had shaped their peoples' history with the region, causing grief and despair in equal parts with triumph.

This part of the story explained the enormous body of water that stretched out below their campsite: the Salton Sea, formed just a few short years before. The boys looked curiously out at the sea, stretching to the horizon, while their elders explained its provenance, telling about the riches culled from a once-dry landscape in the form of salt. The biggest risks of the floods, the elders posited, were to their peoples' capacity to make money: "When no money was invested in the desert," one explained, "an increase in the desert lake caused no uneasiness. Being a desert country, it made no difference how large the lake might grow." Continuing in a warning tone, he noted that "considerable money had been invested," so any flooding now caused "grave alarm." He recounted the epic flooding that washed away profitable saltworks and farms alike, and he detailed the heroic attempts to turn back the river.[66]

"Were they finally able to stop the opening?" one of the boys asked breathlessly. They were, the storyteller told him; if they had not been successful, this small group camped above the sea's southeastern shore would not be able to be there to learn from the desert and its denizens.

These stories, in many ways, were as shallow as their people's history with the region, which consisted of little more than a handful of years. The region's history began, according to their stories, in 1857, when an intrepid explorer crossed a "dry, salty basin" and found profitable deposits of table salt; the stakes of their story rose with the profits of the saltworks, crested with the floods that drove settlers away, and ebbed into a peaceful denouement as settlers "turned the desert into a flowing Eden."

The boys—Norman, Rob, and, Happy—were the protagonists of *The Land of Drought; or, Across the Great American Desert*, the second installment of Edwin Houston's Young Mineralogist series. The elder storytellers were a mineralogy professor and a mining engineer, tasked by Houston to tell the settler story of the rise of the Salton Sea and the stakes of controlling the Colorado River. During their fictional visit to the Colorado Desert, they camped above the Salton Sea, learned to shoot ducks in the Imperial Valley, and hopped on the Southern Pacific at Yuma. They encountered a range of archetypical adult teachers, like the professor and engineer, through whose mouths Houston told his story of the Colorado Desert. For color, Houston included characters he considered essential to explaining the nature of this place: "Colorado Bill," a Texas cowboy; "Sam Ling," a Chinese cook; and "Awake in the Night," whom Houston unhelpfully described only as "an Indian."

The stories the boys heard, and the morals imparted by Houston's adult characters, represented a fair summary of settler origin stories for the Salton Sea just a few years after its creation. Like many origin stories, Houston's tale blended facts with cultural meaning, offering an illustration of humans' relationships to the natural environment, and to each other, from the perspective of a particular worldview. Like other origin stories, settler and Native alike, this one revealed more about the people telling it than about the physical world around them.

AFTERLIVES OF A DELUGE

Among the Cahuilla settlements scattered throughout the Coachella Valley in the years before the great flood, one in particular drew settlers' attention—and their imaginations. In that valley large stands of fig trees and mesquites threw shade over an oasis in a field of sandy desert ground. Water bubbled up from a natural spring and evaporated in the heat almost as soon as it appeared. Branches of the fig trees sagged toward the ground, heavy with bulbous purple fruit as big as turkey eggs. Children played in the shade while their parents and grandparents watched, the adults chatting among themselves.

The proprietor of this homesite, a member of the Paltūkwic kaíkaíawit clan, was known by several names. His Cahuilla name came to be a matter of considerable debate. Some Cahuilla historians have claimed that it is lost to documented history; Serrano elder Dorothy Ramón, however, remembered him being called 'Ishi'vê'.[67] Settler historians have largely referred to him by the Spanish name he used on census records: Juan or Juanito Razón. Writers with a fondness for stories about Native eccentricity insisted that he introduced himself as "Juanita." Journalists often anglicized it—"Juaneta"—and others dispensed with Spanish altogether and called him "John Razón." Most settlers, however, preferred to pivot directly from any question of his given name—Juan, Juanita, Juanito, John—and simply referred to him as "Fig Tree John."

Fig Tree John lived a mythical life as distinct from Juan Razón's real life as the settlers' moniker for him was from his Cahuilla name. Some thought Fig Tree John was an Apache who had fought along-side Geronimo; fans of this notion invented outlandish backstories to explain how he came to live in California, far removed from the Nde (Apache) homeland.[68] Fanciful stories had Fig Tree John as a former scout for General Frémont and the owner of a secret gold mine from which he procured gold nuggets to trade at market.[69] Tourists in the desert wrongly described him as isolated from Cahuilla community life or, in more extreme accounts, "the only red man on the 2000 acre" Torres Martinez Reservation and "the leader of a tribe that is almost extinct."[70] In the early 1900s no one seemed to be able to agree whether he was 90, 100, 120, or 135 years old, but all agreed he was aged, with a craggy face that had born witness to many long decades.[71] Locals thrilled at the ostentatious outfit he wore on his sojourns into San Bernardino or Los Angeles: a long military overcoat fastened with brass buttons, as well as a silk top hat beribboned in patriotic shades of red, white, and blue. These stories fell into motifs that historian Jean O'Brien has dubbed "firsting and lasting," or settler habits of telling stories about Native people in ways that enabled settlers to draw stark lines between Natives who belonged to a fictive romantic past and their own forward-looking modernity.[72]

Like other Indigenous people caught up in local motifs of "firsting and lasting," Juan Razón's real life more accurately reflected the complex history of this ever-changing desert world than the mythical accounts of Fig Tree John ever could. He likely encountered U.S. troops passing through the northern stretches of the Colorado Desert during the U.S.-Mexico War, the provenance of his storied military coat and top hat. During the gold rush, Razón adopted the stray burros whose unlucky owners had perished in the desert en route to the diggings.[73] Later in his life he served as an informant to archeologists and anthropologists who appeared regularly among Cahuilla villages to record their place-names, words in their language, and some Cahuilla stories.[74] In 1914

FIG TREE JOHN AND FAMILY

13. Juan and Matilda Razón, with children, photographed at their homesite. Jocie Wallace, "On the Desert," *Youth's Instructor*, October 17, 1905. Courtesy of the Adventist Digital Library.

he rescued Chaffey Grant, the grandson of the former U.S. president and Civil War hero, from dying of thirst after his car broke down in the desert.[75]

In 1905 Juan Razón and his family watched warily as water began creeping north from the Salton Sink. Many of the residents of the community around Razón's oasis abandoned their homes and moved to higher ground, as their families had during previous floods. As in these previous floods, their caution proved prescient. By early October 1906 Razón's oasis on the desert had been entirely submerged, along with the homesites of a number of other Cahuilla families. His neighbors took refuge in the foothills, where they were lacking in proper clothing and shelter to ward off the cool autumn air. Unlike in previous floods, however, Razón and his neighbors now had significantly fewer options for where to move within their homeland when the water rose. Settler homesites, as well as private and federal land, hemmed them in on all sides. In the years since the last significant flooding, their homeland had been reduced from a broad swath of mountain, valley, and desert, through which they could move in patterns of intranational migration, to a handful of too-small reservations, outside of which Native people could rarely feel safe from settler aggression. For Cahuillas this fundamentally changed an age-old experience of flooding and migration, which had never been free from stress but now presented itself as a life-altering and terrifying displacement.

Furious and worried, Razón donned his overcoat and top hat and traveled to San Bernardino to consult with an attorney and ally with a Cahuilla man, John Brown Jr. With Brown's help, he enlisted journalists from local and regional newspapers to cover the Cahuillas' plight—namely, that they had "all been rendered homeless by the Salton Sea."[76] Razón estimated that at least 150 Cahuillas faced starvation due to the flood that had ruined their homes.[77] Holding court before a handful of reporters assembled at Brown's San Bernardino home, "the old rugged Captain" gave an extended lament of conditions for the desert people. "'Our houses are under water,'" Razón recounted, "'the ground we tilled is the home of the fishes, our little ponies have to seek the hills for the bunch grass, and our women and children lie out under the stars, with no shelter over them but their blankets.'"[78] Journalists waxed nostalgic about Razón's story, seeing him as a stoic and "pathetic" figure representing the inevitability of tribal loss. According to one reporter, Razón's "eyes wandered wistfully off to the distant mountains. He saw a picture of his people, homeless and foodless and hopeless, but he is an Indian, a great brave, and despite his thoughts he remained unmoved." This description dispensed with Razón's urgent plea for his people in favor of a depiction of Fig Tree John that could accurately describe any number of Edward Curtis portraits of Natives that falsely represented the "vanishing" of Native life from the continent.[79] Like this journalist, settlers memorialized Native people prematurely, their nostalgia about Fig Tree John allowing them to disappear whole communities of Cahuilla and Kumeyaay people, many of whom, Razón implored them to understand, were suddenly unhoused in their own homeland.[80]

The Indian Service agent for Southern California, L. A. Wright, reacted with outright hostility to Razón's account and the sympathy it inspired among journalists. Furious, Wright called his own press confer-ence, curtly declaring that Razón had "dreamed" the plight of Cahuilla families and that only Fig Tree John himself and his brother had lost their land to the flooding. According to Wright, Razón and his brother could simply "take up new lands anywhere in the reservation or near the villages and establish a new home just as good as the former one, if he wishes."[81] Wright's protestations ignored facts that should have been obvious to him as the Indian Service representative in charge of this part of Southern California. The flooding that began in 1905 and brought Razón to San Bernardino in 1906 inundated almost half of the Cahuillas' desert reservation, to say nothing of the numerous Cahuilla homesites off the reservation, including Razón's, that dotted the desert near the New Liverpool Salt Works. Cahuillas, under instructions to farm their arid acreage, went from not having enough water one year to having far too much the next. By 1907 Razón's home sat under at least five feet of water.[82]

The rise of the Salton Sea was not the only crucial change in Cahuilla life that Juan Razón experienced in the decades that bridged the nine-teenth and twentieth centuries. To the contrary, Juan and Matilda Razón witnessed firsthand the major transformations that created the Torres Martinez Reservation. The first reservation for desert Cahuillas was established in 1876, consisting of a meager 640 acres. In 1891, the same year that the water rose in the desert and prompted Durbrow's Cahuilla workers to flee to the mountains, a federal executive order expanded the reservation. In 1909, as settlers and Natives alike grappled with the watery consequences of nearly two years of floods, the Interior secretary expanded it again, by ten thousand acres. Nearly all of this acreage, plus a good portion of the 1891 expansion, sat underwater and remain inundated for the rest of the century, thanks to Imperial and Coachella Valleys.[83]

In the midst of these changes to their community's landholdings, the Razóns raised three children during the ascendancy of Indian boarding schools: John Mack, born around 1874, followed three years later by Jake Juan, and Lario, born in 1890. In subsequent years the removal of children from their families changed the shape of familial relations and life chances among Cahuillas, as it did throughout Indian country. The removal of children coincided with their families' relegation to small reservations that had little access to water for irrigation; as federal agents noted in 1908, Native adults were "compelled by want of reservation to earn most of their living elsewhere and send their children to boarding schools." The same report noted offhandedly that parents moved so as to live near the boarding schools, seeking off-reservation wage labor that would keep them as close to their children as possible.[84]

Lario Razón, born the same year St. Boniface Indian School opened, would have grown up alongside the institutions that would come to house entire generations of Native children, but he likely never attended them. During Lario's childhood, Indian agents encouraged Cahuilla children to travel to an on-reservation school in Thermal, eight hard miles on bad roads to the north of Torres—a trip most families could not make during much of the year.[85] For this reason, agents advocated for an Indian day school to be built on the Martinez Reservation. Congress authorized construction funds for Martinez Indian School in December 1906, and the school opened in 1907, enrolling students from Martinez, Torres, Augustine, and Cabazon Reservations. The local Indian agent, J. B. Boyce, presided over the school as superintendent.[86]

The children arrived to find a one-room adobe building with a sharply peaked roof. A straggly fence of barbed wire enclosed a yard of loose dirt, presided over by a single tree. At the school the children likely had the hallmark experience of Indian education in the United States: cultural assimilation, with a particularly keen assault on Native gender norms and Indigenous languages. Boys and girls occupied separate physical and instructional spheres; rather than weaving, grinding mesquite bean pods, and preparing for important ceremonies, girls learned to sew, clean dormitories, and cook meals from canned foods.[87] Rather than learning rabbit-hunting skills and Cahuilla oral history, boys learned agriculture and the maintenance of mechanical farm equipment. In this way schools sought to instill American-style "usefulness and citizenship" through gendered instruction in maintaining a "well regulated home," among girls, and mastering "habits of industry," among boys.[88] In private, however, those in charge of the Indian school system doubted

14. Charles C. Pierce, *Group of Students with Their Teacher in Front of the Indian School at Martinez*, circa 1900. California Historical Society Collection, 1860–1960; Title Insurance and Trust, and C. C. Pierce Photography Collection, 1860–1960. University of Southern California Libraries. California Historical Society.

the inherent intelligence and ability to learn of the youngest members of what one school superintendent called "'the child race.'" In many Indian schools the lofty ideals at the heart of the federal government's assimilationist program devolved into racist attitudes resulting in violent discipline, gender segregation, insult, and harm for Indigenous nations' youngest members.[89]

In addition to acting as the school superintendent, J. B. Boyce served as the federal Indian agent for Martinez. In this role as agent, his primary focus remained on the problem of water: too much of one kind and not nearly enough of the other. Boyce wrote to his supervisors, complaining, like Juan Razón had to San Bernardino journalists two years before, that the Salton Sea had not only flooded Cahuilla land but covered "a fine belt of artesian water"—the same water Cahuillas had accessed via the deep walk-in wells they had built over hundreds of years in between periods of flooding. Everything possible, Boyce insisted, should be done to "ensure to the Indians a permanent water supply," since the Salton Sea had deprived them of the water that flowed below the desert's surface.[90] Boyce, like the Cahuillas he represented, assumed that the water flooding the Cahuillas' land would quickly evaporate under the hot sun; after all, as Cahuilla history documented, it had done just that over and over again for hundreds of years.

The answer from the federal government to complaints from Boyce and others, like Juan Razón, followed a curious kind of logic. In 1909 the Department of the Interior added twelve thousand acres to the Torres Martinez Reservation, and three-quarters of that area lay under the water.[91] At the same time, sixty miles to the south, the Imperial Irrigation District busily negotiated contracts to ensure that the Salton Sea would stay at its current depth and area and thus that the federally guaranteed Torres Martinez Reservation land would remain at the bottom of a lake.

Over the course of the five years that followed the flooding in the Salton Sink, Razón, repeatedly facing the kind of obstinate denial on the part of federal agents that he received from Wright, returned to San Bernardino in repeated attempts to enlist white allies in his struggle to achieve "redress from the government" on behalf of himself and other Cahuilla families who "had been dispossessed of the homes where for generations their tribe has dwelt."[92] Razón, meanwhile, had moved his family a few miles north of his drowned home to Agua Dulce Springs, where a few years hence an "officious government agent" sold part of his land out from under him—one of any number of such instances of encroachment and dispossession in the area.[93] Again, Razón traveled to San Bernardino to lodge a protest. Settlers would come to refer to his new homesite near Agua Dulce as "Fig Tree John." Appropriately to the fiction of Fig Tree John overlaid on Juan Razón's real life, the place that came to be named for him was neither his original home-site (which would remain underwater) nor land that he could legally claim as his. As in other places, Native toponyms, like local histories of vanishing Indians, obscured more about Indigenous life and history than they memorialized.[94]

By 1911 newspaper stories about Razón's visits to protest these kinds of injustices increasingly focused on his eccentricities and his misfortunes, rather than his demands for redress. Journalists underscored his poverty, in stark contrast to stories two decades prior that celebrated his windfall of prospectors' burros, fresh water from his artesian well, and shade from his fig trees. Now, "old age, the depredations of the Salton sea and other misfortunes, have swept most of his belongings away."[95] "Juanito Razon," one journalist declared, "doesn't have much opportunity to smile these days for of late the palefaces have been working havoc with his rights and those of his people. And not only with his rights, but with his dignity too."[96] Razón, however, demonstrated in subsequent years that his dignity remained intact. If the flooding of the Salton Sea inspired him to engage in multiple forms of political protest as a leader of his community, other threats to Cahuillas' ownership of land would continue to figure strongly in his life. Razón's story did not begin with the flooding of the Salton Sea nor did it end with the water flooding his land; rather, the themes of his story—assertions of his claims to land in the face of dispossession, leadership of his desert community, alliance with sympathetic white allies, and confrontation with federal authorities—endured.

PART 2

3

BIRDS

These are not the only relations possible.

—Dian Million, "'We Are the Land and the Land Is Us,'" 2018

THE DESERT WRAITH

In the summer of 1882 an eleven-year-old boy crept through a thicket of spiny desert plants in an arid valley southeast of San Gorgonio Pass, near the settlement of Banning, California. His imagination ran wild, chasing ghost stories about who, or what, he might encounter. He had been told of a "Mexican horsethief who had died with his boots on" (surely a euphemism for some kind of grisly end) "and been buried somewhere among the creosote bushes and squat mesquite trees."[1] Creeping through the underbrush, his senses strained for evidence of this phantom. Suddenly, a trilling whistle sent a jolt of adrenaline through his young body.

He ran for it. As he crashed through the brush, he hoped against hope that the whistle had come from someone summoning him home to the nearby ranch house. Discovering no one there, he felt as sure as he had ever been of anything that the whistle was the beckoning of "the Mexican ghost."[2]

Two decades later the boy, now a rancher and amateur ornithologist, heard the same haunting whistle in the depths of the Salton Sink, carried to him across drifts of white sand on a cool evening breeze. In 1902 the Salton Sink held much promise for those who, like him, were interested in birding. Winters in the desert provided shelter and forage for a startlingly diverse array of winged fauna: from poetically named species of geese (snow goose, white-fronted goose, white-cheeked goose, cackling goose) to majestic blue herons in more consistently watered parts of the arid ecosystem, to the underappreciated but admirably resourceful white-necked raven in the desert's spare lowlands. When winter rains brought bursts of wildflowers and grasses to the desert's nooks and crannies, sandhill cranes deigned to visit during daylong sojourns from the Pacific. Black-throated sparrows sought out the meager shade from bushes throughout the desert, as did yellow-headed tits, hummingbirds, orioles, finches, jays, woodpeckers, warblers, flycatchers, wrens, buntings, bluebirds, and quails. Some savvy birds made their nests among the prickly branches of mesquites or between cactus spines high off the ground. Others took their chances laying eggs in ground nests, a bold choice in a place where rattlesnakes outnumbered eggs by a two-to-one margin.[3] Nightfall revealed that the more regal and deadly members of the bird world also reigned here; in the moonlight, red-tailed, Swainson's, sparrow, ferruginous, and rough-legged hawks kept a close eye out for creatures skittering across the dusty ground, competing in the hunt with short-eared, barn, and pygmy owls.[4]

French Gilman, the amateur ornithologist poking around the Salton Sink in 1902, was looking for evidence of any of these many bird species when he heard again the eerie whistling from his boyhood. This time, however, he did not suspect a Mexican ghost. Rather, he attributed the call to a strange-sounding mockingbird "whose individuality had been developed by the desert solitudes." Some casting around for the source revealed the truth: he had heard a LeConte's thrasher, a desert-dwelling bird with a rare trilling song "indistinguishable" from a person whistling for their dog—or from something more spectral, for an errant boy losing himself in search of ghosts.[5]

Gilman never forgot the sound of that call in the Salton Sink, perhaps because it came to him across what he called "a most lonesome,

God-forsaken" spot, "near an ancient Indian encampment and burial ground," across which he trespassed in search of bird and plant specimens.[6]

Known for thriving in the most waterless of environs, surviving on not much more than the sustenance provided by insects foraging along the ground, these sand-colored birds could be found throughout the sink in those years before the flooding, nesting close in between the spines of cholla cacti or nestled in the prickly crooks of mesquite trees. Their range extended as far west as Banning, where cowboys got their afternoon entertainment by chasing the birds until they took flight. As ground dwellers unaccustomed to spending much time aloft, the birds had wings that eventually "failed altogether" as they fled the cowboys, and they would fall to the ground in exhaustion, perhaps taking refuge in a bush before being captured.[7]

Three years after Gilman discovered the bird that he had twice mistaken—once for a Mexican ghost and once for a mockingbird—this bird species' life in the desert came to be shaped by a force larger than the games of bored cowboys. The flooding that created the Salton Sea in 1905 made this northern part of the LeConte's thrasher territory an unattractive one for a bird so thoroughly acclimated to the desert. The runaway Colorado River brought with it transformations of many kinds: fish and fowl, plant and human, in addition to no end of brackish water. In the early years of the twentieth century the thrasher and other desert birds came to share territory with all manner of avifauna that arrived at the Salton Sea through grand regional and global machinations of the human and natural worlds. Pelicans, sandhill cranes, seagulls, and thousands upon thousands of ducks arrived in the Colorado Desert, called by the creation of new ecosystems, new feeding grounds in the form of vast Imperial Valley farms, and a massive new water resource during a time when water resources rapidly vanished or became unusable for birds as new settlements and cities spread throughout the West.

Even while Gilman would always associate the bird with Mexican ghosts, Indian burial grounds, and cowboys' devilment—spectral signifiers of a frontier past—the thrasher itself remained a vibrant part of

15. LeConte's thrasher. U.S. Department of the Interior, *Report on the United States and Mexican boundary survey, made under the direction of the secretary of the Interior by William H. Emory*, vol. 2, part 2, "Birds," edited by Spencer Fullerton Baird (Washington DC: A. O. P. Nicholson, 1859).

the region's avifaunal ecology, despite the massive changes brought by the formation of the Salton Sea. As this part of California came rather suddenly to host a crowded register of bird species, ornithologists and hunters alike sought to collect birds and bird bodies as evidence of the new abundance brought by the Salton Sea and by the arrival of settlers in the Imperial Valley. As *Forest and Stream* magazine crowed in 1910, "When the water came, [the birds] saw it from afar and followed man in his pioneering."[8] If desert birds, to Gilman and others, would always carry echoes of the Mexican and Native past of the region, migrating water birds were "pioneers" and "citizens" of a newly watered land.

In 1930 the importance of birds to the region, and the importance of the Salton Sea *to* those birds, was formalized with the creation of the Salton Sea National Wildlife Refuge.[9] The refuge existed as part of a larger network of managed wetlands for migrating birds and other wild avifauna along the Pacific Flyway. At the same time that considerable state and federal resources went into maintaining refuge for these birds, other birds were targeted for extermination as "winged miscreants" and pests that plucked profits from farmers' fields.[10]

This chapter traces the meanings made of birds and bird bodies at the Salton Sea in the first half of the twentieth century. Throughout this history, birds have mediated settlers' ideas about race and gender, standing in for or shoring up a range of racial and gender identities: from white masculinity as "pioneers," to white feminine vulnerability as "innocents" in need of protection, to racialized and nativist depictions of birds as greedy invaders that threatened farmers' profits. This history of meanings made out of birds reveals how ideas about race and gender have been projected onto human and nonhuman bodies and how those projections determined who lived and who died, humans and nonhumans alike. At the Salton Sea racial and gendered meaning shaped human engagements with birds in sometimes surprising ways— from French Gilman's ghosts and burial grounds to understandings of ducks as invading armies.

In 1902, when Gilman chased his thrasher past "an ancient Indian encampment and burial ground" across a sink that would in three years' time be covered by forty feet of water, birds signified very specific meanings to the Indigenous communities who lived in and near the desert.[11] The mockingbird he thought he heard was a member of the Kumeyaay nation—*tipai*, or people; they held it in high regard and never used it as food. Mourning doves, white pelicans, crows, and eagles held the same favored status. Birds figured centrally in Kumeyaay, Cahuilla, and Serrano origin stories, often being among the original animal people of the land before the gods made some of them into humans. Birds therefore symbolized the relations between humans and nonhumans in entirely different ways: as familial relations and as reminders of a people's original animal forms. When the desert Kumeyaay deity Warharmi arrived in what is currently Imperial Valley, the two-spirit being, before teaching the Kumeyaay people about agriculture, arrived bedecked in sacred bird feathers.[12]

In 1931 a desert Kumeyaay woman named Rosa Narpai explained to a wandering anthropologist one detail of this complex Kumeyaay cosmology as it related to birds. "If a bird flew into a house," Narpai explained, "it was an omen of impending evil" for the family who lived there. "It meant that one of the family would die soon, and that not even a shaman could prevent it. Such a bird was thought to come from a long distance and to already embody the soul of the doomed person. It was believed that the person's soul had left sometime before and returned temporarily in bird form on this occasion. Such a bird was not harmed, though it inspired fear."[13] Narpai's recounting of Kumeyaay relations to birds illustrated vital antidotes to Gilman's various macabre and moribund bird stories: birds as ghosts, birds as denizens of burial grounds, birds as helpless fodder for cowboys' entertainment.

As Narpai's knowledge attested, settler relations to birds did not constitute the only—or even the primary—relations between humans and birds at the Salton Sea and the surrounding desert. They were not even the only *ghost* birds. In fact, local Indigenous nations carried complex histories of human relationships to birds, many of these stories, like Narpai's, signifying not only familial intimacy but also spectrality. Birds drew their power in part from the ability to pass between human and animal worlds and beyond into the spiritual realm.

For Serranos to the north of the Cahuillas' homeland, birds similarly performed the role of intermediary between life and death, serving as guides that taught earthbound spirits how to find the road to the world of the dead. Serrano origin stories teach that human spirits long ago roamed the world, unable to go home. Their living relatives asked birds for help on behalf of the dead. They painted the birds' bodies for their journeys to the underworld. One by one the birds—crows, doves, and others—failed to reach their destination. Then the humans sent a lark, who died on the journey and arrived in the underworld as a spirit. There the lark discovered two roads for the dead to walk: a straight road for good people, a crooked road for bad. The lark returned and taught the dead people how to leave the earth along these roads. "The Earth," recalled Serrano elder Dorothy Ramón, "has been tranquil ever since. That's how it will be through all eternity."[14]

Cupeños also mapped their relations to birds through story, ceremony, and careful ecosystem management. When federal agents forced Cupeños from their homes in 1903, elder Cecilio Blacktooth shamed the government for its cruelty by invoking his community's relationships to both mountains and birds; when asked where he and his people would like to go, he replied, "We do not want you to buy us any other place. If you do not buy this place, we will go into the mountains like quail and die there, the old people and the women and the children."[15] His ire linked the fate of their precious bird relations—the quail—to his fellow community members who suffered a devastating displacement at the hands of settlers.

Cahuillas, like their Kumeyaay, Serrano, and Cupeño neighbors, maintained familial relationships to birds that stretched back to time immemorial. Birds figured centrally in Cahuilla origin stories: a woodpecker took on the solemn role of ordering the death of their creator, Múkat; the condor singed the feathers off of his head while writhing around in mourning at Múkat's cremation; the people then dispersed around the world, taking flight like birds (hence the origin of the name Bird Songs for the Cahuillas' musical oral history); humans sometimes turned into owls; quails rescued people and were rewarded with songs; and roadrunners brought wisdom and good luck.[16]

The regular inundations of the Salton Sink played a key role in

Cahuillas' relationships to birds. Just as the twentieth century's Salton Sea brought new species of water birds to commingle with desert species like Gilman's reclusive thrasher, previous bodies of water in the desert brought gulls, cormorants, grebes, pelicans, and blue herons. Cahuillas honored these birds with ceremonial songs and developed complex guidelines regarding which birds could be hunted and eaten and which could not. When ethnologists and anthropologists arrived in the desert to study Cahuilla culture, frequent references to aquatic birds in ceremonial songs seemed confounding in this dry desert world. To outsiders, this offered further confirmation of Native stories that the desert had once housed a vast body of water and that the people had in times past adapted to their lacustrine environment as well as they had to the desert.[17]

Among all the birds of the Cahuillas' world, however, eagles received the most reverence. Cahuilla *nets* (elected clan leaders) lived together with eagles in clan ceremonial houses, raising and caring for the regal birds. Eagle ceremonies honored the bird's role in the Cahuilla world as a member of their community.

In the early 1920s the future *pul* (spiritual leader or shaman) Ruby Modesto was just a child when her great uncle found a dead golden eagle in the hills north of San Bernardino. Heartbroken for the loss of the majestic bird, he placed its body in a wooden crate and sent it by train to his brother, Francisco Nombre, the *net* of the dog clan. Nombre brought it from the train depot by buggy. When he arrived with the bird at the ceremonial house, "the people sang and cried all night long" over its body, thanking Múkat for sending the eagle to them. Nombre tenderly removed the eagle's feathers. He anointed its body with a salve made from greasewood, a sacred plant, and wrapped it in white linen. Remembering this event from her childhood, Modesto recalled how the people gathered around the small shrouded body and "sang ceremonial songs for the dead, just like they would for a human." They crafted a small coffin for the bird and buried it in the tribal cemetery alongside its human ancestors and relations. Afterward they honored its life by using its feathers in ceremonies.[18]

The eagle made for a different kind of ghost bird: not a fictive and wraith-like symbol of the past, like Gilman's spectral thrasher, but rather part of a living memory for Cahuillas of the maintenance of Cahuilla relations, among humans and between humans and birds. The eagle's body, and the collective human grief for its death and gratitude for its life, brought the community together. Its feathers, as Modesto attested, continued to do so for decades after its burial. "We still use the feathers," she noted solemnly in her autobiography. They used the feathers and they remembered the bird and its kin, all "bound together," as Modesto put it, "in happiness or grief" as one people.[19]

SAVE THE SONGBIRDS, WEAR THE EGRETS, EAT THE DUCKS

The LeConte's thrasher found ways to live its desert-bound life after the creation of the Salton Sea and the subsequent arrival of seabirds by the thousands. For a century after French Gilman chased a thrasher across the Salton Sink, these birds remained key denizens of the arid land-scape. The story of birds at the Salton Sea tends to privilege the stories of larger and more conspicuous creatures: pelicans, ducks, cormorants, and quails. The slight, deft thrasher rarely showed itself, a ghost in the desert whose presence was "most often revealed by footprints on the sand."[20] The bird's rarity made the area a popular destination for orni-thologists, who chased it through the underbrush with guns in hand.

In 1923, two decades after Gilman stumbled across his thrasher in a part of the desert that would soon sit under water, another of these thrasher-obsessed ornithologists arrived in the Colorado Desert to seek out the scarce bird. He spent the morning tramping through the creosote bush to find just one of these "wraith[s]." When at long last he heard the bird's trilling call, "murder rose in [his] heart." It died quickly when he considered the shy frailty of his small, dun-colored prey—lamenting, for a moment, "the whole d—d business of bird-killing."[21]

The moment passed, and he fired on the thrasher anyway.

As evidenced by this turn to guns, in the context of a larger "business of bird-killing," guns had become a central and devastating mediator of the relations between humans and birds in the Colorado Desert. In 1901, as dusty Imperial Valley settlers fervently imagined their baths, boulevards, and cablegrams, they put themselves to the task of forming a gun club, an institution that would become crucial to the valley's identity and development.

Settler Californians had a complex and long-standing relationship to guns, almost always involving the racial violence of settling a territory claimed by both Indigenous nations and Mexican ranchos. As historians have pointed out, gun ownership and gun control in the United States writ large emerged not only out of cultures of hunting game but also out of anxieties around defending white supremacy against potential insurrection by the members of nonwhite groups that the white settlers sought to dominate.[22] In California the fact of a heavily armed settler populace mattered a great deal in how genocide against Native people proceeded from 1848 to the mid-1870s.[23] In fact, among the first laws pertaining to gun ownership in the state were those enacted to make it illegal for Native people to arm themselves against settler violence, and settlers justified some of their bloodiest attacks on Native communities by accusing them of keeping firearms.[24]

By the end of that century settlers in California were bearing arms at startling rates. Cities and rural areas alike bristled with guns. Increasingly, settlers turned their weapons on birds and other game as a form of recreation and leisure. Gun clubs formed in nearly every California settlement from 1877, when the first such entity, the California Gun Club, gathered for a shooting competition in San Francisco, on into the next century. Hunting gradually transitioned from a matter of subsistence to one of sport. In this gradual change, gun ownership continued to signify settler masculinity—as it had during the long and murderous attempted extermination of the state's Indigenous people—but membership in one of California's gun clubs also spoke to class status. In a settler world that required less and less direct interpersonal violence, bird hunting satisfied the natural "instinct to kill something" that sat "dormant in every boy's breast," as one editorial put it in 1905.[25] This coincided with trends in most states around the turn of the twentieth century to more intensive management of hunting and the enactment of laws that governed where, when, and how one could shoot for sport or for food.[26]

The growth of agriculture likewise brought together settlers, guns, and birds, with bloody consequences. The late 1800s saw massive declines in bird numbers across the country, in large part because of extensive settlement across the West and the environmental changes settlement entailed but also because farmers saw birds as pests and often sought to eradicate them. Declines in bird numbers were helped along by the popularity of feathers and bird bodies on hats as an important symbol of femininity and wealth for American women.

During the Progressive era birds became an important site of preservationist angst nationwide, and campaigns to protect birds became darlings of clubwomen. Schools hosted "Bird Days" that taught children that "it is wrong to disturb breeding birds, or rob birds' nests" and that, in fact, "it is wrong to destroy any harmless living creature not properly classed as game, except it be to preserve it in a museum," as noted by the conservationist William Temple Hornaday. Framing bird conservation as both an educational concern and a "moral imperative" situated it firmly in the white feminine realm, part of the Cult of True Womanhood's sphere of childrearing, good works, and moral rectitude.[27] Even while the men of the Audubon Society turned to preservationism as a plausibly masculine political project, "men who saved birds and flowers were subject to potential scorn by those who saved big game, forests, and mountains," according to historian Carolyn Merchant.[28]

Throughout the United States at this time, race, gender, and class collided over interpretations of birds and their worth.[29] In the Imperial Valley these debates played out on farms, in stores and restaurants, and on the pages of local newspapers. Editorials published in the *Imperial Valley Press* chided middle- and upper-class women as "savages" for their conspicuous consumption of feathered hats for fashion.[30] Clubwomen implored farmers to stay their rifles when songbirds picked at their crops, all the while acknowledging that men would deride this as a deeply sentimental plea for "little feathered songsters" and other "nonsensical things."[31] Meanwhile, hunting game birds became a primary way in which settlers cultivated a sense of gentlemanly vigor in the context of a (mostly) ungentlemanly life in the nascent Imperial Valley. In the Progressive era in general the leisure produced by industrial economies prompted middle- and upper-class white men to exercise their masculinity and connections to nature through hunting. Hunting, in turn, ostensibly encouraged soulful connections between man, beast, and wilderness.[32]

Few scenes showed off these conflicting interpretations of birds in the Imperial Valley better than one of the many duck blinds constructed by the valley's gun clubs. As Imperial Valley settlers strove to douse themselves in the veneer of middle-class gentility—willful denial of their dusty and often thirsty reality—the formation of gun clubs for trophy hunting played a key role in their mimicry of civilized life. Duck hunting in the gun clubs was considered a gentleman's sport, requiring skills directly in line with refined settler masculinity.[33] Much was made of the manly skills required to bag fast-flying ducks in particular. During the mornings and evenings, "when the [ducks] are plentiful and are whizzing past the gunners at express speed," the local press noted, "it is an expert shot who can be sure of bagging the limit or anything near it."[34] Ducks made for "quick, difficult shooting, for the birds were usually flying at full speed."[35] And, duck hunting being a sport, hunters needed practice. Upon its formation, the El Centro Gun Club immediately began raising funds to purchase clay pigeons and secure a shooting range, which were needed before the real "fun [could] commence." The clay pigeons were necessary to give the club members "valuable practice that can be turned to good account on the ducks and quail a little later on."[36]

Ducks, for their part, made worthy adversaries to armed men. They were often described as being not only smart but possessed of a downright canny intelligence. Other birds lacked the ducks' savvy and thus ranked lower in hunters' esteem. "The mud hen," wrote one reporter observing a hunt at the Alamo River, "has learned that she is not a duck and is no good, and she paddles and fusses about within a few yards of a [duck] blind, paying no attention to the guns or to the fall of ducks around her." Further considering the mud hen's human corollaries in his own profession, the reporter opined, "She always reminds me of a 'Woman's Press Club'—oblivious and audible, but not to be taken seriously."[37]

If ideas about birds shored up ideas about gender, birds' bodies constituted a highly material manifestation of this relationship between birds and men: whereas bird bodies on hats signified femininity, bird bodies on the plate signified something else entirely. In justifying and encouraging hunting in and around the Imperial Valley, gun clubs and their advocates underscored that "any fresh-water duck killed in Imperial Valley is good to eat . . . and the sprig, widgeon, best mallard and teal that feed in the [Imperial Valley] barley fields are equal to the best canvas-back that ever flapped a wing over the Chesapeake," making Imperial Valley ducks "much superior on the table" to ducks of the coastal regions.[38] Other reports from hunting excursions noted that the ducks' "flesh . . . proved to be very tender and finely flavored."[39] Women's uses of birds, in short, were savage. Men's uses of birds were not only gentlemanly; they were downright delicious.

In addition to birds being used to shore up a kind of privileged white masculinity both ideationally (as worthy adversaries to powerful men) and materially (in the form of meat), gun clubs and bird hunting provided opportunities to commune with nature for Imperial Valley settlers. As they waited in boats and behind duck blinds for the birds to reveal themselves, hunters enjoyed hearing the "wind in the tops of the forest trees" and watching "the rosy glow of dawn" in the early morning hours. Foreshadowing the tourism on the Salton Sea that would become its most lucrative industry in the 1950s, enterprising residents of the Imperial Valley began taking tourists out on the sea by boat as early as 1909. One such boat, provocatively dubbed "The Mayflower of Colton," began its tours in October 1909, setting out on the sea "in quest of the festive duck."[40] While ducks were fair game to those boating on the sea, other kinds of birds were not; in 1910 a whole line of boats was launched, each with capacity for carrying fifty tourists, with the goal of visiting the sea's "most striking scenes." The highlight of the excursions was Pelican Island, "the shores of which are lined with these birds." In marked contrast to the treatment of ducks, it was "hoped no firearms [would] be allowed to be used" on pelicans, "for if they are shot at, one of the most interesting features of the trip will be a thing of the past."[41] The pelicans, in contrast to the ducks, were a key part of experiencing nature on the Salton Sea.

The nature in question, however, was not quite the untouched wilderness such descriptions might suggest. Along the Alamo River, which coursed through the Imperial Valley and into the Salton Sea, the El Centro Gun Club spent several years carefully curating hunting grounds. These "extensive improvements" served to make the area simultaneously more attractive to birds and more conducive to hunting. The labor involved in these improvements seems daunting, including "clearing out jungles of tules and young willows, building dikes to hold water in the ponds when the river is low and," lest the birds' preferences be forgotten, "fixing things to the liking of ducks." Not everything would be to the ducks' liking, however: for the convenience of the shooters, hunters installed blinds "'unbeknownst' to the ducks . . . and a lot of 'phony' ducks are on hand to be staked out for the inveiglement and undoing of the wily mallard."[42]

The racial undertones of California's gun culture did not entirely pass into the ether during this buildup of a sport hunting life in Imperial Valley. If egrets and doves represented helpless victims when they wound up on women's hats, ducks that were hunted adjacent to the Salton Sea's shores were viewed more like soldiers in an enemy army. In one account of a morning duck hunt on the Alamo River with members of the El Centro Gun Club, just as the sun crested the horizon, "the men stood up, their shoulders level with the tops of the tules, and faced the east, looking up the river, alert and intent, with guns at the 'ready.'" When "a small, black spot suddenly darted across the light, the twenty-bore went swiftly to the shoulder and instantly cracked, swinging to the left, and a second later there was a splash in the water behind the tules"— "'a noise like a man killing a teal.'" This was merely the opening shot, to hear the author tell it, of a day that would bring a series of war-like skirmishes between men and birds. The ducks arrived in an "army, accurately aligned and dressed." Onward the birds flocked, "rank after rank," as they were "advancing," in this author's fanciful imagination, on the hunters who awaited the enemy army with shotguns in hand.[43]

The morning ended in victory for the hunters, who, having defeated the winged troops, finally "pulled their boat back to the camp landing, carrying loads of game and appetites for coffee and flapjacks that pressed the limit."[44] Having violently vanquished an antagonistic and wild enemy, their bags full of bird bodies and their stomachs empty from the exertion of their war games against a feathered nemesis, these men embodied the symbolism as well as the substance of hunting in the early twentieth-century settler experience.[45] Their deadly engagements with birds substituted for much larger experiences with nature, gender, and race in the West.

BIRDING ON THE SALTON SEA

In late April 1908 Joseph Grinnell, an ornithologist who was editor of *The Condor* magazine, arrived at the shore of the newly formed Salton Sea, his boots crunching across the gravel-crusted muck that made up the sea's westernmost beach. He surveyed the scene unenthusiastically. A pile of sandbags kept the wind-blown waves from inundating the nearby railroad. His boat had been pulled from the shore by those same waves overnight and was now caught, half underwater, in a stand of prickly mesquite trees. Overall it made for an inauspicious start to the day's voyage.

Grinnell and his companions disentangled and righted the boat and clambered aboard, launching into the muddy shallows. Their destination lay forty miles across the water: Echo Island, where pelicans reportedly gathered to lay their spring eggs.[46] The group motored sluggishly across miles and miles of newly formed lake, tracking their progress by counting half-submerged telegraph poles, still standing sentinel over the now useless course of the Southern Pacific roadbed. Here and there the upper branches of dead cottonwood trees breached the sea's surface, marking drowned homesites far below. The boat's propeller snagged in chicken wire that had been pulled to the surface by an orphan fencepost. The men disentangled the wire and chugged onward.

The early morning breeze flagged. The waves guttered and the sea's face turned to glass, a mirror for the sun's ferocious heat. In his journal Grinnell described this part of the day as "a dead red hot calm."[47] The telegraph wires dipped rhythmically down to the surface of the glassy water, their reflections marred only by the rippling wake of the boat. Angry red burns flared on the men's exposed skin. They shot down three cormorants and spent the next few hours laboriously scraping grease from the birds' flesh, leading Grinnell to issue a gloomy warning to future ornithologists: "Scraping grease from fishy seabirds on an open boat in the frying sun is one phase of collecting well worth avoiding—if one can."[48]

Toward the north end of the sea, the Southern Pacific railway passed close enough to the water for passengers to fling their refuse into it from the windows. Carp, perch, and catfish flocked greedily to the shallows and were rewarded with chunks of stale bread, apple cores, and carcasses of roasted chickens. Birds in turn formed a buffet line on telegraph wires above the thrashing carp and catfish, feasting on the fish that made themselves easy pickings. The railroad and the sea together created marketplace of food and fish that was equal parts chimera and cyborg: part animal, part human, part technology.

This scene was remarked upon by nearly every observer of the Salton Sea in those years—part of the area's growing reputation for weirdness. Railroad passengers looked eagerly for birds and fish, sometimes saving scraps of food specifically for this purpose. They also kept keen eyes out for alligators, which, having reportedly escaped from a curio display at a saloon in Yuma, made their way through irrigation canals downstream to the shallow brackish water at the edges of the Salton Sea. Rumors flew that many of the fenceposts and railroad ties floating on the sea's surface were actually these displaced reptiles. In 1910 employees of the federal Weather Bureau station along the Southern Pacific line caught one, the alligator having been lured by food waste flung from the trains to hungry fish.[49]

As Grinnell and his crew made their way clumsily across the vast body of water, they encountered no alligators but did witness a cornucopia of seabirds: cormorants, great blue herons, ducks, eared grebes and western grebes, common loons, terns, ring-billed gulls, and, finally, the birds they had come specifically to observe: white pelicans. Nine hours after setting out, the boat alighted on Echo Island and the travelers disembarked to find a vast colony of the fish-eating water birds, so many of them that on first sight the island looked like a frosted cake.[50] The pelicans, none too pleased with their visitors, took flight en masse—"they wheeled in great circles overhead, crossing and re-crossing over their breeding grounds," their wings making "quite a roar" when they were all flapping and a "whispering whistle" when they coasted—abandoning their nests to form a flotilla on the water away from the island.[51] Grinnell delighted at what they left behind for his observation: a seemingly infinite network of groundling nests, with one to four eggs in each. "We had discovered," Grinnell reported triumphantly, "the southernmost recorded nesting-colony of the American White Pelican, and we set about taking a census of it." The census revealed nearly a thousand nests, representing more than two thousand pelicans living on Echo Island. Evidence abounded of the *human* colony surrounding the sea and submerged by it, including flotsam railroad ties and building planks interspersed with the pelicans' nests.[52]

Their excursion to Echo Island ended the same way it started: with their boat taken hostage by the Salton Sea. They awoke to the sound of waves pounding the boat's sides, and so they rushed from their open-air beds to its rescue. Despite frantic "bailing and heaving," during which they "enjoyed a prolonged bath in the tepid brackish waters of Salton Sea," the boat filled with water.[53] Its batteries were ruined. From here on, their progress across the sea would be not only hot and slow but also powered only by the sweaty labor of rowing. The next morning, sleep deprived and sunburned, they found themselves bending oars to Pelican Island, three miles away. Pelican Island, ironically, revealed scant evidence of pelicans but instead hosted hundreds of cormorants, numerous great blue herons, and a smattering of gulls. They took samples and photographs and returned to their humbled boat, rowing the final nine miles toward the mainland—which they could only reach by trudging and wading the last few hundred yards after nightfall, arms straining to hold their gear aloft, because the water was too shallow to allow the boat to reach dry ground.

Grinnell's expedition was physically grueling, frustrating, and full of obstacles thrown in his path by sea, wind, sun, and birds. In these ways it echoed central tropes of Progressive-era environmental writing: white settler men sharpening their wits against the natural world. Despite these passing similarities, however, Grinnell's recounting of his expedition was not the stuff of Progressive-era preservationists' fantasies. His exhausting and gloomy story bore almost no resemblance to John Muir's exultations from the Sierras, for example; little here reflected the face of the divine. It was instead littered with the detritus of settler life, which had been dislodged and displaced by the Salton Sea: railroad ties and fenceposts, chicken wire and food waste. And *alligators*, of all things. The greedy carp feasted on scraps while the birds, in turn, feasted on them—the birds and fish themselves brought here through the intemperance of land developers, the tragedy of land lost to flooding with only the chicken wire remaining. All of it painted a bleak and uninspiring scene.

Grinnell, however, seemed unbothered by this lack of natural purity. Unlike Muir, Grinnell was not holding out for something of pure nature in the frantic flight of birds from the ringing shots of his gun, in the eggs he confiscated as scientific samples, or in the beak marks in the dirt around pelican nests. Instead, his role resembled exactly what he described himself performing among the pelican nests: a census taker, a dutiful recorder of facts and figures.[54]

Grinnell's very presence at the Salton Sea in 1908 reflected yet another shift in settler engagements with birds and bird bodies emerging in the early decades of the twentieth century, both locally and nationally, that complicated the already complex rubric of social meaning (race, gender, class) projected onto birds.[55] At a time when settler men increasingly saw themselves as middle-class managers rather than yeoman farmers, and as conservationism followed Gifford Pinchot's lead in pursuing what he famously called "the wise use of the earth and its resources for the lasting good of men," scientific management of those resources became a central concern.[56] Census-taking among wild bird populations supplanted the loving romanticism of clubwomen's pleas for the lives of songbirds and sought to counteract the "savage" poaching of birds for milliners' production of fashionable hats. As evidenced by Grinnell's sweaty and exhausting mission, bird conservation could be real work for middle-class settler men, neither cruel excess nor mere pastime. State-sponsored conservation practices also served as a marker of civilization for the editors of the *Imperial Valley Press*, who opined in

1910 that "civilized states are legislating for the protection of birds and animals, but Mexico, the country that legalizes bull-fights and fosters the cock-pit, takes a step backward and promotes the unspeakable cruelty of sordid bird-murder."[57] At a time when the borderland communities of Imperial Valley sought to differentiate themselves from Mexico in an attempt to shore up their plan for the All-American Canal, birds served the purpose of drawing racial lines between "civilization" north of the border and its perceived absence to the south.

Grinnell, sitting down to record his trip to the Colorado Desert, his adventure on the Salton Sea, and the fieldwork around its shores, mused on the qualities of sea, climate, and desert that drew birds to this perhaps unlikely place: "The Colorado desert from the Colorado converging up to San Gorgonio Pass," he wrote, "acts as a sort of funnel thru which the migrants pour, condensing towards the west. And Mecca itself is a tarrying place because of the cottonwood trees, grass and mesquite and screw-bean thickets and the abundant fresh water from the constantly flowing artesian wells. I have never before seen the great numbers of migrants, either resting, or in passage, as here."[58] In Grinnell's estimation, the Salton Sea functioned as one part of a larger geography of crossings—offering sanctuary for migrating bird populations and native species alike, part of a network of resources that fit the natural conditions of the larger desert region. As he sat nursing his sunburns and fastidiously stuffing the bird specimens he had collected on his trip, it was the theme of migration that rose to the fore of the lessons gleaned from this expedition across the surface of the newly formed Salton Sea.

REFUGE

When Joseph Grinnell finally waded to the shore of the Salton Sea after his long journey of soggy mishaps in the summer of 1908, he could not have known what kinds of fraught futures bird populations would have—and the many uses to which bird bodies would be put in managing the contested social relations of Imperial Valley. But he probably *could* have intuited the idea of the Salton Sea as a kind of bird refuge and the notion of the sea as a place of safety for birds. The pelicans of Echo Island let him know in no uncertain terms that he and his crew were intruding on their sanctuary; whether or not their nests were bordered by railroad ties and tangled in chicken wire, what disturbed their peace was the arrival of humans bent on counting and collecting their eggs. This was clearly a place where the ideals that organized early conservation efforts, including the creation of the first wildlife sanctuaries, would thrive—if of course the Salton Sea did not evaporate in the meantime.

Conservation in the federal Biological Survey, the precursor to the Fish and Wildlife Service, emerged from exactly this kind of work to measure and account for bird populations, many of which were in dramatic decline in the early decades of the twentieth century.[59] Members of the Biological Survey recognized that habitat loss, expansions in agriculture, disease, and hunting were all factors that combined to dramatically reduce wild bird populations in North America.[60] National concerns over "duck slaughter," moreover, led to more stringent changes in federal duck hunting policy.[61] In 1930 many in California thought that even these stricter federal regulations did not go far enough to protect ducks and other wildlife; in that year Proposition 11 pushed to vest plenary power in the state's Fish and Game Commission for control of all wildlife in California. The proposition failed, but its advocates successfully raised the issue of wildlife conservation across the state.

In part due to this kind of political activity, several sites across California were considered for bird refuges under the federal Migratory Bird Conservation Act of 1929. The Salton Sea seemed an obvious choice; it was already known for its diverse bird populations and was a popular haunt of ornithologists like Gilman, Grinnell, and C. Hart Merriam.[62] The Salton Sea Wildlife Tract was established on the southern shore of the sea in 1930 and lauded as "an important place in the network of refuges to be established in the west coast region."[63] The shimmering desert sea, bordered as it was by Imperial Valley's "mantle of green," was already one of the few wetlands remaining for California's water birds and was somewhat ironically deemed "the only area in Southern California meeting all the requirements of an ideal game refuge."[64] As in other parts of the West in these years, carefully managed wildlife areas like bird refuges could serve dual purposes: conservation of bird and other animal populations and recreation in the form of hunting.[65]

The artificial mantle of green marked a stark difference between the area surrounding the Salton Sea and other areas withdrawn by the federal government for wild bird refuges. Elsewhere, farmers systematically drained wetlands to create more land for agriculture.[66] Here and in other places that relied on desert irrigation, the opposite was true. Birds, being sensible creatures, followed the water.

If this move to protect the birds of the Salton Sea pleased conservationists at the federal and state level and local and regional hunters who enjoyed its promise of sport, it enraged Imperial Valley farmers. The farmers made quick enemies of the birds, and ducks in particular, insisting that the damage they caused to their crops that was both expensive and maddening. To this complaint, the federal Biological Survey representatives could only respond that establishing a controlled reserve that fed the birds *and* allowed for them to be hunted would ease the "pest" problem over time. Moreover, no one agreed about the extent of the pest problem itself; refuting the accounts of farmers, Harold Bryant, a zoologist with the University of California's Museum of Vertebrate Zoology, conducted four days of field research in the area, finding that "statements regarding the damage to crops caused by ducks [are] exaggerated." Given the volume of consternation about ducks and other birds, the researcher was "surprised at the relatively few birds eating in the area investigated."[67]

Unsurprisingly, farmers were disgruntled with the plan to create a wildlife refuge at the sea. By the early 1950s even several decades of "rabid" duck hunting on and near the Salton Sea had not reduced the population of ducks to farmers' satisfaction. Hunting seasons from the 1930s to the 1950s seemed to follow a predictable pattern: federal conservationists restricted the length of the hunting season and the number of birds any given hunter could kill. Hunters and farmers alike protested, claiming that "the birds are heavy and in full bloom" and the federal regulations were too "stringent" given the abundance (and, to their minds, pestilential nature) of the birds.[68]

The stakes in this debate—too many birds or too few?—in essence came down to the meaning that was made out of the Salton Sea's seemingly abundant bird population. Farmers and hunters observed quite rightly that the bird population around the Salton Sea was dense and possibly growing denser year by year. Conservationists, however, noted that this increase of birds at the sea was "due to the concentration of the birds on fewer and smaller bodies of water" in California and throughout the West.[69] Their assessment of the bird situation, in short, was the opposite of that of farmers and hunters: increases in bird numbers at the sea, according to conservationists, indicated major problems for bird populations elsewhere. The total number of birds, conservationists pointed out, was actually dangerously low, and their density at the Salton Sea reflected troubling impacts on the birds' other water resources in the West.[70]

Unmoved by such logic, farmers maintained that ducks were pests to be eradicated—not a wildlife resource to be conserved. By the early 1950s ducks were again being represented as an invading army at the Salton Sea and the Imperial Valley. Individual hunters with guns, however, were no longer adequate in this "aerial war." Instead, farmers turned to "searchlights. Batteries of guns. Bursting flares. Air-breaking bombs. And armies of men." The Imperial Valley, according to the *Los Angeles Times*, had become a "battleground of armies equipped with the implements of war"—literally so, as many of the weapons they turned against the flying "miscreants" were army and navy surplus supplies.[71] A Fish and Wildlife report noted in 1940 that "an Army Rifle with tracer ammunition was used to good advantage" in duck-ridden fields. "Bombs," the report added, "were also used effectively."[72] The farmers got their hands on grenade launchers with phosphorus flares, shotgun cartridge blanks, and flare bombs, all intended to "frighten the daylights out of the feeding birds." The "honkers," farmers insisted, were "'worse than a swarm of locusts'" and thoroughly deserved this alarming barrage of artillery.[73]

The Imperial Valley was not the only place where farmers and other private landholders resented and reviled the winged "trespassers"; in the face of their fury, it fell to federal managers to try to compel the birds to "heed the most important borders of all: the ones between private and public land."[74] With the California system of refuges under particular pressure from irate farmers, FWS personnel got into planes to survey farmlands and refuges from above, trying to visualize how the landscape would look to a hungry bird. Indeed, as wetlands dried up in California and throughout the West, federal biologists conceded what farmers already knew: that the transformed landscape itself was irresistible to birds. In one report's attenuated phrasing, the birds "as always took to irrigated fields and were apparently satisfied with what they had to offer."[75] Green, well-watered farmlands glistened below them, far outnumbering the islands of green that marked either the refuge or gun club reserves.

Rather than seeing the Salton Sea as one of the few remaining water resources for these birds, as the federal biologists and conservationists did, farmers saw the sea as an oversized enabler for the winged "miscreants." Ducks, they reasoned, were smart enough to avoid the bird refuge during hunting season, when they would "'wing it out to the middle of the water'" to wait out the shooting, as one game manager said.[76]

By the 1950s the farmers' paranoia about migrating ducks—wily and pestilential in their eyes, migrating to the Imperial Valley to take advantage of the green abundance the farms provided—mirrored their anxieties about migrating humans. In the early 1950s, as the Bracero Program created both sanctioned and unsanctioned streams of migrant laborers to the United States (many of them employed at Imperial Valley and Coachella Valley farms), nativist racism among white Americans reached a crescendo. Mexicans in particular tended to be animalized in white rhetoric, treated as a subhuman racial group "swarming" or "invading" the United States.[77] In this context descriptions of the conflict between men and ducks were racially coded. The conflict was not just with birds, for example; it was between the farmers and their "sworn enemies."[78] Unsanctioned flows of Mexican labor, a result of the Bracero Program, created a category of "illegal" immigration for the first time, igniting and codifying racism against migrant laborers as both unwelcome and undeserving of the privileges of permanent status in the United States. In a region that was both directly adjacent to the U.S.-Mexico border and highly dependent on the exploitation of Mexican laborers, consternation about legal status and perceived threats of "illegal" workers abounded in this decade. At the Salton Sea Wildlife Tract, refuge managers in 1955 acknowledged the widespread angst in the area over migration with "the worst 'pun' of the season," joking that "all of those illegal characters we discuss so often are sick birds . . . (ill-eagles that is)."[79] A groan-worthy pun indeed, but also a gag that underscored the parallels being drawn between birds and people in the area at the time.

Moreover, just as nativist white Americans tended to view conditions in the United States as too good for Mexican laborers (whom they saw as undeserving)—conditions that would make the workers want to stay rather than to return to Mexico—the Salton Sea Wildlife Tract was credited for making life perhaps a bit too cozy for ducks. Local observers fretted that the tract was changing the birds' very migration patterns because they suddenly preferred to stay in California rather than migrate back across international borders.[80] "The sea attracts them here," one California Fish and Game Commission agent conceded. "'That sea's safety . . . and they know it.'"[81] Ducks, plucking the profits from farmers' fields, were ascribed human characteristics in ways that resonated with the racial logic that saw Mexicans in the fields—sanctioned through the Bracero Program or unsanctioned and undocumented—as a troubling threat.

If farmers described ducks in ways that blurred the boundaries between human and bird migrants, federal conservationists began to manage their conservation areas in ways that blurred the boundaries between refuge and farm.[82] Refuges across the West came to resemble the cultivated fields of agricultural regions like Imperial Valley, complete with tree rows and farm fields dedicated to growing crops specifically to feed wild birds. They used farm machinery and chemical pesticides. They also dug ponds and canals, maintained water levels, and treated visibly diseased birds. Each year the refuge managers authored narrative reports that meticulously documented the acreage under cultivation, mostly tracts of alfalfa, millet, rice, and barley meant to draw birds away from Imperial Valley fields.[83] When refuge managers opened headgates to flood the fields, carp that had wound their way from the Colorado River through the Imperial Valley's canal system into the New River flopped around and tried to spawn amid the stalks of millet and barley.

This work created what historian Robert Wilson has called a "duck farm" for conservation.[84] It was met with the obstacles inherent to the sea's ecological conditions and its environmental history. In addition to maintaining a wetland in a desert, the conservationists grappled with politically powerful private entities—farmers and hunters—and a constantly changing desert world. The water of the refuge constantly rose and fell with the tides of agricultural runoff from the Imperial and Coachella Valleys. The pesticides sprayed on the ducks' crops mingled with the pesticides drifting along in the water and air flowing north from pesticide-giddy growers. Tourists and farmers alike brought invasive species and new diseases, including avian cholera and avian botulism, both of which began to cause devastating die-offs in the decades toward the end of the twentieth century. Some of the sea's conditions could be considered useful: the constant stocking of the sea with African tilapia for sport anglers, for example, kept fish-eating birds happy and well fed.

Wild bird populations continued to decline throughout the West. By the end of the twentieth century the Salton Sea refuge, which had by then been renamed the Sonny Bono National Wildlife Refuge (after the singer–turned–member of Congress who took up the sea as a personal cause), sat in the thick of dramatic die-offs of fish and birds alike. Refuge managers' responsibilities would include maintaining the last communities of endangered birds, such as the Yuma clapper rail. Grinnell's experience of witnessing clouds of pelicans soaring over Echo Island while he fastidiously measured their nests had given way to significantly depleted populations of pelicans and other fish-eating birds.

In the waning years of the twentieth century, the Salton Sea came to be known for regular die-offs of the very birds the refuge was designed to protect. Images of Fish and Wildlife officials straining to collect dead birds along the sea's shoreline, with carcasses stretching into the distance, added to a general public distaste for the Salton Sea and a sense that this was a body of water in decline.[85] The cause of these die-offs,

Pacific Flyway

16. The Pacific Flyway. U.S. Fish and Wildlife Service.

according to biologists, often remained as murky as the sea's bacteria-choked water. Toxic levels of bacteria, heavy metals, and pesticides all seemed to be major factors, but no single culprit could explain the overwhelming numbers of bird bodies piling up on the shoreline.[86]

The bird and fish die-offs that would give the Salton Sea the reputation for being an infamous environmental disaster began in the early 1980s. Official reports and unofficial rumors alike began to tell of "mysterious biological 'anomalies'" among the sea's birds. In 1986 the California Department of Health Services recommended that pregnant women and children avoid eating Salton Sea fish. In 1988 a thousand birds, mostly dabbling ducks, perished of avian botulism. In December and January 1989 fish began to succumb to the sea's troubling conditions as well; tilapia perished en masse, floating to the surface and leaving the shoreline thick with rotting fish, at which point "swarms of insects . . . fled the sea's brackish waters, took wing and descended on homes and vehicles for miles around."[87] In February twenty thousand eared grebes died, their bodies, like those of the tilapia, washing to the shore to rot under the bright winter sun. By the end of 1989, 4,500 cattle egrets had died of salmonellosis.

By December 1992 the number of eared grebe fatalities had risen to a hundred thousand. U.S. Fish and Wildlife biologists estimated that this constituted as much as 4 percent of the whole North American population of eared grebes. This die-off confounded conservationists. The birds' livers contained elevated levels of arsenic, chromium, DDE, mercury, selenium, and zinc, but none of these toxicants seemed to exist in their bodies at lethal levels. That winter two thousand other birds succumbed to avian cholera. The birds, noted one wildlife biologist, were "'dying faster than we can pick 'em up.'"[88]

The numbers, and bodies, continued to pile up: in 1994, 20,000 birds died from a range of causes, some as mysterious as the 1992 loss of the eared grebes. In 1995 as many as 3,000 birds died of avian botulism. Botulism struck again the next year, claiming 14,000 birds in 1996, including 8,500 white pelicans and more than 1,000 brown pelicans—marking "the first time fish-eating birds had succumbed to the disease."[89] The scale of the 1996 die-offs could be measured by a particularly grisly rubric: in that year there were so many dead birds that the incinerator the refuge workers were using to dispose of bird bodies could not keep up, even when running twenty-four hours a day.[90] In 1997, 1,900 double-crested cormorants perished, as did an additional 2,500 eared grebes. In 1998, 8,000 more birds were lost to avian cholera, and 6,000 cormorants fell to Newcastle disease.

To be sure, die-offs have occurred regularly at the Salton Sea since its formation. From 1907 on, die-offs occurred in regular annual cycles as the water in the sea, with no natural outlet but evaporation, built up bacteria that could rise to toxic levels. Bacterial overload, however, was not the only cause of bird deaths over the course of the twentieth century. Managers of the Salton Sea Wildlife Refuge frequently examined birds that died of lead poisoning from the excessive quantities of lead shot that made their way to the sea from the barrels of hunters' weapons. Pesticides and other toxicants played their part, too. Overall, the numbers of die-off events have *decreased* since the 1950s, but the sheer numbers of fatalities dramatically *increased*. The only decades in the twentieth century in which die-offs occurred that involved more than ten thousand individual bird deaths were the 1980s and the 1990s. These dramatic incidents, according to one biologist, reflected the "severe stress" of the Salton Sea's ecosystem.[91]

As U.S. officials investigated the die-offs of the 1980s and 1990s, gathering dead bird bodies on the shores of the Salton Sea under a sweltering sun, they primarily recorded the loss of water birds around the wildlife refuge—the birds the refuge had been designed to protect: pelicans, dabbling ducks, grebes, and so on. Farther to the north Cahuilla historian Katherine Siva Saubel noticed a different though related trend: the sudden disappearance of desert birds. "Long ago there used to be a lot of them," she recalled. "You could see them playing around in the morning."[92] Robins, desert wrens, meadow larks, and others had all gone away, Saubel lamented. She missed hearing their chirping and watching them flit among the branches of mesquites and junipers in the early morning light.

She knew the cause: "Nowadays the white man is spraying his crops with that poison." The birds eat it, she averred, "and so then they die."[93] In Saubel's account, the looming threat of a silent spring like the kind that Rachel Carson had used to spur environmentalists to action had already arrived in the Cahuillas' homeland on the northern edge of the Salton Sea.[94] She did not share biologists' hesitancy to pinpoint the cause of bird deaths on the pollutants that had been forced on their world; while scientists mostly demurred when it came to blaming the sea's toxins for die-offs, Saubel knew that one way or another, this loss had to do with "that poison" and settlers' agricultural practices.

Like duck-hating farmers and federal conservationists, Saubel had been watching the birds for signs of distress. For her, these feathered relations revealed a larger picture of ecological imbalance in ways that connected the sea to mesquites, shy thrashers, pesticides, and people. The birds, in short, mattered.

4

CONCRETE

The death of the desert will be a beautiful one.
—Arthur J. Burdick, *The Mystic Mid-Region*, 1904

In early December 1906 the California Fruit Growers Association gathered in Hanford, California, for their annual meeting. Amid a crowded agenda one item raised a raucous debate: whether or not the association should advocate that the state of California be exempted from the Chinese Exclusion Act.[1] The act, passed by the U.S. Congress in 1882, barred the entry of Chinese immigrants to the United States and constituted the first racially exclusionary immigration policy in the country's history.[2] By the time California's fruit growers met in 1906, two decades of exclusion of Chinese workers had pitted the white population's nativist racism against their desire for exploitable labor. This debate was nowhere in evidence so much as on California farms.[3] The association's report in favor of the exclusion law decried the latter position, characterizing it as permitting "the dark flood of Chinese millions [to] break over all barriers and flood this fair land of ours."[4]

At the California Fruit Growers Association meeting, the debate reached a fever pitch. Impassioned speakers on either side of the issue emphasized, on the one hand, the dire conditions of farmers who did not have labor enough to work the land and, on the other, white Californians' aversion to Chinese people. At one point Judge W. H. Aiken insisted on having the floor, delivering a three-minute speech that riffed on a common comparison of Chinese immigration to a "flood" by using a metaphor torn from the state's most recent headlines: the out-of-control Colorado River flooding the Imperial Valley. The people of the Imperial Valley, he cautioned his audience, had been so greedy for water that they convinced themselves that they could control the mighty Colorado. When they started to get the water, however, insisting they would only get a little, the whole river poured in. "And then," Aiken cried, "they sat down in sack-cloth and ashes and said, 'For God's sake, we made a mistake. Can anybody remove this great flood from us?'"[5]

Aiken paused for dramatic effect. "Now," he went on, surveying the room, "here are gentlemen who come here and say that that great dam against the Chinese shall be removed to get a restricted supply of Chinese labor. When the hordes of five hundred millions step against that restriction they will destroy that dam and overflow our fair land, and we will be in a worse condition than the men in Imperial Valley. Let us be men, and let us first protect Americans from the Chinese." Judge Aiken resumed his seat as applause broke out around him.[6]

Aiken's use of the Colorado River floods as a metaphor for Chinese immigration spoke volumes about prevailing understandings of race and nature among white settlers in California in the early 1900s—notions that collided in the Imperial Valley in the decades after the flooding. Racist fears of being overrun by laborers of color, including the Chinese but also South Asians, Mexicans, and African Americans, facilitated a pressing demand for control over the *nature* of the Colorado River as well as over nonwhite people. Here, life in the borderlands for white settlers meant the need for racial hegemony and protection from the menace of the natural world, and what ensued took the form of what literary theorist Phillip Round calls a need for "technological and racial reclamation": material and metaphorical dams made of concrete, iron, racist ire, and, if Judge Aiken had his way, inflexible restrictions against immigration—his "great dam against the Chinese."[7]

This chapter considers how attempts to exert control over nature in the form of dams, diversions, and canals converged with attempts to control nonwhite and Indigenous people in the areas connected by land and by river to the Salton Sea.[8] As racial control in domestic and immigration policies converged around practices of segregation, exclusion, dispossession, and disenfranchisement, control of nature took the form of reclamation via the expedient of dams and canals. As declared by Arthur Burdick in *The Mystic Mid-Region* in 1904, reclamation would spell the "death of the desert." That death would be a "beautiful one," producing a landscape rich in crops, lined with roads, and presided over by rows of majestic trees: the transformation of a "region of death," as Burdick described the desert, "into a kingdom of life."[9] Concrete, poured into riverbeds and adhered to the sides of canyon walls, would be the instrument of the desert's death blow.

By the early 1920s, right about when most observers anticipated the Salton Sea would dry up entirely if left to the forces of evaporation, writers and policy makers were worrying more and more about further threats of flooding from the Colorado River. Given the scale of profit being picked from Imperial Valley farms, could their fate be left to the whims of nature and the potential for the Colorado to spill over its banks yet again? The "extraordinary picture of a great railroad being chased over a bone-dry desert" by the sea's rising waters had stuck in the minds of Imperial Valley investors and state and federal policy makers.[10] The Colorado River existed in these accounts as a malignant menace, a specter of disaster embodied as an uncontrollable and unpredictable force of nature. This represented a stark shift from the ways the river had been depicted in previous decades as an industrious maker of history, a kind of liquid pioneer "constantly tearing away and grinding up boulders and earth, in its onward course through countless ages past," for the noble purpose of, as one writer had put it, "slowly developing a plan to provide homes for a favored race."[11] Dams and canals would return the Colorado to this noble work. Making sure that work provided "homes for a favored race" would entail different—though related—processes in the Imperial Valley.

In Burdick's "kingdom of life," whiteness was overdetermined ideologically, if not in actual reality.[12] In an era that regarded Native people in the West primarily as a barrier to settlement and an anachronistic emblem of the region's frontier past, Burdick and others saw Cocopahs, Mojaves, Kumeyaays, Cahuillas, and Cupeños as people from whom land could rightly be wrested. But the racial and ethnic demographics of the settlers who would deal the desert's death blow did not always match white supremacist ideals. In the 1880s and 1890s the U.S.-Mexico borderlands constituted a place of complex racial and ethnic diversity. In borderland communities like those in the Imperial Valley, white supremacy and power over people of color needed to be negotiated and constructed over time, built into the unsteady firmament of desert soil and new settler institutions.[13]

In the broader context of settler colonialism, in which settlers dispossess Indigenous peoples of their homelands and then coerce non-Native labor to "make the land produce, and produce excessively," the multiracial and multiethnic world of the borderlands presented an opportunity—workers.[14] "Now the day has come," crowed the *Calexico Chronicle* in the wake of the flooding, "when every inch of ground must be forced to do its utmost."[15] In a system that resembled what Marxist political theorist Cedric Robinson has called "racial capitalism," in which organizing people in hierarchical racial strata itself produces profit, growers hired nonwhite laborers in the fields because their labor was less expensive. Making the land produce excessively—forcing it to do its utmost—relied on the exploitation of racialized and underpaid laborers in a system that profited off of racial as well as class-based oppression.[16]

Throughout the late nineteenth century and into the twentieth, California institutions and cultural practices revealed the malleability of racism in its ability to control various nonwhite populations in ways that sought to balance the state's reliance on a large labor force with white Californians' investments in white supremacy. In 1854 California's Supreme Court ruled that Chinese people could not testify against white persons in courts of law; the rationale supporting this decision emerged from the fact that since Natives were barred from testifying, and since, according to prevailing race theories, Chinese and Natives shared the same Asiatic racial ancestry, the restriction could be extended to both groups.[17] The state's Anti-Vagrancy Act of 1855 (commonly known as the "Greaser Act") related to police harassment and incarceration and in effect focused on the heritage of individuals targeted by police and vigilantes. The activities of the latter led to lynchings across the West, terrorizing Native, Mexican, and Chinese people.[18]

In Imperial Valley this California-wide racial caste system was entangled in ideas about race and nature.[19] Boosters debated plans to incentivize Black laborers to come to California from southern fields; local newspapers hummed with competing opinions about the relative prowess of Chinese, Japanese, Indian, and Native pickers, particularly in light of the boom in cotton production in their fields.[20] These racial ideas thrived in the valley in part because many of the landowners had come from cotton-growing states like Texas and Georgia, where divisions of labor were both deeply entrenched and profoundly racist, and had followed "King Cotton" to "his most recently acquired dominion in the American Nile country": Imperial Valley.[21] As Imperial Valley farmers began to invest in cotton, they actively recruited African American laborers from southern states. As a result, the Black population went from 65 in 1910 to 1,648 in 1920.[22] Pursuing King Cotton west to California, the growers brought their notions of racism, hot climates, and fieldwork with them.

Meanwhile, Mexican migration across the border escalated after 1910 with the onset of the Mexican Revolution and increased further still as instability in Mexico reached a crescendo during the war years. From 1910 to 1920 the Mexican population of the Imperial Valley increased from 1,461 to 6,414.[23] Anti-Mexican sentiment among white settlers escalated in kind, eventually lending support for increased control over the U.S.-Mexico border and increased policing of Mexicans seeking to cross that line.[24]

Changes in nonwhite population were not all increases. Japanese labor decreased in the wake of the 1907 "Gentlemen's Agreement" between the United States and the empire of Japan, in which Japan agreed to prevent its citizens from migrating to the United States if the federal government agreed not to adopt formal exclusion policies, as it had against China. In the Imperial Valley decreases in the numbers of

Japanese laborers were followed by increases in those from India and Korea in a pattern of ethnic succession that effectively kept wages as low as possible.[25] In addition, the Chinese population of California was dramatically curtailed—though never fully blocked, as historian Beth Lew-Williams has noted—by the national policy of Chinese exclusion.[26] However, even with these population-specific changes, racism remained a driving force of labor exploitation on Imperial Valley farms.

Concern about the Colorado River's unpredictable power—like the concern that Judge Aiken invoked in his anti-Chinese speech to the California Fruit Growers' Association in 1906—did not necessarily follow from concern for individual farmers living out a Jeffersonian agricultural dream in the desert, although that might have been the intended impression. By the mid-1920s the vast majority of Imperial Valley acreage was owned by absentee landlords who employed tenants to farm their land.[27] Big landowners quickly bought out their smaller neighbors, consolidating much of the profit-producing property in the valley in fewer and fewer hands. Tenancy in the valley meant instability and high degrees of competition. Most leases only lasted three years, particularly when the landlord was a corporation. This meant high pressure on tenants to produce and little guarantee of longevity.[28] The California Alien Land Law of 1913 codified this leasing system for all "aliens ineligible for citizenship." Immigrants subject to the 1913 law were now barred from owning land, but they *could* take out the three-year leases, a system that primarily impacted immigrants from Asian countries. These leases became increasingly common in the Imperial Valley.[29] Combined with the racist preferences of corporate lenders for white farmers, the leasing process compounded an emergent racial caste system.

The specter of a repeat of the 1905 floods hung over the valley in these years, making the farms and fences seem uncomfortably contingent on the whims of a malign external force.[30] In the 1910s and 1920s writers tended to ascribe to the Colorado River qualities frequently used to target and control nonwhite migrants and laborers from various parts of the country and world. In some of the more explicitly racialized rhetoric, the "savage" river "invaded" the newly settled valley, its "tawny" waters threatening the homes and property of thousands of residents.[31] California senator Hiram Johnson urged that the river, "devilish in character," be made "a servant to mankind."[32] This thinly-veiled racist rhetoric echoed Imperial Valley settlers' sense of being under siege by nonwhite people.[33] The settlers would not be flexible in the face of centuries-old cyclical forces of flooding and evaporation.

Leaving the river in peace simply would not do.

The answer to the river's threat, from local settlers and the federal government, seemed obvious to Imperial Valley residents and California politicians: what they needed was more control. More dams, more canals—enough to hem in the might of the region's most forceful river. The early twentieth century had brought a dam-building frenzy that radically remapped the riverine West, ignited on June 1, 1902, when President Theodore Roosevelt signed the Reclamation Act. The act's grand vision to corral the rivers and lakes of sixteen western states and make possible the irrigation of family farms on arid lands came to form a cornerstone of western settlement.[34] Roosevelt declared that reclamation would enable "the settlement of the great arid West by the makers of homes," putting a fine point on the settler colonial logic of the federal policy with a clear, though unstated, preference for *white* homemaking on ostensibly empty land.[35] Over the course of the ensuing century, more than eight thousand large-scale dams appeared throughout the United States, hundreds of them causing immediate dispossession for Native communities.[36] Thousands more small-scale dams magnified the larger consequences of hydrologic infrastructure throughout the West. This reclamation movement reflected a turn-of-the-twentieth-century vision in which, as historian Donald Pisani has put it, "government could turn nature into a productive machine" not unlike a factory assembly line.[37]

The consequences of two converging projects—damming rivers and maintaining white supremacist racial hierarchies—appeared in the most violent way possible on the side of an Imperial Valley road in the early spring of 1910. A foreman for the California Development Company (CDC) named M. A. McKinnon, employed to oversee construction of a dam on the Alamo River, attacked a man named Bert Almer, one of several hundred Black laborers in Imperial Valley in 1910. Using a four-pound iron bar he had snatched from a nearby car, McKinnon leaped on Almer, cracking the victim's skull and causing further, extensive injuries. Almer was rushed to the nearest hospital for emergency treatment, which saved him from death.

McKinnon explained his violence by insisting that he "was from the South" and—turning to the most hackneyed of pretexts for white people's racist assaults on Black men—that Almer had acted disrespectfully toward a white woman in a local store. One white witness called it a "most brutal and cowardly attack" but, rather than suggesting that McKinnon should not have beaten Almer at all, stated that the victim could have simply been "whipped with the fists" rather than with a weapon.[38] Local police charged McKinnon with attempted murder and arrested him, setting his bond at $1,000. However, the CDC intervened on behalf of its employee, advocating for his freedom. The attack took place on a day in late spring; before the summer weather had a chance to take hold in earnest, McKinnon was free and facing nothing more than a brief probation.[39] By the first week of June he was back at the dam site overseeing the workers—most of whom were nonwhite—whose efforts helped control the Colorado River water flowing through the Alamo to growers' fields.

This violent attack put on full display the intersections of race and labor as they played out alongside white settlers' attempts to force the land—and water—to "do its utmost." In the valley the privileges of whiteness were consolidated to the exclusion of African Americans, Natives, and immigrants of color, and racism itself produced additional profits by making nonwhite labor cheaper. Racial power, like power over nature, would never be a fully successful project. Aiken's "great dam" against the Chinese—anti-immigrant legislation—would not end in full exclusion, and the exercise of white supremacist power over workers occurred in the context of knowing that the system required highly exploited laborers to continue to function.[40] Meanwhile, the "death of the desert" would follow the concrete-lined walls of canals and barriers that dammed waterways, with the intent of controlling white settlers' power over water in their "kingdom of life."

Water, however, was not so easily corralled. Dams and canals seeped and leaked.[41] River water brought debris that built up in unexpected places. Labor shortages required the cutting of corners in canal construction. Unlined sections of canals set water free, letting it to soak through the dry soil far from the crops for which it was intended. The ongoing work to corral the water sat at the heart of the region's settler history in these decades. Properly managed, it would make the desert bloom for the "favored race." The river water would become canal water, which then became irrigation water. The wastewater left over at the end of this ambitious hydraulic process would be bound for a single destination: the Salton Sea.

THE VALVE AND THE DRAIN

When Charles Rockwood of the CDC regarded his company's silt-clogged canal system in the autumn of 1904 and decided to dig the ditch that would clear the Colorado River's path to the Salton Sink, he had dams on his mind. More accurately, he had one dam in particular on his mind: the Laguna Dam. Designed to provide water to Arizona farmers from the Colorado River, the Laguna Dam had yet to be built but had been authorized by one of Rockwood's various nemeses, the U.S. Bureau of Reclamation, just a few months before. For Rockwood and, to his consternation, for the settlers whose futures relied on the CDC's muddy canals, the Laguna project presented a stark contrast between private irrigation operations and those backed by the might of the federal government. While Rockwood had tried and failed to get the Colorado River to deliver water to the Imperial Valley—and then tried and failed to get it to *stop* doing so during the floods that created the Salton Sea—the Bureau of Reclamation had both the money and technology to make good on the promise the CDC had laid at settlers' feet.[42] This federal capacity for large-scale projects, added to the unyielding might of the Colorado River that bedeviled his daily life, drove Rockwood to distraction.

Rockwood had good reason to fret about the unfair fight between private irrigation concerns and those backed by Reclamation. By the 1920s, more than a decade after the completion of Laguna Dam and long after Rockwood's choices had forced him out of the valley's story, the Imperial settlers banked on a burgeoning system of dams and federal irrigation projects. Reclamation had become, here as elsewhere in the West, a governmental concern wrested from the private projects that had, one after another, failed in increasingly spectacular ways. Federal engineers hired local crews to pour concrete, construct dikes, and weld headgates, all in pursuit of control over the West's rivers and streams. For residents of Imperial Valley, none of these projects eased fears of the Colorado's might and unpredictability. They believed unequivocally, and with good reason, that the river remained outside of human control, despite a growing—and federally subsidized—reclamation infrastructure. In 1918 the director of Reclamation, Arthur Davis, proposed a solution: a massive dam to bring the river in its entirety under federal control.[43] Although it would be planted far away from the Imperial Valley in a little known spot of sharp canyon walls in the homelands of the Southern Paiutes, Haulapis, and Chemehuevis, the most immediate beneficiaries would be the settlers raising crops on the northern and southern edges of the Salton Sea.

In the years that followed, advocates of a dam in Boulder Canyon consistently framed the project as a means to protect the Imperial Valley from floods like those that created the Salton Sea. In 1922 the Interior Department submitted its report, "Problems of the Imperial Valley and Vicinity," nicknamed the Fall-Davis Report after its most vocal proponents. It proposed Reclamation's dream project, the Boulder Dam (later renamed the Hoover Dam). It also included plans for the single piece of infrastructure most desired by Imperial Valley settlers: the All-American Canal, which would bring the valley's canal system— and thus control over Colorado River irrigation water—north of the U.S.-Mexico boundary line.[44] Events that would determine the fate of the river moved quickly over the next several years. In the fall of 1922 representatives of the seven states in the Colorado River basin gathered in Santa Fe, New Mexico, to sign the Colorado River Compact, and Congress acted on the Fall-Davis Report by introducing a bill to begin construction of the Boulder Dam. Two years later a new study expanded on the findings of the Fall-Davis Report and underscored support for

17. Boulder Canyon Dam map, showing the benefits that the dam would ideally produce for Las Vegas, Los Angeles, and Imperial Valley. "Map of Southwest Showing
the Colorado River with the Boulder Canyon Dam and the All American Canal. As
provided for in Senate Bill 727 and House Bill 2903." "The Boulder Dam All American
Canal Project: Facts." Imperial Irrigation District, 1924, pages 10–11. Special Collections & Archives, UC San Diego, La Jolla, 92093-0175 (https://lib.ucsd.edu/sca).

both dam and canal. The Boulder Canyon Project Act (BCPA) passed
Congress in 1928. President Calvin Coolidge signed it into law in the
waning days of the year.[45]

In the course of these conversations the BCPA emerged from a desire
to curb and control the West's most powerful waterway in the service
of existing agricultural empires like the Imperial and Coachella Valleys
and the promise of more like them.[46] Southern Californians certainly
viewed the BCPA through an Imperial-centric lens. Local boosters published pamphlets and view books extolling the project's usefulness to

the Imperial and Coachella Valleys for agriculture, providing desert denizens with glossy images of a grand river, and inviting them to dream of the shining fields it would water in perpetuity.[47] None of these rose to the sophistication of the campaign later launched by the Los Angeles Department of Water and Power under a title that crystallized how Southern California utilities saw the Colorado: in their plans for their rapidly growing cities and towns, it truly was *The River of Destiny*.[48] In the words of historian Donald Worster, the Boulder Dam, as it was then known, would turn this great, wild waterway into "a managed ditch running meekly from its headwaters to its mouth under the strict supervision of the federal engineers."[49]

The great dam would serve as a valve for the Colorado River. The Salton Sea would be its drain. The results of the Colorado River Compact, which divvied up the river's water among the southwestern states and Mexico, delivered more than three million acre-feet of water to the Imperial Valley, and that water would need to drain off of the fields lest it swamp the crops. To irrigate its most important agricultural region, the Mexicali Valley, Mexico received less than half that amount.[50] The Imperial Valley's millions of acre-feet of water would soak through its notoriously alkaline soil, with evaporation and crops taking the pure water and leaving even more salts behind. Over time the groundwater would contain more and more of this briny runoff, threatening the profitability of acre after acre of Imperial Valley farmland. The Colorado's water, so hard won, would poison the very crops it nourished. Without a drain for the valley's liquid waste, the efforts of the federal government to manage the Colorado would be lost in one of the country's most potentially profitable, and politically powerful, agricultural regions.

The Salton Sea, that "dead sea in an uninhabitable desert," finally had a purpose: to bless the farmers with a "natural dumping basin for the entire valley."[51] In 1923 the problem of building a drainage infrastructure to properly utilize that "natural dumping basin" was taken on by the new Imperial Irrigation District (IID), which quickly became the largest irrigation district in the country; it controlled more than half a million acres of farmland.[52] In time the IID would oversee a complex system of drainage canals that would draw wastewater away from Imperial Valley farms and down into the Salton Sea.

In the Imperial Valley the work of bringing the Colorado River firmly under control was manifested in one particular infrastructural project: the All-American Canal, the "pet scheme" of the valley's elites.[53] The canal made for a frequent conversation topic in Southern California from the earliest years after the flooding until it began to deliver water from the Colorado River to their communities. Settlers in the Imperial Valley had long debated the canal's pros and cons, their opinions largely falling along the lines of local concerns. Calexico residents tended to disapprove of the plan because of the costs involved. The east mesa settlements, particularly Holtville, the only exclusively white town in the valley, favored it first and foremost because it would improve their own irrigation projects.[54] Large and small landowners, if not their tenants, strongly supported it because the canal—and the control of the Colorado River it brought with it—would open up loans from the Federal Land Bank.[55] The construction of the All-American Canal came much later than most Imperial Valley elites would have wanted, however, as larger dam construction projects took priority in the federal agenda.[56]

The Salton Sea in the meantime was in the process of rapidly evaporating under the glare of the intense desert sunlight. As had happened so many times in the past, the water would vanish entirely within a relatively short number of years. Because the Salton Sea had (and has) no natural inflows except for the desert's anemic annual rainfall and agricultural drainage from the New and Alamo Rivers, most observers predicted that without efforts to artificially sustain it, the sea would evaporate entirely by the early 1930s.

A 1924 study by the Interior Department confirmed the Salton Sea's rapid decline, finding that in one year alone, its depth at the shoreline had dropped a full foot. The sea now sat, the report noted, 248 feet below sea level. Since its high point in the years after the flooding, receding water left thirteen thousand acres of shoreline newly exposed. At this rate, observers fretted, evaporation would mean losing the farmers' "natural dumping basin." For the more sentimental among them, it would also bring to a close a quintessential drama that had occurred in "the most genuine desert region in the United States." The 1905 floods had brought a "sudden inrush of the most vital factor in desert life"—water.[57] Losing it would mean an anticlimactic end to this particular melodrama of westward expansion and desert reclamation. The sea's fortunes clearly were imbricated in the settler narrative of the valley that saw how "hardy, courageous men and women . . . wrung a livelihood from Mother Nature in her fiercest phase, and made a spot of beauty on her breast."[58] The wastewater from the IID thus seemed to serve the multiple purposes of artificially sustaining the sea's water level, saving Imperial Valley farmers from alkaline-clogged fields, and sustaining a narrative of settlers "wresting victory from the desert wastes."[59]

The Salton Sea, however, did not evaporate as it had in the past. For part of the Colorado River project, the Coolidge administration penned a series of executive orders that designated the Salton Sea as a permanent drainage basin, a move justified in large part by the widespread notion that the "Salton Sea furnishes a *natural* outlet" for drainage.[60] In the 1920s the Salton Sea's role in Colorado Desert agriculture came to be seen as both natural and, counterintuitively, worth artificially sustaining. In fact, when Imperial Valley farmers began to find ways to conserve water in the mid-1920s, which resulted in less runoff into the Salton Sea, farmers were chided that their conservation had single-handedly caused the sea to drop even more rapidly than had been anticipated.

The use of the Boulder Dam as a valve for the Colorado River, and the Salton Sea its drain, belied federal promises to the Torres Martinez Cahuillas that they would have access to their underwater reservation just as soon as the Salton Sea evaporated. Together, the dams and canals associated with the BCPA guaranteed the longevity of irrigation water for agriculture in the Colorado Desert. It also guaranteed the use of the Salton Sea as a sump for wastewater and, not incidentally, the continued inundation of the Torres Martinez Cahuillas' reservation land. Seeing the Salton Sea as part of the history of dam building and subsequent displacement of Indigenous communities and environmental damage to landscapes throughout the West connects the experiences of the Cahuillas to a much larger pattern of environmental injustice for Native nations.

In fact, reclamation for non-Native settlers has been a primary means by which Native dispossession has occurred throughout the twentieth century and into the twenty-first.

As policy makers began to push Boulder Canyon dam as a flood control effort to protect the Imperial Valley, the rhetoric surrounding the dam's benefits drew explicitly racial lines around the need to control the Colorado River. In the context of the Mexican Revolution, the rationale for controlling the river often came down to preventing it from being abused by "bandits" and "revolutionaries" from Mexico.[61] Anxiety abounded that the canals would be "cut by playful revolutionaries on the southern side"; the border-crossing canal system dreamed up by engineer George Chaffey meant that "the settlers were never sure what the Mexican Government or Mexican bandits might do to their life-sustaining irrigation."[62] This speculation reached the floor of the U.S. House of Representatives in 1922, where one member fretted that, because Mexico was "subject to sudden uprisings of various kinds," there "would be a golden opportunity for a band of insurrectos . . . to destroy with a stick of dynamite the canal or some of its principal works."[63] Without the canal, newspapers blared, the Imperial Valley remained "at the mercy of a foreign government, or of the first anti-American fanatic who can wield a shovel along the levees."[64]

The more pressing desire to control all of the Colorado River's water stemmed not from anxieties about Mexican "fanatics," "bandits," or "insurrectos" illegally cutting more than their share of water from the Imperial Canal south of the border but from the desire to get out from under a concession made by the CDC to the Mexican government that guaranteed half of the flow diverted from the Colorado through the canal to farms on the Mexican side.[65] Of lesser importance but still more of a factor in the desire to build the All-American Canal than spectral fears of Mexicans stealing water was the United States' own border control policies and those of Mexico. As Representative Philip D. Swing summed up the problem in a hearing before the House Committee on Irrigation of Arid Lands, doing business under "two flags" had begun to cause the Imperial Valley's irrigation needs to become hopelessly

18. Stereotypical imagery is used to depict a U.S.-versus-Mexico tug-of-war over the Colorado River, issued by the Colorado River Commission of Arizona in 1983. Folder 20: Colorado River, international problem, Box 58, Papers of Delph E. Carpenter and Family, Colorado State University Water Resources Archive, Fort Collins.

tangled up in the "red tape of the customhouses." CDC-owned dredges had to cross the border to clear silted-up canals. Their laborers had to cross back and forth across the border along with the equipment, and they had any number of headaches trying to replace workers who inevitably deserted their hot and dusty jobs on both sides of the border. "The immigration laws of two nations," Swing complained, "have to be complied with every time a laborer goes across." Therefore, "the interminable delays," he concluded, "are not only costly but at times make operation well-nigh impossible."[66]

Swing and those whose complaints he channeled were in for more frustration in the coming years. As border policing escalated at crossings to include inspections, customs duties, and multiplying regulations for people and goods alike, U.S. companies increasingly found the situation too cumbersome to navigate.[67] Pressure to build the All-American Canal and thus keep control of the Colorado River's water on the U.S. side of the international boundary kept building.

Construction on the long-awaited All-American Canal began in 1934 and continued for nearly a decade. Its completion in 1942 brought control of Colorado River water entirely north of the border, just as Imperial Valley settlers had hoped. It also left Mexicali dependent on the United States to fulfill its obligations under the 1944 Water Treaty to deliver 1.5 million acre-feet to Mexico every year. The 1944 treaty had notoriously been based on gross overestimates of the capacity of the Colorado River and overpromised its regular volume by at least four million-acre feet.[68] In subsequent years the All-American Canal became a means of controlling the Colorado and consolidating both power and water north of the border, part of settlers' demands for "racial and technological reclamation" in the Imperial Valley.[69]

The canal was the manifestation of Imperial settlers' wishes to bring the Colorado River fully under control—wishes that spurred construction of the massive Boulder Dam, the river's valve, and guaranteed continued inflows to the Salton Sea, its drain.[70] Once completed, it would carve a straight line through the Quechan homeland, forsaking the path of the Colorado River that the Quechans' god Kumastamxo had etched into the ground to lead water to Kumeyaay land in the Imperial Valley.

Juan Razón spent the years after the rise of the Salton Sea protesting the incompetence of local and federal officials, who could not or would not take steps to rectify the problem of the desert Cahuillas' flooded lands. He continued to press his people's case, repeatedly traveling to nearby cities and towns and seeking out conversations with lawyers and journalists who might increase pressure on officials. The journalists more often than not preferred to write about him as "Fig Tree John," a romantic fiction considered a symbol and sentinel of the region's Native past.[71]

Locals familiar with the press's version of Fig Tree John—odd and lamentable—must have felt a jolt of shock in the fall of 1921 when they opened their morning newspapers to read that Razón had been arrested by federal marshals and thrown in the Riverside County jail. Along with fourteen other local Native leaders, Razón faced charges of criminal conspiracy to deprive a white settler of his land. A judge set each of their bonds at an astronomical $2,500. An additional charge accused Jonathan Tibbetts, a white "friend of the Indians" from Riverside, with conspiracy to defraud the government and "seeking to alienate the loyalty of the California Indians from the government."[72] In its annual narrative report the Mission Indian Agency called Tibbetts's prosecution "the most important action" needed in Native Southern California, because of "his plotting."[73] The white settler complainant, a Coachella Valley man named P. A. Skelton, claimed that Razón and others had entered his property, "drove [him] from his home," and "refus[ed] to allow him to farm the place." The perpetrators, Skelton alleged, were members of a newly formed organization called the Mission Indian Federation (MIF), which had begun resisting Office of Indian Affairs (OIA) land policies on reservations throughout Southern California.[74]

The public objected to Razón's incarceration—though not to that of the others—because of his fame and his advanced age. "Free 125-Year-Old Indian from Jail" demanded the Los Angeles Herald, for "Fig Tree John, whose real name is Juan Ravon [sic]," was "one of the most noted characters in the West."[75] The jail's "close atmosphere," fretted the Riverside

Daily Press, was "causing him to become ill."[76] The public pressure to free Razón worked; the U.S. attorney ordered him freed by the first days of October. The rest remained in jail except Tibbetts, whose sister had managed to pay his bond.

The conflict that landed these members of the MIF in jail had been simmering for nearly two decades. In the summer of 1907, as the new Salton Sea crested over Juan Razón's homesite and drowned Durbrow's saltworks and the homes of scores of Cahuilla families, a growing sense of consternation and resistance characterized much of Native life in the desert. While the federal government busily remade the riverine West, damming waterways at every turn, Native people in Southern California developed a robust political culture of resistance to the OIA that emerged out of their frustration with the Indian agency and its representatives. This political culture hinged on rights to water and land. Water usage in this desert world had long required expansive territorial holdings; the arid region's sparse rainfall and dry climate required a light human touch spread over a wide swath of land—a lesson the desert Cahuillas and Kumeyaays had learned over the course of hundreds of years.

For all of these reasons, the water of the Salton Sea was not the only thing rising in the desert in those years; so too was impatience among Cahuilla people and other Native desert communities with the federal government and its Indian agents. Throughout Native Southern California the waning years of the nineteenth century saw the formation of reservations that repeatedly failed to fulfill the needs of the people they purported to support. The Campo Reservation for Kumeyaays, for example, was established by executive order as a federal trust reservation in 1891 and occupied a single square mile of dry desert land. Even after the federal government expanded Campo in 1910 to twenty-five square miles, the reservation had no easy or inexpensive access to water for anything more than bare subsistence. To the north, the establishment of the Agua Caliente Reservation in 1877 set off legal and interpersonal conflict over water rights that have endured for more than a century and dispossessed the Cahuillas of that area of water for sustenance as well as sacred hot springs for ceremonial, medicinal, and cultural

FREE 125-YEAR-OLD INDIAN FROM JAIL

"Fig Tree John," Indian chief and one-time Fremont scout, who is released from jail because of his age, 125.

uses.[77] This pattern across Native Southern California led to a region-wide phenomenon in which Indigenous families routinely lived away from their reservations in the early twentieth century, largely out of necessity. In the growing towns and communities of settler California, Native people labored as gardeners, domestics, industrial workers, and builders, unable to remain home due to lack of water, among other necessities.[78]

Adding to this already existing pattern of problems, when Native people did not or could not attempt to farm their land for want of expensive irrigation infrastructure, they faced losing their water rights. Non-Native settlements nearby had both the capital and the political influence to redirect water to their thirsty populations. In turn, the loss of water rights on already parched reservations made the reservations nearly uninhabitable, which, in turn, negated their stated purpose of providing homes for Native people.[79]

By the time the 1887 General Allotment Act, more commonly known as the Dawes Act, was being put into effect in California, frustration among Native people in Southern California had boiled over. The persistent aridity of reservation land and the vicious cycle produced by a lack of support for expensive irrigation schemes and subsequent theft of water rights by settlers became a profound inspiration for activism that gripped the so-called "Mission Indians." The directive of the Dawes Act to parcel collectively held tribal lands into individually owned allotments—effectively hollowing out tribal lands—promised to make this bad situation profoundly worse.

In 1919 Cahuillas, Kuupangaxwichems, Cocopahs, Payómkawichums, and Kumeyaays organized their collective resistance under the banner of the MIF.[80] Joe Peet served as the first leader of the organization, dubbing himself a "headman" for several reservations. Tibbetts advised the group. Not all the leaders were men; a number of women attended their regular meetings and participated in developing their agendas,

19. Police photograph of Juan Razón published after his release. Razón's arrest and incarceration scandalized local settlers, who called him "Fig Tree John." "Free 125-Year-Old Indian from Jail," *Los Angeles Herald*, October 1, 1921, 125.

building on a long history of influential, though informal, political power of women in these nations. Women like Agnes Balenguila and Flora DeBears went to MIF meetings to demand voting rights for Native women and worked to maintain Cahuilla cultural resources as both an anticolonial project and one designed to promote their people's sovereignty.[81]

The MIF functioned as part of the national umbrella of the American Indian Federation, which forged alliances across Indian Country to oppose the Indian New Deal and to advocate for the removal of OIA chief John Collier and the dismantling of the OIA itself for mismanagement of the federal trust relationship with tribes. MIF leaders quickly earned a reputation for running the most aggressive and persistent campaigns for self-determination in the early twentieth century. The MIF continued traditions of political activism that had been present throughout the U.S. colonial period in this part of California, with their efforts characterized by civil disobedience and uncompromising—and savvy—political platforms that centered on land rights and self-determination.[82] Its leaders made their antiallotment agenda clear. As they described their position in 1923, "We are unalterably opposed to allotment of our reservations as being against our future interest. We must have our reservations left to us without any [government] opportunity to take our birth right."[83]

Juan Razón had participated in the early activities that culminated in the formation of the MIF. In 1912 he hosted representatives of the Serranos and other Cahuilla bands at the Martinez Reservation's day school to listen to a presentation by the local Indian agent, Coggeshall, who acquiesced to their requests to see official maps of their reservation boundaries and assured them that he shared their worries about the lack of access to the still-plentiful aquifer under their land. The agent also made it a point to remind them—though they likely did not need reminding—of the OIA's insistence on "the requiring of children to attend the schools, the strict police regulations against the introduction of liquor on the reservations, and the barbarous features of Indian fiestas."[84]

Much of their organizational work happened at these "fiestas," which the Cahuillas called *kewéts*. They were annual or semiannual transnational gatherings that involved celebration, ceremony, dancing, and political organizing. Indian Service personnel loathed these gatherings, grumbling about the need for "control of the obnoxious 'fiesta,'" which they actively attempted to do through a policy to "convert them into agricultural fairs, baby shows, and the like."[85] Southern California tribes were not alone in experiencing federal crackdowns on dances and other forms of community gatherings; during these decades Bureau of Indian Affairs personnel and policy focused intensely on ending traditions like the kewét on Native lands across the United States.[86] By the early 1920s the policy to discourage Southern California kewéts had shown "splendid results"—they had limited the occurrence of these cherished gatherings into a single annual affair, thick with Indian Service–trained tribal police officers who broke up rowdy groups, interrupted gambling, confiscated alcohol, and dispersed meetings they deemed suspicious. Despite these "splendid results," the Indian Service maintained that the kewéts should be ended entirely because they "interfere[d] with the farming or other work of the Indians" and likely also because they provided a singularly convenient opportunity for the MIF to organize and promote itself.[87]

Between its formation in 1919 and the arrest of its top leaders in 1921, the MIF focused on defeating allotment schemes on reservations and tackling the problem of water rights. One of the organization's early mottoes—"More Land – More Water"—succinctly addressed the primary demands of the organization. Mission Indian Agency personnel noted glumly that under the MIF's leadership, "the Indians have assumed an aloofness towards the Government and its employees which makes it difficult to do business with them, as they ignore the officials and refuse to talk about their affairs."[88] The MIF's newsletter described this dynamic between local tribal councils and federal Indian agents as one of endurance against exhausting obstacles. "They took our lands, our homes," the newsletter recounted, but the tribal councils continued to lead their communities, despite being "under years of intimidation and fought on every hand by the Bureau."[89] During these decades, the Mission Indian Agency sought to wrest authority from the MIF, grappling with the antagonism to federal authorities they (often rightly) perceived among people they considered wards of the government.

The general attitude of "suspicion and discontent" led many on Mission reservations to "refuse to recognize the authority of the Government police," a problem that caused no end of consternation at the Mission Indian Agency.[90] The agency supervisor in 1922, C. L. Ellis, advised his colleagues that federal personnel should not attempt to arrest or detain Natives when they were on the reservation; for offenses committed off the reservation, the San Diego County sheriff deputized a local farmer to "act anywhere in the county" and "attend the fiestas and other places where Indians gather." This, Ellis believed, could be a useful deterrent to bad behavior. "Indians are clannish," he advised, "and resentment is easily aroused by prosecution of one of them, no matter how guilty."[91] All of these police matters, in Ellis's estimation, served the same purpose as other federal policies such as allotment, rigorous health screenings, and sending Native children away to school: they supported the "Indian farmer" in achieving self-reliance and trust in the good graces of the government.

However, as the MIF earnestly pointed out, the lack of water on many reservations, perhaps especially Torres Martinez, meant that farming was out of the question. By the 1910s and early 1920s most Native people of working age had had to leave their reservations for wage labor in nearby cities and towns. Natives from Mission reservations engaged in a wide range of jobs. Women made lace, wove baskets to sell in town, and traveled to cities to work as domestics; men picked oranges, canned vegetables, packed crates of figs and dates, paved roads, herded cattle, strung power lines, dug fire lines, and labored on dams and canals. In 1921 seventy Native men made up a good chunk of the crew that assembled Warner's Dam, a sixty-foot-high concrete wall holding back the San Luis Rey River.[92] Their labor would provide irrigation water to Perris, California, for farmers wanting to harvest alfalfa.

Meanwhile, the Natives' water rights on their home reservations suffered. The Mission Indian Agency blamed them for "neglecting" their dry farms in favor of wage labor: "Indians are being warned," Ellis noted, "that all land under ditch must be irrigated in order to maintain their water rights." He had in mind the Pala and Rincon Reservations, which could get water only from a local river. That river would soon be dammed miles away, and then their water and water rights would dry up as they commuted away from the reservation for work. The agency would try to negotiate some water rights, Ellis promised, but the dam project "has been under consideration for years," and without active farms on Pala and Rincon the prospects seemed dim.[93] Two years later Rincon workers poured and smoothed the concrete that lined a canal from that dam through the middle of their reservation, the dam now a solid monolith on the San Luis Rey River and impounding the thousand-plus-acre Lake Henshaw reservoir. Their water would now come from the concrete system of dam and canal, and from there alone.

Agents pushed for allotment as a solution to these problems of water rights, under the logic that parcels of land left over after sections had been divvied up could be sold off for water rights. The MIF pushed back. "Some of their leaders," a seemingly incredulous Ellis noted, "openly assert[ed] they want the boundaries of their reservation shown to them" and then for "the Federal and State authorities [to] withdraw and leave them alone to occupy the reservations without outside help or interference."[94] His unbelieving tone reflected the vast chasm between the desires of the MIF for self-government and the desires of federal Indian policy makers to convert the Native people into dryland farmers—dryland farmers, that is, without enough land or enough water to produce a crop.

THE PROBLEM OF TOO MUCH WATER

Juan Razón lived for six years after his incarceration, dying of influenza on April 11, 1927, at the age of 89 according to census records. Reports of his age in local newspaper accounts suggested he was at least 130 years old, but that wound up being part of the larger fiction of Fig Tree John rather than the lived experience of Juan Razón. His family buried him in the Torres Martinez Reservation's Catholic cemetery next to his wife, Matilda, who had died in 1923.[95]

A decade after Juan Razón's death, the desert world in which he lived would be transformed again by Colorado River water—this time, brought to the north end of the Salton Sink by settlers on purpose, rather than by accident, via a channel that branched from the All-American

Canal. Construction on this channel, the Coachella Canal, began in August 1938. It was designed to divert Colorado River water along the east side of the Salton Sea up to the Coachella Valley, where settlers had spent decades pumping fresh water from underground aquifers onto land that had been recently taken from desert Cahuillas. The Mission Indian Agency declared in 1936 that the "Indians" were learning "how to work competitively with their alert and aggressive white neighbors."[96]

Those neighbors expressed their aggression in a variety of ways. Most pressingly, perhaps, they had pumped so much water out of the aquifer that by the 1920s the water table had dropped precipitously. As a result, the Cahuillas' aquifer wells had "ceased flowing as the area of irrigated lands was extended by the surrounding whites"—making water nearly impossible to access.[97] Their cattle wandered far afield in search of greenery, making boundary negotiations with those "alert and aggressive white neighbors" distinctly worse. As Cahuillas' wells dried up, victims to an aquifer under too much pressure from so many new settlers, the Indian Service installed electric pumps to facilitate the extraction of water from wells that were not completely dry. Then they charged the Cahuillas for the electricity. After a few years of trying and failing to get the Torres Martinez residents to repay them for their use of the electricity to draw water from their own aquifers, the agency removed the pumps, commenting sourly that it should not have been a hard deal for "the Indians" to accept.[98] Access to water on the reservation, already a troubling problem, became worse.

The rapid depletion of the aquifer that ran underneath Coachella Valley threatened to make white settlement there impossible. The Colorado River Aqueduct, which had been completed in 1939 to deliver water to Southern California from the Parker Dam on the California-Arizona state line, passed along the northern end of the Coachella Valley. But that water was reserved for the thirsty city of Los Angeles; Coachella would have to get its water elsewhere. The Coachella Canal project came to the rescue.

Federal grants provided the money for what turned out to be a massive undertaking. From 1938 to 1942 between six hundred and one thousand workers at a time poured concrete for the canal, as farmers in

Coachella eagerly awaited the promised Colorado River water. World War II interrupted the Coachella Canal's slow progress along the Salton Sea's eastern shoreline. By 1942 this and other reclamation projects had been put on hold so that money and labor could be redirected to the war effort. In 1943 the Interior Department announced that work on the canal could resume, with a goal of completing the project by 1945. However, Interior placed a strict limit on the number of workers who could be employed on the canal construction: no more than 175 laborers per day, not counting "war prisoners, Japanese evacuees or conscientious objectors."[99] Well practiced in putting vulnerable people to work in constructing an irrigation infrastructure that would benefit settlers in the desert, the managers of the Coachella Canal had little problem initiating the work once again.

The Colorado Desert was far from the only site where these politics of water and concrete built Indigenous dispossession into the very landscape of the West. By midcentury a veritable tsunami of reservoir water had inundated reservations, treaty lands, unceded lands, and sacred sites across the United States (as well as in Canada), held in place by thousands of tons of concrete. As Boulder Dam, the Salton Sea, the All-American Canal, and the Coachella Canal transformed the land tenure of Colorado Desert Indigenous nations, seemingly solidifying their dispossession by building these structures into the very landscape of the West, their experience echoed the course of—and literal concretization of—settler power for other Native nations in the twentieth century.

This widespread dispossession figured into the most controversial dam-building projects in U.S. history. Perhaps most controversial among them was the O'Shaughnessy Dam on the Yosemite Valley's Tuolumne River. The dam's impoundment created Hetch Hetchy Reservoir in 1923, displacing Ahwahneechee Miwok people and flooding their village sites, food sources, sacred sites, and burial grounds.[100] Half a continent and two decades removed from Hetch Hetchy, the massive Pick-Sloan Missouri Basin Program would drown more than three hundred thousand acres of Oceti Sakowin land utilized by the Santee Sioux, the Yankton

Sioux, the Sicangu Oyate, the Lower Brule Sioux, the Crow Creek Sioux, the Cheyenne River Sioux, and the Standing Rock Sioux.[101]

From 1944 to the mid-1960s the displacement of families and flooding of reservations occurred time and time again: at the Fort Berthold Indian Reservation, by the Garrison Dam; at the Crow Creek and Lower Brule Reservations, by the Big Bend Dam; and at Standing Rock and Cheyenne River, by the Oahe Dam. In the Pacific Northwest the Columbia Basin Project authorized construction of The Dalles Dam, the Grand Coulee Dam, the Wapato Dam, and the Bonneville Dam, producing similarly devastating consequences for the Yakama Nation, the Confederated Tribes of Warm Springs, the Confederated Tribes of the Umatilla Indian Reservation, and the Nez Perce, Colville, and Spokane Nations.[102] Meanwhile, the Moses-Saunders Power Dam drowned 1,200 acres of Akwesasne Reservation land and 15,000 acres of traditional-use land. The 1960s and 1970s brought additional dams and flooding. The Tennessee Valley Authority dammed the Tennessee River, flooding Cherokee sacred sites as well as the historic townsites of Chota, Tanasi, Toqua, Tomotley, Citico, Mialoquo, and Tuskegee. Construction of the Kinzua Dam on the Allegheny River in Pennsylvania inundated the historic Cornplanter Tract of the Seneca Nation.[103]

As a result, by the 1970s dams had become a central focus of Indigenous activism and scholarship and a key locus of Indigenous environmental politics.[104] During the 1970s and 1980s the Native-run newspaper *Akwesasne Notes* kept close track of struggles over dam authorization and construction in the United States, Canada, and beyond, finding a common colonial threat to Indigenous worlds in the dams that alternately flooded and desiccated Native communities the world over, from British Columbia to Arizona, and from the Philippines to the Amazon.[105] Writ large, dam construction brought together two pressing environmental justice concerns for Indigenous nations in the U.S. West: energy injustice, through their use for hydroelectricity, and dispossession from traditional homelands, through flooding upriver and desiccation downriver.[106] Likewise, dam construction constituted a recognized link in the larger chain of Indigenous experiences of settler colonialism, contributing to the social, political, economic, cultural, and psychological conditions of Native peoples' lives.[107]

Many dams, Boulder Dam chief among them, became tourist attractions in their own right, part of the national mythology of the New Deal and evidence of Americans' infrastructural triumph over nature.[108] Tourists roamed over these concrete leviathans, marveling at bronze placards that meticulously listed the weight of materials used, the total numbers of workers who labored (if not those who died) creating them, and the unprecedented engineering heroics that went into wrangling the West's great rivers.

In the case of Indigenous communities downriver from the Boulder Dam, these impacts of the Boulder Canyon Project were felt in deeply dispossessive ways. As historian Donald Worster has explained, "No one asked [the Native nations of the Colorado basin] to participate in the Colorado compact negotiations, and the Bureau of Indian Affairs . . . failed to look out for their interests there. What's more, much of their reservation land, in that watershed as elsewhere in the West, was taken from them and sold to whites, who developed irrigation farms on it."[109] Juan Razón's story reverberates in Worster's description, echoing through the history of reclamation decades after his death. His protests against the flooding of his land draw him—and the Salton Sea—into this larger geography of dams and dispossession over the course of the twentieth century.

In 1996, ninety years after the rising water drove Juan and Matilda Razón and scores of other Cahuilla families out of their desert homes, the chairperson of the Torres Martinez band of the Cahuilla Nation traveled to Washington DC to testify before the Senate Committee on Indian Affairs. Chair Mary Belardo represented roughly 140 tribal members and a 24,800-acre land base, approximately 11,000 acres of which still sat beneath the Salton Sea. Three years before her arrival in DC, the state of California had declared the Salton Sea officially "impaired" due to water quality and threats to wildlife. Before the full committee, presided over by Arizona senator John McCain, Belardo laid out the ninety-year-old complaint of the Torres Martinez Cahuillas regarding the Salton Sea: "Most desert Indian tribes," she began, "share the common problem of insufficient water. Our Tribe has the unusual problem of too much water." Since it flooded Torres Martinez Cahuilla land in 1905, Belardo explained, the Salton Sea had "been maintained largely because of irrigation discharges into the Salton Basin by non-Indian farmers." These farmers, Belardo emphasized, had been doing exactly "what the Federal Government has encouraged them to do. Irrigation discharges into the Salton Sea," she pointed out, "have long been supported by various Federal Government actions." She listed them: the Coolidge administration's executive orders declaring the Salton Sea, even as it inundated half of the reservation, a drainage sump; the passage of the BCPA and construction of Hoover Dam, which dramatically increased drainage to the Salton Sea; and federal support for increased acreage in the Imperial and Coachella Valleys.[110]

Belardo's testimony showed how Juan Razón's experience of the Salton Sea floods persisted over the course of nearly a century and constituted a link in a longer chain of Indigenous experiences of dams, flooding, and reclamation throughout the West. Her account connected the continued existence of the Salton Sea on Cahuilla land to a broader geography of settlement in California and throughout the U.S. West. More than that, she spoke pointedly to the role of the federal government in creating this dispossession-by-inundation. From this point of view, the Salton Sea resulted from interconnected systems of corporate agriculturalism, massive technological manipulation of environmental resources, and settler colonial reservation land systems for Native peoples. The concretization of power across the West drew water to the Salton Sea in ways that directly resulted in dispossession for Torres Martinez Cahuillas. In the meantime, the benefits of the water that sustained it were drawn against the labor, the physical health, and the economic vitality of racialized laborers whose exploitation shaped the water's flow from river to farm to sea.

5

BODIES

Your soul worships at the shrine of pure nature.

—Robert J. Burdette, *American Biography and Genealogy: California Edition*, 1910

A GEOGRAPHY OF ILLNESS

One Monday evening in November 1910 a young woman named Nettie Ingersoll failed to show up for her shift as a waitress at the brand-new Hotel King Cotton in Imperial, California. Although she had trained as a teacher in Colorado, Ingersoll's health had "broken," leaving her with few employment options. She traveled to Southern California with the hope that rumors of the salubrious nature of its warm, arid climate would prove true. Perhaps the rumors about the social world of Southern California would also prove true; the attractiveness of the state to people suffering from ill health derived in part from the notion that "the sufferer who comes here is surrounded, not by a foreign people whose every question is repulsive, but by people of refinement and education, who represent the best social and intellectual conditions to be found anywhere in the United States."[1] "Prospective settlers," historian Emily Abel observes, "were assured that they would associate only with whites."[2]

Ingersoll was doomed to disappointment. By 1910 people in ill health found themselves unwelcome in communities throughout Southern

149

California, whereas just over a decade earlier the whole region had touted itself as a vast "resort" for health seekers. Now, however, communities from Los Angeles to Yuma were passing ordinances that sought to segregate "invalids" in tent communities outside of town or otherwise prevent their access to public spaces.[3] In 1902 the town of Redlands, California, where Nettie Ingersoll's sister lived and taught, outlawed the establishment of any "hospital, sanitarium or place for the reception or treatment of tuberculosis," violation of the law being punishable by a fine of up to $300, three months in prison, or, if the violation was particularly irksome, both. The *Imperial Valley Press* weighed in on this strict new measure, the first of its kind in California, opining that Redlands was justified in its actions because "the presence of any large number of consumptives in any town is a serious menace to the public health. A town is no place for them anyway; they ought to go out in the desert country. . . . And so far as possible they ought to live out of doors."[4] In 1909 the Yuma County Board of Health ordered anyone with symptoms of tuberculosis to register with the county supervisor of health within a week of entering the county. By the end of that year Yuma's antagonism toward people with tuberculosis had escalated considerably: the town leased a tract of land on a mesa outside of town and ordered tuberculosis patients there to erect their own tents in an effort to "prevent consumptives living in the Yuma hotels and rooming houses."[5]

In the context of this newly unwelcoming climate for people of poor health throughout Southern California, Ingersoll's illness and the segregation of "invalids" like her to open-air desert communities led her to the newly founded community of Imperial. She may well have come to the wrong place. Whereas many Colorado Desert communities had catered to sanatoriums and health resorts in places like Indio, the popularity of health resorts in the desert waned in the 1910s as they were supplanted by other, more profitable and less contagious economic pursuits. Moreover, as general rule, the town of Imperial tended to avoid associating itself with the socially maligned as part of its general pursuit of respectability.[6]

Unable to secure a job as a teacher, she instead served clientele at the Hotel King Cotton. The hotel had barely been open two months when Ingersoll failed to appear for her shift downstairs. She was found dead in her room hours later, having cut her own throat with a penknife while kneeling by her bedside.

At first glance this story seems to have little to do with the freshly flooded Salton Sea fifteen miles to the north of where Ingersoll died. It certainly seems distantly removed from the *environmental* history of that body of water. To the contrary, the patterns of health, ableism, mobility, disease ecologies, and theories of climate and health that created the conditions of Ingersoll's life—and quite likely contributed to her death—followed the warp and weft of the environmental conditions that created and sustained the newly formed Salton Sea. This chapter explores the history of the Salton Sea through the framework of various kinds of bodies, ranging in size and scale from humans and livestock to bacteria and viruses. Throughout its history, the Salton Sea has shaped and been shaped both by physical bodies in all of these scales *and* by human ideas about them. What constituted a body that belonged and one that did not? What kinds of bodies could be seen as pathogenic? How could people keep their bodies pure or unpolluted by vectors of many kinds? In the end, the Salton Sea's influence, both ideationally and materially, on the embodied interaction of disease ecologies, plant ecologies, and human demographics of the region relied in surprising ways on notions about what kinds of bodies polluted "pure nature."[7]

The history of the Salton Sea and pathogen-bearing vectors began before its formation. Prior to the flooding that formed the sea, the Colorado Desert was, as a whole, considered singularly healthful for people suffering from conditions ranging from tuberculosis to rheumatism, a reputation it inherited from its more densely populated coastal counterparts in Southern California. That whole part of the state had for decades been viewed as a regional health resort for easterners who suffered from ill health. Boosters touted the glories of the state's fresh air for "debilitated mankind."[8] Railroad companies were a powerful institution in promoting the region in ways "to catch the early influx of invalids" from the East.[9] The vigorous, outdoor lifestyle that characterized Southern California was seen as a powerful counterpoint to the closed-in, crowded lifestyle of eastern cities, with their foul and polluted air.[10]

With the rise of germ theory and the growing understanding of the communicability of illnesses like tuberculosis, people suffering from the symptoms of disease became increasingly unwelcome in communities across Southern California. Sending "consumptives" to the desert served two ends: removing the risk of contagion from the more densely populated coastal cities, particularly Los Angeles, and increasing the possibility of their being "cured" by what were seen as the preferable environmental conditions of the desert climate. As one observer wrote, "The Colorado Desert," by the mid-1890s, was "now conceded to be the ideal location for the planting of tuberculosis," which was an "imperative" move "when we come to consider the formidable numbers that come to this Coast every year from all parts of the world—come here in all likelihood to die."[11] In time, some suggested, "the high mountain regions of Southern California and out on the desert" would have whole "settlements" for invalids "where diseases of the lungs will be made a specialty."[12] Palm Springs, for example, was touted as having mineral springs with "waters [that] are most efficacious for the cure of rheumatism."[13] At Indio a large hotel catered to "such invalids whose presence by reason of their infirmities would be irksome to the general public."[14]

The aridity of the Southern California desert area, the "disinfectant of sunshine," and low population density were not the only reasons for its reputation as a salubrious place for people with respiratory diseases.[15] The Salton Sink also had the curious novelty of being several hundred feet below sea level, creating a high-pressure environment touted as uniquely beneficial to people with asthma or tuberculosis.[16] The low elevation of the sink, according to one doctor, functioned to create "nature's pneumatic cabinet," where the additional air pressure forced oxygen into all parts of afflicted lungs. In addition, the chlorinated gases emanating from the salt beds supposedly rendered the air "nearly aseptic."[17] In Indio, observers marveled at the number of "asthmatics, rheumatics, and consumptives [who] reported wonderful recoveries."[18]

These kinds of climatic theories contributed to Southern California's popularity as a regional health resort. That attractiveness in turn contributed to rising rates of tuberculosis, as that disease spread to new populations. By 1915 California was third in death rates from tuberculosis, outranked only by North Carolina and Kentucky.[19] Over the course of the early decades of the twentieth century, so many people moved to rural and arid areas like the Colorado Desert because of beneficial climate conditions for diseases like tuberculosis that government researchers had to include a caveat in their data sets cautioning researchers against drawing conclusions about climate and "cure" because "states and cities which show exceptionally high death rates are not always those in which conditions are most favorable to the development of tuberculous diseases, but in some instances are those to which patients resort in search of cure."[20]

The Salton Sea changed both the material conditions of the Colorado Desert and its reputation as a natural sanatorium. Boosters fretted that the creation of the Salton Sea had changed the very climate of the area, to the detriment of health seekers. The sea and Imperial Valley irrigation increased the air's humidity, which "render[ed] the summer heat much more unbearable." Suddenly people with tuberculosis did not recover with quite the same rapidity and frequency as before the flooding. "Heat prostration" became a problem. So did pneumonia, peaking in the winter and spring "with a rather high mortality even for that disease."[21] Much of the decline in the area's healthfulness resulted from increases in the settler population, rather than from the sea itself. The vectors that caused scarlet fever, measles, and typhoid all followed settlers to the desert, and incidents of these diseases increased alongside increases in the human population. In an early suggestion that the new lake could affect the health benefits of the Colorado Desert, one physician wrote of the 1891 flooding that the lake "manifests its presence by the enervating and depressing influence it has upon man and beast, for instance, of the superabundance of sensible perspiration."[22]

By the time Ingersoll arrived in Imperial, the area's reputation for promoting good health had declined precipitously. So had its actual health conditions. By 1919 the area was considered "entirely unsuited to the tuberculous."[23] While this was most often attributed to the changing climatic conditions of the area—notably, increased humidity due to the Salton Sea and widespread irrigation—the shift in attitudes toward the influx of people of ill health probably emerged more from residents' pursuit of respectability than any real changes in climate. In the twentieth century, particularly with the rise of germ theory, tuberculosis went from being understood as a "white plague" to being associated with poverty, filth, and, increasingly, people of color. This was a perception that created very real impacts across California. Laborers of color relied heavily on public health care and were thus subject to intense, and highly visible, treatment. White persons, on the other hand, could often afford private health care that guaranteed them some degree of anonymity.[24]

In the course of the twentieth century, the contours of disease in and around the Salton Sea followed those of race, labor, and other forms of social inequality. In the sanatoriums that sprang up across the Colorado Desert people with infectious diseases were catered to and treated by workers who were frequently nonwhite and often Native, Mexican, or Chinese.

In the early decades of the twentieth century tuberculosis hit Indigenous nations particularly hard. Indian Service agents and Public Health Service doctors and nurses, aware of the problem, sporadically sought to visit reservations to measure the spread of outbreaks and treat those infected. Each of the four major health surveys conducted on Native land in the early twentieth century zeroed in on tuberculosis as a significant threat to Native health.[25] The influential Meriam Report singled out tuberculosis as the single most prevalent disease among Native peoples in the United States.[26] This finding was borne out in Southern California, where by the early decades of the twentieth century tuberculosis was the leading killer of the area's Native peoples.[27]

In the Mission Indian Agency, which covered health services for members of the Cahuilla, Kumeyaay, Cupeño, Luiseño, and Chemehuevi Nations, tuberculosis caused more deaths than any other infectious disease between the 1920s and the 1940s, and the number of deaths among children was particularly high.[28] In addition to the Colorado Desert being identified for the "planting" of tuberculosis and thus bringing the threat of contagion in the form of health seekers' bodies, "the reservation system," as anthropologist Clifford Trafzer has noted, "had created deplorable conditions conducive to the spread of disease and death."[29] At the Sherman Institute, a boarding school for Native youth, tuberculosis posed enough of a threat to students and staff that rigorous health protocols were put in place. Despite these measures, the student body in the 1910s experienced 250 cases of tuberculosis and numerous other cases of what was probably tuberculosis but was recorded as something else.[30] This was by no means the only troubling health problem at Sherman; in 1913, for example, a congressional investigation discovered that a full quarter of Sherman students suffered from trachoma, a bacterial infection that can lead to blindness.[31] Together, these diseases "ravaged" pupils in Indian Service schools across the United States, according to the commissioner for the Bureau of Indian Affairs.[32]

The labor of building and maintaining the Imperial and Coachella Valleys—from reaping the salt harvests of the New Liverpool Salt Works to landscaping sanitariums in Palm Springs and Indio, to maintaining the tracks of the Southern Pacific, to picking crops in the Imperial Valley—fell largely to Native workers. This in turn meant that these laborers were particularly susceptible to infection. Men and women who worked in settler communities fell victim to tuberculosis at rates second only to students at Indian Service schools.[33]

In the fall of 1910, after staff of the Hotel King Cotton discovered Nettie Ingersoll's body on the floor of her room, the *Imperial Valley Press* reported her death as a "peculiarly sad case" of a young teacher whose health had "broken."[34] The tragic death of a young white woman touched on larger cultural notions circulating in the early twentieth century about gender and bodily health.[35] The cultural figure of the sickly young waif, unfortunate and wretched in her condition of "broken" health—in other words, a cultural figure not unlike Nettie Ingersoll herself—came to shape larger understandings of disease and ability in the area surrounding the Salton Sea, even if they did not necessarily match the empirical conditions of illness and death.[36]

BELONGING AND POLLUTION

An essay published in *The History of Imperial County, California,* on the county's medical past addressed concerns about the declining health conditions of the communities surrounding the Salton Sea. The essay's author, Dr. F. W. Peterson, suggested that rising humidity from expanding farms had degraded the climatic conditions for people with tuberculosis, making the air less beneficial for them after the flooding than it had been before 1905. He noted the rise of diseases that corresponded to the growing population: pneumonia, scarlet fever, measles, and influenza.

The presence of typhoid fever, however, sparked a separate set of concerns for Peterson. Typhoid fever, a dangerous bacteria-borne illness communicable through water and food tainted with urine and fecal matter, had been a menace in Imperial Valley since the arrival of its first white settlers. From 1900 to 1920 the *Imperial Valley Press* reported on typhoid more often than any other major disease—more than tuberculosis, diphtheria, scarlet fever, influenza, or pneumonia. A 1910 report on the county's health written by the county physician and presented to the Imperial County Board of Supervisors indicated the major health concerns of local residents: in the latter half of that year there were six new cases of typhoid; another six of pulmonary tuberculosis; three cases of influenza; two cases each of pneumonia, rheumatism, and impetigo; and a single case of syphilis (which marked the one and only time the prim *Imperial Valley Press* deigned to report on this or any other sexually transmitted infection in those early years).[37]

It was clear from the first years of settlement that household use of untreated canal water posed the primary threat of typhoid.[38] County authorities urged residents to filter their water through charcoal and sand, boil it, or, during one particularly nerve-wracking county-wide outbreak, do both. In 1908 typhoid-causing bacteria in canal water inspired some of the county's first sanitation regulations, which included prohibiting people from bathing in canal water, letting their livestock go into canals, or burying animals under fewer than three feet of dirt. Violations were punishable by a $300 fine, six months in prison, or both.[39]

By the time Peterson's essay was published in 1918, these kinds of precautions had not entirely alleviated the problem of regular typhoid outbreaks. A new theory emerged: that the waterborne bacteria bringing typhoid into the Imperial Valley came not from Imperial Valley farmers' livestock but from Mexico. "The water," wrote Peterson, "is in most cases already polluted before it crosses the line into American territory." Local health authorities, therefore, were not to blame for the failure of sanitation regulations, for "this, of course, is something over which the health authorities of the county have no control. They may guard ever so zealously the water supply within our own borders, but if indiscriminate pollution is permitted to go on unchecked south of the line, the danger will ever be with us."[40] For Peterson, as well as for many others across Southern California, this threat of waterborne disease flowing across the border constituted yet another reason for the construction of the All-American Canal, because it would effectively move control of the Colorado River entirely north of the border. Peterson urged, moreover, that "this should be one of strongest reasons for eliminating at the earliest possible moment the necessity for securing our water supply from foreign soil."[41]

Blame for the spread of typhoid, according to Peterson and others, lay with nonwhite residents across the border and within the Imperial Valley itself. In 1919 J. Smeaton Chase associated typhoid with the Cahuilla people and their past use of artesian wells. "The water supply" for Cahuilla communities like Martinez, Chase wrote, was "now the commonplace one by pipe and bucket, no longer *per* squaw, marching picturesquely with *olla* through thickets of arrowweed and mesquit [*sic*] to draw from the pool at the foot of the earthen stairway, returning with plentiful germs of typhoid fever."[42] The prose was poetic, but the message was clear: typhoid was indigenous to the land and water of the desert and associated with Indigenous women and their ecological practices.

These kinds of worries about threats of infection and nonwhite peoples, and particularly Peterson's anxiety about polluted water crossing the border from the south, resonated with larger concerns about immigration, race, and public health. Historians have extensively studied the ways in which public health concerns and particularly the fear of contagious diseases prompted American officials and the public to blame, surveil, and police immigrants at border entry points and within the United States.[43] At the U.S.-Mexico border, racial difference was often measured in terms of health and illness; racist stereotypes of Mexicans relied on associating them with disease, filth, and contagion. At a time when Mexican Americans were included in the legal category of whiteness in the United States, their social and cultural exclusion from whiteness often occurred through policing in public spaces: with the state's so-called "Greaser Act," for example, the California legislature in 1855 had made one of its first orders of business to deputize local police to arrest anyone deemed a "vagrant," "vagabond," or "dangerous and suspicious" person—categories of racialized criminality that were formally and informally interpreted as Mexican and Native. At the border a rapid escalation of inspection protocols subjected Mexican and Mexican American border crossers to humiliating rituals of public suspicion.[44]

This pattern of nativist fear of nonwhite immigrant people extended to Calexico, which was among the busiest entry points along the U.S.-Mexico border.[45] In 1922, for example, the Calexico city trustees sent a telegram to the U.S. surgeon general requesting his assistance in protecting Calexico from a smallpox outbreak in Mexicali. The trustees wrote to "respectfully petition [him] to immediately take such steps as will prevent the passage across the boundary line at this point of persons without a certificate of vaccination."[46] Under the advice of a doctor from Los Angeles, the trustees actually desired much more serious action to be taken at the border: a complete quarantine of Mexican border crossers. Inarguably, however, this would devastate the local economies of both communities—hence the more conservative request to the surgeon general, even while local elites and border officials continued to push for a full quarantine.[47] The requirement for vaccination at the border had significant effects on both the human population and the economies of Calexico and Mexicali; in just under two months twenty thousand people underwent smallpox vaccinations. Residents of communities north of the line did so voluntarily. Residents south of the line took the injections because they were a requirement if one wanted to cross the border for work or to visit family.[48]

Policing the bodily health of people crossing the border went both ways in the years that followed. In 1924 Imperial County's horticultural commission and members of the sanitary department met with a number of officials from Mexicali—the customs collector, the president of the chamber of commerce, and the Mexican consul—to discuss preventing the spread of foot and mouth disease across the border into Mexicali. Mexican rules required southbound cars to be stopped and fumigated en route to the border and passengers disinfected.[49]

For the most part, though, the effects of regulations imposed by one or both nations went one way: to control people and animals coming from Mexico into the United States. A 1928 treaty ostensibly imposed by both nations had the effect of restricting how animals could cross the border. It provided for quarantine stations, a "livestock sanitary police service," supervision of animal waste and the importation of animal products, the disinfection of railroad cars transporting livestock, and a reporting system for disease outbreaks. These measures primarily sought to ensure the health of more than 216,000 livestock animals that crossed the line into the United States each year.[50]

Dr. Peterson's concerns about typhoid crossing into the United States via irrigation canals are mirrored in concerns about livestock crossing the border. U.S. officials and the public fretted about all sorts of nonhuman contaminant-bearing entities crossing the border. As historian Mary E. Mendoza has pointed out, concern about the diseases borne by ticks stowing away on the bodies of livestock preceded and prefigured concerns about humans as disease vectors at the border.[51] In communities surrounding the Salton Sea, these concerns clustered around threats to human health, such as waterborne typhoid, as well as threats to agriculture. As in other places along the U.S.-Mexico border, control of these nonhuman bodies inspired significant buildup of border fences, customs houses, and human enforcement.[52]

In the late 1910s, for example, the federal government established a strict quarantine on Mexican cotton as a means of protecting U.S. cotton crops from two insect pests: the pink bollworm, an invasive species that had spread from Mexico to the U.S. Cotton Belt in the Southeast, and the cotton boll weevil, an enduring frustration for cotton farmers everywhere.[53] In the Imperial Valley, where cotton had quickly risen to the top of the list of profit-making crops, the specter of bollworms and weevils was magnified by the fact that the valley was the only place in the United States where cotton crops remained unaffected by the devastating outbreak of these pests in places like Texas.[54] In response, farmers in Baja California sought to double down on inspections of their products before they could even reach quarantine stations at the border. In 1922, for example, the governor of Baja California formed a quarantine board in Mexicali with the goal of establishing inspection points to oversee every shipment of cotton and alfalfa that left the valley, thus ensuring "that every pound of either product is free from any infection of any kind."[55] Ultimately they sought to "make the phrase 'grown in Baja California' a synonym for purity and safety."[56] Employees of the U.S. Department of Agriculture noted with delight the cooperation between Mexican and American officials in protecting the Imperial Valley from the menace of both the pink bollworm and the boll weevil.[57] This cross-border collaboration reaffirms the argument made by borderlands historians that, although border communities shared many things—ecologies, labor forces, economies, to name just a few—officials on either side of the line worked hard (although sometimes unsuccessfully) to create discernible divides between the United States and Mexico. They did this by surveying the border, building up ports of entry, and deploying law enforcement to enforce immigration law.[58]

The *Calexico Chronicle* parsed no words in communicating the stakes of cross-border quarantines to its readers, stating that "there is a direct responsibility on every resident of the valley to cooperate in securing the strict enforcement of the quarantine regulations. Any individual who knowingly violates the laws, is an enemy to every legitimate rancher in the community, and should be treated as such. Imperial Valley must maintain its freedom from the weevil menace. Its failure to do so will very quickly eliminate this valley as a cotton-growing district."[59] The *Chronicle* in its earnestness missed the irony of the situation: that after so much investment in the region to make the desert landscape bear literal fruit—the price of which was the Colorado River itself—an organism as small as a bollworm could pose an existential threat so great it could eliminate agriculture in the region.

In the first scorching week of August 1922, a conflict broke out among Imperial Valley elites regarding the proliferation of johnsongrass, another invasive species that beleaguered farmers seemingly everywhere.[60]

Imperial Valley officials blamed the spread of the pestilential grass on seeds arriving via Mexican products and floating along canals from Mexicali as the water crossed the border. One deeply irritated official, F. W. Waite, demanded a course of action that might strike the reader as a disproportionate response to a weed: total quarantine "against everything grown in Mexico" until Mexicali landowners could get the johnsongrass under control.[61]

This type of blanket quarantine would likely have done no good, however. Johnsongrass and other "noxious weeds," as valley officials called them, often arrived in Imperial County from other parts of the United States—not necessarily from Mexico. Johnsongrass seeds intermingled with alfalfa and sorghum seeds shipped in from other agricultural districts for Imperial Valley farmers, often by state and federal agricultural agencies. Johnsongrass, moreover, was far from the only unwanted seed to arrive with "legitimate" agricultural imports. Morning glory stowed away in shipments of hay. Wild mustard seed and sunflower seeds hid in sacks of barley. Livestock ranging up to the mountains and back to the desert carried cockleburs on their flanks.[62]

Weeds also came by water, to be sure—though not always in the ways Imperial Valley farmers imagined: directly from Mexico to their fields. The water of the Colorado River flooding that created the Salton Sea carried wild asparagus and other unwanted seeds.[63] To control erosion along the banks of its canals, CDC employees planted Bermuda grass, which would go on to endlessly annoy local farmers. The sea also played a more unexpected role in dispersing the seeds of weeds that then took hold in the newly irrigated valley: according to the *Imperial Valley Press*, the flooding that created the Salton Sea "caus[ed] great discouragement among the people" and "the weeds received very little attention and seed was scattered from one farm to another and from one field to another and to the public highways, along the canal banks and few farmers made any effort to keep them down."[64]

Taken together, these efforts to control the movement of particular kinds of plants, animals, insects, viruses, bacteria, and people in the newly watered agricultural districts of the Colorado Desert reveal a deep consternation about belonging and pollution in a place that hinged on in-migration of bodies of many kinds. The success of Imperial Valley agriculture relied on the influx of humans, flora, and fauna from else-where—to say nothing of water. Seeds came from private companies as well as government agencies. The state agricultural commission distributed insects such as ladybugs to control *other* insects that damaged crops, which had in turn been imported for planting in this dry world of mesquites and ocotillos. Laborers came from Indigenous and non-Indigenous communities to the south, east, and north, or from Los Angeles, San Diego, and Baja California, and from places as far afield as Japan, China, and India. Livestock traveled by rail from distant rangelands.

But that reliance on the in-migration of outsiders of all kinds in turn inspired deep anxieties about threats and perceived threats that such an influx presented to settlers. They wanted the state agricultural commission to send barley to be planted where no barley had existed before but did not want the wild mustard seed that came with it. They wanted cheap labor but did not want the burden that came with racial integration, equitable compensation, and more diverse disease ecologies from different parts of the country and world. The movements of unseen "pollutants"—things that did not belong, whether plants or illnesses—inspired efforts to control the region's borders and triggered anxieties about what kinds of migrations the settlers could and could not regulate. The border-crossing canal system and border-crossing laborers rose to the fore of these concerns, prompting support for the All-American Canal (to control the river and everything it carried) and increased surveillance and policing at the border (to control flows of people and everything they carried with them). The health of farmers and their farms hung in the balance.

Or did they? In reality, health conditions in the Imperial Valley deteriorated in an inverse relationship to its growing population. Weeds seemed to flourish or perish based more on the amount of attention settlers paid to them than on control over the dispersal of their seeds by farmers to the south (in fact, any meaningful control of unwanted plants came only with the development and widespread use of chemical pesticides in the late 1940s). Rather, epidemics of typhoid, influenza, smallpox, and the proliferation of unwanted plants and insects occurred with or without strict control of the county's borders. The projection of social meaning onto viruses, animals, insects, and weeds often governed how settlers responded to those various pests and the degree of threat they posed to the health of farmers and their fields.

As tuberculosis, typhoid, and other diseases came to be closely associated with poverty, laboring classes, and immigrants of color, policing the movement of nonwhite people and plants, animals, and germs that migrated from nonwhite geographies (or seemed to) came to be a central way in which white settlers negotiated racial notions of belonging. Sickness became a sign of racial otherness. Robust bodies, of human and plant varieties alike, came to signify whiteness. Exceptions were troubling. Ranchers from Imperial to Mexicali described American-owned cattle as "thoroughbreds" and Mexican-owned cattle as "scrubs."[65] Weeds such as johnsongrass "contaminated [farmers'] clean fields" and required a robust policing of unwelcome versus—as the county's agricultural commission put it in 1948—"certified" seeds.[66] Throughout, negotiations of purity and pollution in the valley often depended on white settlers' understandings of who, and what, belonged.

VIM, VIGOR, VITALITY!

In the wake of the flooding that created the Salton Sea, boosters imagined new potential for the existing network of sanatoriums and health resorts. In 1911 a group of physicians from Los Angeles visited the town of Mecca to explore the "possibilities in this combination of desert air and the inland sea." Impressed with what they found, they selected a site two miles south of Mecca, imagining the profitability of a "recreation grounds" complete with boats on the sea and comfortable facilities on the shore.[67]

Recreation opportunities would not be limited to people in ill health, however. In 1911 brothers E. G. Murray and J. A. Murray from Los Angeles completed work on an eighteen-foot launch for motorboats on the south shore of the sea. With the launch and nearby camping and picnic areas, they envisioned capitalizing on an opportunity for Imperial Valley residents "to enjoy the long neglected opportunities of motor boating on the Salton sea."[68] They were not the only ones devising ways to market "one of the most picturesque locations in the world for those who enjoy the beauties of nature, especially when viewed from the comfortable cushions of a speedy motor boat."[69] J. W. Yokum spent the summer of 1911 seeking out a good spot at the mouth of the Alamo River in the Salton Sea for a boat launch of his own, believing that the Alamo was a prime locale for tourists to gather and explore the sea on board his "pleasure craft."[70] Elsewhere, two promoters calling themselves the Salton Sea Pleasure Company set out on a venture to make an empire of boating and fishing on the sea. Their endeavor ended abruptly when the financier of the pair landed himself in a Yuma jail for six months, having gotten himself "mixed up in some [unspecified] trouble."[71]

In 1916 area boosters actively sought to bring tourists in on sponsored trips to experience the Salton Sea's wonders and its oddities. Members of the Automobile Club of Southern California came to the sea to experience firsthand the cool breezes that skated over the water and tempered the dry desert air. They waded and swam while their host caught fresh mullet for their dinner. When night fell, exhausted and full of fish, they slept under the moonlight in cots placed in lines under a breezy ramada. The entire experience added up to "a touch of the seemingly impossible": a desert idyll with "all the advantages of an ocean resort."[72]

If the new environmental conditions created by the Salton Sea drew tourists to the desert and thus transformed the social conditions of the area, tourists themselves had their own impacts on the disease ecologies of the desert. As local and state horticultural commissioners sought to control the movement of pests that harmed crops—from Mexican fruit flies, alfalfa and boll weevils, to Japanese beetles, and so on—the steady increase in tourist traffic made their work increasingly difficult. Meanwhile, tourists also brought contagious diseases, and officials struggled to find ways to control the flow of tourists during outbreaks of invasive weeds and disease-causing viruses alike.[73]

The years after the flooding that created the Salton Sea saw a shift that the sea itself inspired: from recuperation to recreation. Both involved the relationships of bodies and health to the natural environment—first to the environment of the desert and sink, and second to the sea itself. The resort experience, from the tingle of cool air on one's skin on a hot day, to the taste of freshly caught fish, to the view of the stars from an outdoor bed in isolated desert country, leaned on the interplay between bodies, air, and water. The Salton Sea supplied crucial transformations to the desert, and boosters relied on the surprise to the human senses created by the interactions of this vast body of water with its unlikely surroundings.

By midcentury the striking paradox of sea air and desert heat no longer constituted enough of a draw in the eyes of area promoters. While "the cool sea breeze [was] always a delight," the makeshift accommodations and open-air cots simply no longer seemed like enough. Beginning in 1930 and escalating dramatically after World War II, hoteliers and resort owners, mostly San Franciscans and Los Angelenos with deep pockets, put up the money for yacht harbors to be dredged, streets laid out, concrete foundations poured, towns zoned, and bare desert landscaped with trees and shrubbery.[74] Resort promoters advertised showers, steam baths, cafés, clean drinking water, roads, shade, piers, and swimming areas, all of which depended on securing titles to land and ensuring "uncontested possession" of seaside properties.[75]

In the wake of World War II the county established the Master Committee of Imperial County on Salton Sea Development to resolve these issues of title and possession by undertaking surveys of land for resorts, setting aside areas for agricultural or mining ventures, and negotiating with potential investors. They envisioned the Salton Sea as "a health center" complete with "exclusive resort hotels, water sports facilities, beaches, and every other type of service and accommodations that will attract winter tourists and health-seekers."[76]

"Health-seekers," however, no longer meant well-off easterners suffering from tuberculosis. Now the quest for good health had more to do with middle- and upper-class white Americans' bodily engagement with pastoral landscapes of all kinds, from forests to beaches. Spending one's vacation breathing fresh air, exercising one's body, and taking in grand views had become by midcentury a quintessential ingredient of American life.[77] Perhaps the best illustration of this shift in how health seekers were imagined, and to whom Colorado Desert resorts were marketed, came from a prescient early take on the sea and desert published in *The Outlook* magazine in 1914: "To the lover of the strenuous life," the writer mused, "the desert makes offerings": "restored nervous vigor and a balanced sense of life's proportions, and when he went back to his city desk it was with the mental freshness of one who had drunk at the Fountain of Youth."[78]

Lovers of the strenuous life—particularly those with bountiful salaries and the luxury of paid vacation time—found much to celebrate at the Salton Sea. The land for Date Palm Beach, the first resort at the sea, was purchased in 1926 from the Southern Pacific. Located on the sea's north shore, it became renowned for its sponsorship of boat races on the sea. During World War II, when hundreds of soldiers were stationed in the area, the resort offered free swimming to soldiers. Renamed Desert Beach in 1946, the resort eventually expanded to include a yacht club, clubhouse, and boat mooring. In the subsequent two decades more resorts joined Desert Beach on the Salton Sea's shores, including Bombay Beach, the North Shore Yacht Club, and various hotels along the beach at Salton City. Photographs of fit, young (white) bodies symbolizing the robustness of the "lover of the strenuous life" featured celebrities on vacation; Frank Sinatra, Jerry Lewis, Rock Hudson, George Nader, and others were frequent visitors to the Salton Sea resorts.

As late as 1959 *Time* magazine described the benefits of Salton Sea resorts to urban tourists in ways that directly reflected boosters' promotion of the Colorado Desert six decades earlier: "Once a death trap to pioneers, the desert's rock and sand wastes, with their harsh beauty, dry, pollen-free air and brilliant sunsets, are a delight and a refuge to smog-smothered inhabitants of Los Angeles and other coastal cities."[79] Just as people with tuberculosis, asthma, weak constitutions, and poor health fled eastern cities due to concerns about foul air and cramped quarters, the "smog-smothered" people of LA sought out the "dry, pollen-free air" of the desert for their bodily health.

The Native history of the region played directly into this boom in tourism in the 1950s and 1960s. Brochures, pamphlets, and tour guides directed visitors to places where they could experience the Indigenous history of the desert. The Imperial Valley Chamber of Commerce boasted in its brochure that "Indian life, in its more or less primitive form, proceeds on all sides of the Imperial Valley." The brochure's cover image depicted a caricature of an Indian brave, standing barefoot over the distinctive tendrils of an ocotillo.[80] Other tourist guides pointed the way for tourists to locate "Indian picture writings" and other evidence of the desert's Native past.[81] One brochure gave visitors directions to places where they could see Cahuilla fish traps, the shoreline of Lake Cahuilla, and the sacred trails that connected Indigenous nations throughout the desert world.

Other enticements involved making sure that tourists had things to do on the Salton Sea itself. In the 1950s, in its attempts to make the Salton Sea a pleasing environment for tourists, the state and federal fish and game authorities undertook plans to make the sea suitable and pleasant for fishing. From 1947 to 1951 state personnel introduced into the sea's waters more than seven thousand individual fish of more than a dozen varieties, more or less to see which would do well. They tried anchovies, shrimp, mussels, oysters, and clams, in addition to sargo and bairdiella. To keep these creatures well fed and happy, they also introduced worms and filter-feeding mysids from as far away as Texas.

Along with the species they brought to the sea on purpose, state Department of Fish and Game personnel also transported any number of other types of plants and animals by accident. For example, when they planted shoal grass from Texas to entice waterfowl, the grass had stowaways: amphipoda, a type of crustacean that grazes on algae in aquatic environments.[82] The amphipods proliferated, providing a rich food source for the sea's growing population of sargo. Barnacles, too, wound up in the sea by accident, transported on the hulls of boats from marinas in San Diego and elsewhere. Barnacles thrived in the warm water, spreading throughout the shallows in mere days and collecting on any hard surface they could find—mostly the wet undersides of docks and boats. When all else failed, they attached to each other, forming clumps that rolled to the shore on waves, much to the disgust of tourists.[83] None of the fish brought in by state wildlife managers ate the barnacles, thus aiding their rapid proliferation. As the barnacles washed up on the sea's shores in low mounds, their shells broke down into a coarse sand that made up most of the beaches on which sunbathers reclined.[84]

The through line of recuperation and recreation brought together these histories of health, bodies, desert, and sea under the rubric of a particular kind of whiteness: able-bodied and affluent, traversing the dichotomous worlds of city and nature to revive health and restore vivacity. Like hunters a generation before, white settlers lived out their privilege through experiencing nature as *recreation*. Tourists came away from Salton Sea resorts with tanned skin and sun-bleached hair, their legs tired from waterskiing, their ice chests packed with freshly caught fish, their systems occasionally hungover from the waterfalls of martinis poured in hotel cocktail lounges. These experiences might not line up with what we could call experiences of the natural world—the vacationers' energy having been expelled splashing in a sump for farm water runoff, their fish imported from distant places and kept alive for them by state and federal conservationists—but they remained those of the midcentury "lover[s] of the strenuous life."

The yacht clubs and health resorts that made the Salton Sea a famous retreat for beautiful people of robust health for the most part all suffered the same fate: gradual, unavoidable, wholly devastating inundation. Increases in irrigation for agriculture in the Imperial Valley increased agricultural runoff, raising the level of the sea above the foundations of all the resorts' proud buildings. Wind-blown waves sloshed through the Desert Beach clubhouse. The club at Bombay Beach met a similarly soggy fate, as did Lido Palms, Desert Shores, and Salton City Yacht Club. Hotel furniture washed away or succumbed to bloat, mold, and rot. Whole subdivisions that boosters had plotted out in the desert soil washed away either in the rising water or in flimsy financial schemes—or sometimes both.[85]

Slowly but surely the sea that had sculpted the muscles and cooled the tanning skin of so many vacationers' bodies overtook the built environment that housed and fed them. Just as the Colorado River took boosters' dreams of lakeside resorts down to the Salton Sink in

20. In the 1960s increases in irrigation in the booming Imperial and Coachella Valleys had an adverse effect on tourism at Salton Sea beach resorts. More drainage from the fields meant that the water level rose year after year, inundating tourist-serving businesses like this hot dog stand. Sid Avery / mptvimages.com.

1905, the Salton Sea had drowned dreams of a "California Riviera" by the late 1960s. In both inundations, dreams of coupling healthy settler bodies and bodies of water in the desert succumbed to larger forces of agricultural development and water use that first created, then swelled, and finally brought about the precipitous decline of the Salton Sea.

BODIES AT WORK

As tourists sunned their bodies on the beaches of the Salton Sea's resorts, other people to the north and south worked in the agricultural fields from which the sea's water flowed. In Coachella and Imperial Valleys vast amounts of water poured onto crops maintained and harvested by an even vaster workforce of laborers.

By the 1950s landowners in the Imperial and Coachella Valleys could lean even harder into their expansive agricultural operations in the desert. After all, they were now fortified by a guarantee of water from the dammed Colorado and the network of canals carved into the desert. Add to that the bonanza of chlorinated hydrocarbon pesticides that burst across western farms in the aftermath of World War II, and large landowners in this part of California saw nothing but fortune in their future. In fact, it was this combination of factors that led to the expansions of irrigation in Imperial and Coachella and the subsequent dramatic rises in the Salton Sea's water level in the 1950s.

Federal policy aided the expansion of agriculture here and elsewhere by facilitating a labor program designed to make a large pool of inexpensive and exploitable workers available to farm owners. The Bracero Program, which began in 1942 as a collaboration between the United States and Mexico to ease wartime worker shortages in U.S. fields, expanded through the 1950s until by the end of the decade it was bringing in nearly half a million Mexican farm laborers annually. This contributed to a labor system in the Imperial Valley that was already deeply racialized. Whereas prior to World War II the workers in Imperial Valley fields had been a mixture of white, Chinese, Japanese, Mexican, Native, South Asian, Filipina/o, and Black, the postwar period saw an increased reliance on two of these groups: Mexicans and Filipinas/os.[86] Meanwhile, reliance on agricultural labor in the state as a whole increased dramatically: by the early 1980s California growers were employing 200 percent more farmworkers than they had in 1940, almost all of them engaged in transient, seasonal labor.[87]

At the same time, agriculture throughout the Southwest became increasingly dangerous. In California agriculture lagged behind only two other industries in the state—construction and mining—in rates of disabling injuries among workers. In Imperial Valley many of the most debilitating injuries occurred when farm owners and operators compelled workers to operate equipment they were neither certified nor trained to use. By 1961 the state had recorded nearly seventeen thousand farm worker injuries in California, with causes ranging from vehicles (2,136 injuries) to ladders (1,449 injuries) to "Chemicals and Hot, Injurious Substances" (966 injuries).[88] The consequences of worker exploitation in the fields did not stop at bodily injury. In the Imperial Valley in 1959 two workers bled to death from injuries they sustained while trying to operate cattle feed grinders. Beginning in 1957 a pattern of farm laborers dying in their sleep—ominously nicknamed "dream-deaths"—led public health experts to realize that at least some of these deaths resulted from acute exposure to insecticides.[89] If the Salton Sea was debilitating to the bodies of human workers, not only because it was a source of health problems but also an enabler of the industry that exploited them, the animal bodies that populated agricultural fields were debilitating to the sea. By 1923 the Imperial Valley was staggering under the numbers of animals it contained. That year the El Centro Chamber of Commerce ticked off a list of these animals, their bodies indicating profit yet to be made: more than thirty-four thousand stock cattle, more than thirty-eight thousand dairy cattle, almost thirty thousand hogs, fifty-four thousand sheep, nine thousand stands of bees, and more than ten thousand horses and mules. All these animals together, moreover, roughly approximated the number of chickens in the valley. For an agricultural region known for touting its cornucopia of fruit and vegetable products—asparagus, sugar beets, tomatoes, watermelons, cantaloupes, carrots, and more— cattle and sheep provided a considerable proportion of Imperial Valley farmers' profits in the 1920s, nearly as much as the next three most lucrative crops (cotton lint, alfalfa, and lettuce) combined.

As the human and animal populations expanded to the north and south of the Salton Sea and the area devoted to farmland increased, water flowed from farms, to canals, into the New and Alamo Rivers, and into the inland sea. Thick with fertilizers and human and animal waste, the water draining from the soil into the canals, rivers, and sea was not just salty and contaminated with pesticides but also rich in nutrients. Bacteria from these nutrients multiplied rapidly, feeding on the phosphorus and nitrogen delivered to the sea from farm fertilizers and sewage. These bacteria exploded to form blankets of foamy slime and scum—green, yellow, or brown—blocking the sunlight from reaching underwater plants at the lake's bottom and depriving them of the ability to photosynthesize. The algae sucked up the oxygen in the water, leaving none for the fish, which, in the summer, died by the millions,

21. Fish die-offs increased to massive mortality rates in the 1980s and 1990s at the Salton Sea, confounding researchers. Photo by Milton Friend. U.S. Fish and Wildlife Service.

whereupon they floated to the surface and washed up on the shore, their decomposing bodies adding yet more nutrients to the water. The chemical changes emitted by this process filled the air with hydrogen sulfide, which choked the surrounding area with the smell of rotten eggs.

This cycle—a process called eutrophication—occurs in bodies of water with a high density of nutrients, largely phosphorus and nitrogen, from farm runoff and human and animal waste. The Salton Sea's warm water, stagnant except when ruffled by winds, made for a perfect breeding ground; think of it as a five-hundred-mile-wide petri dish under a huge heat lamp. In the latter decades of the twentieth century, eutrophication produced the conditions for which the Salton Sea became famous as an environmental disaster: dead fish, putrid smells, and slimy water. More than any other consequence of this process, however, eutrophication became synonymous at the Salton Sea with the massive fish and bird die-offs that came to take over its story in the latter decades of the twentieth century.

By far the most calamitous cause of die-offs since 1979, and the one with the highest body count in these decades of death, began, like the process of eutrophication, in a bacterial cycle. Outbreaks of avian botulism began when *Clostridium botulinum*, a common bacterium virtually ubiquitous in wetland ecologies, emitted a lethal amount of toxins that could cause neuromuscular illness. When this happened in fish such as the Salton Sea's tilapia, they became weak—easy prey for winged predators. After eating fish infected with the bacteria, the birds themselves faltered: first they lost the strength and the coordination necessary to fly, then to swim, then to keep their heads above water. When a bird died, often by drowning when its neck muscles stopped working properly, flies descended on its body to lay their eggs. These eggs hatched maggots. The bacteria-generated toxins concentrated in the maggots' bodies, which were in turn eaten by birds, which also sickened and died. And so on. In the succinct parlance of the U.S. Fish and Wildlife Service, "As the cycle accelerates, major die-offs occur."[90] The Salton Sea by the 1990s had become a laboratory for this kind of bacterial cycle.

Avian cholera, which claimed thousands of birds at the Salton Sea in the 1980s and 1990s, resulted from their exposure to *Pasteurella multocida* bacteria. Transmitted for the most part from bird to bird, this bacteria-borne infectious disease affected flocks most dramatically in stressful environmental conditions: when resources were scarce and when more individual birds had to compete for scarce food and water. During outbreaks, thousands of birds died in short order. Because of avian cholera's lethal potential and rapid spread from sick to healthy birds, experts consider it the "most significant infectious disease of wild waterfowl in North America."[91] Avian salmonellosis (caused by *Salmonella typhimurium*) appeared in 1989, killing nearly five thousand cattle egrets in that year alone.[92]

By the last decades of the twentieth century, the sea that had once been known as a place of recuperation and recreation had come to be known almost exclusively as a lake in decline, an environmental wretch, rotting and redolent. When historian William deBuys summarized the litany of environmental problems at the Salton Sea in *Salt Dreams*, he imagined the sea as a body being wheeled on a gurney through an emergency room, with doctors and nurses running alongside shouting orders for life-saving tests and procedure. A *Los Angeles Times* writer in the 2000s took to describing the Salton Sea as an "environmental invalid."[93] Policy makers demanded to know the "prescription" for saving the sea. The temptation to imagine the sea as a body—debilitated, disabled, sick, or injured—resonated with the Salton Sea's bodily history, one that included the recuperation of sick people, the debilitation of healthy people, and everything in between.

PART 3

6

BOMBS

The horizons of the settler colonial nation-state are total.

—Eve Tuck and K. Wayne Yang, "Decolonization Is Not a Metaphor," 2012

A BOMB'S-EYE VIEW

In late November 1944 a man named Donald Leroy Helfrick piloted an F6F-5 Hellcat over the Salton Sea. Helfrick sat at the controls of the navy's newest model of fighter plane, painted deep blue and built as recently as that summer by mechanics at Grumman Aircraft Engineering Company (now Northrop Grumman). It could carry multiple machine guns and hundreds of rounds of ammunition, as well as racks under each wing that could hold up to two thousand pounds of bombs.

Helfrick was one among any number of navy pilots who took to the skies above the Salton Sea during World War II. They flew routes charted by their commanders above the sea and desert, picking out buoyed targets and land targets and hitting them with heavy dummy bombs crafted from cement and lead. Helfrick's mission, however, was doomed. Just before dinnertime, his new plane careened into the water, with poor Helfrick at the helm, smashing into the surface of the Salton Sea two miles east of the floating target he had put in his sights. When navy divers recovered Helfrick's body days later, the War Department informed his mother in Kansas that his death would be recorded as a casualty of war despite having occurred far from any of the official battlegrounds of World War II.

Less than a month later, near midnight in the bleached light of a full moon that sparkled on the water and illuminated the surrounding desert in a bone-white glow, another plane crashed into the Salton Sea. This one, a Grumman-made TBM-3 Avenger, carried two navy officers. The pilot, W. V. Colbert, and his radio operator, O. F. Brown, crashed two miles from a bomb target bobbing on the lake's surface. This target, a giant wooden structure cast into the sea, was one of many the navy had launched for pilots' training exercises in preparation for bombing raids on the Pacific and European fronts. After the crash, divers plumbed the sea's murky water to recover Colbert's water-logged body; they never found Brown. Like Helfrick, these two also made the official rolls of wartime casualties.

These two crashes, one occurring so soon after the other, signified a change in the Salton Sea's environmental and human history. Around the sea the military reigned from the late 1930s on, creating devastating environmental conditions that irrevocably altered the land and water. The navy first began using the sea for target practice in the late 1930s, launching seaplanes over its northwestern corner to drop bombs into its murky depths or to let service members try their hand at hitting target boats miles from the shore.[1] The navy tested torpedoes in the Salton Sea and skipped bombs on its surface like children skipping rocks on a lake. By the war's end the military had lost at least twenty-four aircraft and thirty-six people in these training exercises.[2]

From a very particular way of looking at things, the Salton Sea made for a useful military target.[3] Seemingly occupying a desert wasteland, unpopulated (or, to military minds, unimportantly populated), the sea created a stark visual contrast to the surrounding desert.[4] Sparse numbers of settlers and Natives on the western and northern shores made it easier to maintain military secrecy. This chapter provides a bomb's-eye view of the Salton Sea, tracing the tangled lines between the sea's story and military history beginning in the mid-twentieth century. The physical changes wrought on the sea by virtue of these overlapping histories shaped its material conditions; at the same time, military uses of the sea for target practice dovetailed with agriculturalists' views of the sea as good for nothing but disposal. In a bomb-centric history of the Salton Sea, however, consequences of environmentally destructive military activities did not stay put. Rather, as this chapter explores, both material and ideological consequences flowed back from the sea to far-flung places, just as they affected local communities.

The navy was far from the only branch of the military that found the Salton Sea a convenient target for defense activities in World War II. Throughout the war air force bombers winged their way toward the Salton Sea from Kirtland Air Force Base, located two states to the east, near Albuquerque. The service members on these missions aimed to drop their payloads on one of the buoyed targets bobbing a mile and a half from the shore.[5] To the north of the Salton Sea, the air force launched and landed planes at an airfield in the heart of the Serranos' homeland beginning in the early 1940s. In 1952, jumping on these other branches' fondness for practicing bombing and fighting in the desert, the marines took over the airfield and designated it the Twentynine Palms Marine Corps Training Center; successive expansions eventually made this one of the largest military bases in the world.[6] Extensive bombing of the area around the Salton Sea likely destroyed sacred Cahuilla historical sites, particularly fish traps along the ancient shoreline of Lake Cahuilla.[7]

In 1942 the army arrived here as well, conducting land war simulations at the Desert Training Center (DTC), a vast area stretching across Southern Paiute, Cocopah, Chemehuevi, and Cahuilla land from western Arizona to within a few miles of the eastern shore of the Salton Sea.[8] Throughout World War II more than a million soldiers trained for combat at the DTC, imagining this desert world as a reasonable ecological facsimile of North Africa.[9] The navy, meanwhile, continued to traverse the Salton Sea by water and by air. By 1945 the navy had cast thirteen wooden targets into the sea like the one that Colbert and Brown had in their sights before their deaths in 1944. The navy then added ten targets on the shoreline. They launched at least twelve boats, mostly landing craft, into the water for pilots to aim at from the air.[10]

The crashes that killed Helfrick, Brown, and Colbert were not the only accidents at the Salton Sea during these early years of the military's

22. The Salton Sea, photographed from above by a U.S. Army Air Forces airplane, June 20, 1941. Record Group 18: Records of the Army Air Forces. National Archives and Records Administration.

tenure in this part of California. Just after Christmas in 1942 a navy lieutenant named W. O. Carlson crashed a PB2Y Coronado, a heavy and cumbersome bomber plane, at the Salton Sea, killing Carlson and his entire crew.[11] In May 1949 a B-30 bomber out of Davis-Monthan Air Force Base, near Tucson, overshot its target on the shoreline of the Salton Sea and accidentally dropped its concrete-filled dummy bomb on a tomato field near the town of Niland, leaving local residents confused and afraid.[12] Witnesses reported seeing an object resembling a rocket plummeting to earth, followed in short order by "armed forces" who cordoned off the giant crater and refused to answer any questions.[13]

This military use of the Salton Sea led to a range of environmental consequences. Enlisted men dumped their waste in it, from kitchen and office trash to car batteries. So did the navy itself, for that matter, tossing waste ranging from vehicle engines, to airplane nose cones, to entire planes into the sea.[14] By 1945 the navy had so extensively bombed the sea that it had depopulated a mullet fishery that had supported the sport-fishing business for three decades. The navy reported making "all possible effort" to recover their bombs once dropped; however, this was almost never possible "due to deep penetrating nature of certain test shapes, shallow subsurface water, and quicksand."[15] Thus, there they remained, aging gracelessly in the Salton Sea's salty—and corrosive—water. Planes, too, sank below the surface, never to be recovered, as did service members' bodies in the aftermath of crashes.

Environmental degradation proceeded along with the growth of these bases and airfields. At Twentynine Palms the marines depleted vast underground aquifers, contributing to the decline of the Agassiz desert tortoise (currently classified as threatened under the Endangered Species Act), and littered the delicate desert ecosystem with spent ammunition from training exercises.[16] When the army abandoned the DTC, it left behind scattered wooden signs that read, "Danger . . . Entering abandoned U.S. maneuver area." Making good on those promises of danger, the army also left unknown quantities of unexploded ordnance.[17]

Meanwhile, back at the Salton Sea, the hulls of navy seaplanes brought in from San Diego Bay introduced an organism that would go on to shape the sea's biological profile, as well as peoples' perceptions of it: striped acorn barnacles (*Amphibalanus amphitrite*), a filter feeder that thrived in the Salton Sea's warm water. Within a few years the barnacles had spread throughout the sea, piling up on every hard surface. Thick crusts of barnacles on docks and boats disgusted tourists and infuriated hoteliers. Barnacle shells crunched under beachgoers' feet and clustered underneath the docks where they strolled. Piles of the shells made habitats for other organisms, mostly invertebrates.[18] Ironically, as filter feeders, the barnacles might have reduced the overabundance of nutrients that leads to algal blooms and die-offs, but the lack of hard surfaces in the sea and the tendency of humans to find the sight of them off-putting meant that they never achieved the critical mass necessary to have a positive impact on water quality.[19]

The Department of Defense has continued to make use of the Salton Sea and nearby desert landscapes well into the twenty-first century, rendering this Cahuilla and Kumeyaay land a kind of military sacrifice zone and training ground for U.S. military adventurism abroad. Soldiers parachuted into the sea, tested water-based survival gear, practiced rescue missions, and trained for desert warfare. By the end of the twentieth century the Salton Sea sat between the Chocolate Mountain Aerial Gunnery Range to the east, the Naval Air Facility El Centro to the south, the Desert Training Center to the north, and the abandoned Salton Sea Test Base to the west. The state of California had more than seven hundred formerly used defense sites (FUDS) tracked by the U.S. Army Corps of Engineers for cleanup; ninety—nearly 13 percent—sat in the two counties adjacent to the Salton Sea, fifteen at or in the Salton Sea itself.[20]

On Christmas day 1999 an elderly couple from Escondido, California, took their two-seater Piper Cherokee airplane—one of at least three Piper aircrafts named after Native nations, along with the Seminole and Comanche—out for a wintry joyride. They were cruising over the hills of Southern California toward the desert when they disappeared. By early February the search for the couple and their plane had turned into a recovery mission. The Riverside County Sheriff's Department eyed the Salton Sea as the most likely place where their ill-fated flight could have crashed; it deployed a team of divers to see what they could find to give the couple's family some closure.

To no one's great surprise, the divers did not find the Piper. Visibility in the Salton Sea's murky water made it almost impossible to see, even near the surface. Farther down the divers could barely see beyond their fingertips with their arms fully extended. They had meager chances of finding the small Piper in such conditions. Sinking down into fifty feet of salty water, however, they did find something else: the ghostly outline of a massive military plane, covered in silt and mud. It was a World War II–era Avenger, exactly like the one that had carried W. V. Colbert and O. F. Brown to their deaths half a century before. From what the divers could tell, the plane remained perfectly intact, as though its pilot had accomplished a perfect water landing and then sunk straight to the bottom. This may very well have been close to what happened; the pilot and gunner canopies had been opened and the divers found no evidence of human remains.[21]

This was one of at least ten Avengers lost during war training exercises at the Salton Sea. Half a century after they crashed, some carrying military personnel to the bottom with them, little information existed about where they could be found. Due to the cost and logistics, the Avenger found in 1999 would not be hauled to the surface but left at the bottom beneath its thick blanket of sludge. Together with the other artifacts of military uses of the Salton Sea, it had become part of the physical world of the sea, its outline inscribed in mud and muck.

THE MONSTER THAT CHALLENGED THE WORLD

In 1957 an earthquake rocked the Salton Sea—a temblor of the kind that in prior years might have collapsed one of the Cahuillas' walk-in wells. Deep under the brackish water, the ground cracked and gave way. Water—warmed from the sun, salty from agricultural runoff, and slightly radioactive from secret atomic experiments conducted at a nearby military test site—gushed into the new undersea fissures.

As it flowed into one of these newly opened faults deep below the surface, the water splashed over a nest of prehistoric eggs, creating a warm and irradiated incubator. In due course the eggs hatched. From them emerged huge and terrifying monsters, hungry for human flesh. Shaped like mollusks with bulbous glowing eyes, the monsters towered over their human victims—boaters, sunbathers, illicit lovers—leaving nothing behind but trails of radioactive slime. With each attack, they grew larger and stronger, moving from water to land and back again. The Salton Sea's resorts and yacht clubs closed their beaches, keeping their sweaty and disgruntled customers inside in 120-degree heat. The tourists who did sneak away to take their chances with the sea met unfortunate, and mucilaginous, ends.

But that was not the nightmare scenario. The nightmare scenario, as outlined by frantic military officers, involved the All-American Canal: should the monsters make their way into the Imperial Valley canal system, and from there into the All-American, and then up the Colorado River and down into the Gulf of California, "this species could threaten the entire world, devouring all life in the ocean and then foraging on land." That scenario prompted panic. "Can you imagine," one officer

23. *The Monster That Challenged the World* sought to make sense of military and nuclear uses of the Salton Sea in the late 1950s. Arnold Laven, dir., *The Monster That Challenged the World* (Gramercy Pictures, 1957). Wikimedia Commons.

quailed, "an army of these things descending on one of our cities?" Cue a crescendo of ominous music.

Calexico residents watched this drama of monstrous mollusks and irradiated water unfold from their cushioned seats inside the town's lone movie theater, the Capitol. Outside, the glowing marquee blared a title as cumbersome as the film's plotline: *The Monster That Challenged the World*, premiering in a double feature with *The Vampire*. The Capitol advertised each showtime in the local newspaper, bragging that the movie was made in nearby Imperial Valley. On the screen, shots of the familiar Salton Sea and Imperial Valley thrilled moviegoers who regularly saw those vistas in real life.

As the epicenter of an outbreak of overgrown prehistoric snail-like monsters, the Salton Sea in this story became the center of the world and the setting for a chain of events that could lead to apocalyptic mayhem. The canals that delivered pesticide-choked water, heavy with the salts drained from Imperial Valley soil, no longer delivered environmental threats *into* the Salton Sea but suddenly became the conduits for threats moving *from* the sea. The plot of the movie hinged not only on the unique ecological conditions of this part of California but also, crucially, the presence of the Atomic Energy Commission (AEC) and the military there and larger cultural anxieties about nuclearism during the Cold War years.

The radiation that turned the mollusks into flesh-eating monsters came from the tests initiated at the Salton Sea Test Base on the sea's southwestern shores near present-day Salton City. The test base first operated during World War II as the Old Sandy Beach Naval Station and the Naval Auxiliary Air Station. There, Manhattan Project engineers tested ballistics on the Salton Sea's shores and dropped clumsy facsimiles of the first atomic bombs in its water—ten-thousand-pound payloads made of concrete, iron, lead, and rocks, with many of the fake nuclear bombs containing explosives to more effectively approximate the real thing. Multiple replicas of both the "Little Boy" and "Fat Man" bombs that later devastated the Japanese cities of Hiroshima and Nagasaki crashed into the Salton Sea during these years.

At the end of World War II, on the recommendation of Commodore

24. After World War II, the Sandia Corporation took over the naval base on the west shore of the Salton Sea. The Salton Sea Test Base became one of the most important sites for ballistics testing in the early years of the atomic era. Courtesy of the San Diego History Center.

William S. Parsons, control over these two naval stations passed to the AEC, which gave management of the new Salton Sea Test Base to the New Mexico–based Sandia Corporation.[22] Under the administration of Sandia National Laboratories, thousands of bombs — inert and otherwise — landed in the Salton Sea after being rigged up with telemetry devices to provide information to engineers about everything from the drop to the impact. Sandia personnel ran test shots throughout the year from 1947 to the mid-1950s, with a peak of 223 tests in 1952.[23]

Locals witnessed firsthand the silence and secrecy that had come to characterize AEC projects in the postwar period. Newspapers published conflicting accounts about the uses to which the base was put and whether radiation posed any risk to the humans and nonhumans who lived nearby. Some accounts held that the base would be used to develop "peacetime" applications of atomic energy; locals excitedly conjectured that this might entail an atomic process of desalinating salt water.[24] Others reported that the base would merely be used for equipment tests and storage. No matter the rumor, the overarching message to the public underscored one central claim: that "fish in the waters of Salton Sea and jackrabbits in the brush of the surrounding desert are safe. And so are the people."[25] Down at the Salton Sea Refuge, refuge managers went a step further, speculating that the presence of the AEC might aid their conservation efforts because trespassers would now think twice about bothering the birds at Pelican Island while dummy atomic bombs dropped from the sky.[26] In 1949 the AEC disclosed that it had been engaged in nuclear experiments in two locations: the Marshall Islands and the Salton Sea. They denied, however, that these experiments involved the use of radiation. Confusion abounded among locals, as it did in communities surrounding other sites of atomic secrecy.[27]

In a quintessential example of the tensions of knowledge and power in a newly atomic world, in the fall of 1951 an El Centro bus driver named T. D. Jones noticed a plume of smoke on the horizon as he neared the town of Indio. Curious, he drove toward it until he reached the fence of the test base, beyond which rose a pillar of smoke he described as towering four thousand feet in the air. It originated, according to Jones, from a giant fire that seemed to float on the surface of the Salton Sea about ten miles south of Sandia headquarters. Jones called the police in a panic. The test base's manager, however, denied the existence of a fire or a giant plume of smoke—or that anyone had been working at the base that day at all.[28]

As the secrecy of the Salton Sea tests began to slowly thaw over the course of the 1950s, Sandia decided to stage a demonstration for local reporters. They fed the reporters lunch and then trooped them out to the beach, where the journalists witnessed a bomb emerge from the bay of a B-47. The massive wooden target lay some four thousand feet from the shore, but the bomb plummeted into the water more than seven hundred feet shy of the intended spot. Unabashed by the miss, the Sandia personnel assured reporters that the previous week they had gotten within twenty-five feet of the target. Many of their tests at the Salton Sea, it turned out, were "spectacular misses"; one bomb even landed in the middle of the base's tennis court.[29] No one seemed to mind much—the journalists remained captivated by the "deadly arc of the dead-white dummy atomic bomb" and the panels of beeping, clicking, and whirring equipment that tracked its fall into the Salton Sea, adding "another bit of information . . . to what must be an immense fund of secret data."[30]

Sandia's purpose at the Salton Sea Test Base was to evaluate the drop capabilities of a range of different types of bombs. Test base personnel rigged up bomb facsimiles of various shapes, sizes, capacities, and purposes and shot or dropped them one by one into the water. They photographed the bombs' descent, tracked them by radar, and took meticulous measurements. Afterward they tried to recover the remains of the projectiles, with varying degrees of success. What came up from the dark depths of the water came up in fragments.

The AEC subsequently claimed that no radioactive materials were included in those tests, but evidence suggests that those claims were not entirely true. As the Environmental Protection Agency reported in 1993, Department of Energy employees reported having used uranium in bombs at the Salton Sea and elsewhere, primarily (and somewhat ironically) for reasons of expediency and expense: uranium was useful for ballast because it was "less expensive than concrete and easier to use than lead."[31]

Like the navy on the opposite shore, Sandia personnel dropped, crashed, and dumped a wide range of materials into the Salton Sea, many of them toxic. In addition to bombs rigged up with electronics and encased in heavy metals, the Salton Sea Test Base dumped motor oil, trash, and construction materials into the water. They buried disposal tanks with unknown contents along the beach, and several of those tanks remained there until well into the 2010s. In the late 1960s the California Regional Water Quality Control Board had to issue a cease and desist order to get the navy, which was by then overseeing the test site, to stop discharging sewage effluent from the base into the sea.[32]

The enthusiasm with which the Sandia Corporation shot and dumped things into the Salton Sea made for a running joke among its personnel.

Since they spent their days busily dropping "everything but the kitchen sink" into the water, it was only a matter of time until one enterprising (or bored) test base resident hauled a sink onto an airplane, opened the bomb bay doors high above the Salton Sea, and shoved it out. Cheering and laughing, other employees watched it splash down and then went about their business. Or so the story went.[33]

This context sparked the mad brainstorm that manifested ultimately in shots of giant carnivorous mollusks, incubated in radioactive water, emerging to feed on comely sunbathers along the sea's shore. *The Monster That Challenged the World* deployed familiar tropes and metanarratives common to midcentury monster movies, in a genre that often nakedly responded to prevailing cultural anxieties with metaphors of monstrosity, apocalypse, and terror. Monster films in general have functioned as a kind of shadow history of economic stress, political strife, racial conflict, technological revolution, and other challenges and upheavals in American life. To be sure, the radioactive, bug-eyed krakens that feasted on alluring young sunbathers on the beaches of the Salton Sea gave form to the atomic terror that gripped Americans in the post–World War II years. Like the better-known slime-covered monsters of *The Blob* fame, these prehistoric krakens from the depths of the Salton Sea served as thinly veiled stand-ins for the public threat of Cold War confrontation and technological revolutions.[34]

The key difference between the Salton Sea's krakens and the blobs of *The Blob* has to do with both the environment and the history of the Salton Sea itself. Whereas *The Blob* featured monsters from outer space, totally foreign to Earth and a clearly xenophobic metaphor for immigration, *The Monster That Challenged the World* showcased threats specific to the environmental conditions—both human-made and otherwise—of this unique place. Drawing on the mollusks that originally inspired William Phipps Blake to collect and study these remnants of a long-gone inland sea, as well as the risks of radioactive adventurism at the test base and the complex network of canals that distributed the lifeblood of river water to Imperial Valley farms, these monsters embodied nearly every major element of the Salton Sea's settler history.

Like the terrifying giant ants of *Them!* (1954), the irradiated octopus from *It Came from Beneath the Sea* (1955), the three-story spiders of *Tarantula* (1955), and the towering praying mantis of *The Deadly Mantis* (1957), the Salton Sea monsters represented the consequences of meddling overmuch with the environment. In each of these examples of the monster movie genre, military, atomic, or agricultural technology ran amok to threaten devastation and death by oversized pincers, limbs, and tentacles.

Unlike these other movies, however, *The Monster That Challenged the World* was not set in a city. In each of the films mentioned above, apocalypse mainly came in the form of devastation to densely populated and geopolitically important urban areas: San Francisco, New York, Los Angeles, and so on. In this regard, the giant ants, spiders, mantises, and octopi stood in for bomb or air assaults that would be, in effect, limited in terms of their geographical impact. The Salton Sea, however, posed different kinds of apocalyptic possibilities and thus symbolized different kinds of socioecological threats that might come of new technology. If the urban environments being destroyed by overgrown critters in other films made them apocalyptic by virtue of the sheer numbers of people they killed and displaced, the Imperial Valley and its interlinked web of canals offered a different kind of apocalypse: an ecosystemic one. The canal system that linked the Salton Sea to its larger limnological ecology, up the Colorado River and down to its delta in the Gulf of California, remapped the Southwest as a contiguous region with connections across the continent and ultimately a geography that had the potential to challenge—and maybe destroy—the entire world.

CONSEQUENCES

Just over a month before the United States entered World War II, a construction crew broke ground on a recently purchased site near the southernmost corner of Nevada, in the homeland of the Southern Paiutes. Within a year the factory they built there would churn out a metal alloy that would provide a key ingredient of President Franklin Roosevelt's "arsenal of democracy." At the time, however, it was little more than a hopeful investment in a desert world just a few miles from

Las Vegas—still a dusty little town occupied mainly by the families of workers who had come to Nevada to build Hoover Dam.

Around this factory a new community would be built from scratch: schools, hospitals, churches, grocery stores, and gridlines of smooth-paved roads. The town would be one of many "family-centered, consumer-oriented communities" that rose up during and after the war. They were communities in which companies created a comforting veneer of "monoclass affluence" for their mainly working-class employees.[35] Of course all of this began with jobs—hence, the construction crew skittering like fire ants over the dry desert soil of the northern Mojave in the late autumn of 1941, laying the foundations of a new factory and its soon-to-be-thriving company town.

This town—Henderson, Nevada—rapidly grew into the third-largest city in the state. More than five thousand workers arrived here with their families in the early 1940s, ready to work, live, pray, study, and shop in the brand-new buildings sprouting from the desert soil. On the first anniversary of the factory's opening, more workers walked its floors than had labored at the Hoover Dam site on the busiest day of construction. By 1943 more hydroelectric power flowed from that dam's turbines to this Henderson factory than went to the entire city of Los Angeles. A quarter of the electricity harnessed from the rushing water of the Colorado River came here to power the plant that, just eighteen months earlier, had not existed at all. All of that human and river energy went into processing raw magnesite ore, blasted from the ground in Gabbs Valley several hundred miles northwest of Henderson, into magnesium. Basic Magnesium, Incorporated (BMI), a subsidiary of the monolithic Anaconda Copper mining company, had been charged by the federal Defense Plant Corporation to produce the silvery "miracle metal" that, when alloyed with aluminum, created products as strong as steel but half as heavy.

On December 7, 1941, the Henderson facility immediately gained new heights of urgency and purpose. The Imperial Japanese Navy Air Service's bombing of Pearl Harbor, the U.S. naval base on Kānaka Maoli land on the island of Oahu, Hawai'i, came a mere three weeks from the beginning of construction in this stretch of Southern Paiute land.

Suddenly, the production of the "miracle metal" from Gabbs Valley magnesite became a wartime necessity. During the war magnesium alloys would go directly to the War Department as key ingredients in airplanes and then in helicopters and rockets as well.

Demand for magnesium, like demand for other wartime alloys, did not drop off when the fighting stopped. Instead, in the decades after the war, magnesium would travel to the suburbs that blossomed all across the country, appearing in products ranging from cars and household tools to sports equipment and beer cans.[36] Aerospace companies partnered with the federal government to send magnesium alloys into space and all over the world in the form of airplane parts. When ignited, magnesium sparked into bright white flares that transformed the production of fireworks and thus transformed Fourth of July celebrations in municipal parks across the country.[37]

These postwar applications of the miracle metal, however, did not come from Henderson; by 1947 the Henderson facility was careening toward the inauspicious fate of being declared surplus war property by the federal War Asset Administration. Nevada lawmakers stepped in, transferring control of the erstwhile defense plant to the state's Colorado River Commission. Surely such a state-of-the-art facility could find a postwar life in the new Cold War industrial landscape. After all, not far away the U.S. Navy was busily erecting its own facility to process an inorganic compound called ammonium perchlorate, which it used in rocket fuel. In only a handful of years a new company took over the BMI facility and, drawing inspiration from the navy plant just a few miles to the west, began making its own perchlorate.[38] By the early 1960s the Pacific Engineering Production Company of Nevada (PEPCON) was supplying the bulk of federal purchases of this highly combustible compound. The chemical giant Kerr-McGee later took over the navy plant and promptly bestowed upon the newly formed corporate endeavor a name right out of science fiction: Tronox.

Ammonium perchlorate dissolves easily and moves quickly from soil to groundwater. From both facilities, PEPCON and Tronox, the toxic rocket fuel ingredient seeped into the ground and moved downhill to the Las Vegas Wash. From there it trickled into Lake Mead.

Perchlorate-contaminated river water rushed through the Hoover Dam, churning through its turbines to generate electricity that powered the Southwest from Las Vegas to Los Angeles and coursing through the Lower Colorado River basin below Lake Mead.[39] Some twenty million people relied on Colorado River water for drinking, bathing, and farming, including the Colorado River tribes who lived directly *on* the water where the river knits together the states of California and Arizona.

Health problems trailed along behind the chemical processing operation. Perchlorate inhibits the uptake of iodide by the thyroid, which can result in hypothyroidism, a condition associated with metabolic problems in adults and developmental problems with infants. Low levels of thyroid hormones can cause cardiovascular problems, disrupt kidney function, harm reproductive systems, and have negative impacts in one way or another on almost all other systems of the body.[40] During pregnancy, hypothyroidism can cause a range of cognitive impairments for a developing fetus. In the postwar years, public health experts became particularly concerned about concentrations of perchlorate in human breast milk because of its clear threat to infant neurodevelopment.[41]

The Colorado River Aqueduct delivered perchlorate into the Los Angeles Metropolitan Water District, a problem that was not discovered until 1997, when it inspired the Environmental Protection Agency to examine how and why this toxic substance had traveled so far from its source. By then PEPCON no longer operated in Nevada; in 1988 its facility exploded when a worker got too close to the perchlorate with a welding torch. The explosion killed two people and injured more than a hundred others, rocking this part of the Mojave like an earthquake. PEPCON waited a year, announced it would not reopen the plant, and moved to Utah.

Below the diversion of the Colorado River Aqueduct, perchlorate-polluted river water coursed through the All-American Canal and onto the lush green croplands of the Imperial Valley. Animals ingested it as they drank contaminated water and ate contaminated plants, meaning that the chemical passed into their eggs, milk, and flesh. Perchlorate seeped through the soil, wetting the roots of spinach, lettuce, lemon trees, and orange trees and spreading into these plants' leaves and fruit.

Humans likewise consumed the chemical in their water and food. It accumulated in human thyroid tissues, mammary glands, placentas, and saliva.[42] In 2003 researchers found perchlorate in 100 percent of the samples of supermarket milk they tested.[43] The water drained into the valley's complex system of canals, running eventually into the New and Alamo Rivers and downhill into the Salton Sea.[44]

Imagine a map of perchlorate's meandering journey: moving with groundwater from the Henderson factories into the Las Vegas Wash and down through the Colorado River's lower basin, seeping into the soil of riverbanks and farms, being sprayed on crops, absorbing into human and animal bodies, flowing from Los Angeles taps, pouring into glasses from gallons of supermarket milk—and of course draining into the Salton Sea. Such a map would make a serviceable illustration of the Colorado River's reach and power after a century of being bent to settlers' purposes in the West. It might offer a better way to visualize the long reach of Colorado River water than geophysical maps of its early-twenty-first century riverbed—a sobering reality, given that it would be a map of a *toxin* illuminating the reach of a waterway.

A perchlorate map would also reflect the larger ecological consequences of military industries—and their afterlives—in the West. Few of the toxic contaminants produced by industrial development spurred by World War II stayed where companies or the government put them. Rather, they moved downwind, downriver, and downhill, tracing the contours of the physical landscape in ways that created vast and often poorly understood environmental health risks for humans and nonhumans.

This became clear in the late 1990s, when federal regulators discovered that the local water source perhaps most directly affected by perchlorate ran through the taps of the Torres Martinez and Agua Caliente bands of the Cahuilla Nation and their neighbors in the Coachella Valley. The Coachella Valley Water District (CVWD), facing water shortages and ongoing depletion of groundwater by increased settlement since the completion of the Coachella branch of the All-American Canal in 1948, had begun to try to mitigate groundwater shortfalls by pumping in more water from the Colorado River. They did this at four "recharge stations," effectively replacing high-quality, drinkable aquifer water with untreated river water containing dissolved solids, pesticides, nitrates, and perchlorate. From 1996 to 2015 the Agua Caliente band demanded that the CVWD stop replenishing their groundwater with water that "failed to satisfy the EPA's recommended secondary standards for contaminants."[45] At the very least, the tribe argued, the water should be treated first. The water district ignored them for nearly a decade, until the Agua Caliente Cahuillas won a landmark federal lawsuit acknowledging that tribes had a sovereign right to drinkable groundwater underneath their reservations.

On the Torres Martinez Reservation, at the south end of the Coachella aquifer, the tribal EPA found that the groundwater, replenished by CVWD, contained dangerous levels of perchlorate.[46] They advised the reservation's residents not to drink their tap water and provided bottled water to elders. The Torres Martinez Cahuillas faced greater risks, it turned out, because of their proximity to the CVWD's recharge stations, one of which sat directly along the ancient shoreline of Lake Cahuilla, a sacred site for this Native group.[47] A spokesperson for the water district suggested that perchlorate should not worry the tribe; all they had to do was take iodine tablets—a dangerous and misguided recommendation that contributed to an atmosphere already rife with confusion and mistrust.

The lack of federal regulation of toxic chemicals compounded the problem of perchlorate in the drinking water. Perchlorate was discovered in public water systems as early as 1992, but the federal EPA did not determine that perchlorate met the criteria for regulation as a contaminant under the Safe Drinking Water Act until 2011. As of 2019 the EPA had yet to establish a federal maximum contaminant level (MCL) for perchlorate.[48] In the absence of federal regulation California tried to develop its own criteria. In 1997 the state's Department of Health Services declared that perchlorate in drinking water should not exceed 18 parts per billion (ppb). The next five years, however, revealed the potency and environmental health consequences of perchlorate contamination. In 2002 the state realized that its initial assessment had set the upper threshold for action more than four times higher than it should have. They lowered it to 4 ppb. However, without the power of a federally backed MCL designation, California had no authority to actively regulate perchlorate contamination; therefore, the threshold limit of 4 ppb served only as a guideline for utilities.[49] By 2012, when the Torres Martinez EPA studied the groundwater that had been replenished with water from the Colorado River, it contained upwards of 6.9 ppb of perchlorate, nearly 3 ppb higher than the state's guidelines.[50] In 2015 researchers concluded grimly that, although the chemical was "fast becoming a threat to the environment . . . prescribing a permissible limit of perchlorate in drinking water to avoid health problems remains a distant reality."[51]

When researchers discovered elevated rates of perchlorate in the Salton Sea, it imbricated the sea in this broader swath of U.S. history. Taking a bomb's-eye view of the Salton Sea envelops in this larger geography and history the magnesite mines on Southern Paiute land in Gabbs Valley; the infrastructure built by the labor it took to turn magnesite into rocket fuel; the energy wrested from the Colorado River to power the machines that processed the ore into an alloy; the transformation of a World War II factory town into a Cold War cog in the military industrial complex; the distance traveled by magnesium alloys and perchlorate alike in the form of airplane parts, consumer goods, and rocket fuel; and the final settling of perchlorate in downriver bodies and ecosystems. Although it originated far from the Colorado Desert, the perchlorate production in Henderson is also the story of the Salton Sea and the troubled, and troubling, relationships between Native peoples, settlers, and water in the West.

THE VIEW FROM MALKI

Two months before World War II ended in Europe, a shipbuilder in South Carolina launched a new ship for the navy's fleet: the USS *Cahuilla*. The *Cahuilla* was not destined for the front lines; it served instead as a support vessel to larger ships. The navy deployed it as an antisubmarine teacher and tow boat. It tugged bigger vessels between California, Hawai'i, and Guam and was thus a small contributor to the defense of the outposts of U.S. empire in the Pacific. Scholars have reflected on the U.S. military's habit of giving Native names to its boats, planes, and helicopters.[52] In World War II the *Cahuilla* joined the USS *Geronimo*, the *Wampanoag*, the *Navajo*, the *Paiute*, the *Luiseno*, the *Papago*, and the *Salish*, among many others. These Native names did not appear among the big destroyers, battleships, cruisers, and destroyers; instead, they graced the hulls of tug, rescue, and salvage ships.

The use of their name for a navy tugboat made for an odd kind of homage to Cahuilla people, who experienced the war in ways dramatically removed from a relatively small vessel dragging vast ships of war across the Pacific.[53] Throughout the war Cahuillas encountered rapid militarization in ways similar to people of other Native nations: as enlisted soldiers and as workers in factories and fields.[54] In addition to the sudden ubiquity of the navy, AEC, air force, army, and marines on and near Cahuilla land in California, the war shaped Cahuilla life in a range of ways, as it did in other Native communities in the United States. Not all of the effects were unambiguously negative; Katherine Siva Saubel remembered that rations during the war prompted Cahuillas to return to harvesting traditional foods.[55]

Prior to the U.S. entry into World War II the number of Natives in the U.S. military sat at around five thousand. Four years later that figure had jumped to more than forty-four thousand and more than 12 percent of the entire Native population.[56] Native people had complex motivations for participating in the war effort, not least of which was that they were subject to the draft. For Cahuillas, World War II pulled young people away from their home communities in dramatic numbers. This departure of the youth was compounded by a prolonged drought that made bad water conditions on their reservations even worse. In 1945 the navy listed eighteen members of Mission tribes as having been wounded overseas and thirteen more killed in action.[57]

Within a decade of Native people's returning from the war and from off-reservation defense factories and farms that provided material support for the war, the Bureau of Indian Affairs (BIA, renamed as a result of a reorganization of the Indian Affairs Office in 1947) greeted them with a new policy: termination of their trust status with the federal government.[58] Termination involved withdrawing federal services and the associated federal spending on tribes—meager though that spending was—under the auspices of encouraging independence among Native people as fully fledged U.S. citizens. In the words of Native studies scholar Vine Deloria Jr., this policy added up to "a modern war of conquest" waged by the United States against Indigenous nations, something not so different, in Deloria's estimation, from "the old systematic hunt and the deprivation of services" that characterized earlier settler campaigns.[59]

Native peoples in Southern California responded to the termination era of federal Indian policy with deep ambivalence. The remaining members of the Mission Indian Federation (MIF), under the leadership of Adam Castillo, saw the termination issue as an opportunity to finally sever ties with the hated BIA. Most tribal councils, however, saw it differently, as a threat to their sovereignties and their connections to their homelands. The tribal chairperson of the Rincon Reservation, Max Mazzetti, argued decades later that termination represented "a continuation of the struggle we and our grandparents, and great grandparents," faced.[60] Alliances formed between Kumeyaays, Cahuillas, Cupeños, Luiseños, and others to oppose any application of the termination policy to their reservations.[61] The conflicts that developed between pro- and antiterminationists during these years caused deep rifts and ignited heated debate within communities and between family members, as they did among other Native nations during the termination period.[62]

In 1955 the BIA sold more than three hundred acres of Cahuilla land, stretching from the north end of the Salton Sea to Indio, and placed the $57,000 it received as profit from the sale in trust for the tribe. This move directly benefited the local water utility, the Coachella Valley Water District, because the tribe had paid no taxes on these acres and thus did not receive water from the Coachella Canal project. Converting the land to private ownership would let the water district pay off part of its $27 million debt by collecting taxes and water usage fees from nontribal users.[63] Three years later the agency turned control of reservation roads in Southern California over to local counties, citing a desire to pull back from management responsibilities on tribal lands. These and other moves constituted a rapid erosion of the federal trust responsibility to fulfill its treaty obligations to Native nations, whether or not they experienced the full effects of termination.

In this context Cahuillas endeavored to develop their own internal support structures. In 1966 workers poured a new concrete foundation on the Morongo Reservation, home to pass Cahuillas, just north of Mount San Jacinto. From this concrete foundation rose a small brick building, painted white with a low roof. Above the door red letters spelled out "Malki Museum, Inc." Inside, the new museum's founders surveyed their accomplishment: a museum housing Cahuilla arts and crafts that had been collected over the course of decades by a handful of Cahuilla women. Margaret Pablo, a member of the Wanikik Cahuilla clan and a grandniece of a *net* who had signed one of the eighteen Lost Treaties in 1852, had gathered pots and *mortreros*. Victoria Weirick, of the Wanikik and Kawasic clans, had collected pots, baskets, clothing, and photographs from William Pablo, an honored *pul*. Jane Penn, also of the Wanikik clan, added her own precious collection, as did Dr. Katherine Siva Saubel. By the time the museum opened, Pablo and Weirick had died, but Penn and Saubel had brought the women's idea to fruition. They surveyed their accomplishment as the museum's curator (Penn) and first president (Saubel). Just steps from the back door, Penn and Saubel planted medicinal and sacred plants in a garden over which hung a wooden board that read "Temalpakh: From the Earth." In the coming decades, Malki Museum would focus on three primary goals in addition to preserving objects of Cahuillas' material culture and history: to publish Cahuilla-authored books about the tribe's history and culture, to revitalize the Cahuilla language, and to record knowledge of their native botanical practices.[64]

Their first order of business was to throw a *kewét*. After decades of pressure from the Bureau of Indian Affairs office and schemes designed to discontinue what federal agents called "the obnoxious 'fiesta,'" kewéts had not been held regularly since the late 1920s. Under the direction of Penn and Saubel, the inaugural kewét of the Malki Museum would honor Cahuilla military veterans, part of a larger Indigenous practice in the twentieth century of revitalizing community gatherings by reframing them through the lens of patriotism.[65] Thousands of people attended,

25. Katherine Siva Saubel and Jane Penn, founders of the Malki Museum, at its future site. Date unknown. Courtesy of Malki Museum.

including hundreds of Cahuillas, Serranos, Kumeyaays, and Quechans. They sang the Bird Songs, danced to drum circles, and wove baskets while children chased each other through a forest of grownups' legs. The aromas of barbecued beef, corn, beans, and fresh tortillas wafted through the crosshatched shade of the willow and palm ramada outside the museum's door. The Malki *kewét* continued to be held on Memorial Day every year thereafter, offering an opportunity to honor military service members, to dance and sing, and to gather families from across Southern California Native reservations.

In 1966 Jane Penn sought to expand the museum and requested support from state agencies, arguing that it would provide much-needed jobs for residents of the Morongo Reservation. Asked to justify her request, she answered straightforwardly: "We are going to give to you—you who are always taking rather than giving. We are going to give you something you can't give to us—our culture." Frustrated with the patronizing tone of the state representatives she faced, she went on to advise, "We are hoping that, with a little more education, you are going to respect our artifacts and culture. . . . If you don't approve this project, you're just going to wait that much longer to understand us."[66] The chastening apparently worked; the state approved the funding on the spot.

Penn's succinct justification for funding the Malki Museum attested to the state of Cahuilla affairs and relations with the state of California and the federal government in the postwar period. In the wake of World War II and the government's push toward termination policies, Cahuillas faced underemployment, thinning support services from the BIA, and the pressure of swelling settler populations across their homeland, from the Salton Sea to Palm Springs to Riverside. In this context Cahuillas sought to underscore the vibrancy of their culture, the teachings of their history, and the inevitability of a robust Cahuilla future. The work of these Cahuilla women—Penn, Saubel, Pablo, and Weirick—provided a crucial counterpoint and epigraph to these years of militarization and termination.

Their perspective from the Malki Museum lay in tension with the bomb's-eye view of the Salton Sea and the Native homelands that surrounded it. The view from above rendered the region an undifferentiated, unendingly beige wasteland, crinkled here and there with mountains ringed around an oversized wastewater sump fed by smears of green fields to the north and south. The view from Malki showed the lie in this perspective, revealing the detailed history, complex present, and rich future of the Cahuilla world in the California desert.

7

CHAINS

Violence and American nationhood, in short, progressed hand in hand.
—Ned Blackhawk, *Violence over the Land*, 2006

FINDING TACHO

In late April 1890 a twenty-nine-year-old Cahuilla man named Tacho reclined by a fire in the northern reaches of the Colorado Desert, surrounded by friends. The dry Salton trough stretched to the south, sinking down into a low horizon illuminated dimly by a first-quarter moon. Perhaps some of Tacho's companions had spent their day harvesting salt for George Durbrow, escaping after their shifts into the cool night air to get some respite from the white-hot heat of the salt rows. Between wafts of campfire smoke, the air carried their voices and quiet laughter along a breeze scented with California sage and mesquite.

The sudden sound of horse hooves traveling across the desert in the direction of their camp might have surprised Tacho and his group—then again, maybe not. Tacho had been fleeing those horse hooves for several days, having been accused by ranchers in Banning of stealing some of their horses. When a constable and deputy from that nearby town arrived to seize Tacho from his spot beside the fire, the young man might have been ready to make his case to the officers. If he did, they did not listen. Instead, they promptly abducted him, tying him up and hauling him north toward distant hills.

Upon returning to Banning with Tacho in tow, the constable tied the Cahuilla man up in the train depot and fitted him with an "Oregon boot"—a heavy cast-iron ankle shackle with a bar under the instep designed to keep imprisoned people from running. Tacho and the constable were not alone; the ranchers from whom Tacho had allegedly stolen horses stood in a ragged group outside the depot door, looking on in silence. The constable left, skirting the menacing crowd outside the depot door. The ranchers watched him go. Then they dragged Tacho from the depot, shackles and all.

When the sun rose on the morning of April 29, Tacho's body hung by his neck from a telegraph pole above the railroad. His hands had been tied behind his back. His murderers, the same local stockmen who had looked on as the constable clamped chains around Tacho in the train depot, had pinned a paper to their victim's coat warning all "horsethieves" to leave town as soon as possible. The heavy Oregon boot still encircled one of his ankles. The local train, heading into Banning just after dawn, slowed to a stop. Passengers leaned out windows, craning to get a glimpse of the grim scene. The engineer telegraphed the San Diego coroner's office to report the body, asking plaintively, "Must I cut him down?"[1]

With this murder, Banning residents had, in the cruel words of one local historian, "celebrated [their] only public lynching."[2] Weighing the morality of what it called a "hanging bee," the San Bernardino newspaper demurred, describing the victim as a "bad Indian." His murderers had "sent [Tacho] to the happy hunting ground, where he would never again steal horses." The writer described the lynching as a "summary dealing out of justice" that, "while not according to the laws of the land, rid the county of one of the worst desperadoes on the Coast."[3] The Banning newspaper went further; even as it acknowledged ambivalence about Tacho's guilt, the editors opined that "now-a-days we may well afford to have one innocent man suffer for the sake of convicting 99 criminals."[4]

Two stories circulated to explain away the brutal spectacle of Tacho's death, both baldly ludicrous: first, that he had committed suicide, and second, that he had escaped his chains in the train depot and made a run for freedom in the desert. These thinly veiled lies barely stood up to even the scant evidence available about his death, including the note pinned to his body declaring him a horse thief and the Oregon boot, designed specifically to hamper prisoners' ability to escape on foot, since every stride would drive the metal bar deeper and more painfully into an escapee's instep.

Newspaper accounts of the murder gave Tacho a number of different names. In addition to calling him Tacho or Anasthacio (no surname), they dubbed him Tacho Razón and Anatacio Lugo. One account described him as Fig Tree John's youngest brother—perhaps an indication of close community ties between Tacho and Juan Razón or simply the result of settlers knowing of only one famous Cahuilla with whom to associate Tacho. Settler stories of his death amounted to a handful of newspaper articles and local histories of dubious reliability. The agent for the Mission reservations at the time of his murder, Horatio Rust, dismissed the lynching by describing Tacho to the local press as a "member of a gang of horse-thieves who have infested San Bernardino and San Diego Counties." Rust claimed Tacho had escaped—"with an Oregon boot on," the agent huffed incredulously—whereupon "citizens of Banning turned out, hunted him down and hung him."[5] In short, Rust viewed Tacho as a gang member with superhuman abilities to escape justice, in contrast to "citizens" of Banning, who had little choice but to find and execute him.

This interpretation of justice, delivered outside of official legal channels yet nonetheless sanctioned by every level of state and federal officialdom, reflected a cruel reality about race, colonialism, and incarceration in California. In their earliest years of incorporation, most California towns prioritized building jails as proof of their carceral priorities. No town or city without a jail, in late nineteenth-century California, could fully consider itself a civilized place, at least by the logic of the time. Jails functioned as mechanisms of social control that maintained strict class and race hierarchies. Those confined behind their bars were transgressors of particular varieties, such as those referred to simply as drunkards, Indians, and hobos.[6] In California, jails performed barely concealed settler colonial work of Indigenous dispossession and erasure and later the disciplining of workers.[7] As a central component of California history, jails and their correspondent ephemera—chains, police, judiciaries, sentences, and fines—also played an important role in the history of the Salton Sea and its surrounding communities.

Social control, racial violence, and Indigenous dispossession figured into the violent murder of Tacho in 1890 in ways distinct from but related to systems of incarceration. Lynchings in California and other western states and territories functioned as extralegal forms of violence that terrorized nonwhite and Indigenous communities.[8] From the outset of California's admission to the Union, Californians matched codified control of Natives with this form of extralegal violence, while many white Californians declared that, when it came to the state's Indigenous people, "any other but Lynch Law, was a damned humbug."[9] This chapter explores how different forms of carceral violence—codified and extra-legal alike—functioned as technologies internal to settler colonialism in the communities surrounding the Salton Sea. The sea's history has been tied to jails and chains in often surprising ways: as the body of water around which this history played out, as the ecological enabler of settler life in its agricultural zones, and as a physical feature of the landscape that shaped and was shaped by patterns of incarceration and the experiences of incarcerated people.

The details about Tacho's death offered by Agent Rust and local news-papers, though sparse, represented a veritable archival deluge in comparison to accounts in the settler archive of his life. Beyond scat-tered descriptions of him as a "desperado" and one transcription of his first name, hurriedly scrawled on an Indian census record next to those of his family members, Tacho might seem to have no story other than the self-serving accounts of his death, written by those who shared interests with his murderers.

Horse thief or not, Tacho deserved a better story.

The name Tacho appeared twice in Indian census records compiled before his death: one in 1886 and the other in 1888. The closest name to Anasthacio, as he was dubbed by the editors of the *San Diego Union and*

Juana	John	Son	m	16
Jose	Joe	"	m	10
Polenario		Grand Pa	"	82
Johivis		" "	"	76
Pio Lugo	Pino Lugo	Father	"	41
Maria Lugo	Mary	Mother	F	38
Pedrito Lugo	Little Peter	Son	m	15
Ambrosio		Father	"	24
Augustino		Mother	F	21
Teresa		Grand Pa	m	86
Pio		Father	"	65
Maria	Mary	Mother	F	50
Ventura		Son	m	18
Calistro		"	"	13
Victoria		Daught	F	10
Vicente		Father in	m	69
Catalina	Catharine	Mother	F	66
Margarita	Margaret	Daught	F	23
Polonia		"	"	6
Infant		"	"	2
Marallo		Husband	m	48
Isaabella	Isabel	wife	F	45
Antanacio		Father	m	60
Dorila	Dorothy	Mother	F	60
Tacho		son	m	25
Mantusal		"	"	14
Ignacio		Grand Pa	"	80
Miguel	Michael	Father	"	46

26. Indian census roll, 1886, showing Tacho's name and the names of his family members. Indian Census Rolls, 1885–1940, National Archives Microfilm Publication M595, Record Group 75, Records of the Bureau of Indian Affairs, National Archives and Records Administration, Washington DC.

Daily Bee, was that of his father, Antanacio, who was likely named after *his* father, and Tacho's grandparent, Ignacio. The census taker in 1886 anglicized Tacho's mother's name, Doreta, making it "Dorothy." Neither parent, like so many of the Cahuillas listed in this incomplete record, was given a surname in the census record. Tacho's brother, Mantasal, was eleven years his junior. The advanced ages of his parents—both sixty in 1868, with a twenty-five-year-old Tacho and a fourteen-year-old Mantasal still living at home—suggest that perhaps Tacho had older siblings as well; the lack of surnames throughout the census, however, makes it impossible to know what other households might have held their closest relations.

The younger brother gave Tacho a future as well as a past. By 1892, just two years after Tacho's death and perhaps still mourning the murder of his brother, Mantasal married a woman named Lula and lived with her and their newborn baby, Eunice, at Torres, north of the Salton Sink and Durbrow's saltworks. In census records, which are the only transcribed records by which to trace Mantasal, Lula, and Eunice, the family had no surname. That changed in 1902, when the census takers who arrived to enumerate the community members bestowed on Tacho's brother, sister-in-law, and niece the same surname given to almost a third of all Cahuillas on the reservation: Torres.[10] Tacho retroactively became not a Lugo or a Razón (as he had been dubbed in the newspapers) but a Torres. Being associated with these three surnames applied by settlers carried with it a bit of inadvertent poetry: by linking him to the three most common surnames among the desert and pass Cahuillas, settlers made him kin to nearly the entire Cahuilla Nation.

Mantasal, Lula, and Eunice gave Tacho a future. Doreta gave him a past. Tacho's mother would have arrived in the world around 1826, in the denouement of the mission system that sent its shock waves from the coasts to her desert home. She likely saw at least three small overflow lakes created in the Salton Sink as she grew. She would also have seen them slowly evaporate. She would have learned to weave tight baskets, to haul heavy water pots by using a sling that balanced the water's weight against her forehead, and to harvest and cook mesquite beans. She would have undergone the Cahuillas' puberty ceremony for girls as they became women, just as Tacho's father, Antanacio, would have gone through the ceremony to celebrate boys' passage into adulthood.[11]

By the time Doreta gave birth to baby Tacho, around 1861, her world would have undergone dramatic changes. Soldiers had passed through the desert en route to fight the U.S.-Mexico War in 1846. In 1848 more newcomers passed through the desert—or died trying—in search of gold. Smallpox epidemics had come and gone, although the largest and most devastating was yet in the offing. When a terrible outbreak struck the desert Cahuillas in 1863, the death and disease must have been terrifying for both Doreta and Antanacio, with two-year-old Tacho, and perhaps older children, in their care.

Like Juan and Matilda Razón, Doreta and Antanacio belonged to the last generation of Cahuilla parents who did not have their children forcibly removed to boarding schools. Tacho would have been too old to have been taken away to the St. Boniface, Perris, or Sherman institutions; Mantasal would have avoided this fate too, having turned eighteen the year St. Boniface opened. As children, the boys probably learned some English and Spanish but primarily spoke Cahuilla in their daily lives. Tacho's niece, Eunice, born in 1892, likely attended the Martinez Indian School when it opened in 1908, perhaps with Juan Razón's youngest son, Lario, who would have been two years her senior.

Whereas the settler archive reflected little about Tacho's life, and only offered troublingly skewed accounts of his death, Cahuillas remembered him. Cahuilla historian Katherine Saubel retold Tacho's story without even using his name, calling him simply "the man hanged in Banning." Elders in her family—her husband's grandfather, her mother-in-law, and others—had told Saubel about him, stories about "the olden days," when "they arrested him [Tacho]" and "hanged him in town." These elders, Saubel reported, remembered Tacho's death as a key incident that illustrated conditions of anti-Native violence at a time when "it was awful" for Native people. "'They would abduct women. They would take them. They mistreated them any way they felt like. . . . There was nothing,'" she concluded, "'the (Indian) men could do.'" Saubel's informants and relations, in other words, not only remembered Tacho and his death, but also connected this murder to the racial, colonial, and gendered implications of violence against their people during this time period.[12]

Tacho's murder crystallized important lessons among the Cahuilla and other Indigenous people of desert California. He was far from the only Native victim of this form of extralegal violence during those decades. Lynching occurred from the very outset of the American period of California history, becoming commonplace in Los Angeles and San Diego in the 1850s. Like lynching in other places and in other times in the United States, these spectacles of violence were often about racial control, functioning as a form of racist terrorism designed to spread fear that would shore up white supremacist economic, political, and cultural institutions.[13] In California "the primary victims" of lynchings, as one historian has noted, "were Latinos and Indians," though certainly there were Asian and Black victims too.[14] As Saubel's account attested, however, his brutal killing also illustrated how racist violence intersected with gender-based violence in the settler order of things in the region. The ranchers' singling out of Tacho for allegedly stealing settlers' property reflected a desire to maintain white men's relations of domination over Native men, in a pattern of coercive control described by Native feminist scholars Maile Arvin, Eve Tuck, and Angela Morrill as settler heteropaternalism, or "the presumption that heteropatriarchal nuclear-domestic arrangements, in which the father is both center and leader/boss, should serve as the model for social arrangements of the state and its institutions."[15] Tacho's alleged theft of settler property violated heteropaternalistic norms. The spectacle made of his murder—meant to be seen as a threat of more violence against other Native men who violated settlers' ideas about their own invulnerability—sought to reinforce those norms. As such, it illustrated the larger gendered politics of incarceration and punishment in colonial and white supremacist contexts.[16]

It mattered that Saubel's account of Tacho's death, passed down to her by her parents' generation, folded his murder in with stories about attacks on Native women.[17] Just as the violence directed toward Tacho was gendered, organized around policing his masculinity and access to settler men's property, the violence enacted against Native women and girls was gender based, motivated by a desire to maintain settler-defined gender roles and hierarchies.[18] Cahuillas remembered patterns of assaults on Native women and girls despite the fact that relatively few reports of those kinds of violence made their way into the settler archive, let alone rich accounts of the victims' and survivors' lives. This latter-day vagueness matched the obtuseness of the documentary record; newspapers tended not to report the assaults white men committed against Native women, and official Indian Agency reports also elided this violence. When they did, they obscured the horrors behind euphemisms and victim-blaming rationalizations.[19] In the late twentieth century and early twenty-first, Native feminists folded this horrifying silence of settler documentary records into ongoing patterns of sexual and gender-based violence against Native women and girls underpinning colonialism, organizing around the searing problem of missing and murdered indigenous women and girls (MMIWG).

Like her latter-day Native feminist counterparts, Saubel remembered these stories of violence and how the gendered nature of genocidal campaigns against Native peoples in California had continued to shape the contours of Indigenous life for generations.[20] Whether or not Tacho and other victims of extralegal violence have been named in their accounts, their lives—and deaths—echoed through Cahuilla stories about the deep currents of violence and brutality that structured (and continue to structure) settler colonialism. The broad brush strokes of these power relations reveal how extralegal and codified forms of control over Native life constituted their relationships to individual settlers and settler institutions. Cahuillas' own histories, however, held these victims of violence as their ancestors and family relations and also held settler colonialism accountable where the U.S. justice system never would.

JAILS AND THEIR USES

In 1908 young Condino Lubo, son of Ramona Lubo and Juan Diego (the couple of *Ramona* fame), and a friend goofed off for essayist George Wharton James's camera. In the photograph, Condino aggressively pushed at his friend's body, digging his bare feet determinedly into the dirt. His friend, meanwhile, leaned sideways in a posture of passive resistance, his hands clutching at the would-be jailer's arms as though

27. Stereographic images of Condino Lubo playing with a friend. George Wharton James, *Ramona's Son, Condino, and a Friend Playing outside the Jail at Cahuilla*, circa 1899. Huntington Digital Library.

to give himself some scant chance of self-protection. His head drooped off to one side, invisible to the camera. He propped his body slackly against the force of Condino's weight, looking like he might fall to the ground at any moment. For that matter, both boys seemed on the verge of toppling to the ground, balanced against one another in an unsteady, unstable kind of reciprocity: a playful, though ominous, mimesis of the larger patterns of carceral control between settlers and Natives in California in those early years of the twentieth century.

The jail behind them was little more than an oversized box hammered together out of spare wood, with a rectangular hole for a door. Just imagine the sweaty suffering of anyone locked inside. This box represented the carceral system developed by the pass Cahuillas near Indio in the early twentieth century—one of many reservations that built their own infrastructures of policing and caging in the early twentieth century under the encouragement and financing of the Indian Service. Local Native communities on reservations adapted settler systems of incarceration to local contexts, realizing that jails symbolized a key step toward "civilization" in the eyes of the Indian Service agents who controlled their access to much-needed resources.

A casual observer might think of Condino and his friend as playing at a game of cops and robbers; in the context of the Cahuilla Reservation in 1908, however, they might more likely have been playing Cahuillas and settlers. The jail had initially been hammered together under the direction of the Indian Service in the hope that Cahuillas might police each other and thus tread farther down the path toward "civilization" in the eyes of federal agents. However, the structure soon took on a new use in the early years of the twentieth century: as a place to lock up settlers who trespassed on Cahuilla land. As such, this settler-imposed institution ended up being used by Cahuillas to enforce their sovereignty—something they needed much more urgently than they needed a box in which to cage their own people. The reservation captain, Leonicio Lugo, had repeatedly petitioned the Indian Service for help in clarifying and reinforcing the reservation boundaries. He asked for fences, survey lines, and boundary markers to keep out white trespassers and their livestock. His entreaties went unanswered. In frustration, Lugo deployed men to ride along the reservation boundary line on horseback to catch intruders of both the bipedal and hoofed variety. In defense of their land, Lugo and his men threatened human interlopers with violence, claimed wayward livestock as their own, and eventually began to jail wayward white persons in the wooden box that constituted the Cahuillas' prison system.[21] Since the Indian Service provided a jail rather than boundary fences, Lugo used the jail to incarcerate white intruders.

The Indian Service and local white residents did not take kindly to the Cahuillas' defense of their sovereignty by incarcerating settlers or to the use of the reservation jail for locking up white people rather than other Natives. Will Stanley, the local Indian Service superintendent for the Cahuilla Reservation from 1907 to 1911, desperately sought to assert control over Captain Lugo and the government Lugo had set up, in the words of the captain's nephew and advisor, "to look after the interests of the people."[22] Superintendent Stanley did this by arresting and fining Natives for minor offenses (or fictional offenses) with such vigor that his superiors eventually called him home for "stirring up conflicts." His successor, Superintendent Swayne, proved little better.

Under Lugo's leadership, the superintendent grumbled, Cahuillas "really believe that . . . if they decided anything in meeting [their decision] is more binding than any [American] law or rule."[23] Annoyed at these demonstrations of sovereignty and self-determination by Lugo's people, Swayne arrested and prosecuted Captain Lugo himself.

The fact that the Indian Service repeatedly resorted to carceral control over Native people in the mountains north of the Salton Sea reflected larger patterns of settler colonial power in California and beyond. In fact, as argued by historian Kelly Lytle Hernández, prisons and jails functioned as powerful vehicles of settler colonialism in California, as was the case throughout the West.[24]

Even as it served as a means of amplifying settler power over Indigenous people, incarceration played an unexpected role in the material conditions of the nearby Salton Sea. The making of the settler world that came to surround, as well as sustain, the Salton Sea required material changes to the desert. Tourists who cruised into brand-new resort towns in the 1950s on long ribbons of black asphalt, laborers who arrived to pick crops from Imperial Valley fields, and state Department of Fish and Wildlife conservationists who monitored the comings and goings of pelicans all relied on networks of new roads and the built infrastructure of firehouses and town halls, water management systems, and police stations. In the area surrounding the Salton Sea the labor of constructing this world around, because of, and for the Salton Sea often came from a specific category of workers: incarcerated ones.

From the network of lonely roads that circumnavigated its shores to the sprinkling of towns that sprang up around it, the built environment of the Salton Sea followed larger state and national patterns of incarceration. Prison labor has occupied an enduring role in the United States, as section 1 of the Thirteenth Amendment to the Constitution codifies it as an acceptable form of enslavement; the amendment abolished enslaved labor "except as punishment for a crime." This codification of forced work in the prison system drew powerful ties between the now-abolished institution of chattel slavery and new patterns of racial hegemony, unfree labor, and confinement throughout the United States.[25] In the desert world of Southern California, the people forced to work as part of their incarceration were marginalized by class, lack of housing, or, more frequently, by race or nationality. Following these patterns, the imprisoned laborers who built major parts of the region surrounding the sea were thus disproportionately Native, Mexican, Black, and Asian.

Chain gangs functioned as externalizations of the jailhouse, bringing incarcerated people out into the open to perform public service before the public's very eyes. Calexico's chain gang program began in 1909 and before long functioned like a well-oiled machine: on the weekends deputy constables rounded up people they accused of petty offenses—being drunk and disorderly fell in that category—and locked them in jail until Monday morning, at which time they would be marched in shackles before the town judge and ordered to pay a fine or be sentenced to hard labor. This was a false choice. Most of these people, referred to in the local newspaper as the "grist of Mexicali" and "Mexicans and Indians who had imbibed too much mescal," had no money to pay fines; instead, as everyone knew, they would be both incarcerated *and* subject to the fine, to be paid with their labor in lieu of cash.[26] Labor on chain gangs served another purpose from the point of view of the local Mission Indian Agency, whose agents took to punishing Native people they accused of possessing liquor by sending them to work on the "road camp."[27]

True to the description in the *Calexico Chronicle* of the demographics local police considered the "grist of Mexicali," they mostly hauled in Mexicans and Natives on weekend "petty crime" roundups. But others wound up penned inside the Calexico jail until their Monday morning hearings too: "plain drunks," drunk drivers, speeders, vagrants, check forgers, and so on. The system of incarceration and the profit derived from fines served to punish a range of offenses, big and small, interrupting the lives of people of all kinds. By far, however, the stories of those swept up in this era of policing in Imperial and Calexico reflected white settlers' desires to control, dominate, and profit from the nonwhite people who lived among them.

At times the targets of this zeal for policing escaped the labor camps, if not the larger violence of arrest and incarceration. These experiences probably resembled that of Jenny Cruiz, a Quechan woman who "sometimes [came] over" to Calexico "for her firewater." In 1929 Cruiz appeared before the court with "severe facial bruises," which the local newspaper credulously attributed to her having fallen down on the sidewalk. The twelve other defendants ushered with Cruiz into the court that morning paid fines or began their work on the chain gang; the judge ordered Cruiz, on the other hand, to leave town and not come back. Her incarceration, it seemed, served no other purpose than as part of a larger system of temporary catch, confine, and release.[28]

These patterns of incarceration effectively instilled a sense of social control and—as officials bragged—gave people they dismissively called "hobos" pause before they came near their well-policed towns.[29] Like any system of domination, however, this one was far from perfect. Prisoners escaped, ran, fought back, went on strike, and engaged in organized work stoppages. In 1904 Juan Pinon—a "Bad Man from Arizona," as the *Imperial Valley Press* subheadline labeled him—sat in an unguarded cell to await judgment on a charge of public drunkenness. Two friends tried and failed to free him, whereupon he started a fire in an attempt to burn his way out. Not one to give up easily, he eventually managed his escape by scratching through the wall near the door with a knife.[30] In 1905 a Native woman incarcerated in Calexico staged a similar "jail break" when her friends loosened the bricks around the cell's lock, allowing her to simply walk out into the cool night air.[31] The same year and farther to the north in Imperial, two incarcerated men escaped by simply unscrewing the lock from the jail door.[32] In 1915 Calexico's chain gang, mobilized to action by a "big Indian from Oklahoma," decided to go on a collective strike that brought the county's incarcerated labor program to a grinding halt. Their act of rebellion? They "simply [lay] down on the job," dropping their picks and shovels, reclining comfortably on the dusty ground, and calmly "explaining to the guard that they were perfectly satisfied to receive two regular jail meals" a day rather than the three meals served to those who chose to work.[33] Imprisoned people bolted at every opportunity, such as one who took advantage of being temporarily moved outside while the jail was being painted.[34] Another, decades later, disappeared into one of Calexico's grapefruit orchards, prompting a search that turned up only "an elderly Indian woman who had been mistaken for the escaped convict"—a remarkable mix-up, as the escapee in question was a young African American man convicted of possessing "six and one-half reefers" of marijuana.[35]

The labor of building up the public infrastructure of Imperial Valley was not the only resource gleaned from ever-expanding systems of policing and incarceration; the raw material for that infrastructure also came from the valley. In the early 1930s Imperial County officials found a single solution to two of their most pressing problems: a high concentration of unemployed people, including those already living in Imperial Valley as well as new arrivals fleeing the dust bowl and Great Depression, and a dearth of reliable roads cutting across the desert's soft surface.[36] The tourist industry on the shores of the Salton Sea could only develop in fits and starts without well-paved roads. Perhaps more pressingly, the Imperial Valley's booming agricultural fields needed efficient conduits to move their produce to market.

The solution to these problems sat deep within the gentle slopes of Superstition Mountain, a glorified bump of earth directly west of Imperial. Underneath its dune-like top layer, the core of the "mountain" contained vast deposits of granite. In 1932 the county purchased rights to the hill, sent away for a rock crusher, and began to plot how it might use the tons of crushed granite that Superstition Mountain would yield to construct serviceable roads across the soft desert floor. The county applied for state funding to open a relief work camp at the base of the mountain. The first workers, fifty unmarried and unemployed Imperial residents, arrived in the winter of 1933 and received guarantees of board, food, and thirty cents a day for their labor.[37]

By that summer, however, it became clear that few if any Imperial Valley residents would willingly subject themselves to the brutal conditions entailed in blasting granite from the exposed hill in scorching desert heat. On top of the sunburn and grueling effort involved, employees at Superstition Mountain earned less than a quarter what they could at Imperial Valley farms.[38] Free workers would simply not do this labor. Imperial officials turned instead to *un*free ones. By the summer of 1934 work at the granite pit was relying increasingly on incarcerated laborers. Their lack of a choice in the matter, however, did not make their exertions at the quarry and rock crusher any easier. In June the tough conditions under which they toiled prompted eleven prisoners at the camp to go on a hunger strike; one escaped and fled through the desert to Mexico.[39] In the same month Imperial County's board of supervisors doubled down on its insistence that the rock crushers would continue to run, whether or not workers wanted to suffer the conditions at the site. The board passed a resolution that gave the county sheriff the authority to assign anyone convicted in Imperial County of any infraction, including traffic violations and other misdemeanors, to labor at the rock quarry—or indeed on any "public premises in the county."[40]

The rock-crushing operation shut down in 1937, as did the Works Progress Administration offices in Imperial Valley. The rock pit would not stay closed for long, however. By the following year the county was again sending laborers to the granite quarry. In 1938 local newspapers called on "drunk drivers [to] take warning!" because a county judge had begun sentencing people convicted of driving while intoxicated to be taken "under armed guard" to Superstition Mountain.[41] Throughout the rest of the decade imprisoned laborers blasted, dug, crushed, and hauled nearly one hundred tons of granite every day, six days a week, for the benefit of the county's road system. From 1933 to 1939 the county went from having 30 miles of paved rural roads to 107.[42] By the time the county supervisors ended the chain gang program at Superstition Mountain, they had enough rock to repave nearly all county highways and streets, for the benefit of tourists and farmers.

In these ways, in the early decades of the twentieth century much of the public works infrastructure of the area surrounding the Salton Sea came to be built by the hands of incarcerated people. Chain gangs paved roads, painted municipal buildings, maintained their own prisons, cared for irrigation ditches and canals, and blasted from the desert floor the raw material that built Imperial Valley. They did so in a system that presupposed their vulnerability to local and state power and feigned an interest in their personal development, often entrapping incarcerated people in a false choice: work for free or receive less food; work for free or pay fines you have no capacity to afford.[43]

By the late 1930s the Mission Indian Agency was regularly reporting on the "law and order" status of Southern California reservations. Each year agents meticulously tabulated federal and state charges against Native people on and off their reservations. In 1937 alone there were fifty-six federal cases and thirty-six state cases made against Indigenous members of the Mission Indian Agency.[44] In a population of just under three thousand people, this made the rate of incarceration among Southern California Native people three times higher than that for the U.S. population as a whole.[45] Clearly, incarceration had developed as a powerful iteration of colonial power, with the intention of dispossessing and controlling Native peoples through legal channels, according to Salish historian Luana Ross.[46] Around the Salton Sea this brought together the colonial power of the law with physical dispossession effected by farms and by the water that drained from them. All the while, imprisoned people, many of them Native and most of them nonwhite, performed the unfree labor that built an infrastructure of access for settler consumers and tourists and for the flourishing of an agricultural empire in the desert.

CARCERAL CONSERVATION

The early weeks of June 1970 brought strange weather to the Salton Sea. In addition to the customary oven-like heat pressing down on the water's surface, unusually powerful winds gusted off the mountains down toward the desert. The Salton Sea roiled. Deep below the waves, the water—rarely disturbed except by the gradual upward pull of evaporation—churned up thick sediments of decaying algae and other organic matter. The sea's oxygen levels plummeted. Fish suffocated, their bodies floating to the surface and collecting on shorelines.

This was not the first spring fish die-off to result from heavy winds and low oxygen levels. Far from it. Spring and summer had nearly always brought toxic conditions for the sea's fish, and year after year a heat wave or windstorm would send dead fish bobbing up from below. However, when the local warden from the state's Department of Fish and Game stood on the north shore gazing out at the fish floating in like "solid rafts" from the middle of the sea, he could see that this would be the worst loss of fish life yet. Thousands of dead corvina, croaker, and sargo washed up on the beach to decay under the glare of a hot summer sun. Some of the croakers were massive, weighing as much as twenty pounds.[47] The fish lined twenty-five miles of shoreline, stretching from the northern reaches of the Salton Sea down along its eastern edge.

The state sent laborers to the Salton Sea to clear the smelly scene. Together, these workers collectively spent more than two thousand hours collecting rotting fish and hauling them into skip loaders and trucks furnished by Riverside County.[48] The local fire department set up a kitchen for these workers not far from the North Shore Beach and Yacht Club so that the laborers could eat between shifts, all the while trying to ignore the pervasive stench of decaying fish that clung to their clothes as they bolted down their rations.

These workers all came from Southern California prison camps, which, in 1970s California, employed incarcerated people in a wide range of conservation-related jobs. When they were not tramping over miles of beach sand to gather fish carcasses, these imprisoned laborers weeded streambeds, cut fire lines, cleared flood debris, maintained trails and roads, fumigated forests for insect infestations, managed nurseries, and dredged canals. When not on location, they lived at former Civilian Conservation Corps camps that had been taken over by the state government and nicknamed "Honor Camps." Honor Camps housed incarcerated adults and youth wards of the state. From 1946 to 1957 the program grew from a single youth program to seven youth camps, fifteen adult camps operated in partnership by the Departments of Corrections and Forestry, six seasonal camps run in conjunction with the federal Forest Service, and three highway camps.[49]

California state officials crowed over the successes of the program, which utilized, they claimed, "the idle man-power wasted in prisons." The Honor Camps, according to the state, accomplished any number of positive ends: "economy in prison operation," "great quantities of valuable conservation work at economical cost," and—"most of all"— "an inestimable good in human rehabilitation." For all these reasons, the state's Department of Forestry anticipated in 1957 that "the Honor Camp program will certainly long occupy a respected place of California State government."[50] In 1959 alone the California legislature authorized

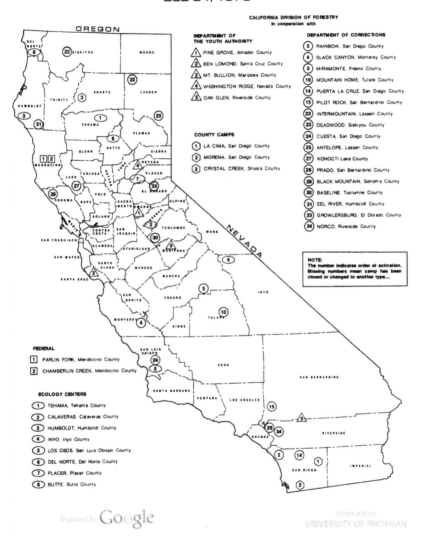

LOCATION OF CONSERVATION CAMPS
AND
ECOLOGY CENTERS
DEC 31, 1973

CALIFORNIA DIVISION OF FORESTRY
in cooperation with

DEPARTMENT OF THE YOUTH AUTHORITY

1. PINE GROVE, Amador County
2. BEN LOMOND, Santa Cruz County
3. MT. BULLION, Mariposa County
4. WASHINGTON RIDGE, Nevada County
5. OAK GLEN, Riverside County

COUNTY CAMPS

1. LA CIMA, San Diego County
2. MORENA, San Diego County
3. CRYSTAL CREEK, Shasta County

DEPARTMENT OF CORRECTIONS

2. RAINBOW, San Diego County
4. SLACK CANYON, Monterey County
5. MIRAMONTE, Fresno County
10. MOUNTAIN HOME, Tulare County
14. PUERTA LA CRUZ, San Diego County
15. PILOT ROCK, San Bernardino County
22. INTERMOUNTAIN, Lassen County
23. DEADWOOD, Siskiyou County
24. CUESTA, San Diego County
25. ANTELOPE, Lassen County
27. KONOCTI, Lake County
28. PRADO, San Bernardino County
29. BLACK MOUNTAIN, Sonoma County
30. BASELINE, Tuolumne County
31. EEL RIVER, Humboldt County
33. GROWLERSBURG, El Dorado County
34. NORCO, Riverside County

NOTE:
The number indicates order of activation. Missing numbers mean camp has been closed or changed to another type....

FEDERAL

1. PARLIN FORK, Mendocino County
2. CHAMBERLIN CREEK, Mendocino County

ECOLOGY CENTERS

1. TEHAMA, Tehama County
2. CALAVERAS, Calaveras County
3. HUMBOLDT, Humboldt County
4. INYO, Inyo County
5. LOS OSOS, San Luis Obispo County
6. DEL NORTE, Del Norte County
7. PLACER, Placer County
8. BUTTE, Butte County

28. Location of conservation camps and ecology centers, 1970. California Division of Forestry, Engineering and Camps Section, "Division of Forestry in the California Conservation Camp Program" (Sacramento: California State Board of Forestry, 1970).

more than $4 million to be spent on conservation camp construction.[51] Then-governor Edmund "Pat" Brown (father of Jerry Brown, who later became famous as the country's "greenest" governor) encouraged the participation of imprisoned people in conservation work because he believed they would benefit from a "healthy outdoor lifestyle." It likely did not hurt that their labor cost the state no more than $2.50 per laborer per day.[52]

By 1966 the number of incarcerated people in conservation camps in California had increased fivefold, from fewer than a thousand in 1959 to more than five thousand. Governor Pat Brown adored the program, pointing out that it had helped the state develop nearly 150,000 new acres for outdoor recreation. In a single year, he declared, "'inmate crews from conservation camps put in more than five million man-hours of constructive work in our forests, work which the taxpayers could not otherwise afford.'"[53] By 1970 the Forestry and the Corrections Departments, along with the state's Youth Authority, were running thirty-three sites that employed two and a half thousand incarcerated minors and adults to fight fires and conserve the state's natural resources.[54] Each year in Southern California prisoners housed in conservation camps participated in demonstrations of their work, for which state authorities would travel to the mountains in Riverside County to witness the skills expected of incarcerated workers: hiking, laying hose, constructing fire lines (which required them to clear an area "a minimum of six-feet wide and 300-feet long down to bare mineral soil," an almost unimaginably grueling task), and off-road driving. The workers were closely watched and their activities "timed and inspected for quality," forcing them to possess the physical prowess required to run this gauntlet of dangerous conditions before an audience of strict overseers and rapt policy makers.[55]

As the program expanded across California, incarcerated workers contributed meaningfully to the material world around the Salton Sea in ways that went beyond firefighting. Puerta La Cruz Conservation Camp and La Cima Conservation Center opened in 1957 and 1966, respectively, in the mountains to the west of the sea. By the early 1970s the California Department of Corrections and Rehabilitation (CDCR) was running the majority of the state's conservation camps and ecology centers. Like Puerta La Cruz and La Cima, the eight located in Southern California mostly clustered in the western reaches of the Colorado and Mohave Deserts in remote mountain outposts. State officials bragged that the people incarcerated in the camps rarely attempted escapes, a situation they attributed to the recuperative effects of strenuous labor in nature. Perhaps a more likely interpretation of the infrequency of escape attempts was that the camps sat in rough landscapes far removed from cities and towns. In essence, the formidable landscape functioned as a helpmate to—or replacement for—iron bars, walls, and chains. In ways that echoed other forms of incarceration in harsh or forbidding places, the environment itself intensified the experience of incarceration.[56]

In autumn of 1976 thirteen youths from one of these Southern California camps—the Oak Glen Youth Conservation Camp in Riverside County—arrived in Coachella Valley, the heart of the desert Cahuillas' homeland, to dig out more than two hundred homes from flood debris after torrential downpours. They ranged in age from late teens to early twenties and had been convicted of offenses from burglary to armed robbery. For their work the state of California paid them seventy-five cents a day. On most days their labor involved cutting fire trails; in this instance, however, they spent their time and energy hauling wheelbarrows full of mud mixed with the detritus of peoples' flood-wrecked homes. Local residents, wary at first of having convicted men and boys help dig out their homes, grew to appreciate how "rehabilitated" the workers seemed.[57] As these local citizens observed the young people engaged in unfree labor in and near their homes, it seemed to them to underscore the similarities between resident and worker—regardless of past transgressions. In fact, however, the youths' exertions drew stronger connections between them and generations of incarcerated people who had labored under the same hot sun to shore up the settler world in this part of California, just a few miles north of the Salton Sea.

By the late 1980s conservation projects throughout the state of California faced problems of underfunding and labor shortages. The Salton Sea Wildlife Refuge was no exception. In 1986 the refuge relied almost exclusively on volunteers and visits from fourteen members of the Youth Conservation Corps, a federal Fish and Wildlife Service program that provided a few months of conservation experience for teenagers. These extra hands performed much of the labor that could not be done by the refuge's nine paid staff members: they cleaned and organized the refuge's headquarters, cleared concrete irrigation ditches, repaired the water system, dug postholes for split rail fencing, cleared brush, marked boundaries, transplanted mesquites and palo verde trees, and worked on a drip irrigation system.

By the early 1990s these labor shortages persuaded the refuge to turn to incarcerated laborers to undertake this kind of work and focus on the many other projects that needed attention. Crews of incarcerated people from the McCain Valley Conservation Camp, a minimum-security state prison in Boulevard, California, rode buses fueled by the refuge-supplied diesel fuel ("to alleviate their transportation costs") to undertake "valuable manpower" for the refuge. Year after year in the early 1990s workers arrived at the refuge in January, after the fire season had passed, and remained there until March. They tackled the refuge's most labor-intensive projects, performing work that otherwise, according to the refuge managers, "would not have been done, due to lack of refuge staff." In 1990 refuge managers estimated that prisoners had done more than 1,500 hours of work: they had raked troublesome stands of salt cedar out of ponds, built a visitor observation tower, installed drainage pipes, cleared ditches, and pruned trees and shrubs.[58] The following year their workload more than doubled; they contributed 3,600 hours doing "yeoman work in supporting refuge projects, frequently those of a time-consuming, labor-intensive nature."[59]

McCain Valley was among the newest of the state's carceral conservation program sites in the late twentieth century. The camp was established in 1986 as a collaboration between the CDCR and the California Department of Forestry and Fire Protection (CAL Fire), to "provide convicted felons with the opportunity to give something back to California citizens while paying their debt to society."[60] Like its predecessor camps, McCain Valley was deputized by the state to furnish local, state, and federal agencies with a labor force for a range

29. McCain Valley Conservation Camp #21 logo. California Department of Corrections and Rehabilitation.

of conservation-related projects. The camp's logo brought together iconography of the American West—most notably a pioneer wagon—with perhaps Southern California's most recognizable image of conservation: windmills, like those that stand in groves outside Palm Springs. Over this updated version of westward expansion, a raven stretched its wings, reaching out with its claws as though to zero in on some unseen prey.

Like other incarcerated conservation workers, those from McCain Valley split their time between providing labor for various state agencies (in this instance, Fish and Wildlife) and fire management. By the early 2000s, as climate change caused temperatures to tick higher and California endured year after year of unprecedented drought conditions, firefighting had become an even more urgent task—and a more dangerous one. Of the twenty largest fires in the state's history up to 2019, fifteen ignited in the 2000s.[61] By the end of those first two scorched decades of the twenty-first century, nearly four thousand imprisoned people had been sent to labor on fire lines across California, making a dollar an hour on active fires and under two dollars a day doing fire prevention work.[62] These workers described their time on the fire line as frightening, grueling, unpredictable, and exhausting; as one man put it to a researcher in 2012, "This is legalized slavery, and that's all it is."[63] Whereas their civilian counterparts underwent three years of apprenticeship to become firefighters, prisoners headed out to confront unpredictable blazes with two meager weeks of fire safety and suppression training.[64] All told, in any given year in the 2010s imprisoned laborers provided up to ten million person-hours fighting fires and undertaking other kinds of conservation-oriented work. The CDCR bragged in 2010 that the program saved the state $80 million a year.[65]

The program—linking incarceration, public lands, fire, and conservation—presented glaring ironies. California's ecosystem, far from being a pure wilderness that would best thrive if only humans could learn to "leave no trace," has been managed and maintained for centuries by Indigenous nations that used fire to care for landscapes from the Sierra Nevada to the coasts and deserts.[66]

Like the Cahuillas who fired palms to protect them from pests, Native peoples deployed fire as mediator of their human relations to their nonhuman world.[67] As settlers privatized California lands or brought them under state control as public lands, settler environmental management practices—from conservation and preservation on refuges and parks, to exploitation in mines, urban areas, ranches, and farms—focused on "uncompromising fire suppression."[68] The dispossession of Native people from their homelands had direct material consequences for ecosystems that depended on regular controlled burns to thrive.[69] While these settler environmental (mis)management schemes caught landscapes up in fire suppression, the laborers who undertook the hot and difficult work of fire suppression were likewise caught up in a settler system of incarceration.[70]

These ironies, crystallized in the confrontation between an imprisoned person and a wall of flames, were present on the Salton Sea's northern beaches in the summer of 1970 as well, as fish bodies drifted to the shore to rot and incarcerated workers gathered them into piles and chucked them into the beds of trucks. Decades of mismanagement of the sea, control over the Colorado River that parented it, and encouragement of Imperial Valley farms that kept the sea full of pesticide-laced water produced this and other cycles of die-offs, which the state had little capacity to clean up. The employment of prison laborers to undertake these clean-ups—or, for that matter, to dredge fire lines through drying and overgrown foothills—functioned, in essence, as a settler answer to a settler problem.

Within a few decades the oversized wooden box that represented the carceral system of the Cahuilla Reservation in 1908 would be swallowed up by a massive network of settler prisons and jails that flourished throughout the area and indeed throughout the United States. This system encompassed vast areas of land and used dramatic quantities of natural and human resources to imprison wide swaths of people. In California incarceration rapidly became a central feature of the state's political economy.[71] By the early decades of the twenty-first century the CDCR had become the largest and most expensive agency in the executive branch. The CDCR employed roughly fifty-six thousand people and ran forty-three facilities that covered thirty-five thousand acres of state land, from the foothills of the Sierra Nevada in Lassen County, to the coastal land surrounding San Quentin, to the low desert in Imperial and Riverside Counties. Echoing its long-standing partnership with state conservation agencies, the CDCR in 2018 declared itself to be an "innovator in sustainability," demonstrating "leadership in environmental stewardship."[72]

The area surrounding the Salton Sea proved no exception.

In addition to the conservation camps scattered throughout the mountains that ringed the sea, several facilities incarcerated people throughout the Colorado Desert from the early years of the twentieth century through the 1970s. The Imperial County Jail, which had been the main Imperial Valley incarceration facility since 1907, was replaced by the Herbert Hughes Correctional Center in the early 1960s. Imperial added the Regional Adult Detention Facility in the late 1970s.

Then came President Ronald Reagan's War on Drugs, which escalated the country's jailed population. The 1980s through the 1990s saw an explosion in prison construction in this part of California. Northeast of the Salton Sea, along Interstate 10, the Chuckwalla Valley State Prison began caging people in 1988. In 1992 and 1993 both Calipatria State Prison and the California State Prison at Centinela opened; these two facilities, Calipatria and Centinela, then spent the next few decades vying for the notoriety of being California's most overcrowded prison.

To complete the transformation of the desert into an extensively carceral landscape, Ironwood State Prison opened in the winter of 1994, just next door to the prison at Chuckwalla Valley.

Calipatria State Prison landed in newspapers all over the country not long after it opened. It was selected to host California's newest experiment in carceral technology: an electrified fence carrying enough volts to instantly kill any person who touched it. California chose Calipatria for this experiment with the "death fence," as its critics instantly nicknamed it, because, below sea level and achingly hot, it was already a difficult place to maintain a reliable workforce of guards. The death fence served the dual purpose of solving Calipatria's staffing issues and allowing the CDCR to step boldly into new frontiers of carceral control of people's bodies and mobility. Up until that point, two states—Indiana and Massachusetts—used electrified fencing to deter would-be escapees, but nothing nearing the lethal totality promised by Calipatria's death fence.

Inside the confines of the death fence the Calipatria facility rapidly devolved into an intensely dangerous environment for humans. California's carceral economy, dependent for its lifeblood on the caging of disproportionately poor, African American, Latinx, Native American, and disabled people, grew rapidly from 1990 to the early 2000s, peaking in 2006 at nearly 163,000 imprisoned people.[73] In California, as in the rest of the United States, the system of incarceration has functioned in an institutionally and systematically racist way, targeting communities of color and disproportionately caging nonwhite men. In 2010, for example, African Americans made up only a little more than 6 percent of the state's population but nearly 30 percent of its jailed population. Three-quarters of all incarcerated men in California by that decade were nonwhite. At Calipatria, prison policies aimed at discouraging "race riots" encouraged segregation, with interpersonal violence maintaining the borders of racial groups—violence that in turn allowed guards to implement increasingly intimate searches of imprisoned people and their visitors. Overcrowding had prompted the warden at Calipatria to institute "double-celling," a system born of desperation in which two people are housed in a cell designed for one, in the prison's earliest years of operation. By 2008, two years after the all-time peak in California's prison population, Calipatria's population stood at 184 percent of its design capacity. Centinela was staggeringly worse at 215 percent.[74]

Guards threw the switch on the death fence in November 1993, sending four thousand volts of electricity through a wire grid thirteen feet high and sandwiched between two other razor wire–topped fences. The force of the electrical current encircling the prison was literal overkill, providing more than four times what it would take to kill a human. Signs posted in English and Spanish warned people away. Observers across the state and country watched, some in disgust, others in anticipation of a plan that would soon sprout similar death fences in prisons all over California and the United States.

What they saw, almost immediately, was death—not of humans but of birds. In the first seven months after the fence was operational at least eighty birds, including several endangered burrowing owls, alighted on the fence and were electrocuted. Despite a "warning wire" along the ground meant to deter terrestrial creatures by delivering a mild shock, several rabbits also died against the fence.

Bird conservationists responded rapidly and fervently. Newspapers carried the story of bird deaths all over the world, publishing for French and German readers the numbers of birds that fell victim to the death fence. Even the prison's spokesperson, an enthusiast of the fence's lethal threat to humans, lamented the loss of bird life: bird deaths were "something we don't want to happen," and the prison committed itself to doing "whatever we have to do to keep [the birds] out of here."[75] Prison authorities protested in their own defense that they had tried to account for the threat to wildlife—just look at the warning wire for bunnies!—but "they figured the birds would know better."[76] As birds died at Calipatria, the state of California was busily erecting death fences throughout the state. Within five years such fences encircled twenty-five of the thirty-three CDCR prisons. U.S. Fish and Wildlife officials estimated the loss of bird life due to electrocution on the fences at three thousand.[77]

In the face of international outrage that a fence designed to kill incarcerated humans turned out to be a threat to wildlife, CDCR sprang into action. Bad press coverage of their death fences simply would not do. They hired an ornithologist to study the fence's design and propose ways to keep birds from coming near it. They consulted with state and federal wildlife agencies. They tried denuding the surrounding landscape of trees where birds might shelter. They tried to clean up food waste in the prison yard, creating new rules about where and when incarcerated people could eat. They installed owl decoys as deterrents. After five years of these kinds of attempts, they arrived at a multipronged, $150,000 solution: a net draped over the fence, strong enough to keep birds away but pliable enough that a person would be unable to scale it without falling into the fence to their death. For good measure, they added antiperching spikes atop the fence's posts, tiny passageways underneath the fence for burrowing owls, and, outside the prison, a duck pond that would entice waterfowl away from the fence's lethal wires. Through years of collaboration between Fish and Wildlife and Corrections and Rehabilitation, the state of California had finally created the world's first "ecologically sensitive death fence."[78]

If all of this feels bizarre, it should. The partnerships forged between state government agencies, such as the employment of incarcerated people to do the labor of maintaining wildlife refuges and the collaboration to build green death fences, reflect long-standing but muted patterns connecting *conservation* and *correction*. Protecting birds under the logic that a death fence should kill only humans might seem at first blush like a logical stance for mainstream conservation organizations; after all, they seek to care for the environment and not people. This perspective on environmentalism emerges from a particular kind of environmental politics that sees human welfare as at best secondary to ecological health and, at worst, a distraction from it.[79]

Even presupposing the claim that environmentalists can, should, and do care about plants and animals in a way that silos them from humans and from larger ecologies, those who are concerned about environmental quality would find much about mass incarceration to be troubling. Prisons commit devastating ecological vandalism.[80] Functioning like very condensed towns or small cities, prisons produce the same kinds of ecological impact as other communities of people but with considerably less regulation: they require vast inputs of resources (food, water, electricity, and raw materials for industrial work—incarcerated workers make products ranging from T-shirts to circuit boards) and produce even vaster outputs (air pollution, chemical waste, solid waste, and sewage).[81] Imprisoned people increasingly undertake highly toxic work, such as electronics recycling. In one Florida women's prison the jailed workers were directed to smash computers with hammers to get at their valuable internal components, a process that released a cloud of cadmium and lead dust into the air, poisoning the prisoners, the staff, and the nearby environment alike.[82]

California's state prison system has been charged with multiple major water pollution problems, including a 700,000-gallon sewage spill into the American River from Folsom Prison and a 220,000-gallon spill from the notorious California Men's Colony facility in San Luis Obispo. Consistent overcrowding in California prisons has meant that prison infrastructure is grossly overtaxed; when it comes to, say, sewage systems, this overcrowding has dramatic ecological consequences. Poorly regulated prison factories emit toxic chemicals and other noxious compounds into the air, soil, and water. Prisons have been fined for falsifying reports on hazardous waste emissions and failing to update infrastructure for properly disposing of noxious effluent. Like the military, prisons have also been exempted from state and federal regulations on the use and disposal of hazardous products and chemicals.[83] Nonetheless, between 2013 and 2018 federal and state environmental agencies made more than 1,300 charges against prisons across the country for violating the Clean Air Act and the Clean Water Act.[84]

These kinds of problems apply to the prisons surrounding the Salton Sea, compounding the area's already daunting ecological challenges.[85] In 2000 the California Environmental Protection Agency initiated a civil liability complaint against the Centinela prison for failing to properly disinfect its wastewater, which it discharges into the New River. It was a situation made worse when the prison also had a sewage spill in the same year.[86] Calipatria failed to meet the state's mandate to divert half of its solid waste destined for landfills numerous years in a row. Chuckwalla Prison has its own EPA identifier as a federally recognized hazardous waste site.[87] Nearby, Ironwood State Prison has been repeatedly cited for overtaxing its sewage system, with orders to undertake conservation measures. To comply with these conservation measures, the CDCR placed limits on imprisoned people's access to water by installing toilets with flush limiters, low-flow urinals and shower heads, and hot water solenoid valves to cut the amount of hot water prisoners can use.[88] In other words, CDCR sought to mediate its own structural problems by passing the burden on to the people whom it caged.

Environmental impacts traveled both ways. Even as the prison created environmental problems for the surrounding area, the Salton Sea and the Imperial Valley created conditions that contributed to the debilitating environment *inside* Calipatria. Nearby livestock feedlots and kill lots produced a pervasive stench of manure, fertilizer, and animal bodies. The sea's frequent bird and fish die-offs and algal blooms smothered the prison with the smell of rotten eggs. Wind storms blew noxious particulate matter across the yard. The pesticide-laced dust crept into all corners of the cell blocks.[89] Signs posted in the Calipatria prison's visitors' waiting room in the 1990s warned them against drinking the water because of contamination, although prison officials did not provide alternative water sources for incarcerated people. These impacts on the bodies and lives of inmates were not unique to those near the Salton Sea. From arsenic-contaminated water in California prisons, to radon gas exposure in a Connecticut facility, to air pollution from toxic ash in a jail sited above a coal mine in Kentucky, prisons have been seething sites of environmental injustice.[90] At times the cycle of environmental harm, from nature to marginalized people, is easy to see: one Central Valley facility had dangerous levels of heavy metals in the prisoners' drinking water, a problem that then passed through imprisoned peoples' bodies into the local ecosystem, polluting the San Joaquin River's delta.[91]

Meanwhile, the same blistering heat waves that accelerated the evaporation of the Salton Sea and contributed to the drought conditions that decrease the amount of wastewater flowing into it from the Imperial Valley also baked the walls of the desert's prisons. Of the five CDCR facilities most vulnerable to extreme heat events, four—Centinela,

Calipatria, Ironwood, and Chuckwalla—sit close to the Salton Sea. By the first decades of the twenty-first century, climate change had already increased the number of days of extreme heat in this part of the state; the CDCR anticipated a fivefold increase in the number of days when the temperature would rise above 112 degrees Fahrenheit after the year 2031. By 2019 most CDCR prisons were relying solely on outdated evaporative cooling systems that, by the agency's own admission, "provide[d] little relief in extreme heat events."[92] Their proximity to the receding shoreline of the Salton Sea meant that in addition to the health risks of extreme heat, prisoners continued to experience noxious dust storms of pesticide-polluted playa and particulate matter—two factors that would likely increase incidents of respiratory disease and other illnesses. This, combined with CDCR's abysmal record of providing adequate health care to imprisoned people, compounded their experiences (and embodiments) of environmental injustice.[93]

Calipatria's electrified fence made fleeing these kinds of conditions a death sentence.[94]

Clearly, around the Salton Sea and elsewhere in the prison systems across the United States the environmental injustices of incarceration ranged from physical conditions in and around prisons, to working conditions for incarcerated laborers, to prison food systems, to poor health care, and beyond.[95] In form as well as function, jailing mass numbers of people relies on problematic, if not dangerous, exertions of power and control over the relationships incarcerated humans have with the natural world. Prisons are designed and imagined as spaces siloed from nonhuman nature; even the language used to describe incarceration ("being inside" versus "being outside") implies that imprisonment entails enclosure from the environment, creating what literary critic Sarah Nolan calls "extreme nature deprivation" as part of an already overwrought system of punishment.[96]

This has created a set of injustices specific to Indigenous people, who are overrepresented in the U.S. prison system and have the highest per capita rate of incarceration of any nonwhite group.[97] Because Indigenous worldviews and religious practices often emerge from close care for human-nature relations, nature deprivation stands in direct violation of Native human and religious rights.[98] As described in a submission to the United Nations Committee on the Elimination of Racial Discrimination by a joint committee of numerous Native organizations and tribes, "increasing restrictions on Indigenous prisoners' religious freedoms pose a direct threat to the cultural survival of Indigenous communities in the United States. Given the large and growing incarcerated Indigenous population, the inability of Indigenous prisoners to freely practice their religion has a potentially severe impact not only on the prisoners themselves but also on the broader, often tribal, communities to which they return."[99] In other words, incarceration poses a direct threat to Indigenous sovereignty, Indigenous survival as individuals and as nations, and Indigenous futures.

In 2008 these concerns rose to the fore within the bird-friendly death fence of Calipatria, the desert prison with a view of the shrinking Salton Sea. Ralph Martinez, an Indigenous man incarcerated at Calipatria, sued CDCR for violations of his and other incarcerated Natives' religious rights, specifically naming their right to access sweat lodges, to smudge, to consult with Native spiritual leaders, to receive sacred objects, to host powwows, and to ceremonially use tobacco. The lawsuit specifically called on the CDCR to provide "buffalo bones, brass beads, goat lace or sinew, wooden beading looms, nylon thread, small sea shells, glass seed beads ('including red and blue beads'), crow beads, needles, rabbit skin, beaver skin, cowhide, rattlesnake skin, deer skin, porcupine quills, coyote teeth, and wire hooks made of silver and gold" for the crafting of religious objects and "pipe, pipe bag, tobacco, kinnikinnick, bitter root, sage, cedar, sweet grass, copal, angelica root, drum and drum sticks, rattles, prayer stick, flute, medicine bag, abalone shell, tree wood/kindling, mo[l]cajete or a stone grinding bowl, eagle feathers, hawk feathers, buffalo or deer skull, antlers, [and] a water dipper" for prison-maintained sweat lodges.[100] Martinez's suit came with the support of 126 other Native people incarcerated by CDCR who signed declarations of support; twenty-five of these declarations came from other people caged in Calipatria. Martinez's case succeeded in getting a judge to order Calipatria to hire a Native American spiritual leader (NASL), host two powwows per year, and allow regular sweat lodge ceremonies. The courts, however, denied his request that the order apply to all Native people incarcerated by the CDCR as a class. Eventually, Martinez and state officials settled.

Three years later the CDCR rolled back all of these provisions, claiming an "emergency" need to remove imprisoned Native people's religious rights to have sacred medicines, prayer ties, beads, and pipes and dramatically curtailing sweat lodge ceremonies. In 2013 the CDCR made these "emergency" restrictions permanent, despite vociferous objection by Native prisoners.[101] Opposition to these renewed restrictions came, again, from inside Calipatria's death fence: in 2017 Gregory Rhoades, another Native person incarcerated in that prison within view of the Salton Sea, filed a writ of habeas corpus demanding his rights to religious objects such as tobacco.[102]

These struggles of imprisoned Native people against the CDCR point to the fact that the injustices inherent to incarceration, environmental and otherwise, are experienced in specific ways by Indigenous people. This reality has carried through the history of the Salton Sea, connecting Tacho's murder to other forms of carceral control in the desert: forced labor on chain gangs, patterns of confinement in and escape from the Imperial Valley's jailhouses, and conservation projects undertaken by unfree workers. The physical world of the sea changed dramatically under the power of these systems of incarceration and the power of incarcerated workers' muscle and grit. In the waning years of the twentieth century, as imprisonment reached a grinding crescendo in California in terms of both political impact *and* numbers of people trapped inside, it became clear that cages, sea, and land would continue to work on one another to produce strange new realities in this part of the state. This settler-built carceral world revolved around environmental degradation, racial domination, and Indigenous dispossession as three prongs of a unified project. The people within this world, however—to say nothing of the birds soaring above it and the winds blowing through it—showed the capacity to move toward something different.

8

TOXINS

The cause and the chemistry vary from my homeland to yours, but each of us can name these wounded places.

—Robin Wall Kimmerer, *Braiding Sweetgrass*, 2013

CAUSE AND CHEMISTRY

Dichlorophenoxyacetic acid—better known as 2,4-D—is among the most effective of what are called "systemic" herbicides. As opposed to contact herbicides, which kill the parts of a plant that come into direct contact with the spray, systemic herbicides seep into the plant itself, moving throughout its tissues, from roots to leaves. Used correctly, these kinds of systemic killers function most effectively to attack perennial dicot (or broadleaf) plants, thus preventing dicots from surviving season to season. The 2,4-D herbicide works by imitating an auxin—a plant hormone—and attacking the cells of a plant that deliver water and nutrients to its leaves. Rather than killing the plant's cells outright, it triggers out-of-control cell growth, functioning as a kind of artificially induced cancer. Drowning in its own nutrients, an affected plant's leaves curl in on themselves, its stem twisting and sinking to the ground. Within ten days or so, it dies.

In 1947, just two years after 2,4-D was made commercially available in the United States, Imperial Valley farmers began dousing a species of dicot plants they considered prickly and prolific nuisances—the desert's mesquite trees—with the new herbicide.[1] The stands of mesquites cultivated over centuries by Cahuillas and Kumeyaays in the area surrounding the Salton Sea had become over a few short decades a pest to settlers who wanted to clear them from the land to make room for non-Native food crops. They soaked the soil at mesquites' roots with up to two hundred gallons per acre of a diluted 2,4-D solution, watched the trees' leaves curl in on themselves and the branches swell and split, and then flooded the area to wash away any residual chemical that might harm their crops. 2,4-D, in turn, drained into the canal system, which carried the herbicide downslope to the Salton Sea.

As it moved from the nozzles of farmers' sprayers, through the cells of mesquite trees, through the soil, into canals, and into the Salton Sea, 2,4-D mingled with a myriad of other toxic substances draining into the sea in the latter half of the twentieth century. The sea's water and soil contained lead, arsenic, bisphenol, selenium, molybdenum, cadmium, copper, nickel, zinc, and polychlorinated biphenyl (PCB), as well as dichlorodiphenyldichloroethylene (DDE), diazinon, sodium hypochlorite, atrazine, cyanuric acid, and chlorate. Close examination of the water's murky depths would yield evidence of toxic levels of ammonium perchlorate, chlorpyrifos, chromium, carbofuran, zinc, malathion, boron, and carbaryl.[2] Waste from the Salton Sea Test Base alone included many of these contaminants, in addition to asbestos, trichloroethylene, carbon tetrachloride, mercury, dielectric fluid, fuel oil, diesel fuel, and petroleum hydrocarbon. In other words, the sea's water and soil told its own history—one that, like the history of the twentieth-century United States, revolved around the industrial pollutants and heavy metals that transformed the country's economy and ecosystems over the course of six decades. In these decades, the sea effectively became an archive of the toxins that had come to characterize the post–World War II industrial economy.

By the end of the century researchers found it nearly impossible to pinpoint the sources of most of these different pollutants. As a sump for agricultural farms in the Imperial Valley and as the terminus of a vast quantity of water from the Colorado River and ephemeral rivers and streams, the Salton Sea served as the final stopping place for a wide range of toxic inflows. After the completion of the All-American Canal, the Colorado drained a remarkable array of industrial pollutants from major swaths of the West through the Imperial Valley's canals and directly into the Salton Sea. The exploitation of farm laborers played a crucial role in toxic pollution coming from both sides of the U.S.-Mexico border, from pesticides sprayed on fields without regard for workers' health, to increasingly toxic workplaces in Mexicali's maquiladora factories. Meanwhile, the noxious conditions of the sea resulted not only from chemicals but from toxic overloads of bacteria. This chapter traces those inflows, looking to the major sources of pollution that have degraded the sea's environmental conditions, as well as the larger social milieu that produced and enabled those toxic flows. Like the combined effects of chemical toxins, heavy metals, and lethal levels of toxic bacteria that killed birds and fish by thousands in the 1980s and 1990s, this history speaks to the deadly new world that emerged from the amalgamation of settler technology, nature, and change over time.

2,4-D was invented for the purposes of war, not food production. In the early 1940s scientists working for American Chemical Paint Company (ACP) sought a good way to clear broadleaf plants from war zones. At the company's headquarters on the Lenni-Lenape Nation's homeland in Ambler, Pennsylvania, ACP chemists formulated 2,4-D as part of their work on synthetic growth regulators. Despite the compound's lethal effectiveness, the strategy of weaponizing chemical defoliants did not alter the course of World War II. Two decades later, however, this strategy—and 2,4-D—*would* become central to the U.S. war in Vietnam. In Vietnam a cocktail of 2,4-D and 2,4,5-T (trichlorophenoxyacetic acid) rained down on the Vietnamese countryside under a now-notorious pseudonym: Agent Orange, just one of a range of weaponized chemical products American companies sold to the U.S. military.[3]

Years before it flowed from low-flying U.S. planes to defoliate enemy lines in Vietnam, farmers across the United States bought up 2,4-D and 2,4,5-T by the millions of gallons, unaware that these herbicides unleashed the chemical compound known as dioxin, a by-product that could harm humans' reproductive systems, immune systems, and hormones.[4] Farmers to the north and south of the Salton Sea sprayed 2,4-D and 2,4,5-T liberally on their own fields, eager to clear the land of what they considered nuisance plants: mustard, star thistle, radish, morning glory, and hoary cress, in addition to mesquites. The ester form of 2,4-D, farmers noted, worked well on the aquatic plants that grew in stands of water along their canals and at the Salton Sea—cattail, tule, burr-reed, and kelp—particularly when they mixed it with diesel fuel. With help from researchers employed by the University of California, they experimented with 2,4-D and 2,4,5-T on their food crops, spraying mixtures of the herbicides on oranges, lemons, apricots, plums, and grapefruits or testing them separately on cereal grains, broccoli, cabbage, sugar beets, tomatoes, and beans.[5] The Agricultural Commission helped, providing power sprayers that could be used by any farmers who wanted to tackle a plant or insect infestation or unwanted growth of plants.

Farmers' giddy deployment of chemical compounds that had been developed as weapons of war did not begin or end with 2,4-D and 2,4,5-T. With support from agricultural researchers and state agencies, Imperial and Coachella settlers dusted and sprayed their fields, crops and weeds alike, with almost every product released by chemical companies in the postwar years.[6] They used organophosphate products like diazinon, parathion, and malathion, which had originally been developed as chemical nerve agents for deployment in war zones before researchers discovered that they harmed insects as well as enemy combatants.[7] They reveled in the effectiveness of organochlorine compounds, a class of chemical pesticides renowned for their toxicity to insects and stability in environments of all kinds. Organochlorine pesticides included lindane, endrin, chlordane, heptachlor, endosulfan, isodrin, and dieldrin, as well as large quantities of perhaps the most notorious banned pesticide ever produced by humans—dichlorodiphenyltrichloroethane (DDT)—all of which emerged from labs doing research and development for the military in World War II.[8]

By 1949 Imperial County officials were approving permits for more than 3 million pounds of insecticides annually.[9] By 1952 that number had skyrocketed: in that year alone Imperial County farmers applied for permits to disperse 9,719,725 pounds of insecticides and 1.5 million gallons of herbicidal sprays.[10] Rather than being put off by the military origins of products like DDT, Imperial residents and farmers found their wartime origins quite alluring. They waited impatiently for that "new wonder insecticide," available on military bases nearby (but not to consumers and farmers), to be approved for sale to civilians.[11] The *Palm Springs Desert Sun* reported on the new dearth of bugs bothering enlisted men after a DDT spraying at the army base outside of Palm Springs, speculating with bated breath about when the new pesticide might be available in town as well.[12] In the *San Bernardino Sun* in a political cartoon feature called "Aunt Het," the titular character gazed at a newspaper with her flyswatter in hand and proclaimed, "'I hope I live 'till this war is over and folks can get that DDT. For once in my life I want to live in a house that flies and ants can't live in.'"[13] Aunt Het would not have to wait long. By the fall of that year consumers would be able to test out the new "wonder insecticide" for themselves.

To be sure, there were objections to this toxic bonanza in those early years, though newspapers picked up few of them in comparison to the rave reviews they enthusiastically published. Among the most outspoken groups immediately after DDT's release to the public were beekeepers, who quite reasonably grumbled about the widespread use of chemicals designed to kill bugs.[14] Some early advertisements by local hardware stores selling pesticides cautioned buyers of their dangers. "We have now in stock the new DDT spray," one Imperial store informed potential shoppers. "It is a good insecticide—of that there is no doubt. However, it has many dangers to people, beneficial insects and plant foliage" and should be used with caution.[15] A study released by the state's Division of Entomology and Parasitology in 1944 offered a milquetoast warning against the unfettered use of DDT, concluding that farmers should consult with their local agricultural commissions— which were enthusiastically in favor of pesticide use—before spraying their fields.[16] These few objections aside, pesticides were treated as miracle inventions and used in products ranging from powders to be dusted under kitchen sinks, to wallpaper and interior paint, to aerial sprays that would blanket streets and farms alike. In the Imperial Valley impatience to use DDT and other new poisons hit an inflection point in the summer of 1948, when a polio scare prompted Calexico officials to spray a 10 percent DDT solution over parks and other public areas. Imperial went further, choosing to err on the side of caution and aerial-spray the entire town.[17]

GEOGRAPHIES OF HARM

As the postwar decades wore on, the fact that a glut of pesticides flowed from Imperial and Coachella Valleys directly into the Salton Sea began to cause some concern, though it was often muted in comparison to the enthusiasm of pesticides' many advocates. By the early 1960s newspapers had begun reporting on studies revealing that Salton Sea fish already carried chemical body burdens from pesticide compounds. These studies alarmed residents to the north and south of the sea as well as the many tourists who visited the area.[18] By the end of that decade academic and government researchers alike were fretting about whether humans should consume Salton Sea fish, given the amount of chemical pesticides flowing into the water from Imperial and Coachella Valley farms.[19] In response to studies like these, locals expressed concerns about the effects of pesticides on the environment and particularly whether the Salton Sea and its fish, birds, and water were safe.[20]

These concerns ran aground against the profit motives of huge business interests. Pesticide companies, as well as growers, food distributors, and other components of the vast web of U.S. agribusiness, had vested interests in countering public anxieties quickly and skillfully, a task at which they came to excel.[21] Deeply committed to seeing pesticides as an overall good for people and for markets, government regulators in the 1950s and 1960s consistently refused to place restrictions on their use and sale; courts demurely declined to punish pesticide companies and applicators when people brought suit.[22] Even environmental organizations, with majority-white membership and leadership, sought to split the difference when they weighed in on pesticide issues at all, calling for bans on spraying in national parks and other wilderness areas but not on food crops or residential areas.[23]

These dynamics played out around the Salton Sea in the 1960s and early 1970s in ways that reflected larger national patterns. In 1966, for example, the chief legal counsel for the Imperial Irrigation District traveled to a conference at the University of California, Davis, on pesticides and agricultural wastewater.[24] He returned to the Imperial Valley to reassure farmers, hoteliers, and tourists that the vast volume of pesticide-laced water coursing through the valley to the Salton Sea posed no threat. The sea was safe, he insisted, for swimming, boating, and waterskiing despite the fact that a full 70 percent of its inflow drained from farms. "Waste waters that travel any distance," he averred, "do not retain harmful effects."[25] Though devastatingly incorrect, this perspective reflected a larger tendency among industry and government stakeholders alike to see pesticides as innocent until proven guilty, as well as then-dominant views about the static nature of pesticide toxicity.[26]

This framing of the issue in terms of proximity to sprayers revealed public officials' conceptions of who mattered and who did not. The race and class politics of who was in regular proximity to the pesticide spraying would not have been lost on Imperial Valley residents and Salton Sea tourists in these booming years of agricultural production. The suggestion that the death-dealing effects of pesticides like DDT, diazinon, and heptachlor did not travel long distances might reassure people who had the time, money, and inclination to recreate on the Salton Sea's beaches, splash in its warm and briny water, and grill its abundant fish for their dinner. It would do nothing, however, to assuage any concerns about exposure for the people working in the fields being sprayed and dusted. In effect, this framing isolated the risk of chemical pesticides to already-vulnerable farmworkers laboring in Imperial and Coachella Valley fields, effectively detoxifying the Salton Sea—in discourse if not in fact—and drawing any sense of risk away from privileged tourists. The workers in the fields where the risk remained, by implication, did not matter much.[27]

Late spring of 1969 brought unusually cold weather to the desert. In an area that sometimes reached 90 degrees Fahrenheit in early May, in 1969 the temperature barely broke into the sixties during the day. At night it dropped an additional twenty degrees. Bundled into blankets and sleeping bags, a group of people slept overnight on the eastern shore of the Salton Sea, staying warm under the meager light of a waning crescent moon.

They had spent the day walking from the north and would continue their march south as soon as the sun rose. They would be joined by thousands of people from either side of the international boundary line in a demonstration of support for farmworker-led boycotts of California-grown crops like grapes. In what came to be known as the "March to the Border," these activists, most of them union organizers and farm laborers from Coachella Valley, would draw wide coverage from media during a time marked by dramatic and powerful labor rights campaigns.

Among these protesters who camped that cold night on the shore of the Salton Sea was a nineteen-year-old farmworker named Amalia Uribe, who had grown up in Coachella fields. Like farmworkers across the state, she spent her days following her parents, siblings, uncles, aunts, cousins, and friends into the rows of tomatoes, beans, and alfalfa that sprouted from the Cahuillas' desert homeland. From the age of ten at the dawn of that decade to its close as she entered adulthood, Uribe witnessed horrifying working conditions. As a teenager, Uribe and other workers experienced itchy eyes, blurred vision, nausea, excessive sweating, and bright red rashes, conditions that worsened when the fields had been freshly sprayed. Their employers refused to provide any information about the pesticides they used. Her brother, who worked in the fields alongside her, suffered acute pesticide poisoning so extreme that any time he returned to recently sprayed or dusted fields, his symptoms flared up again.[28]

Although she had not yet turned twenty, Uribe's fury about exploitative working conditions in the fields spurred her to early leadership in the United Farm Workers (UFW). The activism that would come to be associated with the UFW had been launched in early May 1965, when a Filipino-American labor organizer named Larry Itliong led the Agricultural Workers Organizing Committee (AWOC) in a strike against Coachella Valley grape growers—not far from where Uribe labored with her family. After a weeklong strike, the growers partially conceded, agreeing to increase worker pay from $1.25 to $1.40 an hour, though they refused to draw up contracts with strikers. The following autumn Itliong partnered with Filipino organizers Philip Vera Cruz and Pete Velasco to bring a strike in what would become the most famous stand against farmworker exploitation in California history: the Delano grape strike. Eight days after Itliong, Vera Cruz, and Velasco spurred an AWOC vote to begin their strike, they were joined by Dolores Huerta, Cesar Chavez, and the UFW.[29] Throughout the remainder of the decade and into the 1970s the UFW would emerge as one of most transformative social movements in United States history.

In the May 1969 March to the Border, Uribe walked hand-in-hand with other organizers, singing "De Colores" while wearing a straw hat emblazoned with the UFW eagle.[30] At the end of the march she watched Cesar Chavez and other UFW leaders deliver speeches at a five-thousand-person rally in Rockwood Plaza, named for founder of the California Development Company who made the fateful cut that ushered the Colorado River into the Salton Sink. The following month Uribe and other organizers sought to solicit support among workers at an Indio labor camp run by a notoriously antiunion grower, Mike Bozick. Calling the organizers "agitators" who were "disturbing his workers," Bozick seized Uribe and two other activists (including Cesar Chavez's brother Richard) and held them illegally until the sheriff arrived.[31]

Across the United States and in the Imperial and Coachella Valleys, farmworkers like Uribe and her family were often the first people to identify the human health consequences of widespread pesticide spraying and dusting in fields in which they toiled. In fact, the most ardently antipesticide positions in the United States in the 1960s appeared not in the pages of Sierra Club and Audubon Society publications but in the United Farm Workers' newspaper, *El Malcriado*.[32] Farmworker organizers identified pesticide poisoning as a central labor rights problem in the early part of the decade; by the end of the 1960s the problem of pesticides was positioned at the heart of the UFW's multipronged strategy for wresting power from California growers who exploited their labor.

If marches and unionizing marked two of the major UFW strategies in those years, lawsuits were the third. On April 1, 1969, the month before she marched to Rockwood Plaza with other organizers, camping at the

Salton Sea along the way, Amalia Uribe set in motion a lawsuit that would go on to do more to regulate California pesticide use than nearly any other major lawsuit (including the much better-known case, *Atwood Aviation v. Morley*).[33] On that day Uribe drove to the office of the Riverside County agricultural commissioner, Robert M. Howie, and requested to see reports of pesticide applications filed with the commission by commercial pest control companies. These reports contained a deluge of information: the name of the operator, the location of fields being sprayed or dusted, quantities and concentrations of the pesticides, and to what kinds of crops the chemicals had been applied. Most crucially for Uribe, they contained detailed data about the chemical ingredients of pesticides used in the fields where she and her family worked. With this kind of information, farmworkers experiencing symptoms they suspected of being those of pesticide poisoning could take blood tests that would give them definitive answers. Howie refused to turn them over; Uribe, with the help of a lawyer who worked for the union, sued.

A California appellate court finally decided the case in 1971 in favor of public release of the kinds of spraying reports that Uribe had demanded—although on the grounds that such public access to information could help researchers develop more effective poisons, rather than on the grounds that workers like Uribe and her family needed to know the chemicals they had been exposed to in order to get proper health care. The outcome of this case, launched by a young woman working on desert Cahuilla land in Coachella Valley, put to rest other pesticide-related lawsuits initiated by the UFW Organizing Committee. Although this history is most often remembered in the context of the Delano grape boycotts in California's Central Valley, many of its most transformational components played out in Coachella Valley on the northern edge of the Salton Sea. The bodies of farmworkers, like the sea itself, absorbed the consequences of the bonanza of pesticides in this part of California.

The damage done by pesticides to Indigenous worlds, in the Cahuillas' homeland and beyond, did not go unnoticed by Native peoples. By the 1990s Native weavers in California had organized around toxic threats to culturally sensitive plants.[34] The contamination of local plants like the desert's mesquites posed cultural threats, as they restricted Native peoples' access to crucial resources for maintaining traditional weavings, foodways, and ceremonies. They also created physical threats to the people—mostly to women—who gather and harvest plants. In 1995 these concerns coalesced in a petition from the California Indian Basketweavers Association (CIBA) to the U.S. Environmental Protection Agency. The petition requested the inclusion of their sacred plants—for the most part designated by settler regulatory agencies as weeds—in the category of crops, which would offer some restrictions against the use of herbicides on tule, arrow-weed, mesquite, and other culturally vital plants.[35] Even oak trees, whose acorns are a cultural and nutritive staple for many Indigenous peoples in California, were doused with herbicides under the logic that they competed with settlers' crops, making them dangerous for traditional uses or, perhaps worse, unavailable altogether. Basketweavers and culture bearers worried for their own health, noting that gathering materials and making baskets required putting the plants in their hands and mouths. They fretted for the plants, too. "A major component of being a basketweaver," CIBA board member Dee Dominguez pointed out in 1997, "is ensuring that our basket materials are healthy. . . . We have to have a healthy plant to have a healthy basket."[36]

In 1994 CIBA's board issued a policy statement about pesticide risks, declaring that "when we harvest and use these plants, or take fish or game, we want to know that they are free of poisons. We want the assurance that we are not endangering our health or that of our children and unborn generations."[37] "The costs of pesticide use to people, wildlife, and ecosystems," CIBA noted, "is immense, often personal and tragic, and can never be justified by economic gain."[38] CIBA's anti-pesticide actions revealed the clear interconnections between settler agriculturalism, the health of ecosystems, and Indigenous lifeways. From the point of view of CIBA, pesticides functioned as a physical manifestation of settler colonial power over Indigenous peoples and cultural practices, endangering basketweavers and traditional gatherers as they engaged in crucial activities that maintained cultural continuity and revitalization.[39]

In their condemnations of the costs of pesticides, they might well have been describing the targeted spraying of mesquites by farmers armed with 2,4-D in the 1940s or a cloud of organophosphates blowing off an alfalfa field in the 1990s.

TOXIC INFLOWS, OR, HOW TO LEARN TO STOP WORRYING AND LOVE THE NEW RIVER

The New River, which feeds the Salton Sea from the south, originates in Mexicali. From Mexicali it traverses the international border, skirting the city of Calexico on the west. Just before it crosses Interstate 8—nicknamed the Kumeyaay Highway in this part of California—it curls around the western edge of one of the desert's incongruously green golf resorts. Following an inexorable, downward path toward the Salton Sea, the New River continues to pass by highways and roadways, sliding past sloughs and irrigation canals that serve any number of Imperial Valley croplands. It kisses the western edge of the town of Brawley and courses past yet more thirsty golf greens. Inconceivably straight lines of drainage ditches provide more water to swell its flow downslope. At the end of its journey, as it enters the Salton Sea, it flows directly into an easement for the Sonny Bono Salton Sea National Wildlife Refuge, its effluent swirling into the salty water where hundreds of birds flock every day.

Beginning in the 1970s the New River became widely known, and frequently described, as the most polluted waterway in the United States. The water it dumped into the Salton Sea carried the residues of myriad kinds of human activity upriver: pesticides and alkaline, solvents and acids, and gallon after gallon of untreated human sewage. The New River's reputation was preceded by its stench, which, beginning in the 1940s, turned notoriously foul due to the lack of sewage treatment infrastructure in Mexicali communities south of the border as well as in Calexico and other towns north of the border.[40] During that decade conflicts between Calexico, Brawley, and Westmorland arose from those towns' refusal to adequately update their sewage systems.[41] They did not do so until the late 1960s; before then, their untreated sewage flowed directly into the New River. Communities in the Imperial Valley also

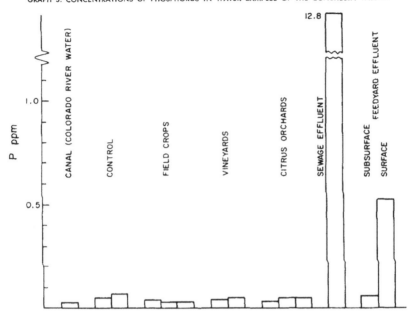

30. This graph from 1973 shows the amount of phosphorus in Coachella Valley water from various sources. Sewage effluent was by far the largest contributor. J. J. Oertli and G. R. Bradford, "Contributions to Water Pollution from Agricultural and Urban Sources in the Coachella Valley," *California Agriculture*, July 1973.

located dumps, with varying degrees of treatment, in the New River floodplain.

By 1992 the New River was carrying between ten million and twenty million gallons of raw sewage across the border every day, and this flow headed directly downhill for the Salton Sea. In the early 2000s the New River grabbed headlines on both sides of the border when liquid discharged from the Don Fileto slaughterhouse in Mexicali, which provided meat to food distribution companies in the United States and Mexico (including two major U.S. meat suppliers: Jensen Meat Company and American Beef), turning the entire river a stomach-churning shade of red.[42]

Deprived of the regular fluctuations of the Colorado River that had formed its channel, the New River has no natural inflow. Every drop of its effluent comes from runoff of one kind of human activity or another. And while environmentalists and policy makers in the United States tend to point to Mexico as the source of the New River's noxious conditions, many of the river's pollutants enter its water *north* of the border. For example, in the early 1990s two tons of the selenium that passed from the New River to the Salton Sea came from the Imperial Valley, and six and a half tons came from the Alamo River. Only half a ton of this pollution originated in Mexico.[43] The Alamo River, whose inflows come almost entirely from farms north of the border, carries dangerous levels of boron, selenium, and DDE; this river, however, is almost never described with the levels of alarm and disgust that characterize the much-maligned New River.[44]

In 1995 the *Los Angeles Times* put a fine point on the disgust with which the New River is generally regarded. "Like a toxic stew," the newspaper reporter opined, "the New River flows inexorably into the United States: pea-soup green in color and texture, laden with fecal matter and carcinogens, topped with detergent foam, and carrying the virus that causes polio and the bacteria that cause typhoid and cholera." The river, the *Times* went on, carried "the human and industrial wastes of Mexicali into the Imperial Valley with impunity . . . run[ning] past schools and tumbledown neighborhoods in Mexicali before reaching the U.S. border at Calexico. Then it winds an additional 60 miles north through some of the richest farmland in the world before dumping its load—now with the added wallop of agricultural pesticides—into the troubled Salton Sea."[45] In this description, the river's pollution appeared as a unilateral, and nauseating, threat, coursing from Mexico to the United States in an unrestrained border crossing that threatened the health of the Imperial Valley and the "troubled" Salton Sea.

The reflex to blame Mexico for the New River's, and thus the Salton Sea's, problems emerged from a deeply rooted trend in American environmental thought: reserving environmental stewardship to whites and blaming environmental ruin on people of color. As ecoliterary theorist Sarah Jaquette Ray has argued, "Disgust shapes mainstream environmental discourses . . . by describing which kinds of bodies and bodily relations to the environment are ecologically 'good,' as well as which kinds of bodies are ecologically 'other.'"[46] Had the *Times* taken a closer look at the characteristics of the effluent that turned the New River so noxious, its analysis might have gone beyond a dichotomy of "human and industrial wastes" on one side of the border and "the richest farmland in the world" on the other. In 2001 the California Environmental Protection Agency summed up the river's troubles in ways that offered a different balance of responsibility for the pollution, noting that while the New River carries waste from Mexico, its pollution mostly derives from domestic wastewater and agricultural return flows from the Imperial Valley.[47]

The combination of noxious chemicals, bacteria, and heavy metals that pass from Mexicali into the United States via the New River has earned it the title of the country's most polluted waterway. The New River's contents reflect ecological, economic, and industrial conditions in its Mexicali watershed as well as in the Imperial Valley. However, while the disgust directed toward the New River tends to suggest—or outright declare—that Mexico is to blame for these conditions, most of the blame for the river's environmental problems originated in one way or another in the United States. The United States and the larger, uneven power relations and economic statuses of the two countries, reinforced and exaggerated by global economic policies, create the conditions that bring the New River and its contaminated contents across the border at Mexicali and into the Salton Sea. No example illustrates this more clearly than the maquiladora industry, which reshaped the Mexicali economic and environmental landscape in the late decades of the twentieth century.

The maquiladora system allows for non-Mexican companies to exploit the lower wages and fewer regulations in Mexico's export processing zones to manufacture goods for easy export to the United States. So that owners and managers, as well as goods (but not workers) can easily cross into the United States, most of these plants were built close to the Mexican side of the U.S.-Mexico divide. The first wave of factory-building was initiated by the Border Industrialization Plan of 1965 and increased dramatically in the wake of the Mexican financial crisis and devaluation of the peso in 1982. A boom in maquiladoras in the 1980s transformed cities and towns along the eastern end of the border, most notably Ciudad Juárez. Western border communities like Tijuana and Mexicali followed suit; by 1988 Mexicali had the third-largest population of maquiladora workers behind Tijuana and Ciudad Juárez.[48]

When the ink dried on President Bill Clinton's signature at the bottom of the North American Free Trade Agreement (NAFTA) in 1994, the die seemed forever cast for the Mexican border region. NAFTA doubled down on the binational view of the region as a manufacturing zone for U.S. consumer goods, transforming the social and ecological landscape of the borderlands. In Mexicali, as elsewhere along the border line, factories sprang up as businesses incorporated for manufacturing goods, from textiles to paper products and from electronics to corrugated steel. By the early 2000s Mexicali was hosting scores of factories that in turn transformed the landscape and the environmental health conditions of what had previously been primarily an agricultural region.[49] Even before NAFTA the maquiladora system had earned a reputation for creating devastating environmental consequences, intensified by dramatic power imbalances between the Mexican government's environmental regulatory body (the Secretaría de Desarollo Urbano y Ecología, or SEDUE) and the non-Mexican-owned companies backed by the economic power of the United States and the enforcement power of free trade mediators like the World Trade Organization and the World Bank.

SEDUE faced the constant challenge of policing illegal and unreported discharges of hazardous wastes from chemical-intensive industrial plants. Witnessing rampant pollution streaming (often literally) out of the maquila corridors, the Mexican government sought to increase its regulatory power, passing stricter environmental controls on toxic waste in 1987 and emphasizing a 1986 international agreement with the United States that included restrictions on transboundary hazardous waste created by U.S.-owned companies in Mexico. Throughout this process, economic and political power imbalances between the United States and Mexico created vast environmental problems with health consequences for humans and nonhumans on both sides of the border.

These consequences, however, did not fall evenly; the environmental impacts of industrialism rarely do.[50] The post-NAFTA boom in industrial facilities along the border did not coincide with a boom in infrastructural development and social support networks; low-income housing, schools, well-lit streets, policing, and plumbing did not follow the hundreds of thousands of workers who arrived in border cities.[51] These workers, often having experienced multiple displacements already, found plenty of work at the border but often resorted to makeshift approaches for necessities such as housing, clean water, food, and schools for their children. Mexicali grew to bursting, from a city of 64,500 that mostly supported local agricultural in 1950, to 510,000 in 1980, to nearly 700,000 in the early decades of the twenty-first century.[52] However, competing free trade opportunities in countries like China, as well as the economic recession in the United States in 2008–10, saw tens of thousands of these jobs fall away, and scores of plants were shuttered, leaving workers again displaced with few options other than to undertake yet another migration for work—this time, typically into the United States.

During the height of the maquila boom, factory managers sought out young women for their workforces, creating a labor environment that was segregated by both race and gender. "'Small, foreign, and female'" became the watchwords for employers seeking out pliable workforces the world over, in what amounted to a feminization of the global assembly line.[53] In Mexican maquilas, such as those in Mexicali, this meant a workforce of young women who were often primary caregivers for young children or who supported other family members—elderly parents, grandparents, and sometimes unemployed spouses or brothers.

Booms in population without corresponding booms in infrastructure development spelled disaster, particularly for women. Major environmental justice concerns arise at both the "core" and "periphery" of maquila and other factory workplaces—at work and at home.[54] In the workplace, underregulated factory environments involve workers spending long days handling noxious chemicals: solvents, paints, acids, and other chemical compounds.[55] Workers reported experiencing headaches; sores on their hands, mouths, and noses; disruption of menstrual cycles; frequent miscarriages—all symptoms of acute exposure to toxic chemicals.[56] This kind of exposure is compounded by other physical stressors present in maquiladora workplaces. Workers are expected to labor for long hours, six or seven days a week, with few breaks. Their work involves repetitive motions, increasing the likelihood of debilitating stress injuries. Workers often report experiencing detrimental impacts on their eyesight from spending many hours focused on small component parts of the products they assemble, leading to shortsightedness and other chronic vision problems.[57]

As this surge of population at the border with no corresponding surge in infrastructure created consternation among binational actors concerned about the New River, few mechanisms existed to measure or regulate hazardous chemical waste from the factories.[58] Maquiladora managers routinely, and notoriously, discharged waste illegally into the nearby arroyos and *colonias*, often waiting until it rained so that liquid waste would mingle with rainwater runoff. Even after rigorous binational efforts at regulation in the 1990s and 2000s, the New River still carried more than 150 cubic yards of trash across the border per year, pesticides remained a problem, and at least 20 percent of the phosphate that drained through the New River watershed eventually reached the Salton Sea.[59]

A view of the Salton Sea as part of the borderlands weaves together the industrial development of Mexicali, and its ecological consequences, with the sea's own history and current conditions. An ecological map of the region, rather than a political map, underscores the relationships between workers in Mexico who are exposed every day to the environmental injustices of industrial work, and the Cahuillas north of the Salton Sea who inhale polluted playa from a rapidly evaporating sea.

CONSEQUENCES

By the last decade of the twentieth century, crop dusting had rendered the air above the Salton Sea, stretching from the Coachella Valley to the north and the Imperial Valley to the south, as saturated with noxious carcinogens as its water—if not more so. Like California's other major agricultural zones, particularly the Central Valley, abysmal air quality created dangerous conditions for both humans and nonhumans. The state's maps of air pollution overlapped with these zones of highest agricultural activity; in a state notorious for air pollution problems in its cities, particularly in traffic-clogged Los Angeles, the rural Imperial and Coachella Valleys rivaled urban areas for the highest rates of airborne class B carcinogens in the state.

For Torres Martinez Cahuillas, the problem of air pollution came from a number of sources. Pesticides blew off of farmers' fields, mingling with dust from the rapidly evaporating Salton Sea, which still covered 40 percent of their reservation. Over the course of the twentieth century settler communities and the state of California had targeted the Torres Martinez Reservation for environmental harm, constructing on their land sources of pollution ranging from a sludge dump to electronics waste facilities. On Torres Martinez land the stench from the Salton Sea's regular fish and bird die-offs competed with the noxious reek of an unregulated, illegal sewage dump, pushing Torres Martinez people and their allies into action to protect their land from ongoing toxic incursions. By the 1990s that reservation had assumed the common designation of "the most polluted tribal land in California," a devastating description for the people who had lived on this land and maintained their relations with its plants and animals throughout their long history.[60] If it was the "most polluted" reservation land in the state, that designation came through no fault of their own but rather from targeted environmental racism combined with the deadly cumulative effects of benign neglect.

The sludge dump was a prime offender. Beginning in 1989, truckloads of a by-product of human sewage processing, known simply and with unfortunate accuracy as "sludge," arrived from San Diego, Orange, and Los Angeles Counties, to be dumped on a 120-acre allotment on the Torres Martinez Reservation. The dump had originally been authorized by the allottee, who had not cleared this with the tribe and who then moved away from her land. As Southern California municipalities faced growing, and self-created landfill crises, producing more solid waste then they had space to dispose of, they pushed the limits of dumping on Native land (and other places they considered marginal) past their legal, ecosystemic, and moral bounds.[61]

In 1994 Torres Martinez people and their allies took a stand against the unauthorized importation of sludge. They formed a human blockade, reinforced with chain-link fencing and railroad ties, to stop huge, sludge-filled trucks from rumbling onto their land. On protest lines and in meetings, activists' fierce determination was met with defiance from industry representatives, militancy from local police, and ambivalence by local, state, and federal stakeholders. The only thing government representatives seemed sure of was that Native protesters were overreacting. Joe Loya, then the Torres Martinez band's tribal clerk, furiously called them out on their hypocrisy: "You can't smell it, you can't see it, you can't feel it, you can't choke on it, unless you're here."[62] Policy makers and business executives, in other words, could feel comfortable denying the extent and danger of the dump because they did not experience it in person. Loya's frustration echoed long-standing concerns about the ways this part of California had in general long been regarded as marginal.

The scene of the 1994 protests could describe any number of standoffs between Native communities and polluting industries throughout the late twentieth century. It could describe the Diné resistance to Peabody Coal mines on the sacred Black Mesa or Northern Cheyenne defiance of fossil fuel companies seeking to mine methane gas from their homeland. These could have been Ajachemen protests against the development of a toll road in coastal Southern California or the efforts of Kānaka Maoli to protect Mauna Kea from the construction of the largest telescope in the world.[63] It could, for that matter, describe the historic—and heroic—assembly of Native Water Protectors against the Dakota Access Pipeline (DAPL) at Standing Rock on behalf of the Missouri River.[64] In each of these instances Native people have gathered to protect sacred sites, water, earth, their families, and neighbors from the onslaughts of environmentally disastrous industrial projects.

A map of these resistance struggles would suffice as a map of contemporary Indigenous experiences of environmental injustice, which occurs when the settler colonial relationship between the United States and Indigenous people facilitates the targeting of Indigenous communities and lands for environmental harm.[65] Like CIBA's efforts to protect sacred plants from pesticide contamination, struggles against these environmental injustices go beyond demands for a clean and livable environment: these Indigenous environmental justice movements desire decolonized human relations to the nonhuman world, promoting what historian Joshua Reid has termed "traditional futures."[66] In seeking out these decolonized relations, these movements place Indigenous ecological knowledge, political sovereignty, cultural practices, foodways, languages, and homelands at the center of what might otherwise be shorthanded as simply "environmentalist" politics. Moreover, the Torres Martinez Cahuillas' protests against the sludge dump shared another quality with those of the #NoDAPL water protectors and other Native environmental justice movements: the end result of their work would create more livable conditions for everyone in the region, not just tribal members.

Creating more livable conditions for people living near the Salton Sea had become a struggle with life-and-death stakes by the opening decades of the twenty-first century.[67] In 2003 a farm-to-city agreement meant to alleviate chronic water shortages in Southern California's densely populated coastal counties diverted irrigation water from Imperial Valley farms to San Diego. Officials knew that this would cut off most inflow to the Salton Sea, so the agreement came with a mitigation strategy to divert additional water to the sea for fifteen years. Even so, between 2003 and 2016 the acreage of exposed shoreline previously covered by water grew from 862 to 16,452.[68] Predictably, as soon as that fifteen-year plan expired in 2018, the Salton Sea began to recede at an alarming rate, exposing more and more shoreline to desert winds. The fine particles of dust stirred up by the desert's windy climate contain salts, pesticide residues, heavy metals, and other toxicants. Studies by the U.S. Geological Survey anticipate that every three-foot decline in the Salton Sea's water level will expose an additional 11,000 acres of lakebed.[69] Other researchers anticipate a 40 percent reduction of the sea's water volume before 2025, which would "expose several square miles" of contaminated dust.[70]

These conditions have created alarming public health concerns for communities all around the sea. Chronic exposure to the particulate matter kicked up in dust storms can lead to negative impacts on cardiac and pulmonary health and may also worsen allergies, vulnerability to allergic diseases, and eye diseases.[71] Probably most distressingly, researchers have linked this kind of windborne air pollution to a range of childhood respiratory illnesses, particularly asthma. By 2017 three times more children were being rushed to emergency departments to be treated for asthma in Imperial County than anywhere else in California.[72] For an area in which the vast majority of residents are nonwhite and most live below the poverty line, these health threats create seething conditions of environmental injustice.[73] Poor air quality is compounded by the combined effects of contaminated drinking water, proximity to hazardous industrial facilities, agricultural pesticide application, low representation or ineffective representation in the governing bodies that make decisions about environmental quality concerns, and so on.[74]

Elevated rates of air pollution impacted the nonhuman world in troubling ways too. High concentrations of noxious particulate matter in the air restricts the photosynthesizing capacities of native desert plants. Meanwhile, sulfur dioxide from power plants in adjacent areas (like the Mojave) and nitrogen from vehicular exhaust have complicated impacts on plants and animals, often to the detriment of the desert's shrubs, grasses, and diverse communities of animals.[75]

Together these factors combine to underscore the urgency, and the intersections, of conservation and public health at the Salton Sea. Community-based environmental justice organizations, and particularly the Comite Civico del Valle, amassed a range of highly impactful programs that serve local residents and address growing problems such as childhood asthma.[76] The Torres Martinez Cahuillas likewise continue to link environmental impacts at the Salton Sea with long-standing impacts of colonization that have undermined their sovereignty and self-determination in ways that link environmental and human health.

These ongoing struggles around pesticides, polluted rivers, farmworkers' health, and sludge dumps have revealed more than the imbrication of environmental and social justice concerns. They have also demonstrated that the Salton Sea, so long a body of water that has influenced the region by what kinds of inflows it has received—inflows of birds, bombs, tourists, and poisons—had in the early decades of the twenty-first century begun to assert its influence via its outflows—evaporation and dust. The desert winds kicked up dust particles that carried the lingering effects of decades of pollution to nearby residents' lungs. As the water evaporated, the Torres Martinez Reservation and other sea-adjacent communities watched the shoreline recede into the distance, disappearing from under the wings of wetland-dependent birds. Meanwhile, the reticence of policy makers to make the Salton Sea a priority for conservation followed unjust contours of representation and privilege; residents of desert towns and cities—overwhelmingly people of color and Indigenous peoples—lacked the political and economic clout of wealthier and whiter communities. Journalists reported the increasingly alarming conditions at the sea, wondering at times, as one reporter did in a headline in 2015, "Why don't Californians care about saving the Salton Sea?"[77] National news outlets ran series on the problem, asking similar questions. Local communities mobilized despite this sense of apathy, developing strategies to care for their families and neighbors through public health initiatives while also partnering with conservation organizations that focused primarily on the Salton Sea as a crucial wetland resource for birds and fish.

One such organization launched a campaign to raise awareness about threats posed to the Salton Sea. The group called the initiative Save Our Sea, or SOS. In 2017 the group formed the letters SOS with their bodies on the shore of the Salton Sea, a human distress signal for the troubled body of water that lapped just beyond the reach of their fingertips.[78] To defend an environmental resource that few see as "pure" nature, that seemingly exists only as a list of incongruous, even comical, contradictions (a sea in a desert, a wildlife preserve that poisons wildlife, a body of water in which fish suffocate, a human-made wetland) has proven to be a nearly impossible project, even when paired with the urgency of a public health crisis.[79] This area has been regarded as marginal, a place where, as Joe Loya framed the problem, not being there to see, smell, and feel the impact of toxic pollution has enabled and preserved the notion that the Salton Sea's evaporation does not matter. Intentionally or not, this creates consequences for the people who live here, breathe the dust in the dry air, and care about the birds, fish, and soil.

The Salton Sea has become an archive of twentieth-century toxins, the drain for the pesticides and industrial pollutants that have shaped and enabled agriculturalism and manufacturing in the post–World War II world. Its water and lakebed index this history and link it to other geographies—other "wounded places," as botanist Robin Wall Kimmerer describes them in the epigraph to this chapter. However, the movement of toxins through the ecosystem—through the tissues of mesquite trees, along the banks of the New River, into the bodies of laborers, and in dumping grounds near the sea's shoreline—illustrates more than the toxicity of the postwar economy. It reveals how the systems that produced these conditions, with their reckless impacts on humans, trees, birds, fish, and water, reflect the broader outcomes of settler colonialism and its toxic relationships to land and people.[80]

CONCLUSION

A HOW-TO GUIDE TO SAVING THE SALTON SEA

Decolonization never takes place unnoticed.
—Frantz Fanon, *The Wretched of the Earth*, 1961

LAKE CAHUILLA: AN UNSETTLED SEA

In 2020 the Torres Martinez tribal council sponsored a poster project to honor the sea and its role in Cahuilla life. They chose the theme "the past, present and future of the Salton Sea." The contest came about as part of a workshop designed to increase awareness about the sea's various environmental problems and to share plans for its future.[1] The art, submitted by children as young as six as well as by adults, teemed with life. One poster depicted blue water coursing under rich brown mountains that glowed in pink and purple sunsets, while people danced around a fire on the water's edge, some shaking the kinds of gourd rattles used in accompaniment to the Bird Songs. In another, mesquite trees dotted the foreground, their leaves rendered as fish along a cracked shoreline, suggesting both a fish die-off *and* a resurgence of bountiful mesquites with full overstories. In one painting a sun glows red, yellow, and orange over cinnamon-hued mountains while a rush of blue water runs by, with brightly colored fish visible on the water's surface; on a nearby hill a family of quail etches a trail to the water along a green riverbank. A collage paired archival photographs of Cahuilla ancestors with contemporary shots of kids learning to shake Bird Song rattles and playing in schoolyards. Another painting showed dancers clad in finely detailed ceremonial regalia spinning against a textured blue background, a giant golden moon hanging over them. In the rich blue paint that represents both the sea and sky, the artist etched the words "I dance."[2]

These artworks represented a view of the Salton Sea that stands in stark contrast to the endless images of rot and decay that regularly color outsiders' perceptions of it. In these Cahuilla artists' eyes, the sea is a vibrant and rich body of water, teeming with fish, birds, trees, and people—an *un*settled sea, contiguous with the body of water that has been used for military target practice and farm water runoff but one that holds different stories and different promises for the future. These might, in fact, be two seas, with differences but not discrepancies—one that reveals the power of settler colonialism to reshape the landscape to its own ends and one that reveals that this has always been and always will be a failed project.[3] Throughout its history, local Native nations have viewed the sea as part of a cycle of flooding that has occurred in their homelands for hundreds of years. Thus, even while its maintenance (and mismanagement) by settlers has created problems of environmental injustice and land dispossession for them, many Native people have considered it part of a larger Indigenous world with which they seek to maintain good relations.[4]

Cahuillas, Kumeyaays, Chemehuevis, Quechans, and the desert's other peoples have done extensive work to give the Salton Sea the future it deserves, as reflected in these artists' vibrant posters. They have regularly petitioned the state of California and the federal government to direct resources to respiratory health care, dust suppression, and soil testing that would lessen the harm the sea's conditions pose. Basketweavers go to the sea's shoreline to gather materials, refusing to see it through the lens of danger and decay that has so shaped many perceptions of its worth. Torres Martinez Cahuillas have partnered with the Salton Sea Authority, the central policy-making team that has been working with state and federal governments in revitalization efforts since the 1980s, to assess mitigation plans to save the sea and reduce the harm of its evaporation on local residents and wildlife.

Indigenous studies scholar Laura Harjo has called these kinds of quotidian practices of asserting Native sovereignty in social, political, and cultural life part of a broader "futurity praxis."[5] In California this praxis has not been limited to actions around the Salton Sea. Through Bird Songs and *kewéts*, ceremonies and basketweaving, language revitalization and political self-determination, Native peoples of the desert establish their sovereignties and build self-determined futures. These assertions of sovereignty are not new but rather part of an unbroken chain of resistance, cultural revitalization, self-determination, and memory-keeping over the course of more than two centuries of colonization.[6] Nor are they unique to the Native nations of the Colorado Desert. Dedication to decolonized Indigenous futures in the first decades of the twenty-first century have been reflected in the "(re)writing, (re)righting, and (re) riteing" of Native worlds all across North America—further evidence that one of the projects at the center of settler colonialism, Native elimination, continues to fail in the face of Indigenous survivance.[7]

This context of assertions of Native sovereignty go a long way toward explaining the stark contrasts between how the Salton Sea is often depicted—as a place marked by rotting debris, foul odors, and little else—and how the Cahuilla artists painted it for the Torres Martinez poster contest. Reflecting on contemporary assertions of Native self-determination, Indigenous studies scholar Audra Simpson wrote in 2014 that "this is political life that, in its insistence upon certain things—such as nationhood and sovereignty—fundamentally interrupts and casts into question the story that settler states tell about themselves."[8] The unsettled sea, this latter-day incarnation of Lake Cahuilla, does the same to the settler Salton Sea, calling into question the stories—about nature, technology, and what it means to live a good life—that settlers have been telling themselves.

LAND BACK, RIVER BACK

Despite the title I used to lure you to this final chapter, proposing a concrete solution to the problems of the Salton Sea goes beyond the capacity of this book. As an environmental history, the narrative provided here instead seeks to examine the changes that took place over time to create the dilemmas and opportunities now present in this part of California.

The Settler Sea does, however, question the overarching context that shapes existing approaches to solving the Salton Sea's many challenges. One thread running through these chapters is a critique of settlers' relationships to the environment around them, as well as their relationships to Indigenous peoples. It follows from such an analysis that settlers' approaches to environmentalism bear critique as well. As environmental justice activists and scholars have been demonstrating for decades, what they call "mainstream environmentalism" has largely been organized around white people's environmental politics and priorities. A more diverse array of perspectives on environmental problems and environmentalist solutions, to be sure, can more effectively address the complex sets of challenges we face.[9]

These questions of *whose environmentalism* we follow when it comes to the Salton Sea—as well as when it comes to myriad other environmental challenges—matters. Vast networks of people, from activists to lawmakers to artists to engineers, have endeavored for decades to find solutions to the sea's many environmental problems. Organizations and individuals alike have undertaken heroic efforts to mobilize resources to conserve the sea's water, protect its bird populations, and curtail the seething environmental health problems threatened by its receding shorelines.[10] Many of these efforts have been in partnership, in consultation with, or led by local Native communities, as well as organizations that represent non-Native residents of the area.

The stakes of this case, however, should remind us to consider solutions in a broader context. To borrow a phrase from Indigenous studies scholar Dean Itsuji Saranillio, the staggering scale of environmental problems created in colonial contexts deserves solutions that "trouble certain commonsense logics that gatekeep the thinkable."[11] In other words, what solutions might exist if we broaden our horizons of possibility? What if the only appropriate solution to the problem of the Salton Sea is decolonization—and what would that look like?

Decolonization is not a metaphor but rather a historical process of repatriating settler-claimed lands, waters, and power (political, cultural, and economic) to Indigenous peoples.[12] As postcolonial theorist Frantz Fanon put it in *The Wretched of the Earth* in the 1960s, quoted in the epigraph to this chapter, "decolonization never takes place unnoticed"; it seeks to do nothing less than "change the order of the world."[13] While there are as many steps toward changing the colonial order of things as there are expressions of colonial power, the ultimate manifestation of it is land return (or, in marine environments, water return).[14] Land return can take a number of forms: on Ohlone homelands in California's Bay Area, some settlers have paid a tax for occupying Indigenous territory; other settlers have made use of protective covenants that allow Native use of their so-called property in perpetuity; and some municipalities have acceded to demands for land return by ceding certain areas to tribes.[15] Cases of land return have produced positive results for environmental conditions as well as for Native sovereignty, functioning as a form of ecological protection as well as decolonization.[16]

[margin annotation: ? Many of this message]

The Salton Sea's story begins with the Colorado River; it must end with the river too. Releasing the Colorado River to its original purpose must be a central component to any purportedly environmentalist solution to the problem of the Salton Sea. The river must be undammed, the massive plugs of concrete and iron removed from canyon walls, and the water allowed to make its own course through the Southwest. In short, decolonization at the Salton Sea and beyond looks like dam removal—not in the sense demanded by Edward Abbey in *The Monkeywrench Gang*, in which his manly settler antihero, George Hayduke, eyed the Glen Canyon Dam with wrath and revulsion. Rather, this kind of undamming would follow generations of Indigenous peoples who have identified dams as key enablers of their dispossession.[17]

Non-Native environmentalists and some environmentally inclined engineers have followed suit, arguing that undamming waterways can often be a fast and remarkably effective form of restabilizing damaged riverine ecosystems.[18] After all, these systems of dams and canals have not delivered on their promise of turning the West into a well-watered Utopia.[19] Instead, they have served to compound the dispossession of Native people from their lands and water sources and grow huge— and hugely unsustainable—settler metropolises in deserts.[20] Nor have dams delivered on promised results in terms of energy production; as of 2020 fewer than 3 percent of dams in the United States provided hydroelectric power.[21] In the first two decades of the twenty-first century Native communities advocated for dam removal as one step that could be taken to weave together land return and the repair of a wide range of damaged ecosystems connected to rivers.[22]

Non-Natives too

Decolonization must also address the militarized build-up of the U.S.-Mexico border and allowing resumption of the human, animal, and plant migration back and forth over that border that constituted its political and ecological reality for thousands of years before being arbitrarily designated in 1848. Border tribes like the Kumeyaay and the Tohono O'odham Nations have long resisted increased militarization of the border, refusing to allow federal agents to pursue undocumented migrants on their border-bisected homelands and protesting any federal infrastructure to be erected to reinforce the line. This work has preserved ecological conditions along the border even as it underscores the fact that the border holds meaning only for the U.S. and Mexican states—not for the long-established sovereignties of Native nations in these contested areas.[23]

The Salton Sea demonstrates the limits of settler forms of environmentalism and environmental management. All the received wisdom of what constitutes environmental action—changes in individual consumption patterns (asking people to be slightly better consumers), engineering miracles, more meticulous wildlife management—falter in the face of this particularly wicked problem. These are short-term solutions that might temporarily stave off disaster or produce "less bad" outcomes but in no way lead to acceptable solutions to environmental challenges. Even broad visions of ecological holism falter because of their naivety regarding local ecological conditions and deep historical knowledge of places and their environmental possibilities.[24] U.S.-style environmentalism has fallen short by virtue of being a political movement that, as noted by environmental historian Paul Sutter, is "dominated by the colonizers, not the colonized."[25]

In short, the Salton Sea functions as a microcosm of the precariousness of the settler world, not just settler approaches to environmentalism but settler epistemologies about human relationships to nature and to one another. Other solutions are needed—and, more important, other solutions are *possible* if we expand our notions of what environmentalism might look like.

The Salton Sea's story revolves around precarity, but it is by no means alone.[26] In fact, the history of settler colonialism in the West tells of little *more* than bare precarity. Pipelines break. Dams crack. Reservoirs fill with silt. Tailings ponds leak. A landscape of dams that do not water the West. Aquifers dry up. The West as a region teems with evidence that the Enlightenment vision of the natural world as a passive and insensate machine that, with its gears properly oiled, could sustain endless human progress has been a shimmering, immaterial, and deadly fantasy.[27] The Salton Sea's very precariousness—the way it sits uncomfortably between worlds, existing always in the interstices of human and natural influences, between desert and wetland, between the skyward pull of the sun and the constant inflow of polluted water—is both a symptom and a symbol of the larger precariousness of settler relationships to the environment, in the West and beyond.

Imagine the river released. Imagine the land returned to its Native relations. These are not impossible futures for the Salton Sea. If the set of proposed solutions to this problem can envisage giant energy-guzzling desalination plants or think about gouging a canal from the sea to the Gulf of California or launching great barges full of water and plants to keep wild birds alive—all solutions to the problem of the Salton Sea that have been proposed in recent decades and could feasibly be part of its short- and medium-term conservation—surely we can also imagine something less radical and more revolutionary: a decolonized future for the river, the desert, and the rest of us.

ENVIRONMENTAL HISTORIES FOR THE FUTURE

The current stand of water in the desert came into being at the beginning of the twentieth century with a quintessential drama of settlers trying their luck at dryland farming with stolen water and on stolen land. It ended that century mired in water shortages and climate change— environmental problems deeply embroiled in settlers' mismanagement of the nonhuman world.[28] In between, as this book documents, the Salton Sea served as a microcosm of the twentieth-century West, reflecting back to us—sometimes with the exaggerated distortions of a funhouse mirror—the major forces that have shaped that century's western environmental history: dryland irrigation, Indigenous dispossession, dam-building, militarization, pesticide-intensive agriculture, labor exploitation, tourism, prisons and policing, and wildlife conservation.[29] The only thing more impossible than saving the Salton Sea is continuing to live with the conditions that made it this way in the first place. Ultimately, we cannot continue to live in a world where colonization and dispossession are built into the landscape in a way that organizes and enables settlers' everyday lives at the expense of Indigenous peoples. In the long term (which is looking shorter every day), these environmental outcomes of colonization go beyond impacts to Indigenous peoples, redounding on all non-Native people, white settlers included. In his 1999 history of the Salton Sea and its surrounding environs, historian William deBuys proposed to think about the Salton Sea, sitting in a basin two hundred feet below sea level, as a place where consequences collect.[30] It is a compelling metaphor. However, it framed the problems of the Salton Sea as an end point—consequences collect here, and wallow in this benighted place, left in their own squalor. As *The Settler Sea* illustrates, consequences may collect here, but they do not stay put. Nor are the consequences of settlers' actions the only way to understand the Salton Sea and its past, present, and future.

Scholars of Indigenous history have shown that our responsibilities as historians must be not only to understand the past but also to understand how stories about the past shape how we collectively imagine the future. Historian Jean O'Brien, for example, has demonstrated how historical narratives of "firsting" (as in settler mythologies of being native to the landscape, or "firsting" themselves) and "lasting" (as in settler stories of Native people belonging only and irrevocably to the past) have functioned as helpmates to colonization and Indigenous dispossession.[31] Shaping history through firsting and lasting makes colonization seem manifestly natural, part of a progressive teleology of history.

Environmental historians understand the stakes and the possibilities in questions about how stories about the past shape the future. We are tired, as a general rule, of stories of decline precisely because these narratives, in which humans endlessly and universally destroy and deplete the natural world around them, leave so little room for hope or a sense of future possibilities.[32] In addition, any investigation of how historical events have been influenced by both nature and humans—a question at the heart of environmental history—reveals that the outcomes of these interactions are rarely predictable. "Following the twists and turns" of environmental history in the United States, as Patricia Limerick has noted, "has the pleasant effect of reviving one's sense of contingency, improbability, and even implausibility."[33] This leaves environmental historians with plenty of good reasons to craft historical narratives that attend closely to the intersectional formations of social power that have made anthropogenic destruction of nature *seem* universal. An approach that attends to diverse environmental histories also provides a narrative infrastructure that allows for future possibilities that are so much more interesting—and hopeful—than decline.

Just as certain kinds of actions on the natural world have foreclosed particular futures—as, for example, the use of the Salton Sea for farm runoff did for its otherwise-guaranteed future of evaporation in the 1920s—certain stories about human relationships to the environment foreclose possibilities for alternative futures. The insistence of many environmental scholars to universalize human harms to the environment (such as they do when they think of the "Anthropocene" without specifying that it has only been particular kinds of humans engaged in capitalist industrialism that has pushed all of us into a new geological epoch) makes it hard to think about a future with reciprocal and more balanced relationships between people and planet.[34] As environmental historian William Cronon reminded us in 1992, historians make important choices about framing their narratives.[35]

These choices have consequences. May we choose well.

NOTES

A NOTE ON NAMING

1. Preston J. Arrow-Weed, "Xa-Wiilth-Kaw-Tai (The Big Water): Lake Cahuilla—The Salton Sea," *Desert Report*, September 2016, http://www.desertreport.org/wp-content/uploads/2016/09/DR-Fall2016-Online.pdf.
2. William Phipps Blake, "Lake Cahuilla: The Ancient Lake of the Colorado Desert," *Out West Magazine*, June 1909.
3. Blake, *Report of a Geological Reconnaissance in California*, 228–29.

INTRODUCTION

1. Schoenherr, *Natural History of California*, 368.
2. Wilson, *Seeking Refuge*.
3. DeBuys and Myers, *Salt Dreams*, 99–121; Zappia, *Traders and Raiders*; Shipek, *Pushed into the Rocks*, 11–13.
4. Roger Birdseye, "America's Dead Sea Is Curbed Forever," *New York Times*, March 29, 1925.
5. "Bill Proposes Salton Sea as Drainage Basin," *Los Angeles Times*, December 8, 1925.
6. Andrés, *Power and Control in the Imperial Valley*, 59–60.
7. McWilliams, *Factories in the Field*; Leonard, *Making Ethnic Choices*; Andrés, *Power and Control in the Imperial Valley*.
8. Mike Davis, "A Prison-Industrial Complex: Hell Factories in the Field," *The Nation*, February 20, 1995. Historian Benny Andrés has traced how growers on either side of the international border line in this region established a "racialized, hierarchical labor force" in what amounted to an "international interracial borderland." Andrés, *Power and Control in the Imperial Valley*, 8.

9. McWilliams, *Factories in the Field*.

10. Hundley, *Great Thirst*, 394–97; Wilson, *Seeking Refuge*, 158–64.

11. Voyles, "Environmentalism in the Interstices," 211. See also Chris Clarke, "Why Don't Californians Care about Saving the Salton Sea?," KCET, October 15, 2015, https://www.kcet.org/redefine/why-dont-californians-care-about-saving-the -salton-sea; Matt Simon, "The Salton Sea: Death and Politics in the Great American Water Wars," *Wired Magazine*, September 14, 2012.

12. Social theorist Jodi Melamed has offered a succinct explanation of the forces undergirding the concept of *racial capitalism*, first developed by Marxist theorist Cedric Robinson in *Black Marxism* in 1983. Capital, Melamed explained, "can only accumulate by producing and moving through relations of severe inequality among human groups. . . . These antinomies of accumulation require loss, disposability, and the unequal differentiation of human value." "Racism," in short, "enshrines the inequalities that capitalism requires." Melamed, "Racial Capitalism," 78. By *nationalist enclosure* I refer to the kinds of enclosures — ideological, representational, and material — that delineate who belongs as a full citizen of the nation and who does not. These kinds of enclosures, which both police and produce the whiteness of citizenship, have occurred through the buildup of borders as well as through carceral control, policing, and immigration and naturalization policy. Mendoza, "Unnatural Border"; Mendoza, "Caging Out, Caging In"; Lytle Hernández, *Migra!*

13. Philosopher Kyle Powys White has argued that colonialism can best be understood "as a system of domination that concerns how one society inflicts burdensome anthropogenic environmental change on another society." Whyte, Adamson, and Davis, "Is It Colonial Déjà Vu?," 5.

14. For example, Indigenous feminist scholars Maile Arvin, Eve Tuck, and Angela Morrill have defined settler colonialism as "a persistent social and political formation in which newcomers/colonizers/settlers come to a place, claim it as their own, and do whatever it takes to disappear the Indigenous peoples that are there. Within settler colonialism, it is exploitation of land that yields supreme value. . . . Extracting value from the land also often requires systems of slavery and other forms of labor exploitation." Arvin, Tuck, and Morrill, "Decolonizing Feminism," 12. For other useful definitions that reflect this complex theorization, see Snelgrove, Dhamoon, and Corntassel, "Unsettling Settler Colonialism," 2; Kauanui, "'A Structure, Not an Event,'" 2; Tuck and Yang, "Decolonization Is Not a Metaphor," 5; and Lytle Hernández, *City of Inmates*, 8. Indigenous studies theorist Audra Simpson has offered an apt description, though not a definition, of settler colonialism as "a sturdy, structuring logic but also a shifting and impossible assemblage" — both concrete and molten. A. Simpson, "Whither Settler Colonialism?," 439–40.

15. For extended explanations of the environmental justice framework, see Pellow, *What Is Critical Environmental Justice?* For applications of this framework in Indigenous contexts, see Gilio-Whitaker, *As Long as Grass Grows*; Greaves, "Damaging Environments"; Hoover, *River Is in Us*; LaDuke, *All Our Relations*; LaDuke, *Recovering the Sacred*; Whyte, "Recognition Dimensions of Environmental Justice in Indian Country"; Whyte, "Indigenous Experience, Environmental Justice and Settler Colonialism," SSRN Scholarly Paper, Social Science Research Network, April 25, 2016, https://doi.org/10.2139/ssrn.2770058; and Whyte, "Settler Colonialism, Ecology, and Environmental Injustice."

16. Voyles, "Man Destroys Nature?"; Di Chiro, "Welcome to the White (M) Anthropocene?"

17. The slowness of environmental historians to take up questions of social power, particularly those organized around race and gender, has been well documented. For critiques of environmental historians' treatments of race, see Limerick, "Disorientation and Reorientation"; Melosi, "Equity, Eco-racism, and Environmental History"; Merchant, "Shades of Darkness"; Fisher, "Race and US Environmental History"; and Chiang, "Race and Ethnicity in Environmental History." For those oriented more toward gender, see Julie Cohn and Sara Pritchard, "Report on Gender and the American Society for Environmental History," February 23, 2017, https://aseh.org/resources/Documents/Report%20on%20Gender%20and%20the%20American%20Society%20for%20Environmental%20History.pdf; and Scharff, *Seeing Nature through Gender*.

18. As historian Kelly Lytle Hernández puts it, settler colonialism is a process in which "settler fantasies perpetually trend settler societies toward [the] ends." Lytle Hernández, *City of Inmates*, 8.

19. There is a range of public health studies that have examined the problem of air pollution connected to Salton Sea evaporation. I provide an overview in chapter 8. For an excellent summary of environmental justice concerns, including respiratory health, north of the Salton Sea in Coachella Valley, see London, Greenfield, and Zagofsky, *Revealing the Invisible Coachella Valley*.

20. For example, the Torres Martinez desert Cahuillas have undertaken an art project, Position Vector Salton Sea, that seeks to educate community members about this "emergent socioecological catastrophe" through both workshops and art. The Position Vector project "combines aspects of social justice, cultural recognition, youth outreach and human health to address the Salton Sea crisis through the lens of Indigenous knowledge and artistic expression." "Overview," Position Vector Salton Sea, https://www.tmsaltonsea.com/the-project. See also the concluding chapter.

21. Crosby, *Ecological Imperialism*, 7.

22. Langston, *Where Land and Water Meet*, 4.

23. Langston, *Where Land and Water Meet*, 5.

24. White, *Organic Machine*; Worster, *Under Western Skies*.
25. Pisani, *From the Family Farm to Agribusiness*; Pisani, *Water and American Government*.
26. DeBuys, *Great Aridness*; Reisner, *Cadillac Desert*.
27. Limerick, *Desert Passages*.
28. Bowden and deBuys, *Desierto*; Kuletz, *Tainted Desert*; Limerick, *Desert Passages*; Logan, *Desert Cities*; Pyne, *How the Canyon Became Grand*; Needham, *Power Lines*; Voyles, *Wastelanding*; Worster, *Dust Bowl*.
29. Limerick, *Desert Passages*; Voyles, *Wastelanding*; Kuletz, *Tainted Desert*; D. Davis, *Arid Lands*.
30. Worster, *Rivers of Empire*, 19–20.
31. Pisani, *From the Family Farm to Agribusiness*; Pisani, *To Reclaim a Divided West*; Pisani, *Water and American Government*.
32. Gifford, *Kamia of the Imperial Valley*, 9.
33. Settler colonial studies, Indigenous studies, and Indigenous history are fields unto themselves, though they are of course not entirely separate. Settler colonial studies has inspired a number of rich theorizations of power relations in settler societies such as the United States, Canada, Australia, and New Zealand. Wolfe, "Settler Colonialism and the Elimination of the Native"; Veracini, *Settler Colonialism*; Hixson, *American Settler Colonialism*. However, Indigenous studies scholars such as J. Kēhaulani Kauanui and Robert Warrior have pointed out the potential for settler colonial studies and some of its most powerful theoretical models to be used in ways that eschew the perspectives, lived experiences, and assertions of sovereignty among Indigenous *peoples* and thus insist that "Settler Colonial Studies does not, should not, and cannot replace Indigenous Studies." Kauanui, "'A Structure, Not an Event,'" 2, 3; see also Tuck and Yang, "Decolonization Is Not a Metaphor," 6. Indigenous history, meanwhile, looks to the ways in which Indigenous worlds have changed over time, including by asserting their sovereignty and contesting colonization. Indigenous history has, as a field, also provided rich frameworks for understanding different epistemological approaches to understanding historical change and how teleological (settler) models of history have been part and parcel of colonization itself. See O'Brien, *Dispossession by Degrees*; Lomawaima and McCarty, *"To Remain an Indian"*; O'Brien, *Firsting and Lasting*; Miller and Riding In, *Native Historians Write Back*; Lonetree, *Decolonizing Museums*; Denetdale, *Reclaiming Diné History*; Mt. Pleasant, Wigginton, and Wisecup, "Materials and Methods in Native American and Indigenous Studies"; L. Brooks, *Our Beloved Kin*; and Estes, *Our History Is the Future*.
34. For recent analyses of settler colonialism as an analytic framework in western history, see the articles in Lahti, "Settler Colonialism and the American West," which is a special issue of *Journal of the West*.

35. Coulthard, *Red Skin, White Masks*, 15.

36. Wolfe, "Settler Colonialism and the Elimination of the Native"; Veracini, *Settler Colonialism*.

37. Reid, *Sea Is My Country*.

38. Million, "'We Are the Land and the Land Is Us'"; LaDuke, *All Our Relations*; L. Simpson, *As We Have Always Done*; Whyte, "Settler Colonialism, Ecology, and Environmental Injustice."

39. See also Rifkin, *Settler Common Sense*; and Morgenson, "Biopolitics of Settler Colonialism." For a generative discussion of the complex and expansive natures Indigenous relations, see Todd, "Fish, Kin and Hope," 107.

40. Pellow, "Toward a Critical Environmental Justice Studies."

41. Lytle Hernández, *City of Inmates*, 8.

42. Lytle Hernández, *City of Inmates*, 7–8.

43. Day, "Being or Nothingness," 113.

44. Coulthard, *Red Skin, White Masks*, 14.

45. David Pellow has summarized the contributions of this scholarship: "Hundreds of studies have documented that people of color, people of lower socioeconomic status, Indigenous and immigrant populations, and other marginalized communities are disproportionately affected by ecologically harmful infrastructures, such as landfills, mines, incinerators, polluting factories, and destructive transportation systems, as well as by the negative consequences of ecologically harmful practices, such as climate change/disruption and pesticide exposure." Those studies have together documented "the troubling depths and breadth of environmental injustice's impact on the lives of people." Pellow, "Toward a Critical Environmental Justice Studies," 2.

46. Pellow, *What Is Critical Environmental Justice?*; Washington, *Packing Them In*; Sellers, *Hazards of the Job*; Mendoza and Voyles, *Not Just Green, Not Just White*.

47. MacGregor, *Routledge International Handbook of Gender and Environment*, 134.

48. Pellow, *What Is Critical Environmental Justice?*

49. Dhillon, "Introduction," 3; Yazzie, "Decolonizing Development in Diné Bikeyah." I discuss Indigenous frameworks for environmental justice more extensively in chapter 8.

50. Stringfellow, *Greetings from the Salton Sea*.

51. Preston J. Arrow-Weed, "Xa-Wiilth-Kaw-Tai (The Big Water): Lake Cahuilla—The Salton Sea," *Desert Report*, September 2016, http://www.desertreport.org/wp-content/uploads/2016/09/DR-Fall2016-Online.pdf.

1. DESERT

1. Patencio, *Stories and Legends of the Palm Springs Indians*, 3.

2. Cohen, "Managing across Boundaries," 135.

3. Walter C. Mendenhall, "The Colorado Desert," *National Geographic Magazine*, August 1909; Seiler, *Cahuilla Texts with an Introduction*; Wilke, *Late Prehistoric Human Ecology at Lake Cahuilla*; Shipek, "Myth and Reality"; Love and Dahdul, "Desert Chronologies and the Archaic Period in the Coachella Valley."

4. Gobalet and Wake, "Archaeological and Paleontological Fish Remains from the Salton Basin," 514.

5. Patencio, *Stories and Legends of the Palm Springs Indians*, 83.

6. Saubel and Elliott, *'Isill Héqwas Wáxish/A Dried Coyote's Tail*, 224.

7. Bean, Vane, and Young, *Cahuilla and the Santa Rosa Mountain Region*, 3-8.

8. Saubel and Elliott, *'Isill Héqwas Wáxish/A Dried Coyote's Tail*, 351, 1136.

9. This is according to Francisco Nombre, whose knowledge of these clans and other parts of Cahuilla culture and history was reported in Strong, *Aboriginal Society in Southern California*, 49. Túva', also spelled Tūva, is near present-day Agua Dulce. Saubel and Elliott, *'Isill Héqwas Wáxish/A Dried Coyote's Tail*, 1136. See also Bean, Vane, and Young, *Cahuilla Landscape*, 99.

10. Blake, *Report of a Geological Reconnaissance in California*, 100. Katherine Siva Saubel described the bathtub-like rings, pointing out that "the water line is clearly marked, showing how far up the water rose." Saubel and Elliott, *'Isill Héqwas Wáxish/A Dried Coyote's Tail*, 236.

11. Gifford, *Kamia of the Imperial Valley*, 12.

12. Schaefer, "'Now Dead I Begin to Sing.'"

13. Saubel and Elliott, *'Isill Héqwas Wáxish/A Dried Coyote's Tail*, 107; Zappia, *Traders and Raiders*.

14. Saubel and Elliott, *'Isill Héqwas Wáxish/A Dried Coyote's Tail*, 1136; Moerman, *Native American Ethnobotany*.

15. G. Phillips, *Chiefs and Challengers*, 26.

16. Gifford, *Kamia of the Imperial Valley*. Few Indigenous nations have been so variously named as the Kumeyaays; in different geographies and time periods, they have been known by non-Natives as the Cumia, the Kamia, the Diegueño, and the Ipai and Tipai Nation. The diversity of these names reflects the wide swath of the Kumeyaays' homeland and their expertise in cultivating a livelihood out of a plethora of ecosystems, stretching from the coast, across the foothills and mountains, to the deserts. Shackley et al., *Early Ethnography of the Kumeyaay*; May, "Brief Survey of Kumeyaay Ethnography"; Miskwish, *Kumeyaay*. For a breakdown of how anthropologists have described the Kamia people and differentiated them as a nation from the Kumeyaays, see Hedges, "Notes on the Kumeyaay."

17. Such conflict rarely escalated to the point of what we would call "war." Walker, *Indians of Southern California*, 10.

18. Trafzer, *Chemehuevi Song*, 17–18.

19. Zappia, *Traders and Raiders*. On the importance of trails and transportation all across present-day California, see Costo and Costo, *Natives of the Golden State*, 27–31.

20. Jerry Schaefer, "Scratching the Surface of Ceramics in the Colorado Desert: Petrographic and Neutron Activation Analysis of Three Lower Colorado Buff Ware Pot Drops," prepared for the Imperial Irrigation District by ASM Affiliates, February 2002.

21. "'Umu' pá' 'ípa' hempí'i' 'ípa' 'úmu' pá' qíqpimwe pá' hemhíchiwenive', pá' taxhemámikwenive' híchaxi' pé'em Táxswetem." Saubel and Elliott, *'Isill Héqwas Wáxish/A Dried Coyote's Tail*, 108.

22. "Kîll mípa' hemhéeñwive' míyaxwe"; "'Umu' tá' pé' hákushwe'." Saubel and Elliott, *'Isill Héqwas Wáxish/A Dried Coyote's Tail*, 119–21.

23. Dozier, *Heart Is Fire*, 86–94.

24. Romero, "World View of Tewa and Cahuilla," 66.

25. Schoenherr, *Natural History of California*, 365.

26. Tuck and Yang, "Decolonization Is Not a Metaphor," 5.

27. Anthropologist Zoe Todd has argued that it is vital to map watersheds and river systems into our understandings of Indigenous territories and homelands, as well as their reciprocal connections to "more-than-human beings" like fish and birds. Certainly the Colorado River's dynamic relationship to the desert world of the Cahuillas, Kumeyaays, and other contiguous nations is one such instance where it is important to "shift our concepts of territoriality to ones that incorporate watershed-level thinking in order to flesh out land-based understandings" of Indigenous worlds and politics. Todd, "From a Fishy Place," 51, 54.

28. Bovey, *Mesquite*, 56.

29. In some parts of the Colorado delta observers have reported mesquites forty feet high and eighty-five feet wide. E. R. Ward, *Border Oasis*, xx.

30. Harden and Zolfaghari, "Nutritive Composition of Green and Ripe Pods of Honey Mesquite," 523.

31. Bean et al., *Temalpakh (from the Earth)*, 63.

32. Moerman, *Native American Ethnobotany*.

33. These are according to August Lomas, a member of the Cahuilla Nation from the Martinez Reservation in the 1910s, as reported to Lucile Hooper. Hooper, *Cahuilla Indians*, 362. See also Heizer and Elsasser, *Natural World of the California Indians*, 109–10.

34. Clan name examples include the Sēwahilem, or the "mesquite that is not sweet clan," or Wavitcem, "many dead branches or mesquite beans." Strong, *Aboriginal Society in Southern California*, 87; Lewis, "Desert Cahuilla," 62.

35. Saubel and Elliott, *'Isill Héqwas Wáxish/A Dried Coyote's Tail*, 1314–15.

36. J. Brown, *The Salton Sea Region, California*, 114–16.

37. Cokinos and Magrane, *Sonoran Desert*, 54.

38. Strong, *Aboriginal Society in Southern California*, 51.

39. Lando and Modesto, "Temal Wakhish," 105.

40. S. Phillips and Comus, *Natural History of the Sonoran Desert*, 146.

41. Patencio, *Stories and Legends of the Palm Springs Indians*, 59; Cokinos and Magrane, *Sonoran Desert*, 24.

42. Kimmerer, *Braiding Sweetgrass*, 183.

43. "Kíll písh hemkenáviwe' pé'iy"; "'Achakwe' pemkúkulwe' pé' 'ílli'." Saubel and Elliott, *'Isill Héqwas Wáxish/A Dried Coyote's Tail*, 202–3, 655. This is a Cahuilla expression of what experts in traditional ecological knowledge (TEK) call the "honorable harvest." Kimmerer, *Braiding Sweetgrass*, 183. In Saubel's words, "Tuháyimani'chi' 'éxenuk taxtéewqa' híchaxi' 'áchakwe'" (Things were always supposed to be treated with respect). Saubel and Elliott, *'Isill Héqwas Wáxish/A Dried Coyote's Tail*, 203.

44. Lando and Modesto, "Temal Wakhish," 106.

45. Modesto and Mount, *Not for Innocent Ears*, 17.

46. Mendenhall, "Colorado Desert," 685.

47. Romero, "World View of Tewa and Cahuilla," 66; Bean, *Mukat's People*, 11–12.

48. Modesto and Mount, *Not for Innocent Ears*, 33–35.

49. Hooper, *Cahuilla Indians*, 329–33.

50. Shipek, *Pushed into the Rocks*, 1–2.

51. Bean et al., *Temalpakh (from the Earth)*, 201.

52. Bean et al., *Temalpakh (from the Earth)*, 149; Patencio, *Stories and Legends of the Palm Springs Indians*, 69; Saubel and Elliott, *'Isill Héqwas Wáxish/A Dried Coyote's Tail*, 102.

53. "Híchami' peqwá'qalipa' meqwá'qalipa' kú'aqalipa', pénga' pé' pé' pemchútwe' pé'iy máawli'"; "'Exenuk pemtéewwe' 'áchakwe' híchaxi' téma'li' yéwi Táxswetem." Saubel and Elliott, *'Isill Héqwas Wáxish/A Dried Coyote's Tail*, 103.

54. Doolittle, *Cultivated Landscapes of Native North America*, 44.

55. Patencio, *Stories and Legends of the Palm Springs Indians*, 94, 101.

56. Doolittle, *Cultivated Landscapes of Native North America*, 103; Lando and Modesto, "Temal Wakhish," 107.

57. Saubel and Elliott, *'Isill Héqwas Wáxish/A Dried Coyote's Tail*, 1156–57.

58. Hooper, *Cahuilla Indians*, 328.

59. Lando and Modesto, "Temal Wakhish," 107.

60. James, *Cahuilla Indians*, 56–58.

61. Hooper, *Cahuilla Indians*, 352–53.

62. Romero, "World View of Tewa and Cahuilla," 65. Francisco Patencio recalled an earthquake—probably before his lifetime—that was said to have changed the courses of streams and rivers, as well as causing "whole mountains [to]

split" and others to "r[i]se up where there had been none before." Patencio, *Stories and Legends of the Palm Springs Indians*, 58.

63. "Pé' témal 'í' peqi' híkusqa." Quoted in Saubel and Elliott, *'Isill Héqwas Wáxish/A Dried Coyote's Tail*, 88.

64. Saubel and Elliott, *'Isill Héqwas Wáxish/A Dried Coyote's Tail*, 1284.

65. Madrigal, *Sovereignty, Land, and Water*, 30.

66. As recorded in Mount, *Not for Innocent Ears*, 30.

67. Miskwish, *Kumeyaay*; Miskwish, *Maay Uuyow*.

68. Doolittle, *Cultivated Landscapes of Native North America*, 268.

69. Carter, *Plant Geography and Culture History in the American Southwest*, 109–17.

70. Doolittle, *Cultivated Landscapes of Native North America*, 44, 73.

71. Carrico, *Strangers in a Stolen Land*, 13.

72. Cuero and Shipek, *Delfina Cuero*; Miskwish, *Kumeyaay*; Miskwish, *Maay Uuyow*.

73. Miskwish, *Maay Uuyow*, 31; Carrico, *Strangers in a Stolen Land*, 11–12.

74. Gamble and Wilken-Robertson, "Kumeyaay Cultural Landscapes of Baja California's Tijuana River Watershed."

75. Gifford, *Kamia of the Imperial Valley*, 9.

76. Cuero and Shipek, *Delfina Cuero*, 29.

77. Carter, *Plant Geography and Culture History in the American Southwest*; Kimmerer, *Braiding Sweetgrass*.

78. Hyer, *We Are Not Savages*, 22.

79. Jackson and Castillo, *Indians, Franciscans, and Spanish Colonization*; Wyman, *Mission*; Haas, *Saints and Citizens*; Jackson, *Regional Conflict and Demographic Patterns on the Jesuit Missions*. Despite this extreme colonial violence, the Native peoples of current-day Baja California still reside in their homelands and still maintain continuous relationships with the local environment. As one Paipai elder commented to a visiting scholar in 2005, "The mission is today nothing more than ruins whereas the Paipai are still here." Quoted in Panich, *Narratives of Persistence*, 6.

80. As one historian put it, "When a native rebellion was being planned the Spaniards ordinarily had informers available who would warn them in advance. Very few Indian revolts (and they were very frequent) took the Spaniards by surprise." Forbes, *Native Americans of California and Nevada* (1969 ed.), 32.

81. Forbes, *Native Americans of California and Nevada* (1969 ed.), 36. Katherine Siva Saubel recounted a family history of the missions, involving kidnap, enslavement, and escape. Her narrative makes clear that knowledge about the missions traveled the length and breadth of inland, desert California to all the Indigenous nations there, regardless of their physical distance from the missions themselves. Saubel and Elliott, *'Isill Héqwas Wáxish/A Dried Coyote's Tail*, 112–15.

82. Haas, *Saints and Citizens*.

83. Forbes, *Native Americans of California and Nevada* (1969 ed.), 37. Hupa historian Jack Norton has argued that the Spaniards, and subsequently the Mexicans, never colonized California's interior world away from the coast and that therefore the United States had no "right by conquest" to those lands at the end of the U.S.-Mexico War. Norton, "If the Truth Be Told," 83–84.

84. Kelton, *Cherokee Medicine, Colonial Germs*.

85. Robertson, "'Crying Rock' Where They Killed the Children," 152. Saubel described how the Payómkawichum people, tending to Spanish livestock, brought their animals east for grazing, eventually marrying into Cahuilla clans and settling in Cahuilla territory. Eventually almost all the Cahuillas left the area. Saubel and Elliott, *'Isill Héqwas Wáxish/A Dried Coyote's Tail*, 126–27; Merchant, *Green versus Gold*; Weisiger, *Dreaming of Sheep in Navajo Country*; Zappia, *Traders and Raiders*.

86. Blackhawk, *Violence over the Land*; Weisiger, *Dreaming of Sheep in Navajo Country*.

87. J. Brooks, *Captives and Cousins*; Zappia, *Traders and Raiders*; Reséndez, *Other Slavery*.

88. Preston, "Serpent in the Garden," 276–77.

89. Miranda, *Bad Indians*; Haas, *Saints and Citizens*.

90. Shipek, *Pushed into the Rocks*.

91. Ethridge and Shuck-Hall, *Mapping the Mississippian Shatter Zone*.

92. Shipek, *Pushed into the Rocks*.

93. Hyer, *We Are Not Savages*; G. Phillips, *Chiefs and Challengers*.

94. "Between 1836 and 1842 warfare was almost continuous from San Diego to San Bernardino, with Quechans, Kamias, Cahuillas, and Hamakhavas becoming even more aggressive. San Diego was virtually captured by the natives at one point and several missions in northern Baja California were permanently destroyed." Forbes, *Native Americans of California and Nevada* (1982 ed.), 63–64.

95. Merchant, *Green versus Gold*. Flight from the missions into the interior desert world was one of most common acts of resistance and survival for peoples of coastal nations. Long histories of commerce and cultural exchange from the coast to the mountains and desert supported these patterns of escape from west to east. Hanks, *This War Is for a Whole Life*, 9.

96. Pisani, *From the Family Farm to Agribusiness*, 89–91.

97. Charles R. Orcutt, "The Colorado Desert," *Tenth Annual Report of the State Mineralogist of California*, 1890, 899–919.

98. Stremlau, "Witnessing the West"; Shaler, "Indigenous Peoples and the California Gold Rush"; S. Johnson, *Roaring Camp*, 58.

99. Guinn, "Sonoran Migration"; Shaler, "Indigenous Peoples and the California Gold Rush," 84.

100. Historian Nayan Shah has examined how this kind of "immense plurality" characterized California and much of the American West, despite myths of a racially homogenous settler society. Shah also examines how white settlers marginalized the importance, ubiquity, and contributions of transient nonwhite laborers and also limited their power, because they regarded those workers as unimportant and replaceable. Shah, *Stranger Intimacy*, 2.

101. Shah, *Stranger Intimacy*, 2.

102. Quoted in Gossett, *Race*, 290.

103. Lew-Williams, *Chinese Must Go*.

104. Rawls, *Indians of California*.

105. Costo and Costo, *Missions of California*; Reséndez, *Other Slavery*; J. Brooks, *Captives and Cousins*.

106. Norton, *When Our Worlds Cried*; Costo and Costo, *Missions of California*; Heizer, *Destruction of California Indians*; Lindsay, *Murder State*; Madley, *American Genocide*.

107. Madley, *American Genocide*, 13. See also Norton, *When Our Worlds Cried*; Costo and Costo, *Missions of California*; Heizer, *Destruction of California Indians*; and Lindsay, *Murder State*.

108. Rawls, *Indians of California*, 171; Hurtado, *Indian Survival on the California Frontier*, 134–35; Madley, *American Genocide*, 346.

109. Luiseño historian Olivia Chilcote has traced this history for Luiseño bands that have been denied federal recognition, noting that in San Diego County "sheriffs were supposed to demarcate Indian-occupied lands to prevent encroachment by settlers and the possibility of violent interactions." Chilcote, "'Time Out of Mind,'" 43. They failed to do so time and time again, making it nearly impossible for Luiseños to maintain the land tenure to which they were legally entitled. Cuero and Shipek, *Delfina Cuero*; Shipek, *Pushed into the Rocks*.

110. Quoted in Dozier, *Heart Is Fire*, 135.

111. Hurtado, *Indian Survival on the California Frontier*, 134–35; Shipek, *Pushed into the Rocks*, 111–12.

112. U.S. Constitution, article VI, section 2.

113. "Chéqe' míva' pá' 'énga' pemnénganwe'." Saubel and Elliott, *'Isill Héqwas Wáxish/A Dried Coyote's Tail*, 544.

114. As Andrew Shaler has explained, "California Indian societies . . . contested both the logic and practice of elimination through active and sometimes violent resistance, cultural and social adaptation, negotiation, and unflinching assertions of Indigenous identity." Olivia Chilcote and Theodor P. Gordon have meticulously traced the continuance of sovereignty among the Luiseños and Cahuillas, respectively, arguing that these peoples' contemporary status as nations emerges from ongoing articulations of political and cultural self-determination in the context of two and half centuries of intense colonization.

Shaler, "Indigenous Peoples and the California Gold Rush," 81; Chilcote, "'Time Out of Mind'"; Gordon, *Cahuilla Nation Activism and the Tribal Casino Movement*; Hanks, *This War Is for a Whole Life*, xiii.

115. The Glanton Massacre occurred in April 1850. A Texan named John Glanton ran a ferry business shuttling travelers across the Colorado River; when Quechans began a competitive ferry enterprise, Glanton assaulted and insulted them and their "chief." Quechans reacted by killing eleven Americans, including Glanton. Hyer, *We Are Not Savages*, 57.

116. Lieutenant J. D. Stevenson, quoted in Hyer, *We Are Not Savages*, 51. Garrá's parentage has been debated among historians and anthropologists. He has been described as being of Quechan parentage, Kuupangaxwichem parentage, or some combination of both. Because of his literacy, many assumed he had been educated at Mission San Luis Rey. Cahuilla historian Katherine Saubel insisted that Garrá was Kuupangaxwichem and Cahuilla. Saubel and Elliott, *'Isill Héqwas Wáxish/A Dried Coyote's Tail*, 896.

117. Quoted in Hyer, *We Are Not Savages*, 63; Hanks, *This War Is for a Whole Life*.

118. For assessments of how and why epidemics took such heavy tolls on Indigenous peoples, see Kelton, *Cherokee Medicine, Colonial Germs*, 7–9; and Crosby, "Virgin Soil Epidemics," 289.

119. When Helen Hunt Jackson and Abbot Kinney reported on the conditions of the desert Native nations in 1883, they identified the need for new surveys of land by "ethical men" as "the first and most essential step" in rectifying the injustices committed by settlers against the Cahuilla, Serrano, Luiseño, and Kumeyaay peoples. Jackson and Kinney, *Report on the Conditions and Needs of the Mission Indians of California*, 7–9.

120. Jackson and Kinney, *Report on the Conditions and Needs of the Mission Indians of California*.

121. Crawford, "Records of Local Government and California History," 24. The case was *People v. Sam Temple*.

122. This story is told in many ways, and the facts have often been muddled. This account is taken directly from Sam Temple's testimony in his court hearing in *People v. Sam Temple*, from Crawford, "Records of Local Government and California History."

123. Quoted in Mullenneaux, "Doing Good and Making Trouble," 191. While Jackson's ill-fated love story of "Alessandro" (Juan Diego) and Ramona provided a kind of romantic allegory of Native Californians' experiences of settlement, Temple's story would have provided perhaps the more instructive example. In addition to the murders of Diego and two Chinese men, in 1898 he nearly beat his wife to death in San Jacinto, drawing the attention of the local constable, who shot Temple in the arm. The arm had to be amputated. Later he joined with a group of prospectors and filed a claim on a rich deposit of gold and

copper near Yuma. "Sam Temple No More," *San Diego Union and Daily Bee*, August 25, 1898.

124. "Sam Temple No More," *San Diego Union and Daily Bee*.
125. Cuero and Shipek, *Delfina Cuero*.
126. De Falla, "Lantern in the Western Sky."
127. Leonard, *Making Ethnic Choices*.
128. Bowers, *Reconnaissance of the Colorado Desert Mining District*, 8.
129. The new firms included the Cactus Oil Company, Carrizo Creek Oil Company, Flowing Wells Oil Company, Helvetia Investment Company, Langrehr Oil and Development Company, New York Oil and Improvement Company, Palm Springs Oil Company, San Diego Desert Oil Company, San Diego Oil Belt Company, San Diego Oil and Development Company, Signal Mountain Oil Company, Signal Mountain Exploration and Development Company, Success Oil Company, Vallecito Oil Company, and Yuha Oil Company. Bowers, *Reconnaissance of the Colorado Desert Mining District*, 19.
130. Dozier, *Heart Is Fire*, 65.

2. FLOOD

1. "Along the Coast," *Marin Journal*, May 5, 1893.
2. E. M. Ward, *Coachella*, 72.
3. Bean and Vane, *Ethnology of the Alta California Indians*, 204; G. Phillips, *Chiefs and Challengers*, 178–79.
4. Horatio N. Rust, "The Desert Sea," *California Illustrated Magazine*, October 1891, 103.
5. Gunther, *Riverside County, California, Place Names*, 447.
6. When St. Boniface opened in 1890, it housed 125 Cahuilla, Serrano, and Chemehuevi students. "The St. Boniface Industrial/Indian School," Local History, Banning Library District, accessed February 3, 2021, https://www.banninglibrarydistrict.org/banning/documents/st.pdf; Harley, "Founding of St. Boniface Indian School."
7. Saubel and Elliott, *'Isill Héqwas Wáxish/A Dried Coyote's Tail*, 635, 675.
8. Trafzer, Gilbert, and Sisquoc, *Indian School on Magnolia Avenue*; Trafzer, Keller, and Sisquoc, *Boarding School Blues*.
9. "Salt in the Desert," *Daily Alta California*, February 22, 1886.
10. "A Desert Sea: The Valley at Salton Suddenly Submerged," *Los Angeles Herald*, June 28, 1891.
11. "An Eye-Witness's Story," *Los Angeles Herald*, July 2, 1891.
12. "A Chance for Indio," *Los Angeles Herald*, September 10, 1888; "Eye-Witness's Story," *Los Angeles Herald*.
13. "That Desert Sea," *Los Angeles Herald*, June 29, 1891.

14. "It Is a Sea," *Los Angeles Herald*, July 2, 1891. This notion of a great flood that would kill anyone in its path except those who fled to the mountains is echoed in Francisco Patencio's account of past floods in Cahuilla history: "The water did not come in one moment, no. It came rolling along slowly, so that the people who heard and saw, ran up." Patencio, *Stories and Legends of the Palm Springs Indians*, 83.

15. "That Desert Sea," *Los Angeles Herald*.

16. "That Desert Sea," *Los Angeles Herald*.

17. "It Is a Sea," *Los Angeles Herald*.

18. "Water from the Overflow of the Colorado Continues to Flow," *Sacramento Daily Union*, July 1, 1891.

19. "A Desert Sea," *Los Angeles Herald*; "The Desert Sea," *Los Angeles Herald*, July 1, 1891.

20. One writer described in detail the suddenly brutal heat: "To close a car up it became stifling and unbearable; while to breathe the super-heated air was distressing to the lungs. The eyes became painfully dry and the face and neck burned as though exposed to the direct rays of the sun. No one on the train seemed able to comprehend this strange experience, but gazed out on the watery waste and pronounced it a wondrous and magnificent mirage, where the rays of the sun glistened and flashed with terrible effect, while the hundred fold heated air shimmered and waved over the surface." "A Peculiar Atmosphere," *Los Angeles Herald*, July 2, 1891.

21. "The Salton Sea," *Los Angeles Herald*, June 30, 1891.

22. "Climatic Effects of the New Lake in Southern California," 211; Shugart, "Local Climatic Effect of Salton Lake," 522–25; "The Salton Sea: Its Effect on Southern California," *San Francisco Chronicle*, August 21, 1891.

23. Sykes, *Colorado Delta*, 40.

24. "The Herald at the Beach," *Los Angeles Herald*, June 29, 1891.

25. "The Salton Sea: Its Effect on Southern California," *San Francisco Chronicle*.

26. One newspaper report framed this theory of the flooding's provenance: "For a number of years the railroad company has had an artesian well flowing at a little station seven miles east of Indio, which had been sunk at considerable expense. This well had gone dry, it was found, at about the same time that the flow of water had first been noticed at the salt mines. Whether the flow at the latter place was caused by a change in the underground streams which fed the well, of course could not be ascertained." "A Desert Sea," *Los Angeles Herald*.

27. "A Desert Sea," *Los Angeles Herald*; R. L. Duffus, "Putting the Savage Colorado to Work," *New York Times*, August 12, 1928.

28. Cecil-Stephens, "The Colorado Desert and Its Recent Flooding," 367; Sykes, *Colorado Delta*, 40.

29. DeBuys and Myers, *Salt Dreams*, 69–70.

30. Quoted in "The Salton Sea," *San Francisco Chronicle.*
31. "Peculiar Atmosphere," *Los Angeles Herald.*
32. J. H. Gilmour, "The Salt Gatherers: Novel Scenes in and around Salton," *San Francisco Chronicle*, January 3, 1892.
33. Gilmour, "Salt Gatherers."
34. Quoted in the editor's note appended to Cecil-Stephens, "Colorado Desert and Its Recent Flooding," 377, 376, respectively.
35. Drucker, *Culture Element Distributions*, 29.
36. Rust, "Desert Sea," 103.
37. Charles Rockwood, "Statement of C. R. Rockwood: In Matter of the Liability of the California Development Company for the Flooding of Salton Basin" (1907), James D. Schuyler Papers, Water Resources Collections and Archives, Library of the University of California, Riverside (hereafter, Schuyler Papers); Charles Rockwood, "Born of the Desert," *Calexico Chronicle, Second Annual Magazine Edition* (Calexico CA: Calexico Chronicle, 1909); James D. Schuyler, "The Overflow of Colorado River into Salton Basin: Comparison between 1891 and 1905, as Affecting the Responsibility of the California Development Company for Damage Incurred," March 20, 1907, Schuyler Papers.
38. Voyles, "Environmentalism in the Interstices," 211.
39. Quoted in "The Press Honored with a Visit by the Imperial Editorial Party," *Imperial Valley Press*, April 20, 1901; Andrés, *Power and Control in the Imperial Valley*, 41–42.
40. "What Imperial County Offers: A General Review," *Calexico Chronicle, Second Annual Magazine Edition* (Calexico CA: Calexico Chronicle, 1909), 38.
41. "Press Honored with a Visit," *Imperial Valley Press.*
42. "What Imperial County Offers," *Calexico Chronicle*, 37.
43. "Press Honored with a Visit," *Imperial Valley Press.*
44. Said, *Question of Palestine*, chap. 1.
45. Like the "future immense" described by historian Julian Lim ("a vast American empire, rising out of the hard desert ground at the nation's very limits"—the U.S.-Mexico borderlands), Said's "more deserving power" was only white in people's imaginations. Those border areas, including Imperial Valley, "were in fact traversed by a multiethnic and multiracial population that came together dynamically through work and play, in the streets and in homes, through war and marriage, and in the very act of crossing the border." Lim, *Porous Borders*, 1, 2. For detailed accounts of the multiethnic and multiracial nature of Imperial Valley's diverse communities, see Leonard, *Making Ethnic Choices*; and Andrés, *Power and Control.*
46. In Mexican territory the water was technically controlled by a CDC subsidiary because of Mexico's laws forbidding foreign-owned companies from operating along its national borders.

47. Reisner, *Cadillac Desert*, chap. 4.
48. DeBuys and Myers, *Salt Dreams*, 77, 78, 82.
49. Kennan, *Salton Sea*, 23.
50. DeBuys and Myers, *Salt Dreams*, 80.
51. In a congressional hearing to determine whether the CDC had come by its water claims honestly, famed irrigation proponent William Elsworth Smythe testified against the CDC and adequately summarized the government's position with regard to the scheme's legality: the CDC men, Smythe scoffed, "have gone in there and claimed the melting snows of the Rocky mountains as their property." DeBuys and Myers, *Salt Dreams*, 80–81, 92 (quote); Andrés, *Power and Control in the Imperial Valley*.
52. Rockwood, "Born of the Desert."
53. DeBuys and Myers, *Salt Dreams*, 88.
54. "More News of the Valley," *Imperial Valley Press*, October 12, 1901; "Miner's Outfit," *Imperial Valley Press*, November 2, 1901.
55. DeBuys and Myers, *Salt Dreams*, 93–95; Rockwood, "Born of the Desert."
56. Women's National Indian Association, "The Report of Missions," Papers of the Women's National Indian Association, 1880–1951, Reel 3, Cornell University Division of Rare and Manuscript Collections, Ithaca, New York.
57. DeBuys and Myers, *Salt Dreams*, 101–3.
58. Kennan, *Salton Sea*, 33.
59. "Awful Work of the Colorado Flood," *Los Angeles Times*, December 10, 1905; Kennan, *Salton Sea*, 68.
60. "Awful Work of the Colorado Flood," *Los Angeles Times*.
61. Kennan, *Salton Sea*, 73.
62. DeBuys and Myers, *Salt Dreams*, 113–15.
63. John Muir to Helen and Wanda Muir, January 17, 1906, John Muir Correspondence, University of the Pacific, HM 57349-57497, Muir Family Papers, Huntington Library, San Marino, California.
64. Newell, "The Salton Sea," 331, 342. As historian Benny Andrés put it, "Underpaid and segregated native workers saved the project." Andrés, *Power and Control in the Imperial Valley*, 23.
65. "Awful Work of the Colorado Flood," *Los Angeles Times*.
66. Houston, *The Land of Drought*. Subsequent quotations in the main text are from this source.
67. Saubel and Elliott, *'Isill Héqwas Wáxish/A Dried Coyote's Tail*; Ramón with Elliott, *Wayta' Yawa'*, 476.
68. The most notorious of these backstories appears in Edwin Corle's 1935 novel, *Fig Tree John*, which represents Razón as an isolated and often violent White Mountain Apache, rather than the "friendly and gregarious" Cahuilla leader he was generally known to be. Beidler, *Fig Tree John*, xviii.

69. Beidler unpacks this combination of rumors and legends in his book *Fig Tree John*. For instance, the story that Razón had been a scout for General Frémont is probably an apocryphal adaptation of a true story about Razón sheltering and feeding a lost brigade of soldiers led by General Nelson A. Miles in the late 1880s. Beidler concludes that this is the likely provenance of Razón's famous military coat and silk stovepipe hat. Beidler, *Fig Tree John*, 23–24, 26. Beidler found more evidence, surprisingly, for the veracity of a "secret" source of gold nuggets (29–30, 32–33).

70. Both of these descriptions effectively "disappear" Cahuillas from coveted land. Beidler, *Fig Tree John*, 7; "Times' Ocean-to-Ocean Organizer at Brawley," *Los Angeles Times*, May 19, 1912; "Has Coat Presented Him by Gen. Fremont," *Riverside Daily Press*, December 20, 1919.

71. Tribal rolls listed his birth year as 1839, making him nowhere near as old as many white settlers reported. Beidler, *Fig Tree John*, 15–20.

72. O'Brien, *Firsting and Lasting*, xxi.

73. "Stray Burros," *San Francisco Call*, October 14, 1894.

74. Heizer and Nissen, *Human Sources of California Ethnography*.

75. "Grant Boys Escape Horrible Death on Sahara of America," *Sacramento Union*, July 13, 1913; Grant, "A Midsummer Motoring Trip."

76. "Floods Cover Homes of Indians," *San Bernardino Sun*, October 7, 1906.

77. "Says Indians Are Starving," *Los Angeles Times*, October 7, 1906. Agent L. A. Wright of the Indian Service took exception to Razón's account of events, particularly his assertion that "large numbers of the red skins in that section have lost their homes from the ever rising flood." "Indian Agent Says Razon Dreamed," *San Bernardino Sun*, October 9, 1906.

78. "Floods Cover Homes of Indians," *San Bernardino Sun*.

79. "Floods Cover Homes of Indians," *San Bernardino Sun*.

80. This is a fair example of "imperialist nostalgia," a term coined by anthropologist Renato Rosaldo to describe a "mood of nostalgia [that] makes racial domination appear innocent and pure." Rosaldo, *Culture and Truth*, chap. 3; O'Brien, *Firsting and Lasting*; Deloria, *Indians in Unexpected Places*.

81. "Indian Agent Says Razon Dreamed," *San Bernardino Sun*.

82. Beidler, *Fig Tree John*, 15.

83. United States v. Imperial Irr. District, 799 F. Supp. 1052 (S.D. Cal. 1992), No. Civ. No. 82-1790-K(M) (July 17, 1992).

84. "Census of the Santa Rosa Indians of Cahuilla Agency, California, on June 30, 1909, Taken by Francis A. Swayne, Superintendent," Indian Census Rolls, 1885–1940, n.d., Reel 012-Indians of North America—Census, National Archives and Records Administration, Washington DC.

85. United States v. Imperial Irr. District, 799 F. Supp. 1052 (S.D. Cal. 1992).

86. "Indian Agent after Hay," *Imperial Valley Press*, November 28, 1908; "Improvements for Indians," *Imperial Valley Press*, August 28, 1909; "The Trustees of the Coachella School," *Imperial Valley Press*, June 3, 1911.

87. Trennert, "Educating Indian Girls at Nonreservation Boarding Schools"; Trafzer, Keller, and Sisquoc, *Boarding School Blues*; K. Johnson, "'Recruited to Teach the Indians.'"

88. Office of Superintendent of Indian Schools, *Course of Study for the Indian Schools of the United States*, 5–6.

89. Haig-Brown, *Resistance and Renewal*; Lomawaima, *They Called It Prairie Light*; Child, *Boarding School Seasons*; Trafzer, Keller, and Sisquoc, *Boarding School Blues*; Fear-Segal and Rose, *Carlisle Indian Industrial School*.

90. United States v. Imperial Irr. District, 799 F. Supp. 1052 (S.D. Cal. 1992).

91. DeBuys and Myers, *Salt Dreams*, 126–27.

92. "To Seek Aid of Uncle Sam," *San Bernardino Sun*, August 19, 1908.

93. "Noted Indian Has Title of Captain," *San Bernardino Sun*, March 5, 1920.

94. Barnd, *Native Space*.

95. "Fig Tree John Calls on Friends," *San Bernardino Daily Sun*, September 21, 1911.

96. "Noted Indian Has Title of Captain," *San Bernardino Sun*.

3. BIRDS

1. Gilman, "Leconte Thrasher," 95.

2. Gilman, "Leconte Thrasher," 96.

3. Pember, "Collecting in the Colorado Desert."

4. Stephens, "Collecting in the Colorado Desert."

5. Gilman, "Leconte Thrasher," 96.

6. Gilman, "Leconte Thrasher," 96.

7. Gilman, "Leconte Thrasher," 96.

8. Allen Kelly, "Wildfowling below Sea Level," *Forest and Stream*, March 19, 1910, 449.

9. The refuge originally went by the name Salton Sea Migratory Waterfowl Refuge and "would later become the Sonny Bono Salton Sea National Wildlife Refuge." For the majority of the period discussed here, it was the Salton Sea National Wildlife Refuge. Garrett, Molina, and Patten, "History of Ornithological Exploration of the Salton Sink," 20.

10. Cecil Smith, "Imperial Valley Waging Duck War: Guns, Flares, Bombs and Searchlights Used in Battle with 1,000,000 Feathered Visitors," *Los Angeles Times*, January 30, 1950.

11. Gilman, "Leconte Thrasher," 96.

12. Gifford, *Kamia of the Imperial Valley*.

13. Quoted in Gifford, *Kamia of the Imperial Valley*, 74.

14. Ramón with Elliott, *Wayta' Yawa'*, 33.

15. Given in Cupeño and translated by Mrs. Celsa Apapas, quoted in Innis, *San Diego Legends*, 228–29.

16. Saubel and Elliott, *'Isill Héqwas Wáxish/A Dried Coyote's Tail*; Madrigal, *Sovereignty, Land, and Water*, 31–32.

17. Wilke, *Late Prehistoric Human Ecology at Lake Cahuilla*.

18. Modesto and Mount, *Not for Innocent Ears*, 31–32.

19. Modesto and Mount, *Not for Innocent Ears*, 32.

20. Merriam, "The Leconte Thrasher, *Harporhynchus lecontei*."

21. Dawson, *The Birds of California*, 2:710 (wraith), 2:707 (shyest, recluses), 2:708 (murder), 2:709 (business of bird-killing).

22. Winkler, *Gunfight*; N. Johnson, *Negroes and the Gun*; Dunbar-Ortiz, *Loaded*.

23. Lindsay, *Murder State*; Madley, *American Genocide*.

24. In 1855, for instance, settlers of Orleans Bar voted to "'kill on sight all Indians having guns'" and to burn Native communities that harbored — or were suspected of harboring — firearms. Norton, "If the Truth Be Told," 86.

25. Josephine Clifford McCrackin, "The Ornithologist: Save the Song Birds," *Pacific Rural Press*, August 1, 1903. Historian Walter Hixson in his book *American Settler Colonialism* provides a larger context for the relationships between settler colonialism and an "instinct to kill something," as McCrackin put it. Hixson examines the role of violence in settler societies (4–7) and particularly how that violence has hinged on tropes of manliness that emphasize "competition, aggression, control, power" (10).

26. Historian Louis Warren has described this period of increasing federal and state management of hunting laws as "one of the most startling examples of how the nation acquired power over the most intimate of relationships between people and nature." Warren, *Hunter's Game*, 23, 173 (quote).

27. Hornaday, quoted in Armitage, "Bird Day for Kids," 528.

28. Merchant, "George Bird Grinnell's Audubon Society," 6. As environmental historian Adam Rome has explored, environmental preservation in this era was saturated with gender politics, and gender in turn shaped how, when, and by whom environmental protection was taken seriously. Rome, "'Political Hermaphrodites,'" 442.

29. Merchant, "George Bird Grinnell's Audubon Society."

30. "Slaughter of the Innocents," *Imperial Valley Press*, July 23, 1910. As historian Mark V. Barrow has pointed out, the "destruction" of bird life by women for fashion was probably not significantly worse than the destruction caused by men ornithologists for their expansive collections of bird specimens. Women, however, bore the brunt of blame. Barrow, *Passion for Birds*, 112–13. The gender politics of feathered hats are complicated even further by the fact that many women were ardent protesters against the trend. Price, *Flight Maps*, 98–101.

31. McCrackin, "The Ornithologist," *Pacific Rural Press*.

32. Roosevelt, *The Strenuous Life*; Warren, *Hunter's Game*; Merchant, "George Bird Grinnell's Audubon Society."

33. It is important to note that hunting as a masculine exercise was ideational but not necessarily always a strict reflection of lived reality. Women too hid themselves in blinds and turned their guns on birds. In one tragic turn of events at the Salton Sea in 1947, a woman hunter shot and killed her husband, hidden in a blind just feet from where she stood. Garrett, Molina, and Patten, "History of Ornithological Exploration of the Salton Sink," 20.

34. "Valley Gunners and Valley Ducks: El Centro Gun Club Closes Membership List and Goes after the Birds," *Imperial Valley Press*, January 2, 1909.

35. "Submarine Sport," *Imperial Valley Press*, March 12, 1910.

36. "Gun Club Organized," *Imperial Valley Press*, September 29, 1906.

37. "Submarine Sport," *Imperial Valley Press*.

38. "Valley Gunners and Valley Ducks," *Imperial Valley Press*.

39. "Submarine Sport," *Imperial Valley Press*.

40. "A Boat for Salton Sea," *Imperial Valley Press*, October 16, 1909.

41. "Navigation on Salton Sea," *Imperial Valley Press*, July 16, 1910.

42. "Shooting on the Alamo," *Imperial Valley Press*, January 8, 1910.

43. "Submarine Sport," *Imperial Valley Press*.

44. "Submarine Sport," *Imperial Valley Press*.

45. Warren, *Hunter's Game*.

46. It is unclear what part of the sea Grinnell was identifying as "Echo Island"; this name was likely a reference to either Obsidian Butte or Mullet Island. Garrett, Molina, and Patten, "History of Ornithological Exploration of the Salton Sink," 19.

47. Joseph Grinnell, "Salton Sea," in Field Notes (handwritten journal), 1908–9, vol. 1316, sec. 1, April 19, 1908, 14, EcoReader, University of California, Berkeley.

48. Grinnell, "Birds of a Voyage on Salton Sea," 186.

49. "Alligator in Salton Sea," *Imperial Valley Press*, July 9, 1910; "Salton Sea Alligators," *Imperial Valley Press*, July 9, 1910.

50. Grinnell, "Salton Sea," Field Notes, 15.

51. Grinnell, "Salton Sea," Field Notes, 16.

52. Grinnell, "Birds of a Voyage on Salton Sea," 187.

53. Grinnell, "Birds of a Voyage on Salton Sea," 189.

54. Grinnell's expedition was later described as the "first ornithological exploration of the Salton Sea." It would be the first of many, as ornithologists remained fascinated by the rich diversity of bird populations at the sea. Garrett, Molina, and Patten, "History of Ornithological Exploration of the Salton Sink," 19.

55. The Lacey Act (1900) represented one of the first federal conservation efforts, and it specifically authorized restoration of wild bird populations, reflecting both widespread concern about birds and the emerging legislative focus on wildlife conservation. Barrow, *Passion for Birds*, 133.

56. Quoted in Barrow, *Passion for Birds*, 4–5.

57. "Slaughter of the Innocents," *Imperial Valley Press*.

58. Grinnell, "Salton Sea," Field Notes, 26–27.

59. Begun in 1885 as the Section on Economic Ornithology under the Department of Agriculture, the Biological Survey combined with the Department of Fisheries to become the Fish and Wildlife Service in 1939. See Theodore S. Palmer, "A Review of Economic Ornithology in the United States," *Yearbook of the Department of Agriculture* (1899), 264–65.

60. Wilson, *Seeking Refuge*.

61. "Plea Made for Wild Fowl: Biological Survey Chief, Here on Official Mission, Urges Voters to Support Proposition No. 11," *Los Angeles Times*, October 7, 1930.

62. "Plea Made for Wild Fowl," *Los Angeles Times*.

63. "Salton Sea Tract Made Bird Refuge: Hoover Order Creates Important Link in Coast Chain of Protection Areas," *Los Angeles Times*, December 7, 1930.

64. "California News Briefs," *Livermore Journal*, July 30, 1931.

65. Warren, *Hunter's Game*, 112–14.

66. Langston, *Where Land and Water Meet*, 5.

67. H. C. Bryant, "Imperial Valley–Salton Sea, December 16–20, 1919," Harold C. Bryant Field Notes, vol. 3, n.d., Harold C. Bryant Papers, Museum of Vertebrate Zoology Archives, University of California, Berkeley.

68. Al Parmenter, "Duck Plentiful for First Day of Season Monday," *Los Angeles Times*, November 15, 1931.

69. Parmenter, "Duck Plentiful for First Day of Season Monday." Historian Robert Wilson has documented this pattern all along the Pacific Flyway, not just at the Salton Sea. Wilson, *Seeking Refuge*, 88–90.

70. Parmenter, "Duck Plentiful for First Day of Season Monday."

71. Smith, "Imperial Valley Waging Duck War."

72. Luther C. Goldman, "Narrative Report: Salton Sea National Wildlife Refuge, Brawley, California," September 23–October 31, 1940, 4, California Department of Fish and Wildlife.

73. Smith, "Imperial Valley Waging Duck War."

74. Wilson, *Seeking Refuge*, 100.

75. U.S. Fish and Wildlife Service, "Salton Sea National Wildlife Refuge and Waterfowl Development Areas Narrative Report," U.S. Department of the Interior, Brawley, California, August 1949.

76. Quoted in Smith, "Imperial Valley Waging Duck War."

77. Mendoza, "Unnatural Border"; Santa Ana, *Brown Tide Rising*.

78. Smith, "Imperial Valley Waging Duck War."

79. Department of Interior—Fish and Wildlife Service, "Salton Sea National Wildlife Refuge and Waterfowl Development Area Narrative Report," September–December 1955, 20.

80. Opie Warner, "Wild Ducks Hatching Out Many Ducklings," *Sausalito News*, August 12, 1932.

81. Quoted in Smith, "Imperial Valley Waging Duck War."

82. Wilson, *Seeking Refuge*, 100.

83. Department of Interior—Fish and Wildlife Service, "Salton Sea National Wildlife Refuge and Waterfowl Development Area Narrative Report," September–December 1955.

84. Wilson, *Seeking Refuge*, chap. 4.

85. Voyles, "Environmentalism in the Interstices."

86. Cohn, "Saving the Salton Sea."

87. Louis Sahagun, "Salton Sea 'Anomalies' Raise Fears of Start of Its Ecological Collapse," *Los Angeles Times*, April 3, 1989.

88. Patrick McDonnell, "Cause of Bird Deaths at Salton Sea Eludes Experts," *Los Angeles Times*, March 16, 1992.

89. Cohn, "Saving the Salton Sea," 298.

90. Chris Metzler and Jeff Springer, dirs., *Past Pleasures at the Salton Sea* (Tilapia Film, 2009).

91. Friend, "Avian Disease at the Salton Sea," 294.

92. "Yéwi méetechem he'míyaxwe'"; "'Enga' me'téwap míyaxwe' mutúlika' hemkenáviwenipa' 'énga'." Saubel and Elliott, *'Isill Héqwas Wáxish/A Dried Coyote's Tail*, 808.

93. "Pé'ee 'ív'ax Mélkish qahíchay pé'iy 'elélkwi'chi' písh pewíchinqa 'ét hemwáykiñi' Mélkichem hemwésay"; "Pé' mán 'ív'ax nésunngax hemchéxwe." Saubel and Elliott, *'Isill Héqwas Wáxish/A Dried Coyote's Tail*, 807.

94. See Carson, *Silent Spring*.

4. CONCRETE

1. The text of the resolution before the association read, "Whereas, Farm labor is becoming increasingly difficult to obtain, and in California especially the great fruit and wine industries are threatened with disaster unless some remedy be found to get more labor; therefore, be it resolved, That the fruit-growers of California, in convention assembled, favor such modification of the Chinese Exclusion Act as will permit the enactment of laws making possible restricted immigration of laborers irrespective of nationality." "Proceedings of the Thirty-Second Fruit-Growers Convention," 465.

2. Ngai, *Impossible Subjects*.

3. Lew-Williams, *Chinese Must Go*.

4. "Proceedings of the Thirty-Second Fruit-Growers Convention," 465.

5. "Proceedings of the Thirty-Second Fruit-Growers Convention," 467.

6. "Proceedings of the Thirty-Second Fruit-Growers Convention," 467.

7. Round, *Impossible Land*, 11.

8. Historian Christopher Sneddon has traced related patterns of what he calls the "concrete revolution" of the twentieth century as an emergence of intertwined "ideologies and technologies" of control over rivers. Here I examine the role of race as part of that imbrication of ideologies and technologies. Sneddon, *Concrete Revolution*, 1, 55–57.

9. Burdick, *The Mystic Mid-Region*, 234.

10. Roger Birdseye, "America's Dead Sea Is Curbed Forever," *New York Times*, March 29, 1925.

11. This is the description of the Colorado River provided by the secretary of the San Diego Chamber of Commerce, H. P. Wood, in "The Colorado River," *Imperial Valley Press*, April 20, 1901.

12. Jacobson, *Whiteness of a Different Color*, 6.

13. This process often ended in violence. Lew-Williams, *Chinese Must Go*, 5–8; Lim, *Porous Borders*, 4.

14. Tuck and Yang, "Decolonization Is Not a Metaphor," 6.

15. Wilbur Jay Hall, "A Metamorphosis," in *Calexico Chronicle, Second Annual Magazine Edition* (Calexico CA: Calexico Chronicle, 1909), 41.

16. Robinson, *Black Marxism*, chap. 1; Tuck and Yang, "Decolonization Is Not a Metaphor," 6; Arvin, Tuck, and Morrill, "Decolonizing Feminism," 12.

17. Gossett, *Race*, 290.

18. Pfeifer, *Rough Justice*, 32, 85, 87. See also Rodriguez, "Noose That Builds the Nation"; and Lytle Hernández, *City of Inmates*.

19. Historian Benny J. Andrés has stated that these practices in Imperial Valley that maintained white supremacy in California and the West "legitimized the conquest of the landscape." Andrés, *Power and Control in the Imperial Valley*, 4.

20. "The Farm Hand Trouble," *Imperial Valley Press*, April 2, 1904,

21. "Cotton's New Empire," *Imperial Valley Press*, November 6, 1909.

22. Andrés, *Power and Control in the Imperial Valley*, 52.

23. Andrés, *Power and Control in the Imperial Valley*, 52.

24. Lim, *Porous Borders*, 95; St. John, *Line in the Sand*, 182.

25. This pattern of ethnic succession of laborers helped guarantee deeply unjust patterns of racialized labor in California agribusiness more broadly, as argued in McWilliams, *Factories in the Field*.

26. Lew-Williams, *Chinese Must Go*, 7–9, 87.

27. Leonard, *Making Ethnic Choices*.

28. Leonard, *Making Ethnic Choices*, 45. Benny Andrés makes a strong case for how this pattern of lease tenancy emerged in the Imperial Valley more prominently than elsewhere: in the 1910s the Federal Land Bank refused to issue loans to Imperial Valley farmers due to the threat of a repeat of the recent flooding from the Colorado River. In the absence of federal loans, "tenants had to rely on landowners and produce distributors and shippers for loans, resulting in

a loss of control to outsiders who preferred large farms to small family farms to maximize profits. Credit flowed to ethnic and racial groups deemed trustworthy." Andrés, *Power and Control in the Imperial Valley*, 71.

29. Andrés, *Power and Control in the Imperial Valley*, 69.

30. R. L. Duffus, "Putting the Savage Colorado to Work," *New York Times*, August 12, 1928.

31. Duffus, "Putting the Savage Colorado to Work"; R. E. Hodges, "Inexhaustable [*sic*] Power and Water for Southwest," *Pacific Rural Press*, July 16, 1921; Birdseye, "America's Dead Sea Is Curbed Forever." During a time when anti-immigrant politics were firmly couched in arguments about protecting public health from ostensibly disease-carrying foreigners, the depiction of the Colorado as a "feverish" river threatening to "invade" the valley mapped almost exactly onto nativist anti-immigrant racism. Kraut, *Silent Travelers*; Molina, *Fit to Be Citizens?*, 20.

32. Johnson's words are from a 1927 speech supporting the All-American Canal Project, quoted in Andrés, *Power and Control in the Imperial Valley*, 11. Donald Worster describes depictions of the Colorado River at this time as "animistic." Worster, *Rivers of Empire*, 194.

33. Leonard, *Making Ethnic Choices*, 37–42.

34. Pisani, *Water and American Government*, 1–2.

35. Quoted in Pisani, *Water and American Government*, 2.

36. According to the National Inventory of Dams, the United States has 8,100 dams that have more than five thousand acre-feet capacity and are at least fifty feet tall. National Inventory of Dams, U.S. Army Corps of Engineers, https://nid .sec.usace.army.mil/.

37. Pisani, *Water and American Government*, xvi.

38. "A Savage Assault," *Imperial Valley*, April 2, 1910.

39. "McKinnon Held for Trial," *Imperial Valley*, April 16, 1910; "Out on Probation," *Imperial Valley*, May 21, 1910.

40. As noted previously, capital "can only accumulate by producing and moving through relations of severe inequality among human groups." Melamed, "Racial Capitalism," 78.

41. Dams rarely achieved the ends of full control over waterways. They are best conceptualized, according to Sneddon, as agents in the environmental history of rivers and landscapes, rather than as static physical objects. Sneddon, *Concrete Revolution*.

42. In this sense the Imperial Valley sat at the juncture of two major trends in western irrigation schemes: private projects, which proliferated in the last two decades of the nineteenth century, and federal projects, which assumed responsibility for watering the West beginning with the 1902 Reclamation

Act. Worster, *Rivers of Empire*, 129–31; deBuys, *Great Aridness*, 92–93; Reisner, *Cadillac Desert*, 114–17.

43. Hundley, "Politics of Reclamation"; Pisani, *Water and American Government*.

44. The idea for the All-American Canal had been circulating in Imperial Valley almost from its founding, as a way of keeping Colorado River water north of the international boundary line and thus under the control of U.S. concerns. Pisani, *From the Family Farm to Agribusiness*, 309–12.

45. *Problems of Imperial Valley and Vicinity*, 8.

46. "Boulder Canyon Project Act," Pub. L. No. 642 (1928), https://www.usbr.gov /lc/region/g1000/pdfiles/bcpact.pdf; Worster, *Under Western Skies*, 69–78; Worster, *Rivers of Empire*, 208–13.

47. The League of California Municipalities published *The Boulder Canyon Project on the Colorado River and the All-American Canal for Imperial and Coachella Valley* in 1924, and the Imperial Irrigation District circulated a view book, *Boulder Dam, All-American Canal Project, and Imperial Valley Pictorially*, in 1926. Duchemin, "Water, Power, and Tourism," 63.

48. Kinsey, *River of Destiny*.

49. Worster, *Rivers of Empire*, 211.

50. E. R. Ward, *Border Oasis*, 23.

51. Robert Benson, "How the Imperial Valley Is Solving Its Drainage Problem," *Los Angeles Times*, January 27, 1924.

52. "Bill Proposes Salton Sea as Drainage Basin," *Los Angeles Times*, December 8, 1925.

53. Worster, *Rivers of Empire*, 212.

54. "Eastside for All-American Canal for Purely Selfish Reasons and Not for Broad Valley Interests," *Calexico Chronicle*, January 16, 1919; Leonard, *Making Ethnic Choices*, 37–45.

55. Andrés, *Power and Control in the Imperial Valley*, 71.

56. Worster, *Rivers of Empire*, 212.

57. Birdseye, "America's Dead Sea Is Curbed Forever."

58. "Wresting Victory from the Desert Wastes," *Los Angeles Times*, May 17, 1925.

59. "Wresting Victory from the Desert Wastes," *Los Angeles Times*.

60. "Bill Proposes Salton Sea as Drainage Basin," *Los Angeles Times* (emphasis added).

61. Gerhard, "Socialist Invasion of Baja California"; Leonard, *Making Ethnic Choices*, 45.

62. Duffus, "Putting the Savage Colorado to Work"; Hodges, "Inexhaustable [*sic*] Power and Water for Southwest."

63. Statement of Hon. Philip D. Swing, Member of Congress from California, "Protection and Development of Lower Colorado River Basin," Committee on Irrigation of Arid Lands (1922), 8, https://play.google.com/books/reader?id =rFVXeTu_IEYC&hl=en&pg=GBS.PA7.

64. "All-American Canal Favored Plan to Supply Coachella and Imperial," *Riverside Daily Press*, May 7, 1919.

65. "Settlers earnestly desired to control the river to stop flooding . . . but ultimately, what the Imperial Valley and the basin states wanted was to take the river away from Mexico." Andrés, *Power and Control in the Imperial Valley*, 32–33. See also Hundley, *Great Thirst*, 206–7.

66. Statement of Swing, "Protection and Development of Lower Colorado River Basin," 7–8.

67. Thomas H. Means, "Report on the All-American Canal, Imperial Valley, California," December 1930, Box 1, Thomas H. Means Papers, Water Resources Collections and Archives, Library of the University of California, Riverside; Lytle Hernández, *Migra!*, 29.

68. Furnish and Ladman, "Colorado River Salinity Agreement"; deBuys, *Great Aridness*.

69. Round, *Impossible Land*, 11.

70. Hundley, *Great Thirst*, 206–9, 211.

71. As one local newspaper put it, "Old 'Fig Tree John' is the leader of a tribe that is almost extinct," reflecting historian Jean O'Brien's concept of "firsting and lasting." "Has Coat Presented Him by Gen. Fremont," *Riverside Daily Press*, December 20, 1919; O'Brien, *Firsting and Lasting*.

72. "Jonathan Tibbetts Has Put Up Bond," *Riverside Daily Press*, October 3, 1921.

73. C. L. Ellis, "Annual Report for 1922," June 30, 1922, Records of the Mission Indian Agency, Record Group 75, Bureau of Indian Affairs 75.19.61, National Archives and Records Administration, Riverside, California (hereafter, Records of the Mission Indian Agency).

74. "Federal Officers Arresting Indians," *Riverside Daily Press*, September 28, 1921.

75. "Free 125-Year-Old Indian from Jail," *Los Angeles Herald*, October 1, 1921.

76. "Jonathan Tibbetts Has Put Up Bond," *Riverside Daily Press*.

77. Patencio, *Stories and Legends of the Palm Springs Indians*, 91–94; Brumgardt and Bowles, *People of the Magic Waters*, 101–3.

78. Thorne, "On the Fault Line," 186.

79. Thorne, "On the Fault Line," 190.

80. Costo and Costo, *Natives of the Golden State*, 316–18.

81. Hanks, *This War Is for a Whole Life*, 182.

82. Thorne, "Death of Superintendent Stanley"; Thorne, *El Capitan*.

83. Ellis, "Annual Report for 1922."

84. "Indian Council Held Saturday," *San Bernardino Sun*, March 5, 1912.

85. Annual Report for 1921, Mission Indian Agency of California, June 30, 1921, Records of the Mission Indian Agency.

86. Child, *My Grandfather's Knocking Sticks*, 131.

87. Annual Report for 1921, Mission Indian Agency of California.

88. Annual Report for 1921, Mission Indian Agency of California.

89. "Our Duty Lies Ahead," *The Indian*, July–August 1934, 19, in Folder 2, Box 113, Don Meadows Papers MS-R01, Special Collections and Archives, University of California, Irvine.

90. Ellis, "Annual Report for 1922."

91. Ellis, "Annual Report for 1922."

92. Adams et al., *Reports on the Irrigation Resources of California*; Ellis, "Annual Report for 1922."

93. Ellis, "Annual Report for 1922."

94. Ellis, "Annual Report for 1922."

95. Beidler, *Fig Tree John*, 15–20.

96. John W. Dady, Superintendent, "Narrative Report," Mission Indian Agency, California, for the Fiscal Year 1936, Records of the Mission Indian Agency.

97. Ellis, "Annual Report for 1922."

98. Ellis, "Annual Report for 1922."

99. "Coachella Valley Will Get Water by 1945," *Calexico Chronicle*, October 28, 1943.

100. The concrete that made up the O'Shaughnessy Dam not only stemmed the flow of the Tuolumne River, it also instigated the nation's first and, up to that point, largest campaign of concerted environmental activism. Led by John Muir and members of the newly formed Sierra Club, opposition to the Hetch Hetchy dam project arose among affluent preservationists who, inspired by Muir, considered the mountains and valleys of the country's "wilderness" places to be sites of divine inspiration—vast outdoor churches that humans could visit to touch the face of God. No matter that these so-called wildernesses had been complex cultural environments since time immemorial and work sites for Indigenous people who understood the land's ecological quirks and capacity, for Muir and his "nature lovers" the image of pure, untouched nature sat at the heart of their political project. Righter, *Battle over Hetch Hetchy*. In keeping with this preservationist ethic, Muir's contemporaries chose to advocate on behalf of the nonhuman world of Hetch Hetchy without advocating for the homeland rights of Miwok people.

101. More than half of the land condemned in the government's declaration of "eminent domain" for the dams that made up the Pick-Sloan project was crucial bottomlands for these Oceti Sakowin tribes. Lawson, *Dammed Indians*; Estes, "Fighting for Our Lives," 117.

102. Jacob, *Yakama Rising*, 9.

103. Church et al., "Tribal Water Rights"; Billington, Jackson, and Melosi, *History of Large Federal Dams*; Gilio-Whitaker, *As Long as Grass Grows*.

104. This history is "not widely known among non-Indian readers, who are generally more familiar with land losses sustained by Indian tribes in the nineteenth

century than in the twentieth." Danker, "'Violation of the Earth,'" 86. In the western part of the country, hundreds of thousands of acres of land belonging to tribes such as those living on the Fort Mohave, Chemehuevi Valley, Colorado River, Yuma, and Gila Bend Reservations in California and Arizona have been condemned for federal dams and reservoirs. Lawson, *Dammed Indians*, xxix. Key thinkers in the development of Native American and Indigenous studies grounded their work in experiences of dam construction and its consequences. Cook-Lynn, *Anti-Indianism in Modern America*; Cook-Lynn, *I Remember the Fallen Trees*; LaDuke, *All Our Relations*.

105. "Dispossessing the Dispossessed," *Akwesasne Notes*, June 30, 1976; "Slave River Dam Another James Bay?," *Akwesasne Notes*, April 1, 1983; "Tribal Filipinos Face Violent Removal from Land Base: Logging, Agri-Business Spearhead Genocide," *Akwesasne Notes*, April 1, 1983; "Malaysia: Bakun Hydropower Project: 69,000 Hectares or Rainforest to Be Flooded," *Akwesasne Notes*, December 31, 1986; Jim Ransom, "The Poisoning of the Great Lakes: The Nation's Response," *Akwesasne Notes*, June 30, 1988; "Cherokees File Dam Suit," *Akwesasne Notes*, n.d.

106. On energy injustice, see Gedicks, *Resource Rebels*; Goldtooth (Mato Awanyankapi), "State of Indigenous"; LaDuke, *All Our Relations*; Voyles, *Wastelanding*; Grossman, *Unlikely Alliances*; and Gilio-Whitaker, *As Long as Grass Grows*. Additionally, Nick Estes links dams and pipelines in his article "Fighting for Our Lives."

107. Todd Luce and Clifford Trafzer, for example, connect the inundation of Yakama fishing communities by The Dalles Dam that flooded Celilo Falls to an epidemic of suicide among Yakama people. See Luce and Trafzer, "Invisible Epidemic."

108. Edward Abbey dubbed this "industrial tourism," linking it to federal public works projects that ushered in a "new" West where technological advancement met outdoor recreation. Abbey, *Desert Solitaire*, 48–53. See also Hiltzik, *Colossus*.

109. Worster, *Rivers of Empire*, 211. For a rich account of the broader consequences of dam building and energy projects in the southwest, see Needham, *Power Lines*.

110. "Torres-Martinez Desert Cahuilla Indians Claims Settlement Act and Additional Lands within the State of Utah for the Goshute Indian Reservation," Hearing before the Committee on Indian Affairs, U.S. Senate, 104th Cong., 2nd sess., on S. 1893 and H.R. 2464 to provide for the settlement of issues and claims related to the trust lands of the Torres Martinez Desert Cahuilla Indians and to amend Public Law 103-93 to provide additional lands within the state of Utah for the Goshute Indian Reservation, July 18, 1996, 30 (testimony of Mary Belardo).

5. BODIES

1. Orme, "The Climate of Southern California," 155.
2. Abel, *Tuberculosis and the Politics of Exclusion*, 62.

3. Baur, "Health Seekers and Early Southern California Agriculture"; "Against Consumption," *Imperial Valley Press*, April 5, 1902.

4. "Against Consumption," *Imperial Valley Press*.

5. "Consumptives Must Register," *Imperial Valley Press*, February 20, 1909; "Segregate Consumptives," *Imperial Valley Press*, December 11, 1909.

6. Andrés, *Power and Control in the Imperial Valley*, 53–55. For details on exclusionary policies and practices against people with tuberculosis in California, see Abel, *Suffering in the Land of Sunshine*, 78–82.

7. Kosek, "Purity and Pollution."

8. Norman Bridge, "The Sun-and-Air Cure: Out-Door Life in California, and Its Value," *Los Angeles Times*, January 1, 1898; Bridge, "The Climate of Southern California."

9. Baur, "Health Seekers and Early Southern California Agriculture," 347.

10. Abel, *Tuberculosis and the Politics of Exclusion*.

11. J. H. Gilmour, "The Salt Gatherers: Novel Scenes in and around Salton," *San Francisco Chronicle*, January 3, 1892.

12. "Care of the Body: Valuable Suggestions for Acquiring and Preserving Health," *Los Angeles Times*, August 27, 1899.

13. "The Desert Area: Animal Life, Soil and Climate, the Desert for Invalids," *Los Angeles Times*, January 1, 1897.

14. "Progress of the Coast," *San Francisco Chronicle*, December 7, 1897.

15. "Sunbath on the Desert," *Imperial Valley Press*, January 25, 1901.

16. "Imperial Valley, Land of Promise," *Imperial Valley Press*, March 12, 1910.

17. Shugart, "Local Climatic Effect of Salton Lake," 524.

18. Lindley, "Below the Sea—Nature's Pneumatic Cabinet," 381.

19. *Mortality Statistics, 1915*, 26.

20. *Mortality Statistics, 1915*, 26.

21. Farr, *History of Imperial County*, 217.

22. Shugart, "Local Climatic Effect of Salton Lake," 524.

23. Hinsdale, "Atmospheric Air in Relation to Tuberculosis," 88.

24. Abel, *Tuberculosis and the Politics of Exclusion*, 87.

25. The surveys were conducted by Ales Hrdlicka in 1908, the U.S. Public Health Service in 1913, Florence Patterson in 1923, and a commission headed by Lewis Meriam in 1923.

26. Institute for Government Research, *The Problem of Indian Administration: Report made at the request of Honorable Hubert Work, Secretary of the Interior, and submitted to him, February 21, 1928*, https://babel.hathitrust.org/cgi/pt?id=coo.31924014526150&view=2up&seq=9.

27. Trafzer, *Fighting Invisible Enemies*, 229.

28. Trafzer notes that the "occupation" listed in Mission Agency Death Registers during this time for victims of tuberculosis was "child/student" more than a

quarter (28 percent) of the time. Trafzer, "Tuberculosis Death and Survival," 85, 96.

29. The conditions that generated epidemic rates of diseases like tuberculosis, according to Trafzer, included "poor public health, sanitation, housing, medical care, health education, and inadequate traditional diets." Trafzer, "Tuberculosis Death and Survival," 86.

30. Keller, *Empty Beds*, 180.

31. *Impounding Waters and Indian Tuberculosis Sanitarium*, 14.

32. *Impounding Waters and Indian Tuberculosis Sanitarium*, 9.

33. Trafzer, "Tuberculosis Death and Survival," 96.

34. "Suicide at Imperial," *Imperial Valley Press*, November 26, 1910.

35. Abel, *Suffering in the Land of Sunshine*, 38–41.

36. As historian Diane Price Herndl points out, regardless of actual rates of diagnosis of maladies, during this time "invalidism" came to be closely aligned with the image of the middle- or upper-class "sickly woman," trapped in the ideological and embodied effects of the "cult of female frailty." Herndl, *Invalid Women*, 1, 21, 25. Herndl notes that, despite the fact that men's health was probably as bad as or worse than women's, "the public perception . . . was that women were truly at risk" (24). Perhaps the most famous literary depiction of the lived reality of these intersecting ideological and embodied forms of invalidation is Charlotte Perkins Gilman's novel *The Yellow Wallpaper* (1892).

37. "The County's Health," *Imperial Valley Press*, December 10, 1910.

38. "Purify the Water," *Imperial Valley Press*, July 20, 1901.

39. "Sanitary Precautions," *Imperial Valley Press*, February 22, 1908.

40. Dr. F. W. Peterson, "Medical History," in Farr, *History of Imperial County*, 218.

41. Peterson, "Medical History," in Farr, *History of Imperial County*, 218.

42. Chase, *California Desert Trails*, 174.

43. Kraut, *Silent Travelers*; Molina, *Fit to Be Citizens?*; Shah, *Contagious Divides*.

44. Mendoza, "Unnatural Border."

45. The first U.S. customs office in Calexico was built in 1902. By 1910 two more had been established. By the early 1920s a border fence had been constructed to separate Calexico and Mexicali. St. John, *Line in the Sand*, 98, 144–45.

46. Quoted in "Vaccination to Be Required at Border," *Calexico Chronicle*, June 3, 1922. This was truly a cross-border effort, at least among the elites and government officials of both Calexico and Mexicali.

47. "Immigration Men Take Steps to Close Line," *Calexico Chronicle*, June 3, 1922.

48. "Immediate Lifting of Ban on Border Is Recommended by Local Health Officer," *Calexico Chronicle*, July 25, 1922.

49. "Highway into Mexicali to Be Guarded," *Calexico Chronicle*, April 17, 1924.

50. "Pact with Mexico Strengthens Fight on Livestock Diseases," *Calexico Chronicle*, April 24, 1928.

51. Mendoza, "Unnatural Border."
52. Mendoza, "Unnatural Border."
53. "Pink Bollworm," National Invasive Species Information Center, U.S. Department of Agriculture, n.d., https://www.invasivespeciesinfo.gov/profile/pink-bollworm#cit.
54. "Government Is Keeping Watch on Boll Worm," *Calexico Chronicle*, February 1, 1917.
55. Pratt, "Report for Lower California," 48.
56. "Martinez de Castro Is Again Head of Camera [de Diputados]," *Calexico Chronicle*, January 20, 1922.
57. "Keep Weevil Out, Warn[s] U.S. Expert," *Calexico Chronicle*, January 31, 1922.
58. St. John, *Line in the Sand*, 90–91; Truett, *Fugitive Landscapes*.
59. "Constant Vigilance Is the Best Safeguard," *Calexico Chronicle*, March 17, 1922.
60. McWhorter, "Introduction and Spread of Johnsongrass in the United States."
61. "Controversy Is Raised about Grass Seed," *Calexico Chronicle*, August 3, 1922. In fact, the plant had been present in Imperial County for more than a decade; in 1908 Imperial County's horticultural commission saw fit to pass an ordinance requiring farmers to remove it from their land or face six months in jail.
62. "Trees, Plants, Weeds, and Bugs," *Imperial Valley Press*, March 12, 1910.
63. "Trees, Plants, Weeds, and Bugs," *Imperial Valley Press*.
64. "Trees, Plants, Weeds, and Bugs," *Imperial Valley Press*.
65. "Picking a Winner: Mexican Insurrectionists Keep the Otis Ranch Crowd Guessing," *California Outlook*, September 12, 1914.
66. Harrigan, *Agricultural Crop Report*, 7.
67. "Sanatorium Planned for Salton Sea's Shores," *Imperial Valley Press*, July 29, 1911.
68. "Planning Motor Boats for Salton Sea Trips," *Imperial Valley Press*, August 5, 1911.
69. "Planning Motor Boats for Salton Sea Trips," *Imperial Valley Press*.
70. "Planning Motor Boats for Salton Sea Trips," *Imperial Valley Press*.
71. "Pleasure Promoters Run into Trouble," *Calexico Chronicle*, September 16, 1913.
72. "Party Has Fine Trip to Salton," *Calexico Chronicle*, July 11, 1916.
73. These efforts were being made throughout California, causing no end of anxiety among officials in Sacramento. Fleury, "Border Inspection Revelations," 86–88.
74. "Inland Sea Resort Goes in at Salton," *Calexico Chronicle*, May 17, 1930.
75. "Will Improve Mullett Island Health Resort," *Calexico Chronicle*, March 14, 1933; "Amusement Center Gets Wide Support," *Calexico Chronicle*, November 14, 1934.
76. "Plan Revealed for Salton Sea Health, Recreation Resort," *Calexico Chronicle*, January 31, 1946.
77. Rothman, *Devil's Bargains*.
78. Charles Francis Saunders, "The California Desert as a Pleasure Resort," *The Outlook*, August 22, 1914, 1002, 998–99, respectively.

79. "The Desert Song," *Time Magazine*, March 2, 1959.
80. Associated Chambers of Commerce of Imperial County, California, "Scenic Points in Imperial Valley," Folder 18, Box 113, Don Meadows Papers.
81. "Indian Picture Writings in Southern California & Where to Find Them," Folder 18, Box 113, Don Meadows Papers.
82. Barnard, "Introduction of an Amphipod Crustacean into the Salton Sea, California."
83. Linsley and Carpelan, "Invertebrate Fauna," 45.
84. Linsley and Carpelan, "Invertebrate Fauna," 46.
85. Robert Twiss et al., "Outdoor Recreational Use of the Salton Sea with Reference to Potential Impacts of Geothermal Development," April 1978, U.S. Department of Energy Office of Scientific and Technical Information, https://www.osti.gov /servlets/purl/6519621.
86. Ngai, *Impossible Subjects*; Andrés, *Power and Control in the Imperial Valley*; Leonard, *Making Ethnic Choices*.
87. Nash, *Inescapable Ecologies*, 131.
88. Mitchell, *They Saved the Crops*, 317.
89. Mitchell, *They Saved the Crops*, 317.
90. U.S. Fish and Wildlife Service Sonny Bono Salton Sea National Wildlife Refuge Complex, "Wildlife Disease," last updated May 23, 2011, https://www.fws.gov /saltonsea/botulism.html.
91. Northeast Wildlife Disease Cooperative, "Avian Cholera," last updated December 16, 2020, https://www.northeastwildlife.org/disease/avian-cholera.
92. Friend, "Avian Disease at the Salton Sea," 300.
93. See, for example, Tony Perry, "Salton Sea Study Findings Are Encouraging," *Los Angeles Times*, May 23, 1999; and Tony Perry, "A Fresh Battle between Local Water Adversaries," *Los Angeles Times*, October 18, 2010.

6. BOMBS

1. Stringfellow, *Greetings from the Salton Sea.*
2. Tony Perry, "Divers Examine Wreck of Plane in Salton Sea," *Los Angeles Times*, June 15, 1999.
3. For a gendered analysis of this way of looking at the Salton Sea, see Voyles, "Toxic Masculinity."
4. Voyles, *Wastelanding.*
5. Brenda D. Smith et al., "Class I Cultural Resources Inventory of the Salton Sea Region," prepared by Tetra Tech for the Salton Sea Authority and Bureau of Reclamation, August 2002, 4-44, https://www.cvwd.org/ArchiveCenter /ViewFile/Item/603.

6. Encompassing 635,811 acres of Serrano land, the base (called the Marine Corps Air Ground Combat Center as of 2020) is the sixth-largest military base in the United States.

7. Phukan et al., "Shorelines in the Desert."

8. The California-Arizona Maneuver Area and Desert Training Center was General George S. Patton's brainchild and encompassed thirty-five million acres. Smith et al., "Class I Cultural Resources Inventory of the Salton Sea Region," 4-43.

9. Smith et al., "Class I Cultural Resources Inventory of the Salton Sea Region," 4-43.

10 The federal government has speculated that all of these vehicles could feasibly have "dumped materials into the Sea, some of which may be hazardous." U.S. Environmental Protection Agency (hereafter EPA), "Final Preliminary Assessment Report: Salton Sea Test Base, Imperial County, California," EPA Identification: CA 2170023152, Potential Hazardous Waste Site Preliminary Assessment, September 1993, 2-31.

11. *Dictionary of American Military Aviation Squadrons*, chap. 4.

12. "Secret Equipment Was Dummy Bomb," *Santa Cruz Sentinel*, May 27, 1949.

13. "Salton Sea Atomic Energy Base Almost Ready, Report," *Palm Springs Desert Sun*, September 23, 1949.

14. EPA, "Final Preliminary Assessment Report," 2-31.

15. EPA, "Final Preliminary Assessment Report," 2-33.

16. For example, from 1965 to 1975, the marines used so much water that the underground aquifers dropped by an average of thirty-five feet. "Groundwater Resources of the Marine Corps Base, Twentynine Palms, San Bernardino County, California," U.S. Geological Survey Water Resources Investigations 77-37, January 1978, https://pubs.usgs.gov/wri/1977/0037/report.pdf.

17. Matt C. Bischoff, "The Desert Training Center/California-Arizona Maneuver Area, 1942–44: Historical and Archaeological Contexts," report prepared for the Bureau of Land Management and Corps of Engineers, 2000, 49, https://usace.contentdm.oclc.org/digital/collection/p266001coll1/id/5472/rec/1.

18. Boris I. Kuperman et al., "Invertebrates of the Salton Sea: A Scanning Electron Microscopy Portfolio," Salton Sea Authority, 2000, http://www.sci.sdsu.edu/salton/InvertebratePoster.html.

19. Geraci, Amrhein, and Goodson, "Barnacle Growth Rate on Artificial Substrate in the Salton Sea, California."

20. U.S. Army Corps of Engineers, "Formerly Used Defense Sites (FUDS) per State—California," FUDS, September 30, 2015, https://www.usace.army.mil/Portals/2/docs/Environmental/FUDS/FUDS_Inventory/FUDS_Inventory_California.pdf.

21. Perry, "Divers Examine Wreck of Plane in Salton Sea."

22. EPA, "Final Preliminary Assessment Report," 2-31.

23. Leland Johnson, "Tonopah Test Range: Outpost of Sandia National Laboratories," Sandia National Laboratories, March 1996, 16, https://doi.org/10.2172/230348.

24. "Salton Sea Atomic Energy Base Almost Ready, Report," *Palm Springs Desert Sun*, September 23, 1949.

25. "Atomic Energy Commission Salton Sea Base to Be Used for Equipment Tests Only," *Palm Springs Desert Sun*, October 12, 1948.

26. U.S. Fish and Wildlife Service, "Salton Sea National Wildlife Refuge and Waterfowl Development Areas Narrative Report," U.S. Department of the Interior, Brawley, California, August 1949, 9.

27. "Salton Sea Site for Atom Energy Plan," *Calexico Chronicle*, July 15, 1948; "Atomic Designs Being Tested at Salton Sea Base," *Palm Springs Desert Sun*, July 8, 1949.

28. "Probe Mystery Fire in Salton Sea Area," *Madera Tribune*, October 15, 1951.

29. L. Johnson, "Tonopah Test Range."

30. "Gates Open to Press at Formerly Secret Salton A-Bomb Test Range," *Calexico Chronicle*, September 8, 1955; "Salton Sea Test Base Plays Host," *Sandia Corporation Lab News*, September 9, 1955, 4, http://planet4589.com/space/archive/MartinPfeiffer/SandiaNews51-84/C0124_Lab_News_09-09-55.pdf.

31. It is worth quoting the EPA report at length: "Most available records from the time period state that the test shapes were 'inert.' 'Inert' as used in the correspondence from the time period meant not containing explosives or radioactive materials (i.e. non-enriched uranium). However, two memos from the Department of Energy (Department of Energy, Albuquerque Operations, Sandia Area Office: Salton Sea—Expended AEC Payload, July 18, 1978, and Department of Energy file: Letter to Mr. F. M. Keeports, September 12, 1962) indicate that at least one of the test units did contain uranium. Uranium was less expensive than concrete and easier to use than lead. Therefore, it was used as ballast in some of the test units. Specifically, an MK-6 flyaround test unit lost in the early 1950s 'contained 120# of normal uranium.'" EPA, "Final Preliminary Assessment Report," 2-32.

32. "Solid Waste Disposal Problems for Imperial County," *Calexico Chronicle*, June 18, 1970.

33. "Salton Sea Test Base in California 'Phased Out' by Sandia Corporation after Long Colorful History," *Sandia Corporation Lab News*, August 18, 1961, 4, http://planet4589.com/space/archive/MartinPfeiffer/SandiaNews51-84/C0284_Lab_News_08-18-61.pdf.

34. Susan Sontag, Michael Rogin, and Naomi Goldberg have all offered analyses of the 1950s monster movie craze, although each of them also relates the ways

in which the genre offered a more implicit critique of mass culture. See Pitkin, *Attack of the Blob*.

35. K. Brown, *Plutopia*, 4.
36. "Magnesium Statistics and Information," National Minerals Information Center, U.S. Geological Survey, n.d., https://www.usgs.gov/centers/nmic/magnesium -statistics-and-information; Charles Moosbrugger, ed., *Engineering Properties of Magnesium Alloys* (ASM International, 2017), chap. 1, https://www .asminternational.org/documents/10192/22833166/05920G_SampleChapter .pdf/d1a641ad-e4e8-789d-c565-c9c690c1931e.
37. Lelande Quick, "Miracle Metal from Nevada Hills," *Desert Magazine*, June 1944, https://archive.org/details/Desert-Magazine-1944-06/page/n9.
38. Gibson and Thayer, *Brief History*.
39. "Groundwater Perchlorate Map, Shallow Water-Bearing Zone, Second Quarter 2016," Annual Performance Report, Nevada Environmental Response Trust, plate 7, https://ndep.nv.gov/uploads/env-sitecleanup-active-bmi-nert/nert -endeavour-perchlorate-map.pdf.
40. "Toxic Substances Portal—Perchlorates," Agency for Toxic Substances and Disease Registry (ATSDR), September 2008, https://www.atsdr.cdc.gov/toxfaqs /tf.asp?id=893&tid=181.
41. Brechner et al., "Ammonium Perchlorate Contamination of Colorado River Drinking Water."
42. Sijimol et al., "Review on Fate, Toxicity, and Remediation of Perchlorate."
43. Kirk et al., "Perchlorate in Milk," 4979–81.
44. Shoddy regulation led to a widespread footprint from PEPCON and Tronox: "Perchlorate was released to the environment through disposal of wastes into unlined ponds and through other leaks from the facilities and is now found in the lower Colorado River from Lake Mead to the international boundary with Mexico." Holdren, Kelly, and Weghorst, "Evaluation of Potential Impacts of Perchlorate," 174.
45. Bass, "Agua Caliente," 234.
46. Imperial Irrigation District Water Conservation and Transfer Project and Draft Habitat Conservation Plan: Environmental Impact Statement, vol. 2, January 1, 2002, https://play.google.com/store/books/details?id=wQUzAQAAMAAJ &pcampaignid=books_web_aboutlink; Torres Martinez Desert Cahuilla Indian Tribe and Environmental Protection Agency Region IX, email announcing "Tribal Concerns Perchlorate Contamination Conference," in Parker, Arizona, September 2003, http://www.cpeo.org/lists/military/2003/msg00984.html.
47. Coachella Valley Water District, "Thomas E. Levy Groundwater Replenishment Facility," YouTube video, March 15, 2012, https://www.youtube.com/watch?v =KG0msaUptUo.

48. EPA, "National Primary Drinking Water Regulations," accessed October 10, 2020, https://www.epa.gov/ground-water-and-drinking-water/national-primary -drinking-water-regulations#one; EPA, "Perchlorate in Drinking Water: Final Action," accessed October 10, 2020, https://www.epa.gov/sdwa/perchlorate -drinking-water.

49. U.S. Bureau of Reclamation, "Water Conservation and Transfer Project—Final EIR/EIS," October 2002, sec. 3.9–14, https://www.usbr.gov/lc/region/g4000 /IID_FEIS/Vol_2/Sec_03.09.pdf.

50. Terria Smith, "Thirsty for Drinkable Water in Torres Martinez," *Center for Health Journalism* (blog), September 30, 2013, https://www.centerforhealthjournalism .org/2013/09/30/thirsty-drinkable-water-torres-martinez.

51. Sijimol et al., "Review on Fate, Toxicity, and Remediation of Perchlorate," 130.

52. Barnd, *Native Space*.

53. "Cahuilla," Naval History and Heritage Command, accessed October 10, 2020, https://www.history.navy.mil/content/history/nhhc/research/histories/ship -histories/danfs/c/cahuilla.html. The habit of naming tug, rescue, and salvage vessels after Native nations echoes historian Noah Riseman's observation that "government officials discounted the need for, and effectiveness of, indigenous fighters" in World War II, and "the participation of indigenous servicemen in the war did *not* represent widespread appreciation of indigenous culture or fighting skills." Riseman, *Defending Whose Country?*, 5.

54. Franco, *Crossing the Pond*; Bernstein, *American Indians and World War II*; Townsend, *World War II and the American Indian*; Gordon, *Cahuilla Nation Activism and the Tribal Casino Movement*.

55. Dozier, *Heart Is Fire*, 76–77.

56. Franco, *Crossing the Pond*; Bernstein, *American Indians and World War II*; Townsend, *World War II and the American Indian*.

57. Office of Indian Affairs, *Indians in the War*, 16.

58. Fixico, *Termination and Relocation*; Philp, *Termination Revisited*; Arnold, *Bartering with the Bones of Their Dead*; Costo and Costo, *Natives of the Golden State*, 325–27.

59. V. Deloria, *Custer Died for Your Sins*, 76.

60. Mazzetti, "Slavery in the Missions," 154.

61. Daly, "Fractured Relations at Home," 432–33.

62. Arnold, *Bartering with the Bones of Their Dead*; Barker, *Sovereignty Matters*.

63. "$57,721 Worth of Indian Land Sold by U.S. Bureau," *Palm Springs Desert Sun*, November 29, 1955.

64. Dozier, *Heart Is Fire*, 147–50.

65. Ojibwe historian Brenda J. Child describes this reclamation of community gatherings under the mantle of patriotism as "a clever ploy to continue hold- ing traditional gatherings in an era when such activities were being banned

and suppressed" by assimilationist Indian policies. Child, *My Grandfather's Knocking Sticks*, 125.

66. Quoted in "Morongo Indians Win Approval of Indian Village, Museum Plan," *Palm Springs Desert Sun*, April 19, 1966.

7. CHAINS

1. "Lynching or Suicide?," *Los Angeles Herald*, April 30, 1890.
2. Hughes, *History of Banning and San Gorgonio Pass in Two Parts*, 33–34.
3. "Left Dangling," *San Bernardino Daily Courier*, April 30, 1890.
4. Quoted in "No! No!," *San Bernardino Daily Courier*, May 11, 1890.
5. "The Banning Lynching," *Los Angeles Times*, May 1, 1890.
6. Lytle Hernández, *City of Inmates*.
7. As Salish historian Luana Ross put it, "Because we are a colonized people, the experiences of imprisonment are, unfortunately, exceedingly familiar." Ross's work has emphasized the frequency with which Native people "disappeared" into "Euro-American institutions of confinement" and the ties between this frequent disappearance and larger colonial forces. Ross, *Inventing the Savage*, 1. In a different, though related, analysis Kānaka Maoli writer Kalaniopua Young has examined how "the historical linkages between surveillance, criminalization, incarceration, and Native dispossession" have functioned to underpin "U.S. Imperialism in Hawai'i" in ways that are deeply gendered and cis-sexist. Young, "From a Native *Trans* Daughter," 89. For more on the settler colonial context and power of incarceration in Indigenous peoples' lives, see Grobsmith, *Indians in Prison*; Lytle Hernández, *City of Inmates*; and Burch, *Committed*. For broader analysis of incarceration in California, see Gilmore, *Golden Gulag*.
8. Pfeifer, *Rough Justice*.
9. Diary of J. Goldsborough Bruff, 1850, quoted in Heizer and Almquist, *Other Californians*, 25.
10. Indian Census Rolls, 1885–1940, National Archives Microfilm Publication M595, Record Group 75, Records of the Bureau of Indian Affairs, 1793–1999, National Archives and Records Administration, Washington DC.
11. Modesto and Mount, *Not for Innocent Ears*, 56.
12. Saubel and Elliott, *'Isill Héqwas Wáxish/A Dried Coyote's Tail*, 949–50.
13. Karlos Hill provides analysis of what he calls "the racialization of lynching," in which lynching became a technology of white supremacist violence targeting Black people in particular. Hill, *Beyond the Rope*, 10–12; Lancaster, *Bullets and Fire*, 6; Pfeifer, *Rough Justice*; Rodriguez, "Noose That Builds the Nation."
14. Lindsay, *Murder State*, 247; Hanks, *This War Is for a Whole Life*, 20.
15. Arvin, Tuck, and Morrill, "Decolonizing Feminism," 13.
16. Historian Sarah Haley has described this as "the gendered logics of punishment." Haley, *No Mercy Here*, 5.

17. Miranda, *Bad Indians*; Deer, *Beginning and End of Rape*.

18. Documentary evidence that gender-based violence mobilized genocide in California during its earliest years of statehood underscores the point made by Native feminists that settler colonialism has always been a gendered and sexualized project. For sources that document gender-based violence against Native peoples in early California, see Robertson, "'Crying Rock Where They Killed the Children"; Hurtado, *Indian Survival on the California Frontier*, 169–92; Heizer, *Destruction of California Indians*, 278–84; Chávez-García, *Negotiating Conquest*; Carrico, *Strangers in a Stolen Land*, 66–68; Miranda, *Bad Indians*; and Risling Baldy, *We Are Dancing for You*. For Native feminist frameworks that explain the intersections of colonization and patriarchy, see Denetdale, "Chairmen, Presidents, and Princesses"; Arvin, Tuck, and Morrill, "Decolonizing Feminism"; Deer, *Beginning and End of Rape*; and Barker, *Critically Sovereign*.

19. As Cutcha Risling Baldy has noted, violence against Native women was often described in settler accounts as them being "taken"—"something that is not often elaborated in the historical record but usually resulted in forced marriage, concubinage, enslavement, or sex slavery." Risling Baldy, *We Are Dancing for You*, 60–61. See also Miranda, *Bad Indians*.

20. Rawls, *Indians of California*; Miranda, *Bad Indians*; Lindsay, *Murder State*; Madley, *American Genocide*; Risling Baldy, *We Are Dancing for You*.

21. Thorne, "Death of Superintendent Stanley," 239.

22. Thorne, "Death of Superintendent Stanley," 242.

23. Thorne, "Death of Superintendent Stanley," 242.

24. Lytle Hernández, *City of Inmates*.

25. Gilmore, *Golden Gulag*; Alexander and West, *New Jim Crow*; Dilts, *Punishment and Inclusion*.

26. "Locals, Valley Briefs and Personals," *Calexico Chronicle*, March 25, 1909; April 22, 1909.

27. C. L. Ellis, Special Supervisor in Charge, "Annual Report for 1929," Mission Indian Agency of California, Riverside, California, June 30, 1929, Records of the Mission Indian Agency.

28. "Good Morning Judge!," *Calexico Chronicle*, January 15, 1929.

29. "Locals, Valley Briefs and Personals," *Calexico Chronicle*, May 20, 1909.

30. "He 'Flew De Coop,'" *Imperial Valley Press*, October 22, 1904.

31. "Local News," *Calexico Chronicle*, May 18, 1905.

32. "Imperial," *Imperial Valley Press*, April 8, 1905.

33. "Chain Gang Is Out on Strike: Oklahoma Indian Blamed for the Labor Conditions among Members," *Calexico Chronicle*, October 16, 1915.

34. "A Break for the Border," *Imperial Valley Press*, December 7, 1907.

35. "Two Month Liberty Ended for Negro; Captured in Utah," *Calexico Chronicle*, December 18, 1940.

36. "County Applies for $100,000 in Reconstruction," *Calexico Chronicle*, October 29, 1932.
37. "County to Aid Relief Program for Unemployed," *Calexico Chronicle*, November 7, 1933.
38. "Preference Given Farmers' Relief," *Calexico Chronicle*, November 14, 1933.
39. "Mexican Escapes Rock Pit Camp; Police Notified," *Calexico Chronicle*, June 12, 1934.
40. "Prisoners Must Work at Places Sheriff Decides," *Calexico Chronicle*, June 14, 1934.
41. "Prisoners Will Go to Work at Old Rock Quarry," *Calexico Chronicle*, April 27, 1938.
42. "Valley 'Devil's Island' Prison Camp Closed; Hobo Hordes Pleased," *Calexico Chronicle*, May 4, 1939.
43. Indigenous studies scholar Vine Deloria Jr. has aptly described the larger system in which these forms of punishment took place: "America's prison population," he wrote in 1969, "continues to climb as society attempts to punish those guilty of violating its mores. Little is done to restore the victim to his original state." V. Deloria, *Custer Died for Your Sins*, 236, 238.
44. John W. Dady, Superintendent, "Narrative Report for the Fiscal Year 1936," Records of the Mission Indian Agency.
45. The national incarceration rate on state and federal charges combined was 117 per 100,000 people in 1937, or 0.11 percent of the population. "Prisoners 1925–81."
46. Ross, *Inventing the Savage*, 16.
47. "Toxic Water Kills Fish at Salton Sea," *San Bernardino Sun*, June 13, 1970.
48. California Division of Forestry, Engineering and Camps Section, *Division of Forestry in the California Conservation Camp Program*, 66.
49. Raymond, *California Division of Forestry in 1957*, 37–38.
50. Raymond, *California Division of Forestry in 1957*, 37, 38–39.
51. "An Act to Add Chapter 11," 11.
52. McAfee, "History of Convict Labor in California," 28.
53. Quoted in "5000-Man Conservation Corps for Conservation Is Formed," *La Habra Star*, November 2, 1966.
54. California Division of Forestry, Engineering and Camps Section, *Division of Forestry in the California Conservation Camp Program*, 2.
55. "Men to Match the Mountains," *Palm Springs Desert Sun*, May 11, 1973.
56. Chiang, *Nature behind Barbed Wire*.
57. "Paying Their Dues as Flood Clean Up Crews," *Palm Springs Desert Sun*, October 2, 1976.
58. Salton Sea National Wildlife Refuge, Calipatria, California, "Annual Narrative Report Calendar Year 1990," U.S. Department of the Interior Fish and

Wildlife Service, National Wildlife Refuge System, sec. E, https://nrm.dfg.ca
.gov/FileHandler.ashx?DocumentID=7735.

59. Review and Approval, Salton Sea National Wildlife Refuge Calipatria, California, "Annual Narrative Report Calendar Year 1991," U.S. Department of the
Interior Fish and Wildlife Service, National Wildlife Refuge System, sec. E,
https://nrm.dfg.ca.gov/FileHandler.ashx?DocumentID=7919.

60. "McCain Valley Conservation Camp #21," California Department of Corrections
and Rehabilitation, accessed October 6, 2020, https://www.cdcr.ca.gov/.

61. "Stats and Events," CAL Fire, accessed October 6, 2020, https://www.fire.ca
.gov/stats-events/.

62. Goodman, "Hero and Inmate," 357.

63. Quoted in Goodman, "Hero and Inmate," 361.

64. Weill, "Prisoners on the Fireline."

65. Goodman, "Hero and Inmate," 360.

66. Anderson, *Tending the Wild.*

67. Norgaard, *Salmon and Acorns Feed Our People.*

68. Pyne, *Between Two Fires*, 86.

69. Anderson, *Tending the Wild.*

70. For in-depth analysis of fire suppression policy as a central component of
settler colonial power in California, see Norgaard, *Salmon and Acorns Feed
Our People*, chap. 2.

71. Gilmore, *Golden Gulag.*

72. California Department of Corrections and Rehabilitation, "Sustainability
Roadmap, 2018–2019: Progress Report and Plan for Meeting the Governor's
Sustainability Goals for California State Agencies," Green California, June 30,
2018, https://www.green.ca.gov/search/?q=%22sustainability+roadmap%22.

73. Heather Harris et al., "California's Prison Population," Just the Facts (Public
Policy Institute of California), July 2019, https://www.ppic.org/publication
/californias-prison-population/.

74. Data Analysis Unit, "California Prisoners and Parolees, 2008: Summary Statistics
on Adult Felon Prisoners and Parolees, Civil Narcotic Addicts and Outpatients
and Other Populations," Estimates and Statistical Analysis Section, Sacramento, California: Offender Information Services Branch of the Department
of Corrections and Rehabilitation, 2009, accessed March 24, 2021, https://
www.prisonlegalnews.org/media/publications/doc_california_prisoners_and
_parolees_2008_statistics.pdf. In 2014, even after a significant decline in the
state's overall prison population, Calipatria remained massively overcrowded
at 167 percent of its design capacity.

75. "Officials: Prison's 'Death' Fence Is Killing Birds," Associated Press, January
25, 1994, https://apnews.com/article/c63f2285e74328bc0ba1dd087999a94d.

76. "Birds Are Shielded from Electric Prison Fences," *New York Times*, April 13, 1998.

77. Gervais et al., "Burrowing Owl (*Athene cunicularia*)."

78. Mike Davis, "A Prison-Industrial Complex: Hell Factories in the Field," *The Nation*, February 20, 1995.

79. Voyles, "Man Destroys Nature?"

80. In Alabama, for example, prisons have been pumping "extremely high levels of toxic ammonia, fecal coliform, viruses, and parasites into local streams and rivers" since 1991, contributing to algae blooms, killing plants and animals, and rendering water unfit for human use. John E. Dannenberg, "Prison Drinking Water and Wastewater Pollution Threaten Environmental Safety Nationwide," *Prison Legal News*, November 15, 2007, https://www.prisonlegalnews.org/news/2007/nov/15/prison-drinking-water-and-wastewater-pollution-threaten-environmental-safety-nationwide/.

81. As the U.S. Environmental Protection Agency noted in 2002, "Supporting [prison] populations, including their buildings and grounds, requires heating and cooling, wastewater treatment, hazardous waste and trash disposal, asbestos management, drinking water supply, pesticide use, vehicle maintenance and power production, to name a few potential environmental hazards. . . . From the inspections, it is clear many prisons have room for improvement." "Prison Ecology Project | Nation Inside," Nation Inside, 2016, https://nationinside.org/campaign/prison-ecology/facts/. Companies took advantage of a California law that allowed them to employ incarcerated people in manufacturing jobs. A San Diego manufacturing company moved its production facilities from the maquiladora corridor in Mexico to the Calipatria prison, where inmates welded products and made tools. Marc Ballad, "Captive Work Force Filling Labor Gaps," *Los Angeles Times*, September 22, 1999.

82. Thompson, "Prison Industrial Complex."

83. Panagioti Tsolkas, "Incarceration, Justice and the Planet: How the Fight against Toxic Prisons May Shape the Future of Environmentalism," *Prison Legal News*, June 3, 2016, https://www.prisonlegalnews.org/news/2016/jun/3/ncarceration-justice-and-planet-how-fight-against-toxic-prisons-may-shape-future-environmentalism/.

84. Candice Bernd, Zoe Loftus-Farren, and Maureen Nandini Mitra, "America's Toxic Prisons: The Environmental Injustices of Mass Incarceration," *Prison Legal News*, April 2, 2018, https://www.prisonlegalnews.org/news/2018/apr/2/americas-toxic-prisons-environmental-injustices-mass-incarceration/.

85. This is true elsewhere as well: "mass incarceration in the U.S. impacts the health of prisoners, prison-adjacent communities and local ecosystems from coast to coast." Bernd, Loftus-Farren, and Mitra, "America's Toxic Prisons."

86. "Pathogen Total Maximum Daily Load for the New River," draft, California Environmental Protection Agency Regional Water Quality Control Board, April 12, 2001, https://www.epa.gov/sites/production/files/2015-07/documents/17_tmdls_stormwater_sources.pdf.

87. "Hazardous Waste Generators and Facilities," California Office of Health Hazard Assessment, accessed October 6, 2020, https://oehha.ca.gov/calenviroscreen/indicator/hazardous-waste-generators-and-facilities.

88. California Office of Administrative Law, "Regarding Petitioner Tuvalu Tutuila concerning a Statewide Toilet Flushing Policy," *California Regulatory Notice Register*, March 7, 2008, Register 2008, No. 10-z edition.

89. These environmental problems with the capacity to impact the health of imprisoned people are not restricted to Calipatria. The Natural Resources Defense Council (NRDC) has identified a number of federal prisons located on or near toxic waste sites. Nicole Greenfield, "The Connection between Mass Incarceration and Environmental Justice," *onEarth*, January 19, 2018, https://www.nrdc.org/onearth/connection-between-mass-incarceration-and-environmental-justice. California's Central Valley poses similar risks to prisoners—pesticide drift, air and water pollution, dust—but environmental health in the Central Valley is also compromised by numerous waste incinerators. Braz and Gilmore, "Joining Forces," 96.

90. Grenier v. Semple, CT, Amended Complaint, Radon Gas Exposure, 2016, "No Escape: Exposure to Toxic Coal Waste at State Correctional Institution Fayette," Abolitionist Law Center and Human Rights Coalition, n.d., https://abolitionistlawcenter.org/wp-content/uploads/2014/09/no-escape-3-3mb.pdf; David Reutter, "California Prisoners Still Forced to Drink Arsenic-Laced Water," *Prison Legal News*, August 15, 2011, https://www.prisonlegalnews.org/news/2011/aug/15/california-prisoners-still-forced-to-drink-arsenic-laced-water; Prescott, "Prisoner (In)Consideration in Environmental Justice Analyses"; Helppie-Schmieder, "Toxic Confinement."

91. Panagioti Tsolkas, "California Prison Spends $417,000 on Bottled Water as Contamination, Violations Continue," *Prison Legal News*, August 7, 2018, https://www.prisonlegalnews.org/news/2018/aug/7/california-prison-spends-417000-bottled-water-contamination-violations-continue/.

92. California Department of Corrections and Rehabilitation, "Sustainability Roadmap, 2018–2019: Progress Report and Plan for Meeting the Governor's Sustainability Goals for California State Agencies," https://www.green.ca.gov/Documents/CDCR/2018_2019_Consolidated_CDCR_SustainabilityRoadmap.pdf.

93. Calipatria State Prison Medical Inspection Results, Office of the Inspector General, July 2010, https://www.oig.ca.gov/wp-content/uploads/2019/05/CAL-Medical-Inspection-Results-1.pdf.

94. Desante, Ruhlen, and Burton, "Results of the 1991 Census," 59.

95. Vanhouche and Beyens, "Introduction"; Pellow, "Struggles for Environmental Justice in U.S. Prisons and Jails"; Bernd, Loftus-Farren, and Mitra, "America's Toxic Prisons"; Calipatria State Prison Medical Inspection Results, Office of the Inspector General, July 2010.

96. Nolan, "Prison Ecopoetics."

97. Margaret Severson and Christine Wilson Duclos, "American Indian Suicides in Jail: Can Risk Screening Be Culturally Sensitive?," National Criminal Justice Reference Service, U.S. Department of Justice, 2005, https://www.ncjrs.gov/pdffiles1/nij/207326.pdf; Lawrence A. Greenfeld and Steven K. Smith, "American Indians and Crime," Bureau of Justice Statistics, U.S. Department of Justice, 1999, http://bjs.gov/content/pub/pdf/aic.pdf; Todd D. Minton, "Jails in Indian Country, 2011," Bureau of Justice Statistics, U.S. Department of Justice, 2012, http://bjs.gov/content/pub/pdf/jic11.pdf.

98. "Joint Submission to the U.N. Committee on the Elimination of Racial Discrimination: Concerning Religious Freedoms of Indigenous Persons Deprived of Their Liberty in the United States of America, in Relation to the United States' Combined 7th, 8th, and 9th Periodic Reports," United Nations Committee on the Elimination of Racial Discrimination, August 1, 2014, https://www.nativeamericanbar.org/wp-content/uploads/2014/01/8-1-14-Supplemental-Joint-Submission-By-Huy-NCAI-USET-NARF-ACLU-et-al-to-U-N-Committee-on-the-Elimination-of-Racial-Discrimination-Re-American-Indigenous-Prisoners-Rel.pdf.

99. "Joint Submission to the U.N. Committee on the Elimination of Racial Discrimination," 9.

100. Martinez v. Schwarzenegger et al., Southern District of California, casd-3:2008-cv-00565, https://www.docketbird.com/court-documents/Martinez-v-Schwarzenegger-et-al/ORDER-Denying-Plaintiff-039-s-50-Motion-for-Class-Certification-Signed-by-Judge-Roger-T-Benitez-on-3-24-2011-knh/casd-3:2008-cv-00565-00101.

101. "Joint Submission to the U.N. Committee on the Elimination of Racial Discrimination," 11.

102. In Re Gregory L. Rhoads on Habeas Corpus, Court of Appeal, Fourth District, Division 1, California, D070488, decided: March 22, 2017, https://caselaw.findlaw.com/ca-court-of-appeal/1856720.html.

8. TOXINS

1. "Agricultural Crop Report, County of Imperial," Imperial County Department of Agriculture, 1949, https://agcom.imperialcounty.org/crop-reports/; Bovey, *Mesquite*, 122–24.

2. James G. Setmire et al., *Detailed Study of Water Quality, Bottom Sediment, and Biota Associated with Irrigation Drainage in the Salton Sea Area, California, 1988–90*, Report 93-4014, U.S. Geological Survey Water Resources Investigations, 1993, https://nrm.dfg.ca.gov/FileHandler.ashx?DocumentID=8842.

3. Despite causing generations of devastating impacts on Vietnamese people and environments, Agent Orange would not even be the most notorious of these products; *that* designation would go to either mustard gas, invented by Dow for use in World War I, or napalm, also used in the war in Vietnam. Pellow, *Resisting Global Toxics*, 159–60.

4. For context on growers' motivations in applying pesticides, see Pulido, *Environmentalism and Economic Justice*, 73.

5. *California Agriculture* magazine archives, http://calag.ucanr.edu/Archive/.

6. "Agricultural Crop Report, County of Imperial," 1949; B. A. Harrigan, "Agricultural Crop Report," Imperial County Department of Agriculture, 1948; "Agricultural Crop Report, County of Imperial," Imperial County Department of Agriculture, 1952; B. A. Harrigan, "Agricultural Crop Report," Imperial County Department of Agriculture, 1952, all at https://agcom.imperialcounty.org/crop-reports/.

7. Pellow, *Resisting Global Toxics*, 159.

8. Sapozhnikova, Bawardi, and Schlenk, "Pesticides and PCBs in Sediments and Fish."

9. "Agricultural Crop Report, County of Imperial," 1949.

10. Harrigan, "Agricultural Crop Report," 1952.

11. "Farm News," *Calexico Chronicle*, June 20, 1946.

12. "On This Side of the Sun," *Palm Springs Desert Sun*, October 20, 1944.

13. Robert Quillen, "Aunt Het," *San Bernardino Sun*, April 15, 1945.

14. "Beekeepers to Hold Meeting," *Madera Tribune*, January 16, 1945; "Beekeepers from Over California Hold Convention," *Calexico Chronicle*, December 12, 1946; "Poisons Killing Bee Industry, Authority Says," *Calexico Chronicle*, June 15, 1948.

15. Twin Cities Seed and Feed Co., "Archie Says," *Calexico Chronicle*, October 4, 1945.

16. University of California, College of Agriculture, Agricultural Experiment Station, *Investigations with DDT in California, 1944: A Preliminary Report*, Division of Entomology and Parasitology, University of California, Berkeley, 1945.

17. "Polio Scare Brings DDT Spray Here," *Calexico Chronicle*, June 24, 1948.

18. "Opinion on Pollution of Canals and Waterways thru Agricultural Chemicals Will Affect Valley," *Calexico Chronicle*, July 28, 1966; "Salton Sea Not Polluted by Chemicals," *Palm Springs Desert Sun*, January 19, 1963.

19. "Salton Sea, California: Water Quality and Ecological Management Considerations," Pacific Southwest Region: U.S. Department of the Interior, Federal

Water Quality Administration, July 1970, 50, https://nrmsecure.dfg.ca.gov
/FileHandler.ashx?DocumentID=9251.

20. These worries mirrored larger anxieties throughout the United States about the
effects of pesticides on human and nonhuman health. Markowitz and Rosner,
Deceit and Denial.

21. Pulido, *Environmentalism and Economic Justice*, 74.

22. These tendencies reflect what geographer Laura Pulido calls a "dense set
of interlocking relationships between regulators and agribusiness." Pulido,
Environmentalism and Economic Justice, 74. As Pulido and others note, the
major regulatory stumbling block antipesticide activists have encountered in
the United States, but not elsewhere, has been an institutional and ideological
view that chemical compounds are "innocent until proven guilty." Elsewhere,
pesticides have been governed according to a precautionary principle that
assumes that they can cause harm until proven safe. See Pulido, *Environmentalism and Economic Justice*; Steingraber, *Living Downstream*, 287–90; and
Harrison, *Pesticide Drift and the Pursuit of Environmental Justice*, 108.

23. Pulido, *Environmentalism and Economic Justice*, 87–88.

24. "Salton Sea Not Polluted by Chemicals," *Palm Springs Desert Sun*; "Salton Sea,"
Calexico Chronicle, September 29, 1966.

25. "Lawyer Says Wastes Not Hurting Fish: Salton Sea Said to Be Safe for Recreation," *Los Angeles Times*, April 15, 1966.

26. This is often referred to as a "proof of harm" model for regulation of noxious
chemicals and a sharp contrast to the "precautionary principle," or the principle that "public and private interests should act to prevent harm before it
occurs," which many ecologists and public health policy makers have advocated.
Steingraber, *Living Downstream*, 281. For more on changing understandings of
how pesticides move in ecosystems, see Nash, *Inescapable Ecologies*, 170–72.

27. This is a prime example of "linguistic detoxification," a phrase coined by ecologist Barry Commoner to describe what he called a "crisis of environmental
regulation" in which expert policy makers frame the public's understanding
of risk, often in misleading ways, when it comes to their exposures to toxins in
the course of everyday life. Commoner, "After 20 Years," 28. Historian Linda
Nash, while noting the risk to people at the point of application of pesticides
(that is, farmworkers), has pointed out that "regulators did little to assess
the presence of chemicals in the broader environment; they assumed that
the ongoing use of chemicals had no relevance to most people's health." The
brilliance and extraordinary impact of farmworkers' framing of the pesticide
problem in the 1960s derived from their framing of the poisons within "an
ecological model of health"—the exact opposite way of looking at the issue
as that taken by public health officials. Nash, *Inescapable Ecologies*, 172, 164.

28. Pulido, *Environmentalism and Economic Justice*; Uribe v. Howie, 19 Cal. App. 3d 194, 213 (4th District, 1971).

29. Scharlin and Villanueva, "'Most Important $2 in My Life.'"

30. "Coachella to Calexico March—Velasco," Farmworker Movement Online Gallery, University of California, San Diego, https://libraries.ucsd.edu /farmworkermovement/; "March to Mexico Builds," *El Malcriado*, May 1969, Farmworker Movement Documentation Project, University of California, San Diego, https://libraries.ucsd.edu/farmworkermovement/.

31. Newspapers solicitously referred to Bozick's clearly illegal actions as a "citizen's arrest." "Three Union Men Arrested by Citizen," *Palm Springs Desert Sun*, June 13, 1969; "Break Due in Grape Strike? Valley Rancher Calls Conference, Speculation Rife," *Palm Springs Desert Sun*, June 13, 1969.

32. Digitized issues of *El Macriado* are archived at the University of California, San Diego, library's website: https://libraries.ucsd.edu/farmworkermovement /archives/#malcriado.

33. Uribe v. Howie, 19 Cal. App. 3d 194, 213 (4th District, 1971). See also Harrison, *Pesticide Drift and the Pursuit of Environmental Justice*, 148; Pulido, *Environmentalism and Economic Justice*, 96–97.

34. "California Indian Basketweavers Association," *Akwesasne Notes*, June 30, 1995; "Basketry Symposium at the Southwest Museum," *California Indian Basketweavers Association Newsletter*, June 1997.

35. As the organization stated in 1995, "Many of the plants targeted by herbicide spraying of forests are the same plants which provide Native Americans with foods and teas, are used in baskets and regalia, or for healing, ceremonial and other traditional purposes. People may come into contact with the poisons when gathering, processing, ingesting or using the plants or plant products. In preparing basketry materials, the weaver usually places them in her mouth. Basketweavers have complained of numbness and other ill effects after processing materials that may have been sprayed. In addition, crops such as acorns are an important source of food for many tribes, yet oak trees and other broad-leafed plants are often doused with herbicides because they 'compete' with commercially-harvested conifers." "California Indian Basketweavers Association," *Akwesasne Notes*.

36. "Basketry Symposium at the Southwest Museum," *California Indian Basketweavers Association Newsletter*.

37. "CIBA Policy Statement on Pesticides," California Indian Basketweavers Association, https://ciba.org/ciba-policy-statement-on-pesticides/. Elizabeth Hoover notes that the use of the word "poisons" among Indigenous people to refer to pesticides has a specific political and epistemological purpose: to denote these chemicals as "not merely substances out of place, but rather chemicals with the ability to injure, impair, or even kill." Hoover, *River Is in Us*, 124–25.

38. "CIBA Policy Statement on Pesticides," California Indian Basketweavers Association.

39. Historian Joshua Reid describes these practices among Indigenous peoples as building toward "traditional futures." Indigenous studies scholar Cutcha Risling Baldy roots them specifically within Indigenous feminist practices of "(re)writing, (re)righting, and (re)riting" Indigenous culture and self-determination. Reid, *Sea Is My Country*, 277–78; Risling Baldy, *We Are Dancing for You*, 8.

40. The refusal of these communities to put in place sewage treatment infrastructure led to a standoff in the early 1950s, during which Calexico and Brawley resisted coaxing by state and federal officials to treat their sewage because, they insisted, Mexicali did not treat *theirs*.

41. Hahn, *Location of Odor Sources and the Affected Population in Imperial County, California*, 29.

42. California Water Boards, Colorado River-R7, "Introduction to the New River/Mexicali Sanitation Program," n.d., https://www.waterboards.ca.gov/coloradoriver/water_issues/programs/new_river/nr_intro.html.

43. Setmire et al., *Detailed Study of Water Quality*, 1.

44. Setmire et al., *Detailed Study of Water Quality*, 5.

45. Tony Perry, "After 50 Years, New Hope for Detoxifying New River," *Los Angeles Times*, November 4, 1995.

46. Ray, *Ecological Other*.

47. "Pathogen Total Maximum Daily Load for the New River," draft, California Environmental Protection Agency Regional Water Quality Control Board, April 12, 2001, https://www.epa.gov/sites/production/files/2015-07/documents/17_tmdls_stormwater_sources.pdf. See also Vlaming et al., "Irrigation Runoff Insecticide Pollution of Rivers in the Imperial Valley, California (USA)."

48. Sánchez, "Health and Environmental Risks of the Maquiladora in Mexicali," 166.

49. Furnish and Ladman, "Colorado River Salinity Agreement of 1973 and the Mexicali Valley."

50. Pellow, *Resisting Global Toxics*.

51. Sánchez, "Health and Environmental Risks of the Maquiladora in Mexicali," 163.

52. K. Collins et al., "Imperial-Mexicali Valleys," 4.

53. Pellow and Park, *Silicon Valley of Dreams*, 88; Ehrenreich and Hochschild, *Global Woman*.

54. Pellow and Park, *Silicon Valley of Dreams*, 85; Frey, "Transfer of Core-Based Hazardous Production Processes."

55. Sánchez, "Health and Environmental Risks of the Maquiladora in Mexicali," 184.

56. Sánchez, "Health and Environmental Risks of the Maquiladora in Mexicali," 171–72; Pellow and Park, *Silicon Valley of Dreams*; Frey, "Transfer of Core-Based Hazardous Production Processes."

57. "Female Worker in the Maquiladores," *Calexico Chronicle*, March 14, 1985; Sánchez, "Health and Environmental Risks of the Maquiladora in Mexicali"; Pellow and Park, *Silicon Valley of Dreams*.

58. Sánchez, "Health and Environmental Risks of the Maquiladora in Mexicali."

59. "Introduction to the New River/Mexicali Sanitation Program," California Water Boards–Colorado, last updated September 24, 2020, https://www.waterboards .ca.gov/coloradoriver/water_issues/programs/new_river/nr_intro.html.

60. David Kelly, "Reservation's Toxic Dumps a Multilayered Nightmare," *Los Angeles Times*, June 2, 2007.

61. McGovern, *Campo Indian Landfill War*.

62. Quoted in Seth Mydans, "Thermal Journal: Tribe Smells Sludge and Bureaucrats," *New York Times*, October 20, 1994, sec. "U.S.," https://www.nytimes .com/1994/10/20/us/thermal-journal-tribe-smells-sludge-and-bureaucrats .html; Goldberg-Ambrose, "Public Law 280 and the Problem of Lawlessness in California Indian Country."

63. Grinde and Johansen, *Ecocide of Native America*; Gedicks, *Resource Rebels*; Grijalva, *Closing the Circle*; Wildcat, *Red Alert!*; Goldtooth (Mato Awanyankapi), "State of Indigenous America Series"; LaDuke, *All Our Relations*; LaDuke, *Recovering the Sacred*; Vickery and Hunter, "Native Americans"; Hoover, *River Is in Us*; Powell, *Vanishing America*; Gilio-Whitaker, *As Long as Grass Grows*.

64. Estes, "Fighting for Our Lives"; Gilio-Whitaker, *As Long as Grass Grows*; Dhillon, "Introduction"; Estes and Dhillon, *Standing with Standing Rock*; Estes, *Our History Is the Future*; Sherwood, "Political Binds of Oil versus Tribes."

65. This is distinct from non-Indigenous definitions of environmental justice, which explore how racism and classism, distinct from settler colonialism, produce environmental injustices. Gilio-Whitaker, *As Long as Grass Grows*.

66. Reid, "Articulating a Traditional Future."

67. Marshall, "Why Emergency Physicians Should Care about the Salton Sea"; Parajuli and Zender, "Projected Changes in Dust Emissions and Regional Air Quality Due to the Shrinking Salton Sea"; Pavlik, *California Deserts*, 278.

68. Johnston et al., "Disappearing Salton Sea," 812.

69. Johnston et al., "Disappearing Salton Sea," 806.

70. Parajuli and Zender, "Projected Changes in Dust Emissions and Regional Air Quality Due to the Shrinking Salton Sea," 83.

71. Johnston et al., "Disappearing Salton Sea," 804, 814.

72. Marshall, "Why Emergency Physicians Should Care about the Salton Sea," 1008.

73. For example, in the Eastern Coachella Valley 94 percent of the population is nonwhite and 65 percent live below the poverty line; in Imperial County, more than 80 percent of the population is Latina/o and have "some of the highest rates of unemployment and poverty in the nation." London, Greenfield, and

Zagofsky, *Revealing the Invisible Coachella Valley*; Johnston et al., "Disappearing Salton Sea," 814.

74. Huang and London, "Mapping in and out of 'Messes'"; London, Greenfield, and Zagofsky, *Revealing the Invisible Coachella Valley*.

75. Pavlik, *California Deserts*, 278–79.

76. "Programs," Comite Civico del Valle, https://www.ccvhealth.org/index.php #program.

77. Chris Clarke, "Why Don't Californians Care about Saving the Salton Sea?," KCET, October 15, 2015, https://www.kcet.org/redefine/why-dont-californians -care-about-saving-the-salton-sea.

78. "SOS! Action Resources," EcoMedia Compass, https://www.ecomediacompass .org/sos-activist-page.

79. For example, see Ian James, "Plan to Save Salton Sea Called for Creating Thousands of Acres of Wetlands, but Less Than 50 Acres Have Been Built," *Palm Springs Desert Sun*, March 26, 2018.

80. Indigenous studies scholar Max Liboiron has examined pollution through the framework of "colonial land relations" and premised research on pollution and plastics from the understanding that "pollution is best understood as the violence of colonial land relations." Liboiron, *Pollution Is Colonialism*, 5–7.

CONCLUSION

1. "Overview," Position Vector Salton Sea, https://www.tmsaltonsea.com/the -project.

2. Amanda Ulrich, "Torres Martinez Tribe Hosts Poster Contest to Honor 'Past, Present and Future' of the Salton Sea," *Palm Springs Desert Sun*, December 27, 2020.

3. Preston Arrow-weed, a Kumeyaay and Quechan culture-bearer, calls it Xa-Wiilth-Kaw-Tai, "The Big Water." Preston J. Arrow-weed, "Xa-Wiilth-Kaw-Tai (The Big Water): Lake Cahuilla—The Salton Sea," *Desert Report*, September 2016, http:// www.desertreport.org/wp-content/uploads/2016/09/DR-Fall2016-Online.pdf.

4. Arrow-weed, "Xa-Wiilth-Kaw-Tai (The Big Water)."

5. Harjo, *Spiral to the Stars*, 191–94.

6. Hanks, *This War Is for a Whole Life*; Dozier, *Heart Is Fire*; Gordon, *Cahuilla Nation Activism and the Tribal Casino Movement*.

7. Risling Baldy, *We Are Dancing for You*, 8. See also Barker, *Critically Sovereign*, 27–28; Reid, *Sea Is My Country*, 277–78; L. Simpson, *As We Have Always Done*, 40; and Jacob, *Yakama Rising*, 114–19. "Survivance" is a term coined by Indigenous literary theorist Gerald Vizenor to describe "an active sense of presence, the continuance of native stories, not a mere reaction, or a survivable name." Vizenor, *Manifest Manners*, vii. The frameworks for futurity praxis and decolonization proposed by Linda Hogan, as well as by Cutcha Risling Baldy,

Joanne Barker, Leanne Betasamosake Simpson, and Michelle Jacob, emerge expressly from Indigenous feminist theory, which focuses on the "gendered and sexed politics of [settler] state formation" and, in turn, the importance of "a *critical* address to the politics of gender, sexuality, and feminism within how [Indigenous] sovereignty and self-determination is imagined, represented, and exercised." Barker, *Critically Sovereign*, 23, 34–35.

8. Simpson, *Mohawk Interruptus*, 177.

9. Sandler and Pezzulo, *Environmental Justice and Environmentalism*.

10. See, for example, "Proposed Solutions," Salton Sea Authority, https://saltonsea .com/get-informed/proposed-solutions/; "Partner Organizations," Salton Sea Authority, https://saltonsea.com/about/partner-organizations/; California Department of Water Resources and California Department of Fish and Game, "Salton Sea: Ecosystem Restoration Program Draft Programmatic Environmental Impact Report, Executive Summary," State Clearinghouse, October 2006; Kaiser, "Bringing the Salton Sea Back to Life."

11. Saranillio, "Kepaniwai (Damming of the Water) Heritage Gardens," 234.

12. Tuck and Yang, "Decolonization Is Not a Metaphor," 1.

13. Fanon, *Wretched of the Earth*, 35.

14. Indigenous activists in the 2010s proposed a solution that did just this, which they shorthanded with the succinct hashtag #LandBack. For explanations of the crucial importance of land return and some examples of how it can happen, see Curley and Smith, "Against Colonial Grounds"; Middleton, *Trust in the Land*; and Riley Yesno and Xicotencatl Maher Lopez, "Four Case Studies of Land Back in Action," *Briarpatch*, September 10, 2020, https://briarpatchmagazine.com /articles/view/four-case-studies-land-back-in-action. For a deep investigation of the need for water to be included in these visions of spatial justice, see Reid, *Sea Is My Country*.

15. Middleton, *Trust in the Land*; Thadeus Greenson, "Duluwat Island Is Returned to the Wiyot Tribe in Historic Ceremony," *North Coast Journal of Politics, People, & Art*, October 21, 2019, https://www.northcoastjournal.com/NewsBlog /archives/2019/10/21/duluwat-island-is-returned-to-the-wiyot-tribe-in-historic -ceremony; Yesno and Maher Lopez, "Four Case Studies of Land Back in Action."

16. Middleton, *Trust in the Land*.

17. Estes, "Fighting for Our Lives"; Bednarek, "Undamming Rivers."

18. The most high-profile example of dam removal as both a step toward land return and a vital move for ecological conservation has focused on the Klamath River, though dam removal proposals for a number of major waterways, including the Colorado River, gained traction in the 2010s. Barber, *Death of Celilo Falls*; Bednarek, "Undamming Rivers"; Sneddon, *Concrete Revolution*, 156–58; Courtney Flatt, "Northwest Tribes Call for Removal of Lower Columbia River Dams," *Science & Environment*, Oregon Public Broadcasting, October 14,

2019, https://www.opb.org/news/article/pacific-northwest-tribes-remove
-columbia-river-dams/; Diana Hartel, "Doctor's Orders: Undam the Klamath,"
High Country News, May 25, 2011, https://www.hcn.org/issues/43.8/doctors
-orders-undam-the-klamath/?b_start:int=2; Kanehl and Lyons, "Changes in
the Habitat and Fish Community of the Milwaukee River"; Norgaard, *Salmon
and Acorns Feed Our People*, 132; Pess et al., "Biological Impacts of the Elwha
River Dams"; Poff and Hart, "How Dams Vary and Why It Matters"; Joe Rojas-
Burke, "Sonar Shows Celilo Falls Are Intact," *Oregon Live*, November 27, 2008,
https://www.oregonlive.com/news/2008/11/sonar_shows_celilo_falls_are_i.html;
Warrick et al., "Large-Scale Dam Removal on the Elwha River, Washington";
Adam Wernick, "Is It Time to Think about Removing Dams on the Colorado
River?," Public Radio International, July 2, 2016, https://www.pri.org/stories
/2016-07-02/it-time-think-about-removing-dams-colorado-river.

19. Reisner, *Cadillac Desert*.
20. DeBuys, *Great Aridness*.
21. National Inventory of Dams, U.S. Army Corps of Engineers, https://nid.sec
.usace.army.mil/ords/f?p=105:1.
22. Hartel, "Doctor's Orders"; Flatt, "Northwest Tribes Call for Removal of Lower
Columbia River Dams."
23. Piekielek, "Creating a Park, Building a Border"; Ray, "Endangering the Desert"; Anya Montiel, "The Tohono O'odham and the Border Wall," *American
Indian Magazine*, Summer 2017, https://www.americanindianmagazine.org
/story/tohono-oodham-and-border-wall; Max Rivlin-Nadler, "Two Arrested as
Kumeyaay Protests against Border Wall Construction Ordered to Stop," *KPBS
News* (San Diego), September 22, 2020, https://www.kpbs.org/news/2020
/sep/22/border-patrol-arrest-two-kumeyaay-protests-against/; "No Wall,"
Tohono O'odham Nation, n.d., http://www.tonation-nsn.gov/nowall/.
24. Nishime and Hester Williams, *Racial Ecologies*.
25. Sutter, "Reflections," 109.
26. Anthropologist Anna Lowenhaupt Tsing has placed precariousness at the center
of contemporary environmental crises. Among her objects of study, the Salton
Sea would fit right in. Tsing, *Mushroom at the End of the World*, 3–6.
27. A wide range of scholars has examined the origins and consequences of this
Enlightenment perspective on the natural world. A few of the major works
that set out this argument include Merchant, *Death of Nature*; Plumwood,
Feminism and the Mastery of Nature; Cronon, *Uncommon Ground*; and Tsing,
Mushroom at the End of the World.
28. Whyte, Adamson, and Davis, "Is It Colonial Déjà Vu?"; Limerick and Hanson,
Ditch in Time.
29. In his classic environmental history of water in the West, Donald Worster has
singled out the ubiquitous western irrigation canal as the ultimate reflection

of the "face" of the West, reflecting back to us "the qualities of concentrated wealth, technical virtuosity, discipline, hard work, popular acquiescence, a feeling of resignation and necessity" that constitute the region's history. But the Salton Sea, and sumps like it, might make for a better mirror than even irrigation canals, serving as a full inversion that reflects the scale of environmental and social manipulation that has made the West what it is today. Worster, *Rivers of Empire*, 7.

30. DeBuys and Myers, *Salt Dreams*, 3, 8, 13.

31. O'Brien, *Firsting and Lasting*, xxiii, xxiv.

32. Cronon, "Place for Stories." Feminist theorist Donna Haraway has offered a critique of scholarship on the Anthropocene that might also apply to these kinds of declensionist narratives in environmental history: environmental narratives that feature "either 'game over' . . . or 'geoengineers to the rescue' plot lines" do not lead to "better stories imagining 'more livable presents and more livable futures,' but often instead to despair and denial." Quoted in Di Chiro, "Welcome to the White (M)Anthropocene," 494.

33. Limerick and Hanson, *Ditch in Time*, 254.

34. Voyles, "Man Destroys Nature?"; Yusoff, *Billion Black Anthropocenes or None*; Di Chiro, "Welcome to the White (M)Anthropocene?"; H. Davis and Todd, "On the Importance of a Date, or Decolonizing the Anthropocene"; Todd, "Indigenizing the Anthropocene."

35. Cronon, "Place for Stories."

BIBLIOGRAPHY

ARCHIVES AND MANUSCRIPT MATERIALS

California Historical Society Collection. University of Southern California Libraries, Los Angeles.

David Rumsey Map Center. Stanford University Libraries, Stanford, California.

Don Meadows Papers. Special Collections and Archives, University of California, Irvine.

Harold C. Bryant Papers. Museum of Vertebrate Zoology Archives, University of California, Berkeley.

Muir Family Papers. Huntington Library, San Marino, California.

National Archives and Records Administration, Washington DC.

    Indian Census Rolls.

    Records of the Army Air Forces.

Papers of the Women's National Indian Association, 1880–1951. Cornell University Division of Rare and Manuscript Collections. Ithaca, New York.

Peace Collection. Swarthmore College, Swarthmore, Pennsylvania.

Records of the Mission Indian Agency. Record Group 75, Bureau of Indian Affairs 75.19.61, National Archives and Records Administration, Riverside, California.

Special Collections and Archives. University of California, San Diego.

United States Coast Survey. Bancroft Library, University of California, Berkeley.

Water Resources Collections and Archives. Library of the University of California, Riverside.

    James D. Schuyler Papers.

    Thomas H. Means Papers.

Abbey, Edward. *Desert Solitaire: A Season in the Wilderness*. 1968. New York: Ballantine Books, 1990.

Abel, Emily K. *Suffering in the Land of Sunshine: A Los Angeles Illness Narrative*. New Brunswick NJ: Rutgers University Press, 2006.

———. *Tuberculosis and the Politics of Exclusion: A History of Public Health and Migration to Los Angeles*. New Brunswick NJ: Rutgers University Press, 2007.

"An Act to Add Chapter 11 (Commencing at Section 4980) to Division 4 of the Public Resources Code, Relating to California Conservation Camps." In *Statutes of California*, vol. 2. N.p.: California State Printing Office, 1959.

Adams, Frank, Sidney Twichell Harding, Ralph D. Robertson, and Clarence Everett Tait. *Reports on the Irrigation Resources of California*. Vol. 1. Sacramento: F. W. Richardson, Superintendent of State Printing, 1912.

Alexander, Michelle, and Cornel West. *The New Jim Crow: Mass Incarceration in the Age of Colorblindness*. Rev. ed. New York: New Press, 2012.

Allen, Paula Gunn. *The Sacred Hoop: Recovering the Feminine in American Indian Traditions; With a New Preface*. 1986. Boston: Beacon Press, 1992.

Anderson, Kat. *Tending the Wild: Native American Knowledge and the Management of California's Natural Resources*. Berkeley: University of California Press, 2013.

Andrés, Benny J. *Power and Control in the Imperial Valley: Nature, Agribusiness, and Workers on the California Borderland, 1900–1940*. College Station: Texas A&M University Press, 2015.

Anzaldúa, Gloria. *Borderlands/La Frontera: The New Mestiza*. San Francisco: Aunt Lute Books, 2012.

Armitage, Kevin C. "Bird Day for Kids: Progressive Conservation in Theory and Practice." *Environmental History* 12, no. 3 (2007): 528–71. http://www.jstor.org/stable/25473131.

Arnold, Laurie. *Bartering with the Bones of Their Dead: The Colville Confederated Tribes and Termination*. Seattle: University of Washington Press, 2012.

Arvin, Maile, Eve Tuck, and Angie Morrill. "Decolonizing Feminism: Challenging Connections between Settler Colonialism and Heteropatriarchy." *Feminist Formations* 25, no. 1 (2013): 8–34. https://doi.org/10.1353/ff.2013.0006.

Barber, Katrine. *Death of Celilo Falls*. Seattle: Center for the Study of the Pacific Northwest in association with the University of Washington Press, 2005.

Barker, Joanne. *Critically Sovereign: Indigenous Gender, Sexuality, and Feminist Studies*. Durham NC: Duke University Press, 2017.

———. *Sovereignty Matters: Locations of Contestation and Possibility in Indigenous Struggles for Self-Determination*. Lincoln: University of Nebraska Press, 2005. eBook.

Barnard, J. Laurens. "Introduction of an Amphipod Crustacean into the Salton Sea, California." *Bulletin of the Southern California Academy of Sciences* 67, no. 4 (1968): 219–32.

Barnd, Natchee Blu. *Native Space: Geographic Strategies to Unsettle Settler Colonialism.* Corvallis: Oregon State University Press, 2017.

Barrow, Mark V. *A Passion for Birds: American Ornithology after Audubon.* Princeton NJ: Princeton University Press, 1998.

Bass, Dana A. "Agua Caliente: A Case Study and Toolkit for Securing Tribal Rights to Clean Groundwater." *Ecology Law Quarterly* 45, no. 2 (2018): 227–52. https://doi.org/10.15779/Z38BN9X33H.

Baur, John E. "The Health Seekers and Early Southern California Agriculture." *Pacific Historical Review* 20, no. 4 (1951): 347–63. https://doi.org/10.2307/3635436.

Bean, Lowell John. *Mukat's People: The Cahuilla Indians of Southern California.* Berkeley: University of California Press, 1974.

Bean, Lowell John, and Harry W. Lawton. "Some Explanations for the Rise of Cultural Complexity in Native California with Comments on Proto-Agriculture and Agriculture." In *Before the Wilderness: Environmental Management by Native Californians,* edited by Thomas C. Blackburn and Kat Anderson, 41–42. Menlo Park CA: Ballena Press, 1993.

Bean, Lowell John, and Sylvia Brakke Vane, eds. *Ethnology of the Alta California Indians.* New York: Garland, 1991.

Bean, Lowell John, Katherine Siva Saubel, Harry W. Lawton, and Lowell John Bean. *Temalpakh (from the Earth): Cahuilla Indian Knowledge and Usage of Plants.* Banning CA: Malki Museum Press, 1972.

Bean, Lowell John, Sylvia Brakke Vane, and Jackson Young. *The Cahuilla and the Santa Rosa Mountain Region: Places and Their Native American Association.* Riverside: California Desert Planning Program, Bureau of Land Management, Department of the Interior, 1981. https://archive.org/details/cahuillasantaros00bean.

———. *The Cahuilla Landscape: The Santa Rosa and San Jacinto Mountains.* Menlo Park CA: Ballena Press, 1991.

Bednarek, Angela T. "Undamming the Rivers: A Review of the Ecological Impacts of Dam Removal." *Environmental Management* 27 (June 2001): 803–14.

Beidler, Peter G. *Fig Tree John: An Indian in Fact and Fiction.* Tucson: University of Arizona Press, 1977.

Bernstein, Alison R. *American Indians and World War II: Toward a New Era in Indian Affairs.* Norman: University of Oklahoma Press, 1999.

Billington, David P., Donald C. Jackson, and Martin V. Melosi. *The History of Large Federal Dams: Planning, Design, and Construction in the Era of Big Dams.* Denver CO: U.S. Department of the Interior, Bureau of Reclamation, 2005. https://www.usbr.gov/history/HistoryofLargeDams/LargeFederalDams.pdf.

Blackburn, Thomas C., and Kat Anderson. *Before the Wilderness: Environmental Management by Native Californians.* Menlo Park CA: Ballena Press, 1993.

Blackhawk, Ned. *Violence over the Land: Indians and Empires in the Early American West.* Cambridge MA: Harvard University Press, 2006.

Blake, William Phipps. *Report of a Geological Reconnaissance in California: Made in Connection with the Expedition to Survey Routes in California, to Connect with the Surveys of Routes for a Railroad from the Mississippi River to the Pacific Ocean.* New York: H. Baillière, 1858.

Bovey, Rodney W. *Mesquite: History, Growth, Biology, Uses, and Management.* College Station: Texas A&M University Press, 2016.

Bowden, Charles, and William deBuys. *Desierto: Memories of the Future.* Austin: University of Texas Press, 2018.

Bowers, Stephen. *Reconnaissance of the Colorado Desert Mining District.* Sacramento: California State Mining Bureau, 1901.

Braz, Rose, and Craig Gilmore. "Joining Forces: Prisons and Environmental Justice in Recent California Organizing." *Radical History Review,* no. 96 (2006): 95–111.

Brechner, Ross J., Gregory D. Parkhurst, William O. Humble, Morton B. Brown, and William H. Herman. "Ammonium Perchlorate Contamination of Colorado River Drinking Water Is Associated with Abnormal Thyroid Function in Newborns in Arizona." *Journal of Occupational and Environmental Medicine* 42, no. 8 (2000): 777–82. https://doi.org/10.1097/00043764-200008000-00002.

Bridge, Norman. "The Climate of Southern California." *Transactions of the American Clinical and Climatological Association* 17 (1901): 85–96.

Brooks, James. *Captives and Cousins: Slavery, Kinship, and Community in the Southwest Borderlands.* Chapel Hill: Published for the Omohundro Institute of Early American History and Culture, Williamsburg, Virginia, by the University of North Carolina Press, 2002.

Brooks, Lisa. *Our Beloved Kin: A New History of King Philip's War.* New Haven CT: Yale University Press, 2019.

Brown, John S. *The Salton Sea Region, California: A Geographic, Geologic, and Hydrologic Reconnaissance with a Guide to Desert Watering Places.* Washington DC: Government Printing Office, 1923.

Brown, Kate. *Plutopia: Nuclear Families, Atomic Cities, and the Great Soviet and American Plutonium Disasters.* Oxford: Oxford University Press, 2015.

Brumgardt, John R., and Larry L. Bowles. *People of the Magic Waters: The Cahuilla Indians of Palm Springs.* Palm Springs CA: ETC Publications, 1981.

Bullard, Robert D. *Dumping in Dixie: Race, Class, and Environmental Quality.* 3rd ed. London: Routledge, 2019.

Burch, Susan. *Committed: Remembering Native Kinship in and beyond Institutions.* Chapel Hill: University of North Carolina Press, 2021.

Burdick, Arthur J. *The Mystic Mid-Region: The Deserts of the Southwest.* New York: G. P. Putnam's Sons, 1904. https://archive.org/details/mysticmidregion00burdgoog/page/n10.

Byrd, Jodi A. *The Transit of Empire: Indigenous Critiques of Colonialism.* Minneapolis: University of Minnesota Press, 2011.

California Division of Forestry, Engineering and Camps Section. *Division of Forestry in the California Conservation Camp Program*. Sacramento: California State Board of Forestry, 1970.

Carrico, Richard L. *Strangers in a Stolen Land: Indians of San Diego County from Prehistory to the New Deal*. 2nd ed. San Diego CA: Sunbelt, 2008.

Carson, Rachel. *Silent Spring*. 40th anniversary ed. Boston: Mariner Books, Houghton Mifflin, 2002.

Carter, George F. *Plant Geography and Culture History in the American Southwest*. New York: Viking Fund, 1945.

Cass, Valerie J. "Toxic Tragedy: Illegal Hazardous Waste Dumping in Mexico." In *Environmental Crime and Criminality: Theoretical and Practical Issues*, edited by Sally M. Edwards, Terry D. Edwards, and Charles B. Fields, 99–119. New York: Garland, 1996.

Cecil-Stephens, B. A. "The Colorado Desert and Its Recent Flooding." *Journal of the American Geographical Society of New York* 23 (1891).

Chase, J. Smeaton. *California Desert Trails*. Boston: Houghton Mifflin, 1919.

Chávez-García, Miroslava. *Negotiating Conquest: Gender and Power in California, 1770s to 1880s*. Tucson: University of Arizona Press, 2004.

Chiang, Connie Y. *Nature behind Barbed Wire: An Environmental History of the Japanese American Incarceration*. New York: Oxford University Press, 2018.

———. "Race and Ethnicity in Environmental History." In *The Oxford Handbook of Environmental History*, edited by Andrew Isenberg, 573–99. New York: Oxford University Press, 2014.

Chilcote, Olivia. "'Time Out of Mind': The San Luis Rey Band of Mission Indians and the Historical Origins of a Struggle for Federal Recognition." *California History* 96, no. 4 (2019): 38–53. https://doi.org/10.1525/ch.2019.96.4.38.

Child, Brenda J. *Boarding School Seasons: American Indian Families, 1900–1940*. Lincoln: University of Nebraska Press, 2000.

———. *My Grandfather's Knocking Sticks: Ojibwe Family Life and Labor on the Reservation*. St. Paul: Minnesota Historical Society Press, 2014.

Church, Jerilyn, Chinyere O. Ekechi, Aila Hoss, and Anika Jade Larson. "Tribal Water Rights: Exploring Dam Construction in Indian Country." *Journal of Law, Medicine, and Ethics* 43, no. S1 (April 2015): 60–63. https://doi.org/10.1111/jlme.12218.

"Climatic Effects of the New Lake in Southern California." *Scientific American* 66, no. 14 (1892). http://www.jstor.org/stable/26109296.

Cohen, Michael. "Managing Cross Boundaries: The Case of the Colorado River Delta." In *The World's Water 2002-2003: The Biennial Report on Freshwater Resources*, by Peter H Gleick et al., 133–48. Washington DC: Island Press, 2002.

Cohn, Jeffrey. "Saving the Salton Sea." *BioScience* 50, no. 4 (2000): 295–301.

Cokinos, Christopher, and Eric Magrane. *The Sonoran Desert: A Literary Field Guide.* Tucson: University of Arizona Press, 2016. eBook.

Collins, Kimberly, Paul Ganster, Cheryl Mason, Eduardo Sánchez-López, and Margarito Quintero-Núñez, eds. *Imperial-Mexicali Valleys: Development and Environment of the U.S.-Mexican Border Region.* San Diego: San Diego State University Press and the Institute for Regional Studies of the Californias, 2004.

Collins, Patricia Hill. *Black Feminist Thought: Knowledge, Consciousness, and the Politics of Empowerment.* 2nd ed. New York: Routledge, 2000.

Commoner, Barry. "After 20 Years: The Crisis of Environmental Regulation." *New Solutions: A Journal of Environmental and Occupational Health Policy* 1, no. 1 (1990): 22–29.

Cook-Lynn, Elizabeth. *Anti-Indianism in Modern America: A Voice from Tatekeya's Earth.* Urbana: University of Illinois Press, 2007.

———. *I Remember the Fallen Trees: New and Selected Poems.* Cheney: Eastern Washington University Press, 1998.

Costo, Jeannette Henry, and Rupert Costo. *Natives of the Golden State: The California Indians.* San Francisco: Indian Historian Press, 1995.

Costo, Rupert, and Jeannette Henry Costo, eds. *The Missions of California: A Legacy of Genocide.* San Francisco: Indian Historian Press, 1987.

Coulthard, Glen Sean. *Red Skin, White Masks: Rejecting the Colonial Politics of Recognition.* Minneapolis: University of Minnesota Press, 2017.

Craib, Raymond B. *Cartographic Mexico: A History of State Fixations and Fugitive Landscapes.* Durham NC: Duke University Press, 2004.

Crawford, Richard W. "The Records of Local Government and California History." *California History* 75, no. 1 (1996): 21–25. https://ch.ucpress.edu/content/75/1/21.

Crenshaw, Kimberle. "Mapping the Margins: Intersectionality, Identity Politics, and Violence against Women of Color." *Stanford Law Review* 43, no. 6 (1991): 1241–99.

Cronon, William. "A Place for Stories: Nature, History, and Narrative." *Journal of American History* 78, no. 4 (1992): 1347–76. https://doi.org/10.2307/2079346.

———. *Uncommon Ground: Toward Reinventing Nature.* New York: Norton, 1995.

Crosby, Alfred W. *Ecological Imperialism: The Biological Expansion of Europe, 900–1900.* 2nd ed. Cambridge: Cambridge University Press, 2004.

———. "Virgin Soil Epidemics as a Factor in the Aboriginal Depopulation in America." *William and Mary Quarterly* 33, no. 2 (1976): 289–99. https://doi.org/10.2307/1922166.

Cuero, Delfina, and Florence Connolly Shipek. *Delfina Cuero: Her Autobiography, an Account of Her Last Years, and Her Ethnobotanic Contributions.* Menlo Park CA: Ballena Press, 1991.

Curley, Andrew, and Sara Smith. "Against Colonial Grounds: Geography on Indigenous Lands." *Dialogues in Human Geography* 10, no. 1 (2020): 37–40. https://doi.org/10.1177/2043820619898900.

Daly, Heather Ponchetti. "Fractured Relations at Home: The 1953 Termination Act's Effect on Tribal Relations throughout Southern California Indian Country." *American Indian Quarterly* 33, no. 4 (2009): 427–39. https://www.jstor.org/stable/40388480.

Danker, Kathleen. "'The Violation of the Earth': Elizabeth Cook-Lynn's 'From the River's Edge' in the Historical Context of the Pick-Sloan Missouri River Dam Project." *Wicazo Sa Review* 12, no. 2 (1997): 85–93. https://doi.org/10.2307/1409208.

Davis, Diana K. *The Arid Lands: History, Power, Knowledge.* Cambridge MA: MIT Press, 2016.

Davis, Heather, and Zoe Todd. "On the Importance of a Date, or Decolonizing the Anthropocene." *ACME: An International E-Journal for Critical Geographies* 16, no. 4 (2017). https://www.acme-journal.org/index.php/acme/article/view/1539.

Dawson, William Leon. *The Birds of California: A Complete, Scientific and Popular Account of the 580 Species and Subspecies of Birds Found in the State.* 4 vols. San Diego CA: South Moulton, 1923.

Day, Iyko. "Being or Nothingness: Indigeneity, Antiblackness, and Settler Colonial Critique." *Critical Ethnic Studies* 1, no. 2 (2015): 102–21.

deBuys, William. *A Great Aridness: Climate Change and the Future of the American Southwest.* New York: Oxford University Press, 2013.

deBuys, William, and Joan Myers. *Salt Dreams: Land and Water in Low-Down California.* Albuquerque: University of New Mexico Press, 1999.

Deer, Sarah. *The Beginning and End of Rape: Confronting Sexual Violence in Native America.* Minneapolis: University of Minnesota Press, 2015.

De Falla, Paul M. "Lantern in the Western Sky." *Historical Society of Southern California Quarterly* 42, no. 1 (1960): 57–88. https://doi.org/10.2307/41169431.

Deloria, Philip Joseph. *Indians in Unexpected Places.* Lawrence: University Press of Kansas, 2004.

Deloria, Vine, Jr. *Custer Died for Your Sins: An Indian Manifesto.* 1969. Norman: University of Oklahoma Press, 1988.

Denetdale, Jennifer. "Chairmen, Presidents, and Princesses: The Navajo Nation, Gender, and the Politics of Tradition." *Wicazo Sa Review* 21, no. 1 (2006): 9–28. https://doi.org/10.1353/wic.2006.0004.

———. *Reclaiming Diné History: The Legacies of Navajo Chief Manuelito and Juanita.* Tucson: University of Arizona Press, 2015.

Desante, D. F., S. Amin Ruhlen, and K. M. Burton. "Results of the 1991 Census of Burrowing Owls in Central California: An Alarmingly Small and Declining Population." *Journal of Raptor Research* 27, no. 1 (1993).

Dhillon, Jaskiran. "Introduction: Indigenous Resurgence, Decolonization, and Movements for Environmental Justice." *Environment and Society* 9, no. 1 (September 1, 2018): 1–5. https://doi.org/10.3167/ares.2018.090101.

Di Chiro, Giovanna. "Welcome to the White (M)Anthropocene? A Feminist-Environmentalist Critique." In *Routledge Handbook of Gender and Environment*, edited by Sherilyn MacGregor, 487–505. London: Routledge, 2017.

Dictionary of American Military Aviation Squadrons. Vol. 2. Washington DC: Naval Historical Center, 2000. https://www.history.navy.mil/content/dam/nhhc/research/histories/naval-aviation/dictionary-of-american-naval-aviation-squadrons-volume-2/pdfs/chap4-1.pdf.

Dilts, Andrew. *Punishment and Inclusion: Race, Membership, and the Limits of American Liberalism.* New York: Fordham University Press, 2014.

Doolittle, William Emery. *Cultivated Landscapes of Native North America.* Oxford: Oxford University Press, 2000.

Dozier, Deborah. *The Heart Is Fire: The World of the Cahuilla Indians of Southern California.* Berkeley CA: Heyday Books, 1998.

Drucker, Philip. *Culture Element Distributions V: Southern California.* Berkeley: University of California Press, 1937.

Duchemin, Michael. "Water, Power, and Tourism: Hoover Dam and the Making of the New West." *California History* 86, no. 4 (January 1, 2009): 60–89. https://doi.org/10.2307/40495234.

Dunbar-Ortiz, Roxanne. *Loaded: A Disarming History of the Second Amendment.* San Francisco: City Lights Books, 2017.

Ehrenreich, Barbara, and Arlie Russell Hochschild, eds. *Global Woman: Nannies, Maids, and Sex Workers in the New Economy.* New York: Metropolitan Books/Holt, 2004.

Estes, Nick. "Fighting for Our Lives: #NoDAPL in Historical Context." *Wicazo Sa Review* 32, no. 2 (2017): 115–22.

———. *Our History Is the Future: Standing Rock versus the Dakota Access Pipeline, and the Long Tradition of Indigenous Resistance.* London: Verso, 2019.

Estes, Nick, and Jaskiran Dhillon, eds. *Standing with Standing Rock: Voices from the #NoDAPL Movement.* Minneapolis: University of Minnesota Press, 2019.

Ethridge, Robbie, and Sheri M. Shuck-Hall, eds. *Mapping the Mississippian Shatter Zone: The Colonial Indian Slave Trade and Regional Instability in the American South.* Lincoln: University of Nebraska Press, 2009.

Fanon, Frantz. *The Wretched of the Earth.* 1961. New York: Grove Press, 1968.

Farr, F. C., ed. *The History of Imperial County, California.* Berkeley CA: Elms and Franks, 1918.

Fear-Segal, Jacqueline, and Susan D. Rose, eds. *Carlisle Indian Industrial School: Indigenous Histories, Memories, and Reclamations.* Lincoln: University of Nebraska Press, 2016.

Fiege, Mark. *Irrigated Eden: The Making of an Agricultural Landscape in the American West.* Seattle: University of Washington Press, 1999.

Fisher, Colin. "Race and US Environmental History." In *A Companion to American Environmental History*, edited by Douglas Cazaux Sackman, 97–115. Malden MA: Wiley-Blackwell, 2014.

Fixico, Donald Lee. *Termination and Relocation: Federal Indian Policy, 1945–1960.* Albuquerque: University of New Mexico Press, 1992.

Fleury, A. C. "Border Inspection Revelations." In *Report of Stallion Registration for the Fiscal Year Ending June 30, 1926*, Special Publication No. 68. Sacramento: California Department of Agriculture, 1926.

Forbes, Jack D. *Native Americans of California and Nevada.* Healdsburg CA: Naturegraph, 1969.

———. *Native Americans of California and Nevada.* Rev. ed. Happy Camp CA: Naturegraph, 1982.

———. *Warriors of the Colorado: The Yumas of the Quechan Nation and Their Neighbors.* Norman: University of Oklahoma Press, 1965.

Franco, Jere Bishop. *Crossing the Pond: The Native American Effort in World War II.* Denton: University of North Texas Press, 1999.

Frey, R. Scott. "The Transfer of Core-Based Hazardous Production Processes to the Export Processing Zones of the Periphery: The Maquiladora Centers of Northern Mexico." *Journal of World-Systems Research* 9, no. 2 (2003): 317–54.

Friend, Milton. "Avian Disease at the Salton Sea." *Hydrobiologia* 473 (2002): 293–306. https://doi.org/10.1023/A:1016570810004.

Furnish, Dale Beck, and Jerry R. Ladman. "The Colorado River Salinity Agreement of 1973 and the Mexicali Valley." *Natural Resources Journal* 15, no. 1 (1975): 83–107.

Gamble, Lynn H., and Michael Wilken-Robertson. "Kumeyaay Cultural Landscapes of Baja California's Tijuana River Watershed." *Journal of California and Great Basin Anthropology* 28, no. 2 (2008): 127–51.

Garrett, Kimball L., Kathy C. Molina, and Michael A. Patten. "History of Ornithological Exploration of the Salton Sink." In *Ecology and Conservation of Birds of the Salton Sink: An Endangered Ecosystem*, edited by W. David Shuford and Kathy C. Molina. Lawrence KS: Allen Press, 2004.

Gedicks, Al. *Resource Rebels: Native Challenges to Mining and Oil Corporations.* Cambridge MA: South End Press, 2001.

Geraci, J. B., C. Amrhein, and C. C. Goodson. "Barnacle Growth Rate on Artificial Substrate in the Salton Sea, California." *Hydrobiologia*, no. 604 (2008): 77–84. https://doi.org/10.1007/978-1-4020-8806-3_6.

Gerhard, Peter. "The Socialist Invasion of Baja California, 1911." *Pacific Historical Review* 15, no. 3 (1946): 295–304. https://doi.org/10.2307/3635477.

Gervais, Jennifer A., Daniel K. Rosenberg, Lyann A. Comrack, and Thomas Gardali. "Burrowing Owl (*Athene cunicularia*)." In *California Bird Species of Special Concern: A Ranked Assessment of Species, Subspecies, and Distinct Populations of Birds of Immediate Conservation Concern in California*, edited by W. David

Shuford. Camarillo and Sacramento: Western Field Ornithologists and California Department of Fish and Game, 2008.

Gibson, John, and Dave Thayer. *A Brief History: Pacific Engineering and Production Company of Nevada*. N.p.: XLIBRIS, 2016.

Gifford, Edward W. *The Kamia of the Imperial Valley*. Bureau of American Ethnology Bulletin 97. Washington DC: Bureau of American Ethnology, 1931.

Gilio-Whitaker, Dina. *As Long as Grass Grows: The Indigenous Fight for Environmental Justice, from Colonization to Standing Rock*. Boston: Beacon Press, 2019.

Gilman, M. French. "The Leconte Thrasher." *The Condor* 6, no. 4 (July 1904).

Gilmore, Ruth Wilson. *Golden Gulag: Prisons, Surplus, Crisis, and Opposition in Globalizing California*. Berkeley: University of California Press, 2007.

Gobalet, Kenneth W., and Thomas A. Wake. "Archaeological and Paleontological Fish Remains from the Salton Basin, Southern California." *Southwestern Naturalist* 45, no. 4 (2000): 514–20. https://doi.org/10.2307/3672600.

Goldberg-Ambrose, Carole. "Public Law 280 and the Problem of Lawlessness in California Indian Country." *UCLA Law Review* 44 (June 1997): 1405–48.

Goldtooth (Mato Awanyankapi), Tom B. K. "The State of Indigenous America Series: Earth Mother, Piñons, and Apple Pie." *Wicazo Sa Review* 25, no. 2 (2010): 11–28.

Goodman, Philip. "Hero and Inmate: Work, Prisons, and Punishment in California's Fire Camps." *WorkingUSA* 15, no. 3 (2012): 353–76. https://doi.org/10.1111/j.1743-4580.2012.00398.x.

Gordon, Theodor P. *Cahuilla Nation Activism and the Tribal Casino Movement*. Reno: University of Nevada Press, 2018.

Gossett, Thomas F. *Race: The History of an Idea in America*. New ed. New York: Oxford University Press, 1997.

Grant, Ulysses S., IV. "A Midsummer Motoring Trip." *Historical Society of Southern California Quarterly* 43, no. 1 (March 1961): 85–96. https://doi.org/10.2307/41169503.

Greaves, Wilfrid. "Damaging Environments: Land, Settler Colonialism, and Security for Indigenous Peoples." *Environment and Society* 9, no. 1 (2018): 107–24.

Grijalva, James M. *Closing the Circle: Environmental Justice in Indian Country*. Durham NC: Carolina Academic Press, 2008.

Grinde, Donald A., and Bruce E. Johansen. *Ecocide of Native America: Environmental Destruction of Indian Lands and Peoples*. Sante Fe NM: Clear Light, 1995.

Grinnell, Joseph. "Birds of a Voyage on Salton Sea." *The Condor* 10, no. 5 (1908).

Grobsmith, Elizabeth S. *Indians in Prison: Incarcerated Native Americans in Nebraska*. Lincoln: University of Nebraska Press, 1994.

Grossman, Zoltán. *Unlikely Alliances: Native Nations and White Communities Join to Defend Rural Lands*. Seattle: University of Washington Press, 2017.

Guinn, J. M. "The Sonoran Migration." *Annual Publication of the Historical Society of Southern California* 8, no. 1–2 (January 1909): 31–36. https://doi.org/10.2307/41168652.

Gunther, Jane Davies. *Riverside County, California, Place Names: Their Origins and Their Stories*. Riverside CA: J. D. Gunther, 1984.

Gutiérrez, Ramón A., and Richard J. Orsi, eds. *Contested Eden: California before the Gold Rush*. Berkeley: University of California Press, 1998.

Haas, Lisbeth. *Saints and Citizens: Indigenous Histories of Colonial Missions and Mexican California*. Berkeley: University of California Press, 2013.

Hahn, Jeffrey L. *Location of Odor Sources and the Affected Population in Imperial County, California*. Berkeley: California Department of Health Services, 1981.

Haig-Brown, Celia. *Resistance and Renewal: Surviving the Indian Residential School*. Vancouver BC: Tillacum Library, 1988.

Haley, Sarah. *No Mercy Here: Gender, Punishment, and the Making of Jim Crow Modernity*. Chapel Hill: University of North Carolina Press, 2019.

Hanks, Richard A. *This War Is for a Whole Life: The Culture of Resistance among Southern California Indians, 1850–1966*. Banning CA: Ushkana Press, 2012.

Harden, M. L., and Reza Zolfaghari. "Nutritive Composition of Green and Ripe Pods of Honey Mesquite (*Prosopis glandulosa*, Fabaceae)." *Economic Botany* 42, no. 4 (1988): 522–32.

Harjo, Laura. *Spiral to the Stars: Mvskoke Tools of Futurity*. Tucson: University of Arizona Press, 2019.

Harley, R. Bruce. "The Founding of St. Boniface Indian School, 1888–1890." *Southern California Quarterly* 81, no. 4 (1999): 449–66. https://doi.org/10.2307/41171974.

Harrigan, B. A. *Agricultural Crop Report*. El Centro CA: Imperial County Department of Agriculture, 1948.

Harrison, Jill Lindsey. *Pesticide Drift and the Pursuit of Environmental Justice*. Cambridge MA: MIT Press, 2011.

Hedges, Ken. "Notes on the Kumeyaay: A Problem of Identification." *Journal of California Anthropology* 2, no. 1 (1975): 71–83.

Heizer, Robert F., ed. *The Destruction of California Indians: A Collection of Documents from the Period 1847 to 1865 in Which Are Described Some of the Things That Happened to Some of the Indians of California*. 1974. Lincoln: University of Nebraska Press, 1993.

Heizer, Robert F., and Alan J. Almquist. *The Other Californians: Prejudice and Discrimination under Spain, Mexico, and the United States to 1920*. 1971. Berkeley: University of California Press, 2000.

Heizer, Robert F., and Albert B. Elsasser. *The Natural World of the California Indians*. Berkeley: University of California Press, 1980.

Heizer, Robert F., and Karen M. Nissen. *The Human Sources of California Ethnography*. Berkeley: Archaeological Research Facility, Department of Anthropology, University of California, 1973.

Helppie-Schmieder, Brenna. "Toxic Confinement: Can the Eighth Amendment Protect Prisoners from Human-Made Environmental Health Hazards?" *Northwestern University Law Review* 110, no. 3 (2016): 647–77.

Herndl, Dian Price. *Invalid Women: Figuring Feminine Illness in American Fiction and Culture, 1840–1940*. Chapel Hill: University of North Carolina Press, 2000. eBook.

Hill, Karlos K. *Beyond the Rope: The Impact of Lynching on Black Culture and Memory*. New York: Cambridge University Press, 2016.

Hiltzik, Michael A. *Colossus: The Turbulent, Thrilling Saga of the Building of Hoover Dam*. New York: Free Press, 2011.

Hinsdale, Guy. "Atmospheric Air in Relation to Tuberculosis." *Smithsonian Miscellaneous Collections* 63, no. 1 (1914).

Hixson, Walter L. *American Settler Colonialism: A History*. New York: Palgrave Macmillan, 2013.

Holdren, G. Chris, Kevin Kelly, and Paul Weghorst. "Evaluation of Potential Impacts of Perchlorate." *Hydrobiologia*, no. 604 (2008): 173–79. https://doi.org/10.1007/s10750-008-9318-z.

Hooper, Lucile. *The Cahuilla Indians*. Berkeley: University of California Press, 1920.

Hoover, Elizabeth. *The River Is in Us: Fighting Toxics in a Mohawk Community*. Minneapolis: University of Minnesota Press, 2017.

Hornaday, William Temple. *Our Vanishing Wildlife: Its Extermination and Preservation*. New York: Charles Scribner's Sons, 1913.

Houston, Edwin J. *The Land of Drought*. Boston: Griffith & Rowland, 1910. https://lccn.loc.gov/10028167.

Huang, Ganlin, and Jonathan K. London. "Mapping in and out of 'Messes': An Adaptive, Participatory, and Transdisciplinary Approach to Assessing Cumulative Environmental Justice Impacts." *Landscape and Urban Planning* 154 (October 2016): 57–67. https://doi.org/10.1016/j.landurbplan.2016.02.014.

Hughes, Tom. *History of Banning and San Gorgonio Pass in Two Parts*. Banning CA: Banning Record Print, 1939.

Hundley, Norris. *The Great Thirst: Californians and Water, 1770s–1990s*. Berkeley: University of California Press, 1992.

———. "The Politics of Reclamation: California, the Federal Government, and the Origins of the Boulder Canyon Act; A Second Look." *California Historical Quarterly* 52, no. 4 (December 1, 1973): 292–325. https://doi.org/10.2307/25157467.

Hurtado, Albert L. *Indian Survival on the California Frontier*. New Haven CT: Yale University Press, 1988.

Hyer, Joel R. *We Are Not Savages: Native Americans in Southern California and the Pala Reservation, 1840–1920*. East Lansing: Michigan State University Press, 2001.

Impounding Waters and Indian Tuberculosis Sanitarium: Report of the Joint Congressional Commission on Indian Tuberculosis Sanitarium and Yakima Indian Reservation Project. Washington DC: Government Printing Office, 1914.

Innis, Jack Scheffler. *San Diego Legends: The Events, People, and Places That Made History.* San Diego: Sunbelt, 2004.

Jackson, Helen Hunt, and Abbot Kinney. *Report on the Conditions and Needs of the Mission Indians of California.* Washington DC: Government Printing Office, 1883.

Jackson, Robert H. *Regional Conflict and Demographic Patterns on the Jesuit Missions among the Guaraní in the Seventeenth and Eighteenth Centuries.* Leiden: Brill, 2019.

Jackson, Robert H., and Edward Castillo. *Indians, Franciscans, and Spanish Colonization: The Impact of the Mission System on California Indians.* Albuquerque: University of New Mexico Press, 1995.

Jacob, Michelle M. *Yakama Rising: Indigenous Cultural Revitalization, Activism, and Healing.* Tucson: University of Arizona Press, 2014.

Jacobson, Matthew Frye. *Whiteness of a Different Color: European Immigrants and the Alchemy of Race.* Cambridge MA: Harvard University Press, 2002.

James, Harry C. *The Cahuilla Indians.* Riverside CA: Malki Museum Press, 1985.

Johnson, Khalil Anthony. "'Recruited to Teach the Indians': An African American Genealogy of Navajo Nation Boarding Schools." *Journal of American Indian Education* 57, no. 1 (2018): 154–76.

Johnson, Nicholas. *Negroes and the Gun: The Black Tradition of Arms.* Amherst NY: Prometheus Books, 2014.

Johnson, Susan Lee. *Roaring Camp: The Social World of the California Gold Rush.* New York: Norton, 2000.

Johnston, Jill E., Mitiasoa Razafy, Humberto Lugo, Luis Olmedo, Shohreh F. Farzan. "The Disappearing Salton Sea: A Critical Reflection on the Emerging Environmental Threat of Disappearing Saline Lakes and Potential Impacts on Children's Health." *Science of the Total Environment* 663 (May 1, 2019): 804–17. https://doi.org/10.1016/j.scitotenv.2019.01.365.

Kaiser, Jocelyn. "Bringing the Salton Sea Back to Life." *Science* 287, no. 5453 (2000): 565.

Kanehl, Paul D., and John Lyons. "Changes in the Habitat and Fish Community of the Milwaukee River, Wisconsin, Following Removal of the Woolen Mills Dam." *North American Journal of Fisheries Management* 17, no. 2 (1997): 387–400.

Kauanui, J. Kehaulani. "'A Structure, Not an Event': Settler Colonialism and Enduring Indigeneity." *Lateral* 5, no. 1 (2016). https://doi.org/10.25158/L5.1.7.

Keller, Jean A. *Empty Beds: Indian Student Health at Sherman Institute, 1902–1922.* East Lansing: Michigan State University Press, 2002.

Kelton, Paul. *Cherokee Medicine, Colonial Germs: An Indigenous Nation's Fight against Smallpox, 1518–1824.* Norman: University of Oklahoma Press, 2018.

Kennan, George. *The Salton Sea: An Account of Harriman's Fight with the Colorado River.* New York: Macmillan, 1917.

Kimmerer, Robin Wall. *Braiding Sweetgrass: Indigenous Wisdom, Scientific Knowledge and the Teachings of Plants*. Minneapolis: Milkweed Editions, 2013.

Kinsey, D. J. *The River of Destiny: The Story of the Colorado River*. Los Angeles: Los Angeles Department of Water and Power, 1928.

Kirk, Andrea B., Ernest E. Smith, Kang Tian, Todd A. Anderson, and Purnendu K. Dasgupta. "Perchlorate in Milk." *Environmental Science and Technology* 37, no. 21 (November 2003): 4979–81. https://doi.org/10.1021/es034735q.

Kosek, Jake. "Purity and Pollution: Racial Degradation and Environmental Anxieties." In *Liberation Ecologies: Environment, Development, Social Movements*, edited by Richard Peet and Michael Watts, 125–65. 2nd ed. London: Routledge, 2004.

Kraut, Alan M. *Silent Travelers: Germs, Genes, and the "Immigrant Menace."* Baltimore: Johns Hopkins University Press, 1995.

Kuletz, Valerie. *The Tainted Desert: Environmental Ruin in the American West*. New York: Routledge, 1998.

LaDuke, Winona. *All Our Relations: Native Struggles for Land and Life*. Chicago: Haymarket Books, 2015.

———. *Recovering the Sacred: The Power of Naming and Claiming*. Chicago: Haymarket Books, 2016.

Lahti, Janne, ed. "Settler Colonialism and the American West." Special issue, *Journal of the West* 56, no. 4 (2017).

Lancaster, Guy, ed. *Bullets and Fire: Lynching and Authority in Arkansas, 1840–1950*. Fayetteville: University of Arkansas Press, 2018.

Lando, Richard, and Ruby E. Modesto. "Temal Wakhish: A Desert Cahuilla Village." *Journal of California Anthropology* 4, no. 1 (1977): 95–112.

Langston, Nancy. *Where Land and Water Meet: A Western Landscape Transformed*. Seattle: University of Washington Press, 2009.

Lawson, Michael L. *Dammed Indians: The Pick-Sloan Plan and the Missouri River Sioux, 1944–1980*. Norman: University of Oklahoma Press, 1994.

Lawton, Harry W., and Lowell John Bean. "Some Explanations for the Rise of Cultural Complexity in Native California with Comments on Proto-Agriculture and Agriculture." In *Patterns of Indian Burning in California: Ecology and Ethnohistory*, edited by Henry T. Lewis, 1–35. Ramona CA: Ballena Press, 1973.

Leonard, Karen Isaksen. *Making Ethnic Choices: California's Punjabi Mexican Americans*. Philadelphia: Temple University Press, 1992.

Lewis, Larea Mae. "The Desert Cahuilla: A Study of Cultural Landscapes and Historic Settlements." Master's thesis, University of Arizona, 2016. http://hdl.handle.net/10150/294028.

Lew-Williams, Beth. *The Chinese Must Go: Violence, Exclusion, and the Making of the Alien in America*. Cambridge MA: Harvard University Press, 2018.

Liboiron, Max. *Pollution Is Colonialism*. Durham NC: Duke University Press, 2021.

Lim, Julian. *Porous Borders: Multiracial Migrations and the Law in the US-Mexico Borderlands*. Chapel Hill: University of North Carolina Press, 2017.

Limerick, Patricia Nelson. *Desert Passages: Encounters with the American Deserts*. Albuquerque: University of New Mexico Press, 1985.

———. "Disorientation and Reorientation: The American Landscape Discovered from the West." *Journal of American History* 79, no. 3 (1992): 1021–49. https://doi.org/10.2307/2080797.

Limerick, Patricia Nelson, and Jason L. Hanson. *A Ditch in Time: The City, the West, and Water*. Golden CO: Fulcrum, 2012.

Lindley, Walter. "Below the Sea — Nature's Pneumatic Cabinet." *Southern California Practitioner* 3, no. 10 (1888).

Lindsay, Brendan C. *Murder State: California's Native American Genocide, 1846–1873*. Lincoln: University of Nebraska Press, 2012.

Linsley, Richard H., and Lars H. Carpelan. "Invertebrate Fauna." In *The Ecology of the Salton Sea, California, in Relation to the Sportfishery*, edited by Boyd Walker. Fish Bulletin No. 113. California Department of Fish and Game, 1961.

Logan, Michael F. *Desert Cities: The Environmental History of Phoenix and Tucson*. Pittsburgh PA: University of Pittsburgh Press, 2006.

Lomawaima, Kimberly Tsianina. *They Called It Prairie Light: The Story of Chilocco Indian School*. Lincoln: University of Nebraska Press, 1995.

Lomawaima, K. Tsianina, and Teresa L. McCarty. *"To Remain an Indian": Lessons in Democracy from a Century of Native American Education*. New York: Teachers College Press, 2006.

London, Jonathan, Teri Greenfield, and Tara Zagofsky. *Revealing the Invisible Coachella Valley: Putting Cumulative Environmental Vulnerabilities on the Map*. Davis: University of California Davis Center for Regional Change, June 2013. https://regionalchange.ucdavis.edu/sites/g/files/dgvnsk986/files/inline-files/revealing_invisible_coachella_valley%202013.pdf.

Lonetree, Amy. *Decolonizing Museums: Representing Native America in National and Tribal Museums*. Chapel Hill: University of North Carolina Press, 2012.

Love, Bruce, and Mariam Dahdul. "Desert Chronologies and the Archaic Period in the Coachella Valley." *Pacific Coast Archaeological Society Quarterly* 38, no. 2–3 (2002): 65–86.

Luce, Todd C., and Clifford E. Trafzer. "The Invisible Epidemic: Suicide and Accidental Death among the Yakama Indian People, 1911–1964." *Wicazo Sa Review* 31, no. 2 (2016): 13–55.

Lytle Hernández, Kelly. *City of Inmates: Conquest, Rebellion, and the Rise of Human Caging in Los Angeles, 1771–1965*. Chapel Hill: University of North Carolina Press, 2017.

———. *Migra! A History of the U.S. Border Patrol*. Berkeley: University of California Press, 2010.

MacGregor, Sherilyn, ed. *Routledge International Handbook of Gender and Environment*. New York: Routledge, 2017.

Madley, Benjamin. *An American Genocide: The United States and the California Indian Catastrophe, 1846–1873*. New Haven CT: Yale University Press, 2017.

Madrigal, Anthony. *Sovereignty, Land, and Water: Building Tribal Environmental and Cultural Programs on the Cahuilla and Twenty-Nine Palms Reservations*. Riverside: California Center for Native Nations, 2008.

Markowitz, Gerald E., and David Rosner. *Deceit and Denial: The Deadly Politics of Industrial Pollution*. Berkeley: University of California Press, 2013.

Marshall, John. "Why Emergency Physicians Should Care about the Salton Sea." *Western Journal of Emergency Medicine* 18, no. 6 (October 18, 2017): 1008–9. https://doi.org/10.5811/westjem.2017.8.36034.

May, Ronald V. "A Brief Survey of Kumeyaay Ethnography: Correlations between Environmental Land-Use Patterns, Material Culture, and Social Organization." *Pacific Coast Archaeological Quarterly* 11, no. 4 (1975): 1–25.

Mazzetti, Max C. "Slavery in the Missions." In *The Missions of California: A Legacy of Genocide*, edited by Rupert Costo and Jeannette Henry Costo. San Francisco: Indian Historian Press, 1987.

McAfee, Ward M. "A History of Convict Labor in California." *Southern California Quarterly* 72, no. 1 (1990): 19–40. https://doi.org/10.2307/41171510.

McGovern, Dan. *The Campo Indian Landfill War: The Fight for Gold in California's Garbage*. Norman: University of Oklahoma Press, 1995.

McWhorter, C. G. "Introduction and Spread of Johnsongrass in the United States." *Weed Science* 19, no. 5 (1971): 496–500. https://www.doi.org/10.1017/S0043174500050517.

McWilliams, Carey. *Factories in the Field: The Story of Migratory Farm Labor in California*. 1939. Berkeley: University of California Press, 2000. eBook.

Melamed, Jodi. "Racial Capitalism." *Critical Ethnic Studies* 1, no. 1 (2015): 76–85. https://doi.org/10.5749/jcritethnstud.1.1.0076.

Melosi, Martin V. "Equity, Eco-Racism and Environmental History." *Environmental History Review* 19, no. 3 (1995): 1–16. https://doi.org/10.2307/3984909.

Mendoza, Mary E. "Unnatural Border: Race and Environment at the US-Mexico Divide." PhD diss., University of California, Davis, 2015.

Merchant, Carolyn. *The Death of Nature: Women, Ecology, and the Scientific Revolution*. New York: HarperCollins, 2019.

———. "George Bird Grinnell's Audubon Society: Bridging the Gender Divide in Conservation." *Environmental History* 15, no. 1 (2010): 3–30.

———, ed. *Green versus Gold: Sources in California's Environmental History*. Washington DC: Island Press, 1998.

———. "Shades of Darkness: Race and Environmental History." *Environmental History* 8, no. 3 (2003): 380–94. https://doi.org/10.2307/3986200.

Merriam, C. Hart. "The Leconte Thrasher, *Harporhynchus lecontei.*" *The Auk* 12, no. 1 (1895): 54–60.

Middleton, Beth Rose. *Trust in the Land: New Directions in Tribal Conservation.* Tucson: University of Arizona Press, 2011.

Miller, Susan A., and James Riding In, eds. *Native Historians Write Back: Decolonizing American Indian History.* Lubbock: Texas Tech University Press, 2011.

Million, Dian. "'We Are the Land and the Land Is Us': Indigenous Land, Lives, and Embodied Ecologies in the Twenty-First Century." In *Racial Ecologies,* edited by Leilani Nishime and Kim D. Hester Williams, 19–33. Seattle: University of Washington Press, 2018.

Miranda, Deborah A. *Bad Indians: A Tribal Memoir.* Berkeley CA: Heyday Books, 2012.

Miskwish, Michael Connolly. *Kumeyaay: A History Book.* El Cajon CA: Sycuan Press, 2007.

———. *Maay Uuyow: Kumeyaay Cosmology.* San Diego: Shuluk, 2016.

Mitchell, Don. *They Saved the Crops: Labor, Landscape, and the Struggle over Industrial Farming in Bracero-Era California.* Athens: University of Georgia Press, 2012.

Modesto, Ruby, and Guy Mount. *Not for Innocent Ears: Spiritual Traditions of a Desert Cahuilla Medicine Woman.* Riverside CA: Sweetlight Books, 1980.

Moerman, Daniel E. *Native American Ethnobotany.* Portland OR: Timber Press, 1998.

Molina, Natalia. *Fit to Be Citizens? Public Health and Race in Los Angeles, 1879–1939.* Berkeley: University of California Press, 2006.

Moraga, Cherríe, and Gloria Anzaldúa. *This Bridge Called My Back: Writings by Radical Women of Color.* Albany: State University of New York Press, 2015.

Morgensen, Scott Lauria. "The Biopolitics of Settler Colonialism: Right Here, Right Now." *Settler Colonial Studies* 1, no. 1 (2013): 52–76. https://doi.org/10.1080/2201473X.2011.10648801.

Mortality Statistics, 1915: Sixteenth Annual Report. Washington DC: Department of Commerce, 1917. https://www.cdc.gov/nchs/data/vsushistorical/mortstatsh_1915.pdf.

Mt. Pleasant, Alyssa, Caroline Wigginton, and Kelly Wisecup. "Materials and Methods in Native American and Indigenous Studies: Completing the Turn." *Early American Literature* 53, no. 2 (2018): 407–44.

Mullenneaux, Lisa. "Doing Good and Making Trouble: A Look at Helen Hunt Jackson." *Ploughshares* 45, no. 1 (2019): 188–96.

Nash, Linda. *Inescapable Ecologies: A History of Environment, Disease, and Knowledge.* Berkeley: University of California Press, 2006.

Needham, Andrew. *Power Lines: Phoenix and the Making of the Modern Southwest.* Princeton NJ: Princeton University Press, 2014.

Neville, Martha. "Look Who Is Singing the Mexicali Blues: How Far Can the EPA Travel under the Toxic Substances Act?" *Washington University Journal of Urban and Contemporary Law* 50 (January 1996): 265–302.

Newell, F. H. "The Salton Sea." In *Annual Report of the Board of Regents of the Smithsonian Institution . . . 1907*. Washington DC: Government Printing Office, 1908.

Ngai, Mae M. *Impossible Subjects: Illegal Aliens and the Making of Modern America*. Princeton NJ: Princeton University Press, 2014.

Nishime, Leilani, and Kim D. Hester Williams, eds. *Racial Ecologies*. Seattle: University of Washington Press, 2018.

Nolan, Sarah. "Prison Ecopoetics: Concrete, Imagined, and Textual Spaces in American Inmate Poetry." *Green Letters* 18, no. 3 (September 2, 2014): 312–24. https://doi.org/10.1080/14688417.2014.922894.

Norgaard, Kari Marie. *Salmon and Acorns Feed Our People: Colonialism, Nature, and Social Action*. New Brunswick NJ: Rutgers University Press, 2019.

Norton, Jack. "If the Truth Be Told: Revising California History as a Moral Objective." *American Behavioral Scientist* 58, no. 1 (January 1, 2014): 83–96. https://doi.org/10.1177/0002764213495033.

O'Brien, Jean M. *Dispossession by Degrees: Indian Land and Identity in Natick, Massachusetts, 1650–1790*. New York: Cambridge University Press, 1997.

———. *Firsting and Lasting: Writing Indians Out of Existence in New England*. Minneapolis: University of Minnesota Press, 2010.

Office of Indian Affairs. *Indians in the War*. Washington DC: U.S. Department of the Interior, 1946.

Office of Superintendent of Indian Schools. *Course of Study for the Indian Schools of the United States: Industrial and Literary*. Washington DC: Government Printing Office, 1901.

Orme, H. S., M.D. "The Climate of Southern California." *Transactions of the American Clinical and Climatological Association* 4 (1887). https://www.ncbi.nlm.nih.gov/pmc/articles/PMC2526647/?page=1.

Panich, Lee M. *Narratives of Persistence: Indigenous Negotiations of Colonialism in Alta and Baja California*. Tucson: University of Arizona Press, 2020.

Parajuli, Sagar P., and Charles S. Zender. "Projected Changes in Dust Emissions and Regional Air Quality Due to the Shrinking Salton Sea." *Aeolian Research* 33 (August 2018): 82–92. https://doi.org/10.1016/j.aeolia.2018.05.004.

Patencio, Francisco. *Stories and Legends of the Palm Springs Indians*. Los Angeles: Times-Mirror, 1943.

Pavlik, Bruce M. *The California Deserts: An Ecological Rediscovery*. Berkeley: University of California Press, 2008.

Pellow, David N. *Resisting Global Toxics: Transnational Movements for Environmental Justice*. Cambridge MA: MIT Press, 2007.

———. "Struggles for Environmental Justice in U.S. Prisons and Jails." *Antipode* 53, no. 1 (2021): 53–76. https://doi.org/10.1111/anti.12569.

———. "Toward a Critical Environmental Justice Studies: Black Lives Matter as an Environmental Justice Challenge." *Du Bois Review: Social Science Research on Race* 13, no. 2 (2016). https://doi.org/10.1017/S1742058X1600014X.

———. *What Is Critical Environmental Justice?* New York: Wiley, 2017. eBook.

Pellow, David N., and Lisa Sun-Hee Park. *The Silicon Valley of Dreams: Environmental Injustice, Immigrant Workers, and the High-Tech Global Economy*. New York: New York University Press, 2002.

Pember, F. T. "Collecting in the Colorado Desert." *The Semi-Annual* (Agassiz Association, Department of the Wilson Chapter) 3, no. 1 (1891): 30–33.

Pess, George R., Michael L. McHenry, Timothy J. Beechie, and Jeremy Davies. "Biological Impacts of the Elwha River Dams and Potential Salmonid Responses to Dam Removal." *Northwest Science* 82, no. sp1 (2008): 72–90. https://doi.org/10.3955/0029-344X-82.S.I.72.

Pfeifer, Michael J. *Rough Justice: Lynching and American Society, 1874–1947*. Urbana: University of Illinois Press, 2006.

Phillips, George Harwood. *Chiefs and Challengers: Indian Resistance and Cooperation in Southern California, 1769–1906*. 2nd ed. Norman: University of Oklahoma Press, 2014.

Phillips, Steven J., and Patricia Wentworth Comus, eds. *A Natural History of the Sonoran Desert*. Tucson: Arizona-Sonora Desert Museum Press; Berkeley: University of California Press, 2000.

Phillips, Steven J., Patricia Wentworth Comus, Mark A. Dimmitt, and Linda M. Brewer, eds. *A Natural History of the Sonoran Desert*. 2nd ed. Tucson: Arizona-Sonora Desert Museum Press; Oakland: University of California Press, 2015.

Philp, Kenneth R. *Termination Revisited: American Indians on the Trail to Self-Determination, 1933–1953*. Lincoln: University of Nebraska Press; Chesham: Combined Academic, 2002.

Phukan, Anjali, Todd J. Braje, Thomas K. Rockwell, and Isaac Ullah. "Shorelines in the Desert: Mapping Fish Trap Features along the Southwest Coast of Ancient Lake Cahuilla, California." *Advances in Archaeological Practice* 7, no. 4 (2019): 325–36. https://doi.org/10.1017/aap.2019.31.

Piekielek, Jessica. "Creating a Park, Building a Border: The Establishment of Organ Pipe Cactus National Monument and the Solidification of the U.S.-Mexico Border." *Journal of the Southwest* 58, no. 1 (2016): 1–27.

Pisani, Donald J. *From the Family Farm to Agribusiness: The Irrigation Crusade in California and the West, 1850–1931*. Berkeley: University of California Press, 1984.

———. *To Reclaim a Divided West: Water, Law, and Public Policy, 1848–1902*. Albuquerque: University of New Mexico Press, 1992.

———. *Water and American Government: The Reclamation Bureau, National Water Policy, and the West, 1902–1935*. Berkeley: University of California Press, 2002.

Pitkin, Hanna Fenichel. *The Attack of the Blob: Hannah Arendt's Concept of the Social.* Chicago: University of Chicago Press, 1998.

Plumwood, Val. *Feminism and the Mastery of Nature.* London: Routledge, 2002.

Poff, N. Leroy, and David D. Hart. "How Dams Vary and Why It Matters for the Emerging Science of Dam Removal." *BioScience* 52, no. 8 (2002): 659. https://doi.org/10.1641/0006-3568.

Powell, Miles A. *Vanishing America: Species Extinction, Racial Peril, and the Origins of Conservation.* Cambridge MA: Harvard University Press, 2016.

Pratt, O. A. "Report for Lower California." In *Report of Stallion Registration for the Fiscal Year Ending June 30, 1926,* Special Publication No. 68. Sacramento: California Department of Agriculture, 1926.

Prescott, Nathalie. "Prisoner (In)Consideration in Environmental Justice Analyses." *Georgetown Environmental Law Review,* May 31, 2016. https://gielr.wordpress.com/2016/05/31/prisoner-inconsideration-in-environmental-justice-analyses/.

Preston, William. "Serpent in the Garden: Environmental Change in Colonial California." In *Contested Eden: California before the Gold Rush,* edited by Ramón A. Gutiérrez and Richard J. Orsi, 260–98. Berkeley: University of California Press, 1998.

Price, Jennifer. *Flight Maps: Adventures with Nature in Modern America.* New York: Basic Books, 1999.

"Prisoners 1925–81." In *Bureau of Justice Statistics.* Washington DC: U.S. Department of Justice, n.d.

Problems of Imperial Valley and Vicinity, Letter from the Secretary of the Interior Transmitting Pursuant to Law a Report by the Director of the Reclamation Service on Problems of Imperial Valley and Vicinity with Respect to Irrigation from the Colorado: Together with the Proceedings of the Conference on the Construction of the Boulder Canyon Dam Held at San Diego, Calif. Washington DC: Government Printing Office, 1922. https://play.google.com/books/reader?id=k04OAAAAYAAJ&hl=en&pg=GBS.PA8.

"Proceedings of the Thirty-Second Fruit-Growers Convention." In *Second Biennial Report of the Commissioner of Horticulture of the State of California for 1905–1906.* Sacramento: W. W. Shannon, 1907.

Pulido, Laura. *Environmentalism and Economic Justice: Two Chicano Struggles in the Southwest.* Tucson: University of Arizona Press, 1996.

Pyne, Stephen J. *Between Two Fires: A Fire History of Contemporary America.* Tucson: University of Arizona Press, 2015. eBook.

———. *How the Canyon Became Grand: A Short History.* New York: Viking, 1998. eBook.

Ramón, Dorothy, with Eric Elliott. *Wayta' Yawa': Always Believe.* Banning CA: Malki-Ballena Press, 2000.

Rawls, James J. *Indians of California: The Changing Image*. Norman: University of Oklahoma Press, 1984.

Ray, Sarah Jaquette. *The Ecological Other: Environmental Exclusion in American Culture*. Tucson: University of Arizona Press, 2013. eBook.

———. "Endangering the Desert: Immigration, the Environment, and Security in the Arizona-Mexico Borderland." *Interdisciplinary Studies in Literature and Environment* 17, no. 4 (2010): 709–34.

Raymond, F. H. *The California Division of Forestry in 1957*. Sacramento: State of California Department of Natural Resources, 1958. https://hdl.handle.net/2027/mdp.39015069629619.

Reid, Joshua L. "Articulating a Traditional Future: Makah Sealers and Whalers, 1880–1999." In *Tribal Worlds*, edited by Brian Hosmer and Larry Nesper, 163–84. Albany: State University of New York Press, 2013.

———. *The Sea Is My Country: The Maritime World of the Makahs, an Indigenous Borderlands People*. New Haven CT: Yale University Press, 2015. eBook.

Reisner, Marc. *Cadillac Desert: The American West and Its Disappearing Water*. Rev. ed. New York: Penguin Books, 2014. eBook.

Reséndez, Andrés. *The Other Slavery: The Uncovered Story of Indian Enslavement in America*. Boston: Mariner Books, Houghton Mifflin Harcourt, 2017.

Rifkin, Mark. *Settler Common Sense: Queerness and Everyday Colonialism in the American Renaissance*. Albuquerque: University of New Mexico Press, 2014.

Righter, Robert W. *The Battle over Hetch Hetchy: America's Most Controversial Dam and the Birth of Modern Environmentalism*. New York: Oxford University Press, 2005.

Riseman, Noah. *Defending Whose Country? Indigenous Soldiers in the Pacific War*. Lincoln: University of Nebraska Press, 2012.

Risling Baldy, Cutcha. *We Are Dancing for You: Native Feminisms and the Revitalization of Women's Coming-of-Age Ceremonies*. Seattle: University of Washington Press, 2018.

Robertson, Rosalie. "The 'Crying Rock' Where They Killed the Children." In *The Missions of California: A Legacy of Genocide*, edited by Rupert Costo and Jeannette Henry Costo, 151–53. San Francisco: Indian Historian Press, 1987.

Robinson, Cedric J. *Black Marxism: The Making of the Black Radical Tradition*. Chapel Hill: University of North Carolina Press, 2000.

Robrock, David P., ed. *Missouri Forty-Niner: The Journal of William W. Hunter on the Southern Gold Trail*. Albuquerque: University of New Mexico Press, 1992.

Rodriguez, Annette M. "The Noose That Builds the Nation: Mexican Lynching in the Southwest." PhD diss., University of New Mexico, 2008. https://digitalrepository.unm.edu/amst_etds/70/.

Rome, Adam. "'Political Hermaphrodites': Gender and Environmental Reform in Progressive America." *Environmental History* 11, no. 3 (2006): 440–63.

Romero, Brenda. "World View of Tewa and Cahuilla Encourage Adaptation to Place and Resounds in Song." *Wicazo Sa Review* 8, no. 1 (1992): 65–69. https://doi .org/10.2307/1409364.

Roosevelt, Theodore. *The Strenuous Life.* 1900. Stilwell KS: Digireads.com, 2008.

Rosaldo, Renato. *Culture and Truth: The Remaking of Social Analysis.* Boston: Beacon Press, 2001. eBook.

Ross, Luana. *Inventing the Savage: The Social Construction of Native American Criminality.* Austin: University of Texas Press, 1998.

Rothman, Hal. *Devil's Bargains: Tourism in the Twentieth-Century American West.* Lawrence: University Press of Kansas, 2000.

Round, Phillip H. *The Impossible Land: Story and Place in California's Imperial Valley.* Albuquerque: University of New Mexico Press, 2008.

Said, Edward W. *The Question of Palestine.* 1992. New York: Vintage Books, 2015. eBook.

Sánchez, Roberto A. "Health and Environmental Risks of the Maquiladora in Mexicali." *Natural Resources Journal* 30, no. 1 (1990): 163–86. https://digitalrepository .unm.edu/nrj/vol30/iss1/11.

Sandler, Ronald L. and Phaedra C. Pezzullo, eds. *Environmental Justice and Environmentalism: The Social Justice Challenge to the Environmental Movement.* Cambridge MA: MIT Press, 2007.

Santa Ana, Otto. *Brown Tide Rising: Metaphors of Latinos in Contemporary American Public Discourse.* Austin: University of Texas Press, 2002.

Sapozhnikova, Yelena, Ola Bawardi, and Daniel Schlenk. "Pesticides and PCBs in Sediments and Fish from the Salton Sea, California, USA." *Chemosphere* 55, no. 6 (2004): 797–809. https://doi.org/10.1016/j.chemosphere.2003.12.009.

Saranillio, Dean Itsuji. "The Kepaniwai (Damming of the Water) Heritage Gardens: Alternative Futures beyond the Settler State." In *Formations of United States Colonialism,* edited by Alyosha Goldstein, 233–64. Durham NC: Duke University Press, 2014.

Saubel, Katherine Siva, and Eric Elliott. *'Isill Héqwas Wáxish/A Dried Coyote's Tail.* Banning CA: Malki Museum Press, 2004.

Schaefer, Jerry. "'Now Dead I Begin to Sing': A Protohistoric Clothes-Burning Ceremonial Feature in the Colorado Desert." *Journal of California and Great Basin Anthropology,* 22, no. 2 (2000): 186–211.

Scharff, Virginia, ed. *Seeing Nature through Gender.* Lawrence: University Press of Kansas, 2003.

Scharlin, Craig, and Lilia V. Villanueva. "'The Most Important $2 in My Life.'" In *Philip Vera Cruz: A Personal History of Filipino Immigrants and the Farmworkers Movement,* 31–51. 3rd ed. Seattle: University of Washington Press, 2000.

Schoenherr, Allan A. *A Natural History of California.* 2nd ed. Oakland: University of California Press, 2017.

Seiler, Hansjakob. *Cahuilla Texts with an Introduction.* Bloomington: Research Center for the Language Sciences, Indiana University, 1970.

Sellers, Christopher C. *Hazards of the Job: From Industrial Disease through Environmental Science*. Chapel Hill: University of North Carolina Press, 1997.

Shackley, M. Steven, Thomas Talbot Waterman, Leslie Spier, and Edward Winslow Gifford. *Early Ethnography of the Kumeyaay*. Berkeley: Phoebe Hearst Museum of Anthropology, University of California, Berkeley, 2004.

Shah, Nayan. *Contagious Divides: Epidemics and Race in San Francisco's Chinatown*. Berkeley: University of California Press, 2011.

———. *Stranger Intimacy: Contesting Race, Sexuality, and the Law in the North American West*. Berkeley: University of California Press, 2011.

Shaler, Andrew. "Indigenous Peoples and the California Gold Rush: Labour, Violence and Contention in the Formation of a Settler Colonial State." *Postcolonial Studies* 23, no. 1 (January 2, 2020): 79–98. https://doi.org/10.1080/13688790.2020.1725221.

Sherwood, Yvonne. "The Political Binds of Oil versus Tribes." *Open Rivers: Rethinking Water, Place, and Community*, no. 13 (Spring 2019): 48–68.

Shipek, Florence C. "An Example of Intensive Plant Husbandry." In *Foraging and Farming: The Evolution of Plant Exploitation*, edited by David R. Harris and Gordon C. Hillman, 159–70. 1989. London: Routledge, 2016.

———. "Myth and Reality: The Antiquity of the Kumeyaay." In *Proceedings of the 1983, 1984 and 1985 Hokan-Penutian Languages Workshop*, edited by James E. Redden, 4–11. Carbondale: Department of Linguistics, Southern Illinois University, [1992].

———. *Pushed into the Rocks: Southern California Indian Land Tenure, 1769–1986*. Lincoln: University of Nebraska Press, 1988.

Shugart, K. D. "Local Climatic Effect of Salton Lake." *Southern California Practitioner* 6, no. 10 (October 1891).

Sijimol, M. R., S. Jyothy, A. P. Pradeepkumar, M. S. Shylesh Chandran, S. Shabin Ghouse, and Mahesh Mohan. "Review on Fate, Toxicity, and Remediation of Perchlorate." *Environmental Forensics* 16, no. 2 (April 3, 2015): 125–34. https://doi.org/10.1080/15275922.2015.1022914.

Simpson, Audra. *Mohawk Interruptus: Political Life across the Borders of Settler States*. Durham NC: Duke University Press, 2014.

———. "Whither Settler Colonialism?" *Settler Colonial Studies* 6, no. 4 (2016): 438–45. https://doi.org/10.1080/2201473X.2015.1124427.

Simpson, Leanne Betasamosake. *As We Have Always Done: Indigenous Freedom through Radical Resistance*. Minneapolis: University of Minnesota Press, 2017.

Sneddon, Christopher. *Concrete Revolution: Large Dams, Cold War Geopolitics, and the US Bureau of Reclamation*. Chicago: University of Chicago Press, 2015.

Snelgrove, Corey, Rita Dhamoon, and Jeff Corntassel. "Unsettling Settler Colonialism: The Discourse and Politics of Settlers, and Solidarity with Indigenous

Nations." *Decolonization* 3, no. 2 (2014). https://jps.library.utoronto.ca/index
.php/des/article/view/21166.

Spence, Mark David. *Dispossessing the Wilderness: Indian Removal and the Making of
the National Parks*. New York: Oxford University Press, 2000.

Steingraber, Sandra. *Living Downstream: An Ecologist's Personal Investigation of
Cancer and the Environment*. 2nd ed. Cambridge MA: Da Capo Press, 2010.

Stephens, F. "Collecting in the Colorado Desert: Leconte's Thrasher." *The Auk* 1, no.
4 (October 1884): 353–58.

St. John, Rachel. *Line in the Sand: A History of the Western U.S.-Mexico Border*.
Princeton: Princeton University Press, 2017. eBook.

Stremlau, Rose. "Witnessing the West: Barbara Longknife and the California Gold Rush."
In *The Native South: New Histories and Enduring Legacies*, edited by Tim Alan Garrison and Greg O'Brien, 162–80. Lincoln: University of Nebraska Press, 2017.

Stringfellow, Kim. *Greetings from the Salton Sea: Folly and Intervention in the Southern
California Landscape, 1905–2005*. Chicago: Center for American Places, 2005.
Google Books.

Strong, William. *Aboriginal Society in Southern California*. Berkeley: University of
California Press, 1929.

Stroud, Ellen. *Nature Next Door: Cities and Trees in the American Northeast*. Seattle:
University of Washington Press, 2012. eBook.

Sutter, Paul. "Reflections: What Can U.S. Environmental Historians Learn from Non-
U.S. Environmental Histography?" *Environmental History* 8, no. 1 (2003): 109–29.

———. "Seeing beyond Our Borders: US and Non-US Historiographies." In *A Companion to American Environmental History*, edited by Douglas Cazaux Sackman,
635–52. Malden MA: Wiley-Blackwell, 2010.

Sykes, Godfrey. *The Colorado Delta*. Washington DC: Carnegie Institution; New York:
American Geographical Society, 1937.

Thompson, Heather Ann. "The Prison Industrial Complex: A Growth Industry in a
Shrinking Economy." *New Labor Forum* 21, no. 3 (2012): 39–47. https://doi.org
/10.4179/NLF.213.0000006.

Thorne, Tanis. "The Death of Superintendent Stanley and the Cahuilla Uprising
of 1907–1912." *Journal of California and Great Basin Anthropology* 24, no. 2
(2004): 233–58.

———. *El Capitan: Adaptation and Agency on a Southern California Indian Reservation, 1850 to 1937*. Banning CA: Malki-Bellena Press, 2012.

———. "On the Fault Line: Political Violence at Campo Fiesta and National Reform
in Indian Policy." *Journal of California and Great Basin Anthropology* 21, no.
2 (1999): 182–212.

Todd, Zoe. "Fish, Kin and Hope: Tending to Water Violations in Amiskwaciwâska-
hikan and Treaty Six Territory." *Afterall: A Journal of Art, Context, & Enquiry*
43, no. 1 (2017): 102–7.

———. "From a Fishy Place: Examining Canadian State Law Applied in the Daniels Decision from the Perspective of Métis Legal Orders." *TOPIA* 36 (November 2016): 43–57. https://doi.org/10.3138/topia.36.43.

———. "Indigenizing the Anthropocene." In *Art in the Anthropocene: Encounters among Aesthetics, Politics, Environments and Epistemologies,* edited by Heather Davis and Etienne Turpin, 241–54. London: Open Humanities Press, 2015.

Townsend, Kenneth William. *World War II and the American Indian.* Albuquerque: University of New Mexico Press, 2000.

Trafzer, Clifford E. *A Chemehuevi Song: The Resilience of a Southern Paiute Tribe.* Seattle: University of Washington Press, 2015. eBook.

———. *Fighting Invisible Enemies: Health and Medical Transitions among Southern California Indians.* Norman: University of Oklahoma Press, 2019.

———. "Tuberculosis Death and Survival among Southern California Indians, 1922–44." *Canadian Bulletin of Medical History* 18, no. 1 (April 2001): 85–107. https://doi.org/10.3138/cbmh.18.1.85.

Trafzer, Clifford E., Jean A. Keller, and Lorene Sisquoc, eds. *Boarding School Blues: Revisiting American Indian Educational Experiences.* Lincoln: University of Nebraska Press, 2006.

Trafzer, Clifford E., Matthew Sakiestewa Gilbert, and Lorene Sisquoc, eds. *The Indian School on Magnolia Avenue: Voices and Images from Sherman Institute.* Corvallis: Oregon State University Press, 2012.

Trennert, Robert A. "Educating Indian Girls at Nonreservation Boarding Schools, 1878–1920." *Western Historical Quarterly* 13, no. 3 (1982): 271–90. https://doi.org/10.2307/969414.

Truett, Samuel. *Fugitive Landscapes: The Forgotten History of the U.S.-Mexico Borderlands.* New Haven CT: Yale University Press, 2008.

Tsing, Anna Lowenhaupt. *The Mushroom at the End of the World: On the Possibility of Life in Capitalist Ruins.* Princeton NJ: Princeton University Press, 2015.

Tuck, Eve, and K. Wayne Yang. "Decolonization Is Not a Metaphor." *Decolonization: Indigeneity, Education, and Society* 1, no. 1 (2012): 1–40.

Vanhouche, An-Sofie, and Kristel Beyens. "Introduction: Prison Foodways; International and Multidisciplinary Perspectives." *Appetite* 147 (April 2020): 104514. https://doi.org/10.1016/j.appet.2019.104514.

Veracini, Lorenzo. *Settler Colonialism: A Theoretical Overview.* Basingstoke: Palgrave Macmillan, 2010.

Vickery, Jamie, and Lori M. Hunter. "Native Americans: Where in Environmental Justice Research?" *Society and Natural Resources* 29, no. 1 (January 2, 2016): 36–52. https://doi.org/10.1080/08941920.2015.1045644.

Vizenor, Gerald. *Manifest Manners: Narratives on Postindian Survivance.* Lincoln: University of Nebraska Press, 1999.

———. *Native Liberty: Natural Reason and Cultural Survivance*. Lincoln: University of Nebraska Press, 2009.

Vlaming, V. de, C. DiGiorgio, S. Fong, L. A. Deanovic, M. de la Paz Carpio-Obeso, J. L. Miller, M. J. Miller, and N. J. Richard. "Irrigation Runoff Insecticide Pollution of Rivers in the Imperial Valley, California (USA)." *Environmental Pollution* 132, no. 2 (November 2004): 213–29. https://doi.org/10.1016/j.envpol.2004.04.025.

Voyles, Traci Brynne. "Environmentalism in the Interstices: California's Salton Sea and the Borderlands of Nature and Culture." *Resilience: A Journal of the Environmental Humanities* 3 (2016): 211–41.

———. "Man Destroys Nature? Gender, History, and the Feminist Praxis of Situating Sustainabilities." In *Sustainability: Approaches to Environmental Justice and Social Power*, edited by Julie Sze, 196–215. New York: New York University Press, 2018.

———. "Toxic Masculinity: California's Salton Sea and the Environmental Consequences of Manliness." *Environmental History* 26, no. 1 (2021): 127–41.

———. *Wastelanding: Legacies of Uranium Mining in Navajo Country*. Minneapolis: University of Minnesota Press, 2015.

Walker, Edwin F. *Indians of Southern California*. Los Angeles: Southwest Museum, 1937.

Ward, Erica M. *Coachella*. Charleston SC: Arcadia, 2014.

Ward, Evan R. *Border Oasis: Water and the Political Ecology of the Colorado River Delta, 1940–1975*. Tucson: University of Arizona Press, 2003.

Warren, Louis S. *The Hunter's Game: Poachers and Conservationists in Twentieth-Century America*. New Haven CT: Yale University Press, 1994.

———. "Paths toward Home: Landmarks of the Field in Environmental History." In *A Companion to American Environmental History*, edited by Douglas Cazaux Sackman, 3–32. Malden MA: Wiley-Blackwell, 2010.

Warrick, Jonathan A., Jennifer A. Bountry, Amy E. East, Christopher S. Magirl, Timothy J. Randle, Guy Gelfenbaum, Andrew C. Ritchie, George R. Pess, Vivian Leung, and Jeffrey J. Duda. "Large-Scale Dam Removal on the Elwha River, Washington, USA: Source-to-Sink Sediment Budget and Synthesis." *Geomorphology* 246 (2015): 729–50. https://doi.org/10.1016/j.geomorph.2015.01.010.

Washington, Sylvia Hood. *Packing Them In: An Archaeology of Environmental Racism in Chicago, 1865–1954*. Lanham MD: Lexington Books, 2005.

Weill, Joanna M. "Prisoners on the Fireline: The Application of Ethical Principles and Guidelines to Prison Fire Camps." *Ethics and Behavior* 30, no. 2 (February 17, 2020): 112–25. https://doi.org/10.1080/10508422.2019.1579649.

Weisiger, Marsha L. *Dreaming of Sheep in Navajo Country*. Seattle: University of Washington Press, 2011. eBook.

White, Richard. *The Organic Machine*. New York: Hill and Wang, 1995.

Whyte, Kyle. "The Recognition Dimensions of Environmental Justice in Indian Country." *Environmental Justice* 4, no. 4 (December 2011): 199–205. https://doi.org/10.1089/env.2011.0036.

———. "Settler Colonialism, Ecology, and Environmental Injustice." *Environment and Society* 9, no. 1 (2018): 125–44.

Whyte, Kyle Powys, Joni Adamson, and Michael Davis. "Is It Colonial Déjà Vu? Indigenous Peoples and Climate Injustice." In *Humanities for the Environment: Integrating Knowledge, Forging New Constellations of Practice*, edited by Joni Adamson and Michael Davis, 88–104. New York: Routledge, 2017.

Wildcat, Daniel R. *Red Alert! Saving the Planet with Indigenous Knowledge*. Golden CO: Fulcrum, 2009.

Wilke, Philip J. *Late Prehistoric Human Ecology at Lake Cahuilla Coachella Valley, California*. Berkeley: Archaeological Research Facility, Department of Anthropology, University of California, 1978. https://escholarship.org/uc/item/8367m039.

Wilson, Robert M. *Seeking Refuge: Birds and Landscapes of the Pacific Flyway*. Seattle: University of Washington Press, 2010.

Winkler, Adam. *Gunfight: The Battle over the Right to Bear Arms in America*. New York: Norton, 2013. eBook.

Wolfe, Patrick. "Settler Colonialism and the Elimination of the Native." *Journal of Genocide Research* 8, no. 4 (2006): 387–409.

———. *Settler Colonialism and the Transformation of Anthropology: The Politics and Poetics of an Ethnographic Event*. London: Cassell, 1999.

Worster, Donald. *Dust Bowl: The Southern Plains in the 1930s*. New York: Oxford University Press, 1993.

———. *Rivers of Empire: Water, Aridity, and the Growth of the American West*. Oxford: Oxford University Press, 1992.

———. *Under Western Skies: Nature and History in the American West*. New York: Oxford University Press, 1992.

Wyman, Margaret. *Mission: The Birth of California, the Death of a Nation*. Idyllwild CA: Idyllwild, 2002.

Yazzie, Melanie K. "Decolonizing Development in Diné Bikeyah." *Environment and Society* 9, no. 1 (2018): 25–39. https://doi.org/10.3167/ares.2018.090103.

Young, Kalaniopua. "From a Native *Trans* Daughter: Carceral Refusal, Settler Colonialism, Re-Routing the Roots of an Indigenous Abolitionist Imaginary." In *Captive Genders: Trans Embodiment and the Prison Industrial Complex*, edited by Eric A. Stanley and Nat Smith, 83–96. Exp. 2nd ed. Oakland CA: AK Press, 2015.

Yusoff, Kathryn. *A Billion Black Anthropocenes or None*. Minneapolis: University of Minnesota Press, 2018.

Zappia, Natale A. *Traders and Raiders: The Indigenous World of the Colorado Basin, 1540–1859*. Chapel Hill: University of North Carolina Press, 2014.

Zimring, Carl A. *Clean and White: A History of Environmental Racism in the United States*. New York: New York University Press, 2015.

INDEX

avian salmonellosis, 173. *See also* die-offs

B-30 bomber, 180

B-47 bomber, 187

bairdiella (fish), 167

Baja California, xiv, *xvi*, *xvii*, 160, 162; missions (Jesuit), 40, 45; Native nations of, 40–41, 45, 279n79

Balenguila, Agnes, 140

Banning CA, 50, 58, 59, 89, 91, 203–5, 209

Basic Magnesium, Incorporated (BMI), 191–92

basketweaving, 11, 17, *33*, 35, 38, 142, 208; for commerce and trade, 25, 43, 142; and environmental justice, 247–48; as futurity praxis, 199, 200, 262–63. *See also* California Indian Basketweavers Association (CIBA)

Belardo, Mary, 147–48

Bermuda grass, 161

Big Bend Dam, 146

Biological Survey (Fish and Wildlife Service), 108–9, 291n59

Bird Songs, 28, 95, 200, 261, 263

Blake, William Phipps, xiii–xiv, 45–46, 189

blue palo verde, 2, 36, 224

Bombay Beach, 166, 168

bombs: to control ducks, 110; military use and testing of, 177–78, 185–89

bonytail (fish), 23

Border Industrialization Plan (1965), 251

borderlands: history, 160, 285n45; of Indigenous nations in the Colorado Desert, 27, 39, 44; U.S.-Mexico, 107, 122, 252, 254, 271n8

Boulder Canyon Dam (Hoover Dam), 15, 128–29, 133, 147, 148, 191, 193

Boulder Canyon Project Act (BCPA) (1928), 129, 132, 148

Boyce, J. B., 82–84

Bozick, Mike, 243, 316n31

Bracero Program, 111–12, 170

Brawley CA, *xviii*, 16, 248, 317n40

Bureau of Indian Affairs (BIA), 141, 147, 197–99, 201

Bureau of Reclamation, U.S., 127. *See also* Reclamation Service, U.S.

Butterfield Overland Mail route, 46

Cabazon Reservation, 82

Cahuillas: clans of, 3, 56, 199; environmental management practices of, 8, 10–11, 29–37, 48; geographic subgroups of, 3, 8, 23, 33–34, 52, 56, 81, 136–37, 144, 199, 209, 212, 223, 246; gods of, 70, 94; history of, x, 22–28, 63, 82, 284n14; relationships of, to nearby Native nations, 3, 22–28, 39, 45, 52, 80, 198; reservation communities of, 50, 157; sovereignty of, 17, 45, 48, 139–40, 195, 198, 213–14, 256–58, 263, 274n33, 281n114, 319n7. *See also* Torres Martinez Cahuillas

Calexico CA, *xviii*, 16, 69, 122, 131, 158, 160, 185, 215–16, 242, 248, 250, 300n45, 317n40

California Alien Land Law (1913), 124

California-Arizona Maneuver Area and Desert Training Center. *See* Desert Training Center (DTC)

California Department of Corrections and Rehabilitation (CDCR), 222, 224, 226–29, 232–35

California Department of Forestry and Fire Protection (CAL Fire), 224–25

California Department of Health Services, 115, 154, 195
California Development Company (CDC), 64–74, 125–27, 133, 135, 161, 285n46, 286n51. *See also* Chaffey, George; Rockwood, Charles
California Fruit Growers Association, 119–20, 124
California Indian Basketweavers Association (CIBA), 247–48, 256. *See also* basketweaving
California Men's Colony, 231
California Regional Water Quality Control Board, 188
California State Prison at Centinela, 227, 229, 231, 232
Calipatria State Prison, 227–29, 231–35, 311n81, 312n89
Campo Reservation, 137
Castillo, Adam, 198
catclaw, 2
Centinela. *See* California State Prison at Centinela
Chaffey, George, 67–71, 79, 133. *See also* California Development Company (CDC)
Chase, J. Smeaton, 157
Chavez, Cesar, 245. *See also* farm labor movement
Chemehuevis, 3, 22, 27, 44, 50, 128, 154, 179, 262
Chinese Exclusion Act, 119. *See also* anti-Chinese racism
Chocolate Mountain Aerial Gunnery Range, 182
Chocolate Mountains, xiv, 2, 47, 182
Chuckwalla Valley State Prison, 227, 228, 231, 233
Chumash people, 25, 40, 41, 42
Civilian Conservation Corps, 220

Clean Air Act, 231
Clean Water Act, 231
climate change, 9, 225, 233, 267, 275
Clostridium botulinum. See avian botulism
Coachella Canal, 144–45, 198
Coachella Valley, 77, 81, 111, 113, 129, 130, 136, 144, 145, 148, 155, 169, 170, 194, 198, 223, 240, 242–46, 249, 254, 255, 273n19
Coachella Valley Water District (CVWD), 194–95
Cochimís, 40, 46
Cocopahs, 3, 39, 44, 45, 69, 74, 122, 139
Collier, John, 140
Colorado Desert, xiv, 10, 27, 42, 47, 52, 64, 66, 76, 77, 78, 91, 97, 107, 132, 145, 150, 152, 153, 154, 161, 166, 196, 203, 227, 263
Colorado Plateau, 21, 22, 28
Colorado River, xvi, 3–5, 21–29, 63–64, 67, 120–21, 127–35; and Colorado River Aqueduct, 144, 193; and Colorado River Compact, 128, 147
Comite Civico del Valle, 258
conservation, 5, 132, 168, 232, 258, 267–68; and birds, 99, 106–17, 187, 229–30, 259, 290n55. *See also* Sonny Bono National Wildlife Refuge
conservation camps, 219–27, 235. *See also* Honor Camps
corvina (fish), 219–20
creosote, 2, 17, 89, 97
Cuero, Delfina, 38–39
Cult of True Womanhood, 99
Cupeño (people and language), 42, 95, 122, 154, 198, 289n15
Curtis, Edward, 80

Dakota Access Pipeline, 256
The Dalles Dam, 146
dam removal, 265–66, 320n18
dams and reservoirs, 72–74, 127–32, 142–43; and Indigenous environmental justice, 265–66; and settler colonialism, 120–21, 125–26, 145–48
Date Palm Beach, 166
Davis, Arthur, 128. *See also* Fall-Davis Report
Dawes Act. *See* General Allotment Act
DDE (dichlorodiphenyldichloroethylene), 115, 238, 250
DDT (dichlorodiphenyltrichloroethane), 240–43
DeBears, Flora, 140
declensionist environmental narratives, 6–7, 17, 268–69. *See also* environmental history
decolonization, 12, 15, 257, 263, 264–67, 319n7
deer grass, 11, 35
Defense Plant Corporation, 191
Delano grape strike (1965–70), 245–46. *See also* farm labor movement
Department of Defense, 177, 181, 192
desert Cahuillas. *See* Cahuillas
Desert Shores Resort, 168
Desert Training Center (DTC), 179, 181
diazinon, 238, 240, 243
dichlorodiphenyldichloroethylene. *See* DDE (dichlorodiphenyldichloroethylene)
dichlorodiphenyltrichloroethane. *See* DDT (dichlorodiphenyltrichloroethane)
dichlorophenoxyacetic acid. *See* 2,4-D (dichlorophenoxyacetic acid)
Diego, Juan, 51, 211, 282n123. *See also* Lubo, Ramona

Diegueños. *See* Kumeyaays
die-offs, 113–17, 172–73, *172*, 181, 219, 226, 232, 255, 261
dioxin, 239–40
disability history, 154–55
Don Fileto slaughterhouse (Mexicali), 249
Dow Chemical, 314n3
Durbrow, George, 56–59, 62–65, 70, 81, 137, 203, 208. *See also* New Liverpool Salt Company

eagles, 34, 94, 96–97, 112, 234
Echo Island, 103–5, 108, 113
El Centro CA, 100, 102, 171, 182, 187
El Centro Gun Club, 100, 102. *See also* guns and gun clubs
environmental history, 7–8, 11, 12, 13, 28, 113, 151, 263, 266, 268–69, 273n17, 289n28, 321n29, 322n32
environmentalism, 5, 117, 230, 250, 257, 264–66. *See also* preservationism
environmental justice, 146, 256–57, 258, 264, 273n19, 318n65. *See also* Indigenous environmental justice
environmental justice studies, 7, 11, 13–15, 264, 273n15
eutrophication, 172–73. *See also* die-offs

F6F-5 Hellcat, 177
Fall-Davis Report, 128–29
Fanon, Frantz. *See* postcolonial theory
farm labor movement, 244–45. *See also* Delano grape strike (1965–70); United Farm Workers (UFW); United Farm Workers Organizing Committee (UFWOC)

Federal Land Bank, 293n28

fiesta. See *kewét*

Fig Tree John. *See* Razón, Juan

fire: Indigenous use and management of, 41, 48, 226; and prisoners, 220, 222–26

firsting and lasting, 78, 268, 296n71. *See also* Indigenous history

Folsom Prison, 231

formerly used defense sites (FUDS), 182

forty-niners, 46–47, 69, 209

futurity, 263, 319n7. *See also* decolonization

Gabbs Valley, 191–92, 196

Garrá, Antonio, 49–50, 282n116

General Allotment Act, 139–43, 255

genocide, 48–49, 98, 211, 308n18

Gentlemen's Agreement (1907), 123

geologic time, 3, 15, 21–23, 269

geology, 36, 45, 55, 63, 257

Ghost Dance, 59

gold. *See* forty-niners

Grand Coulee Dam, 146

groundwater. *See* water

Grumman Aircraft Engineering Company. *See* Northrop Grumman

guns and gun clubs, 97–100, 102, 289n24

Hanlon Heading, 67, 71

Havasupais, 22, 30

Heber, Anthony, 68. *See also* California Development Company (CDC)

Henderson, Nevada, 191–92, 194, 196

Henshaw reservoir, 143

heptachlor, 240, 243

Herbert Hughes Correctional Center, 227

Hetch Hetchy Reservoir, 145, 297n100

Holtville CA *xviii*, 16, 131

Honor Camps, 220–22. *See also* conservation camps

Hoover Dam. *See* Boulder Canyon Dam (Hoover Dam)

Huerta, Dolores, 245. *See also* farm labor movement

immigration, 47, 51, 111, 157–58, 163, 189, 275n45, 294n31; restrictive policies of, 119–21, 124, 126, 135, 160, 292n1

Imperial County Board of Supervisors, 156, 218

Imperial County Jail, 227

Imperial Irrigation District (IID), 84, 129, 130, 132, 243, 295n47

Imperial Valley, 4–5, 64–68, 70, 99–101, 106–13, 120–35, 153–57, 159–63, 168–71, 217–18, 243, 248, 250–51

Imperial Valley Chamber of Commerce, 167

Imperial Valley Press, 65–66, 69, 99, 106, 150, 155, 156, 161, 216

incarceration, 123, 205–6, 210, 212, 214–19, 226–28, 230, 307n7, 309n45, 311nn83–85, 312n89; and environmental degradation, 230; and environmental injustice, 233–35; and settler colonialism, 219, 233–35. *See also* prisons and jails

Indigenous environmental justice, 146, 256–57, 273n15. *See also* environmental justice

Indigenous feminism, 210–11, 272n14, 308n18, 317n39, 319n7

Indigenous history, 11, 268, 274n33

Indigenous studies, 12, 14, 263, 264, 272n14, 274n33, 297n104, 309n43, 317n39, 319n80

North American Free Trade Agreement (NAFTA) (1994), 252–53
Northrop Grumman, 177
North Shore Yacht Club, 166, 220

Oahe Dam, 146
Oak Glen Youth Conservation Camp, 223
Office of Indian Affairs (OIA), 136–37, 140. *See also* Bureau of Indian Affairs (BIA)
Old Sandy Beach Naval Station, 185, 186
organochlorine compounds, 240
organophosphates, 240, 248
O'Shaughnessy Dam, 145, 297n100

Pablo, Margaret, 199–201
Pacific Engineering Production Company of Nevada (PEPCON), 192–93, 305n44
Pacific Flyway, 93, *114*, 291n69
Paipai, 40, 45
Pala Reservation, 142, 143
Papagos, 30, 74, 197
paradoxes, 1–5, 8, 11, 16, 17, 165
parathion, 240
Parry pinyon, 25–26, 38
Pasteurella multocida. See avian cholera
Payómkawichums or Luiseños, 27, 30, 40, 41, 44, 48, 50, 139, 154, 197, 198, 280, 281n109, 282n119
PCBs (chemicals), 238
Peet, Joe, 139
Pelican Island, 101, 105
Penn, Jane, 199–201
Perris Indian School, 209
pesticides: ecological impact of, 112–13, 115, 116, 170–71, 195, 239–48, 250, 254, 255; and the Salton Sea, 115, 116, 260; and settler

colonialism, 247. *See also* Agent Orange; pollution; 2,4-D (dichlorophenoxyacetic acid); 2,4,5-T (trichlorophenoxyacetic acid)
place-names, xiii–xiv
pollution, 155, 157, 161, 163, 231, 239, 249–52, 254–55, 258–59. *See also* pesticides
postcolonial theory, 66, 265
Powell, John Wesley, 63
precarity, 4–5, 67, 266–67, 321n26
preservationism, 106
prisons and jails, 227–28; environmental consequences of, 228–33; and environmental injustice, 233–35; role of, in conservation, 220–26; in settler colonialism, 214. *See also* conservation camps; Honor Camps; incarceration
Public Health Service, U.S., 154
Puerta La Cruz Conservation Camp, 222–23
pul or shaman (Cahuilla), 36, 94, 96, 199
Purísima Concepción Mission, 41

Quechans, x, 3, 22, 24, 27, 39, 40–44, 45, 49, 61, 67, 71–72, 74, 135, 200, 215, 262, 280, 319n3

racial capitalism, 6, 14, 122, 163, 272n12
racial violence, 52, 123, 204–6, 210. *See also* genocide
racism: environmental, 255; interpersonal, 47, 50–51, 119–20, 123–27; and settler colonialism, 13; structural and cultural, 6, 7, 12, 14, 83, 111, 122, 157, 228, 272n12, 294n31
railroad, xiii, 3, 4, 45, 50, 52, 57, 60, 70, 103–5, 106, 108, 121, 151, 159,

Warharmi (desert Kumeyaay deity), 94
Warner's Dam, 142
War on Drugs (Reagan administration), 227
water: aquifer, 10–11, 29, 53, 140, 144, 181, 195, 303n16; and deserts, 8–11; environmental history of, 8–11; for irrigation, 31, 35, 46, 66, 68, 82, 84, 104, 109, 127–33, 139, 142, 145, 148, 153, 159, 168–69, 248, 257, 268; management and control of, 8–9, 67, 71–75, 119–21, 125–31, 133–35. *See also* dams and reservoirs
weeds (unwanted plants), 247; management of, 161–63, 164; pesticides applied to, 240; social meaning of, 161–64
Westmorland CA, *xviii*, 248
wiregrass, 35
work. *See* labor
World Bank, 252
World Trade Organization, 252
Wozencraft, Oliver M., 46, 53
Wright, L. A., 80–81, 84

Xawiłł kwñchawaay, 25, 40

Yaquis, 47
Yavapais, 27, 30
Youth Conservation Corps, 223–24
Yuma clapper rail (bird species), 113

IN THE MANY WESTS SERIES

The Settler Sea: California's Salton Sea and the Consequences of Colonialism
Traci Brynne Voyles

To order or obtain more information on these or other University of Nebraska Press titles, visit nebraskapress.unl.edu.

CPSIA information can be obtained
at www.ICGtesting.com
Printed in the USA
LVHW030850161221
706292LV00018B/768/J